Laughter Out of Place

CALIFORNIA SERIES IN PUBLIC ANTHROPOLOGY

The California Series in Public Anthropology emphasizes the anthropologist's role as an engaged intellectual. It continues anthropology's commitment to being an ethnographic witness, to describing, in human terms, how life is lived beyond the borders of many readers' experiences. But it also adds a commitment, through ethnography, to reframing the terms of public debate—transforming received, accepted understandings of social issues with new insights, new framings.

SERIES EDITOR: Robert Borofsky (Hawaii Pacific University)

CONTRIBUTING EDITORS: Philippe Bourgois (University of Pennsylvania), Paul Farmer (Partners in Health), Alex Hinton (Rutgers University), Carolyn Nordstrom (University of Notre Dame), and Nancy Scheper-Hughes (UC Berkeley)

UNIVERSITY OF CALIFORNIA PRESS EDITOR: Naomi Schneider

Laughter Out of Place

Race, Class, Violence, and Sexuality
in a Rio Shantytown

Donna M. Goldstein

With a New Preface

UNIVERSITY OF CALIFORNIA PRESS
Berkeley · Los Angeles · London

University of California Press, one of the most distinguished university presses in the United States, enriches lives around the world by advancing scholarship in the humanities, social sciences, and natural sciences. Its activities are supported by the UC Press Foundation and by philanthropic contributions from individuals and institutions. For more information, visit www.ucpress.edu.

University of California Press
Berkeley and Los Angeles, California

University of California Press, Ltd.
London, England

ISBN 978-0-520-27604-8

The Library of Congress has cataloged an earlier edition of this book as follows:

Library of Congress Cataloging-in-Publication Data

Goldstein, Donna M.
    Laughter out of place : race, class, violence, and sexuality in a Rio shantytown / Donna M. Goldstein.
        p.   cm.—(California Series in Public Anthropology; 9)
    Includes bibliographical references and index.
    ISBN 978-0-520-23597-7 (pbk. : alk. paper)
    1. Marginality, Social—Brazil—Rio de Janeiro.   2. Poor—Brazil—Rio de Janeiro.   3. Poor—Brazil—Rio de Janeiro—Humor.   4. Slums—Brazil—Rio de Janeiro.   5. Violence—Brazil—Rio de Janeiro.   6. Sex—Brazil—Rio de Janeiro.   7. Rio de Janeiro (Brazil)—Race relations. I. Title.
    HN290.R5 G58   2003
    305.5'68'098153—dc21

                                                            2003001852

Manufactured in the United States of America

22 21 20 19
10 9 8 7 6 5 4 3

*To my grandparents and my parents,
who all understood the importance
of laughter*

I just want to be happy
Walk with tranquillity
In the favela where I was born
Yeah. . . .
And to be able to take pride
And being aware
That the poor have their place
Faith in God DJ

Dear authorities I just don't know what to do
With so much violence I fear living
Because I live in a favela I get no respect
There, sadness and happiness walk side by side. . . .

I can't take any more of this wave of violence
All I'm asking from the authorities is a little more competence

I have never seen a postcard picturing a favela
I only see those with pretty scenes
Those who leave the favela feel nostalgia for it
The gringo who comes here and doesn't know the reality
He goes to the Zona Sul to have coconut milk
While the poor in the favela are suffocating. . . .

Eu só quero é ser feliz
Andar tranqüilamente
Na favela onde eu nasci
É. . . .
E poder me orgulhar
E ter a consciência
Que o pobre tem o seu lugar
Fé em Deus DJ

Minha cara autoridade já não sei o que fazer
Com tanta violência eu fico medo de viver
Pois moro na favela eu sou muito desrespeitado
A tristeza e a alegria que caminha lado a lado. . . .

Já não aguento mais essa onda de violência
Só peço autoridades sum pouco mais de competência

Nunca vi cartão postal que se destaca uma favela
Só vejo paisagem muito linda e muito bela
Quem vai pro exterior da favela senti saudade
O gringo vem aqui e não conhece a realidade
Vai pra zona sul pra conhecer água de cocô
E pobre na favela vive passando sufoco. . . .

Excerpted from "Rap da Felicidade"
("Rap of Happiness") by
Julio Rasta/Kátia

Contents

Illustrations

TABLE

Foreword

A bold and courageous book by a fresh anthropological voice, *Laughter Out of Place* returns anthropology to what it does best by taking the reader on a no-holds-barred ride into the tragicomic world of a bleak Brazilian *favela*. In Rio's vast subterranean underworld of mean and ugly public housing projects, interspersed with ragtag shantytowns that crop up daily on the northern extensions of the city, Felicidade Eterna (Eternal Happiness) residents struggle to keep their anger and despair at bay by laughing and spitting into the face of unbearable suffering, sickness, chaos, injustice, violence, and social abandonment. Welcome to Lula's Brazil—the inheritor of centuries of race, class, and sexual apartheid—which masquerades as a tropical paradise where neither sin nor guilt exist.

Goldstein stages this brilliant ethnography, which often reads like a novel, around a single protagonist, Glória, a tough-as-nails domestic worker, and her large extended family and network of friends, neighbors, and employers. Glória and her clan form a microcosm of Brazil's vast underclass, and they manage to survive with their wits intact through an earthy and absurdist Rabelaisian humor.

What's so funny about rape, child abandonment, physical abuse, or gang murders? Nothing and everything, as Goldstein shows while unraveling the layers of bravado, anger, defiance, and deep sadness that are built into each complex joke. Central to this book is Goldstein's treatment of humor as resistance. Glória laughs bitterly at the spontaneous

tears shed by her son's long-estranged father when he's told that their son
was murdered on the streets at the height of his career as a young drug
lord. While the man who abandoned his baby son dares to cry, Glória,
who raised the boy to manhood, protecting and defending him as best
she could, has no tears left to shed. Bitter, mocking laugher is all she can
summon at the false tears of this sentimental stranger. Let the dead bury
the dead. Glória still has other children to watch out for.

Laughter Out of Place is not a pretty or inspirational story; the suffering produced on the margins of economic global disorder and urban
desertification is ugly. Goldstein, however, is a master storyteller, and she
brings her favela characters to life. She relates their struggles for decent
wages, in a nation whose formidable economy and whose middle and
upper classes depend on cheap wage labor, and their entanglements in
webs of racial and sexual exploitation. She also recounts their often
backfiring struggles to keep their children safe and out of illegal activities, a situation made worse by the loss of all police credibility among the
poor, which has left the drug-trafficking gangs to fill the void. While
telling these stories, she makes the necessary connections between historical, political, and economic forces and cultural habitus to show how
they shape intimate social relations, emotions, and dispositions. Perhaps
most controversially, she demonstrates that Brazil's self-defining embrace
of sexuality as a life-affirming force also limits the ability of poor women
to resist gender oppression.

Many anthropologists today shy away from the thankless task that
Goldstein has taken on. They take the far-safer route of celebrating the
beauty of exotic others at a distance, spinning idealistic travel tales about
the people they love and build their careers around through blameless,
politically correct, low-stake depictions. Other young anthropologists
avoid the inherent interpretive problems and double binds of studying
poor and powerless people by choosing research subjects who are very
much like themselves. Thus, they cannot be accused of exploiting their
powerless subjects, and the traditional claims of friendship and affection
toward one's fieldwork informants are more easily defended. Anthropology must, of course, be applied in a variety of settings—studying up,
around, and within our own society as well as outside it—and fieldworkers must heed the postcolonial critiques of the classical anthropologist's craft. However, there is still much work to be done unpacking the
structures, meanings, and effects of powerlessness, injustice, and race,
sex, and class apartheid for those millions of people stranded on the

urban peripheries of the global economy. If the anthropologist refuses to enter and document those hidden recesses and peripheral communities unknown to any except those who live there, who else will do so?

Goldstein is not afraid to describe and confront the violence that simultaneously organizes and distorts the lives of the people she befriended. Her graphic stories demonstrate the links between the structural violence of an exploitative global and domestic economy and the intimate brutalities of family life, child rearing, and domestic rape. Although anthropologists cannot presume to speak on behalf of the world's socially excluded, they can, as Goldstein does, speak truth to power and force readers to confront, momentarily, a world where people wash away the bloodstains from the previous night's gang rape or police homicide as they invite wary visitors to come inside. "Enter! It's clean, totally clean, all gone, nothing to fear now."

How will Goldstein's book be read and received by her anthropological colleagues in the United States? Not without controversy. In some quarters she will be painted with the tar brush of the "culture-of-poverty" concept developed by Oscar Lewis in the 1960s to describe the seemingly self-perpetuating aspects of deep poverty, its intergenerational and gestational aspects. In his beautifully rendered but deeply disturbing life histories of urban poor families in Mexico, Puerto Rico, and pre-Revolutionary Cuba, analyzed within the limited framework of the culture-and-personality school of his epoch, Lewis focused on the proximate (and devastating) consequences, rather than the ultimate structural causes, of the social disintegration he described. He failed to demonstrate the relationship between structure and human action, although he recognized that cycles of poverty could be broken by infusions of revolutionary optimism and hope. Lewis's culture-of-poverty thesis offended the sensibilities of the emerging New Left in America. It hit a vulnerable academic, identity politics nerve. Whereas Lewis's books are dismissed by American intellectuals as egregious examples of blaming victims for their own misfortune, they are still widely read in France and in Cuba as a potent critique of bourgeois society's failure to address and remedy the hidden injuries of class-based inequality under free market capitalism.

At the beginning of the new millennium, anthropology is still mired in bitter polemic over how social scientists should or should not observe, document, analyze, and engage politically the brutal facts of poverty, marginalization, and social death. Goldstein refuses to fall into the conventional anthropological traps of celebrating the noble savage or of raising irrelevant and experience-distant research questions about people that do not resonate with their own urgent and heartfelt crises, needs, desires, and dreams. Like Oscar Lewis, Goldstein allows herself to get very close to the intimate pathologies of power as they worm themselves into the shacks, bars, and bodegas of Brazilian shantytown life.

How will *Laughter Out of Place* be read in Brazil? No doubt with considerable pain. A great many Brazilian social scientists and anthropologists share their North American counterparts' decided preference for "studying up" and have consigned the classical ethnographies of the Latin American barrio and shantytown to the dustbins of "politically incorrect" anthropological history. But other Brazilian intellectuals, engaged in a necessary social critique of their own society and its institutions, will, we expect, find in this book much that resonates with their own understandings of Rio de Janeiro's "ground zero." Far more important is how *Laughter Out of Place* will be read by Glória and her relations, for this is a book that should be made immediately available to the people of Felicidade Eterna. We believe that they will accept Goldstein's account as a fair and true portrait of their lives, which have been pushed to the limits of human endurance. We hope that the book will be useful to them, both analytically, as a tool of critical self-consciousness, and politically, as a tool for political mobilization. We expect that it will evoke considerable empathy and solidarity within the favela and in politically conscientious sectors outside of it as well.

As part of the California Series in Public Anthropology, we hope that Goldstein's book will initiate a public conversation about topics so painful that they are almost unspeakable. We welcome and salute this brave new anthropological and ethnographic voice. *Laughter Out of Place* captures what this series stands for—bold scholarship with engagement, excellent writing, and astute critical reflections on the "state of the world." Today, much of the world's population survives precariously in shantytowns, housing projects, tenements, and homeless encampments where mind-numbing, bone-crushing experiences of poverty engulf the socially vulnerable. While conventional academics continue to argue over how to talk correctly about the violence of poverty, in this book Goldstein shows how to do it.

In capturing and translating the strange, bittersweet, edgy humor with which Glória and her family and friends face uncertain lives and certain deaths, Goldstein describes a people who are, despite everything, still in love with life. Her unblinking portrait gives readers a ray of hope.

Laughter Out of Place is a remarkable achievement, an artful and affectionate tale of home life and street life in one of Rio's infamous favelas.

Nancy Scheper-Hughes and Philippe Bourgois
Contributing Editors
Berkeley, California, March 5, 2003

Preface to the 2013 Edition

When the editors at University of California Press invited me to write a preface to *Laughter Out of Place* for its tenth anniversary edition, I was a bit hesitant. Would writing this imply that *Laughter* was a relic of history, an outdated snapshot of the social life of inequality that characterized the early 1990s in Rio? Or would it imply that something about the book endures in situ, in spite of Brazil's spectacular economic achievements over the past decade? In the years that have passed since the first publication of *Laughter,* I have often been asked for an assessment of what appears to be an unwieldy and new Brazilian miracle. Readers and friends want to know if life has improved, if domestic workers like Glória are better off now. Is Brazil's rising economic tide lifting all boats? How will the economic successes and transformations brought on by changes in politics, economics, and the much-anticipated 2014 World Cup and 2016 Summer Olympic Games affect the lives of the people there? What should friends and lovers of Brazil and Brazilians be looking forward to?

This new edition of *Laughter Out of Place* coincides with my return to Brazil, to look again and from another angle at this beautiful awakening giant, a metaphor that has been harnessed during different time frames in Brazil's historical record and that refers to its potential as an economic behemoth.[1] My current research on Brazil's widening engagement with nuclear power is in some ways worlds apart from the work that informed *Laughter,* yet it has given me new perspectives on old questions. As I traveled last summer from the cosmopolitan hub of São Paulo across a forgotten highway to an affluent gated tourist community in Angra, I was reminded all over again of how utterly beautiful, amazing, playful—and dare I say perverse—Brazil is, and I am grateful to have this opportunity to write about the well-debated changes, both real and imagined, that are now taking place there. In my comments below I reflect on the past and present and on some of Brazil's most pressing questions. These are the everyday topics that I addressed in *Laughter Out of Place* and that I hear in the conversations not only of Brazilians and Brazilianists but also of the diverse global audiences that desire contact with the pulse of this rapidly growing economy.

NUCLEAR UTOPIAS

The philosopher and social critic Slavoj Žižek speaks passionately about "the violence of liberal utopia," clarifying the idea that liberal capitalism has benefited from its apparent antiutopian stance and parading today's neoliberalism as the sign of the "new era for humanity" (2008). Žižek asserts that there is indeed a utopian core to this project, one that is accompanied by the socially disruptive effects of capitalism—different forms of violence. What brought me to Brazil during my first research trips that concluded with *Laughter Out of Place* and now brings me back again is the sense that there is a quiet form of violence at the inner core of some of Brazil's most spectacular dreams of liberal modernity, whether they are about racial and economic equality or about harnessing the potentials of nuclear energy. Last summer, these dreams led me to Brazil's nuclear power plant and brought me to the treacherous stretch of road between Cunha and Paraty.

The compass of modernity called Google had shockingly misrepresented that road. I found myself driving on a harrowingly steep, muddy switchback with cliffs that fell off the earth on one side—the last ten kilometers of my route, starting in Cunha and heading toward Paraty through the surreal and tropically gorgeous borderland, in the Parque Nacional Serra da Bocaina, between the states of São Paulo and Rio de Janeiro. This is a stretch of the Caminho do Ouro da Estrada Real (Gold Path of the Royal Road), which marked an initial colonial violence, as it is well known to have carried slaves and gold beginning in the seventeenth century. Google Maps in 2012 makes it look like a viable car route that can save hundreds of kilometers of driving between São Paulo and my final destination of Angra dos Reis—the Anchorage of Kings, or King's Cove—an ecological patch of the Atlantic Forest where some of Brazil's most notorious celebrities own homes. But this was definitely not the "good mommy" trail, a comment I offered to my eight-year-old daughter and my partner as they clung to their grab handles while we slowly bumped along at a 45 degree angle in terror.

I was on my way to initiate research at the Angra dos Reis Nuclear Power Plant and was encouraged at the little prayer spot—was it a chapel?—where the final bit of pavement met the dirt by two enthusiastic dirt-bike riders who had come from the other direction and were resting. They were pretty muddied up and looked to be exhausted; they had obviously found it a challenging ride. They gave us the Brazilian thumbs-up, encouraging us to continue in our tiny Renault rental car, a risk we took because the sun was soon to set and the road back was much longer and had no lighting. I had plans to visit the communities surrounding the nuclear power plant, to speak with its administrators, and to tour its control room and interior. In 2008, the Brazilian government authorized Electronuclear, a government-controlled company, to get back to work on Angra III, a project that lack of money and political disagreement had stalled for twenty-two years. In 2008 and then again in 2013, the government signaled its willingness to involve the private sector in limited stages of the nuclear program, such as fuel production and recycling (Tavener 2013).

Angra is about six meters above sea level and is known for its biodiversity and numerous (more than three hundred) offshore islands. The largest, appropriately called Ilha Grande (Big Island), was one I had come to know well, as I had made an extended visit there in the mid-1990s, to the now-defunct prison of the same name, to visit Glória's infamous gang leader son, Pedro Paulo, a few years before the prison was closed. My current research trip emerged from my growing interest in issues in the field of medical anthropology relating to the history of experimentation, science, and genetics, as well as the links between Cold War collaborations and the development of nuclear energy in places such as Brazil. In following and writing about James V. Neel's work among the Yanomamo (Goldstein 2012), I stumbled upon the life and work of Theodosius Dobzhansky, the revered Ukrainian American geneticist and author of *Genetics and the Origin of the Species* (1937), who went to Brazil with support from the Rockefeller Foundation to forward research on population genetics and genetic responses to environmental change. In six extended trips between 1943 and 1960, Dobzhansky, together with his Brazilian colleague Crodowaldo Pavan, did important work on gene mutations and solidified genetic studies at the University of São Paulo. Although Dobzhansky had originally wanted to work in the Amazon, it is believed that on first seeing the islands of Angra from the air, he began dreaming of the potential in harnessing this multi-island paradise to create a kind of natural population cage for genetic experiments with *Drosophila* (fruit flies). The eventual Angra Project team of 1956 did irradiate fruit flies and set them free on the islands, exploring the effects of radiation in a controlled and isolated natural paradise and comparing them to those in a laboratory. As part of this collaboration, Brazilian students in fields related to genetics were provided with scholarships for study in the United States, and some spent time at Oak Ridge National Laboratory and other key facilities that were part of the Manhattan Project. Their scientific research took form in the larger context of the Cold War and included the development of peaceful uses of nuclear technologies.

This genetics project thus appears to share some important historical landmarks and personnel with the history of nuclear energy in Brazil. Additionally, Angra dos Reis has served dually as one of the country's locations for genetics research and the eventual site of its nuclear power plant. In 1955, Brazil—then under a military dictatorship—entered into a cooperation agreement with the United States that eventually paved the way for the 1970s sale of nuclear reactors to Brazil. Today the complex of two reactors just outside the small city (of approximately 169,000 people) of Angra, in the southern region of the state of Rio de Janeiro, close to the border with São Paulo, supplies about 3 percent of Brazil's energy mix.[2] The visitor center at the nuclear plant is home to a public relations team that has created brochures and films for the public that present nuclear energy as "energy that is in harmony with the environment." These materials assert that the fish and other wildlife in the area are doing extremely well and that nuclear power is generally less disruptive than the many hydroelectric energy plants that are so common in Brazil.

There is much to say about social relations in the *vilas,* or resident communities, that thrive behind the security gates of the nuclear plant, but here I will just note that Brazilian class relations have been remade inside these communities, which lack favelas but have many familiar aspects that coincide with those of the communities I worked in and that I outline in *Laughter.* And, indeed, there are favelas just beyond the gates. In the walled city of the Angra nuclear plant, though, there are scientists and professional administrators as well as working-class people. One theme that ran through my preliminary conversations with workers of different ranks at the nuclear plant was that many contemporary employees have worked for multiple generations of Angra employers, a theme I noted between domestic servants and their bosses in *Laughter*.

During my visit, I hired a private boat for a guided tour around the islands and to see the nuclear plant from the islands' perspective. My guide, a man who had worked at the nuclear plant for more than a decade but then decided that "working behind masks" and "following so many rules" didn't appeal to him, had transitioned to boat operator and was keen on showing me around. He pointed out the painted white numbers on rocks on many of the islands, which he said denoted the testing of water quality and the effects on wildlife being monitored by the plant. Or were these numbers part of Dobzhansky's fruit fly experiments? My guide also took me to a place with many yachts, whose owners were resting or swimming, a spot where the perfectly warmed waters from the nuclear plant reentered the Cove of Kings.

On the day scheduled for my entry inside the plant, where I would interview the director of Angra II, I tried not to think about the possibility of an accident or the need for evacuation. I was suited up lightly with a hard hat, foot coverings, and earplugs; soon after I entered the building, a deafening alarm went off. As I had never been to a plant before, I couldn't tell whether this was an emergency or simply a test. My hosts quickly reassured me that it was just part of the regular ten o'clock safety test and that I should not worry. I had received authorization to see the control room and also to visit the inner sanctum of the plant—the turbines. These giant cylinders of steel were behind dozens of locking doors that my escort ushered me through, each time swiping our badges as we went deeper and deeper into areas that contained fewer and fewer personnel. When I made it through the final door, I could feel the awesome power of the technology and stood alone with my guide in the vast turbine room. I did not feel like lingering there, and after about a minute we headed back. I found it hard to reconcile the different frames of modernity that were so close in space and time: the treacherous road from Cunha on which I had arrived, and alternatively, the humming nuclear turbines in the inner sanctum. During my one minute in Angra II's turbine room, I could not help but think about the road that had led me there, the many people living close to the plant, both inside its securitized gates and beyond, and what the protocol would be in case of an accident. I had a clear memory of Fukushima.

Brazil has played a small but constant role in the development of nuclear energy in the global South, with two reactors in operation on site in Angra dos Reis and now a third under construction at the same location. The area was and still is a favorite tourist destination, known and appreciated for its beautiful beaches and islands, as well as "warm waters, nicely heated by the nuclear power stations."[3] Beyond the gates of the nuclear plant, the tourist economy is in plain sight, as are the more modest communities in Angra. From our guesthouse on the city's outskirts, my family and I were able to see the army of cleaners, gardeners, domestic servants, and boat maintenance workers getting yachts ready for sail and homes in order for the occasional visit from an absent owner. Also lodging in our guesthouse was the helicopter pilot who had brought one of those owners to a vacation home from a residence in Rio. On my boat tour, I had been shown mansions and private islands owned at some point by Ayrton Senna, Xuxa, and Ivo Pitanguy. News sources predict that Angra III may be ready to begin operations by December 2015, just in time for the 2016 Olympics.

MILLENNIAL POVERTY

Any kind of black-and-white assessment of Brazil's present and future is difficult to proffer, as every Brazilian will tell you. For the most part, I find my friends in Brazil and those who write about Brazil to be generously optimistic. Clearly, income inequality as measured by the Gini coefficient has declined in Brazil by an average of 1.2 percent per year over the past twenty years. "Focus: Brazil," a 2011 *Economist* online article, lays out the statistical details of the country's economic achievements: Brazil recently overcame Britain to become the sixth-largest economy in the world, growing at an average annual rate of 1.7 percent since 1990. It is slated to achieve its Millennium Development Goal of the reduction of poverty ten years earlier than expected: that is, by 2015. Rio de Janeiro's unemployment rate hovers at only 5.1 percent, which is half of what it was in 2003 and, in comparison with similar measures in European cities, quite good. In 2013, Brazil raised its monthly minimum wage to 674.96 *reais* ($343 U.S.).[4] According to a 2011 survey carried out by Data Popular and commissioned by the Secretariat of Strategic Affairs of the Presidency of Brazil (SAE), Brazil's middle class (C Class) held more than 46 percent of the country's purchasing power in 2009 and "experienced an increase of more than 40% in household income" between 2003 and 2009. The survey also reported that "68% of C Class youths have more schooling than their parents," "19% of the C Class population (18.1 million) plans to buy property in the coming 5 years," and "strong social mobility in Brazil is causing profound changes in the profile of young C Class workers."[5] Yet even with these advances, as *The Economist* notes, approximately 8.5 percent of Brazilians live on less than seventy *reais* per month, which translates to about $1.70 per day.

These rapid changes, signifying growth in middle-class membership, are indeed astounding and have altered how people think about Brazil and how Brazilians think about themselves. After hearing such optimistic reports, we might ask: What about the domestic workers and the Glórias who animate *Laughter*? Are their boats also rising? We would have to offer a very hesitant yes here, for as Pierre Bourdieu (1984) would have it, we must also consider the new hierarchies and distinctions that are emerging from this economic tidal wave.

Over the years, my friends and colleagues who exchange all things Brazilian have continually sent me a broad range of articles that I would say represent a genre of popular literature about domestic work in Brazil—published as news in venues such as the *New York Times,* the *Washington Post,* and more recently *Forbes.* These articles speak about the changing terms of employment and the notably better wages of domestic workers in Brazil, so much so that some include dirges by middle-class informants who lament having to live "cheek by jowl" in a world that offers fewer opportunities to find and take advantage of cheap domestic service. In a recent sarcastically humorous article in *Forbes,* the journalist Kenneth Rapoza (2013) argues that the poor have more opportunities than ever before and that in the past eight years domestic workers earned approximately 56 percent more on average than they did in the past (citing IBGE, the Brazilian Institute for Geography and Statistics). The author cites a report that says domestic servants nationwide earn an average salary of the equivalent of $360 U.S. per month, but that in large cities such as Rio and São Paulo, it can be double or triple that amount. He notes new legislation that has been passed to protect informal and domestic workers, who are now included in programs for retirement, health care, the "thirteenth" salary, and workers' compensation. These new benefits, he claims, must now figure into any individual employer's understanding of an employment contract. The *Forbes* author therefore predicts that many Brazilians and visiting foreigners, including himself, will no longer be able to afford the domestic help they once enjoyed and that the decline in cheap domestic service will continue as Brazil moves forward. What this means for the A and B (upper) Class Brazilians and the expatriates in Brazil who he imagines constitute the readership of *Forbes* is that their convenience and standard of living will decline and they will no longer benefit from the many pleasures that come with cheap, widely available domestic service.

I like to think that *Laughter Out of Place* captures something tragic and also darkly humorous about the conditions of people—mostly dark-skinned women, but also their broader communities of friends and family—living in marginal and impoverished circumstances in Rio de Janeiro in the early 1990s. My hope was to formulate a sense of their lives and struggles through processes of contextualization—historical and other—familiar to anthropologists interested in thick descriptions and in a critique of the institutions and habits that form subjectivities born amid brutal inequalities, daily humiliations, and everyday drug-gang and police violence. As I also argue, the people I came to know in the favelas of Rio de Janeiro in this time frame offered multiple, even if subtle, forms of resistance to these degradations. But since the early 1990s, Brazil has transformed—whether it is now a giant I cannot say—into a firm and stable economic powerhouse, one that is forecast to remain on the list of the top ten economies for the foreseeable future. What we have witnessed in the late twentieth and early twentieth-first centuries is Brazil unlocking the potential to enact powerful economic and political reforms that may forever improve the conditions of its citizens, relieving the sorts of racialized, classed, and gendered inequalities that *Laughter* highlights. If this fresh Brazilian future means that the poverty depicted in *Laughter* is near death, so be it. Over the years I have received different kinds of feedback about the book; one that sticks with me and causes me some angst was from a reader who called *Laughter* "the saddest book I ever read." So if it proves to be an ethnographic artifact of the past, of the distant, tortured times that once existed for the impoverished of Rio de Janeiro, I will be quite happy to welcome in the new. *Tchau*, poverty! *Tchau*, inequality! I won't miss you!

OLYMPIC PACIFICATIONS

When I returned to Brazil in 2012, I had meaningful interactions and numerous conversations with people who reminded me that the humor I had characterized as something recognizably Brazilian in the early 1990s was still very much alive and well. I also recognized that in spite of all of the positive economic changes, the climb into middle-class lives for many of the people I had known would still be a steep one. While in São Paulo, I often traveled by public bus and metro. One rainy morning I headed for the University of São Paulo, where I hoped to access the extensive archives of the Genetics Department's library and speak with researchers who knew about the history of international collaborations among scientists during the Cold War and the era of nuclear energy development in Brazil. On the bus ride, I found myself sitting next to an upper-middle-class woman from Jardins (an elite neighborhood in the center of São Paulo), who began to chat, addressing me and a few other unsuspecting passengers. She relished having an audience to whom to tell the story of how she had recently received a phone call from a person claiming to have kidnapped her husband—who was napping, even snoring, peacefully on the couch, in full view, during this conversation with his alleged kidnappers. Her story was funny, and it inspired others on the bus to tell their own, many of which were frighteningly similar. One woman who was heading to her domestic service job had received a call on her cell phone from someone who claimed to have her son in captivity and demanded that she deposit money in a bank account so that he would not have to kill the boy. As this woman did not have a son, she stridently gave this criminal a piece of her mind, telling him, "*Mata, mata ele mesmo,*" meaning "Go ahead and kill him, kill him good," and she laughed out loud as she told us that her only child is a daughter. This made for an entertaining bus ride and many smiling passengers.

When I made my last extended field research visit to the favelas of Rio in the late 1990s, I saw how friends of mine living in Felicidade Eterna had been in the wrong place at the wrong time and had suffered the consequences. This was a violent period in the favela. I carried out my last official interviews in 1998 in a seedy hotel room in the Zona Sul, as I knew quite well that Felicidade Eterna, in the embattled Zona Norte, was at war. I also knew that many of my friends who lived there had fled, at least for a time. This sort of temporary dislocation of favela residents was common: whenever there was a violent flare-up in a community, people would leave until things settled down so that they wouldn't be caught in the crossfire. The violence was not only in the favelas, however. A middle-class friend of mine had been kidnapped from the center of São Paulo as she entered her car and was driven to the outskirts of the city and then released; her car was taken, but she was left unharmed. She was emotionally shaken. I had been robbed at gunpoint in Copacabana and had a sliver of glass put to my face by a hungry-looking child at a light in Ipanema. I started to feel that I needed a break from Rio and from some of the difficult aspects of my research.

As the millennium turned, I imagined—quite wrongly—that I might have been one of the last researchers to live and work in a Brazilian favela and that the drug-gang violence that Rio's impoverished neighborhoods harbored would intensify and be forever entrenched. I thought that changes in general safety and security for residents would be slow. I held on to a small glimmer of hope as I watched from afar as Brazil attempted to usher in the first-of-its-kind-in-the-world gun ban through a 2005 nationwide referendum, only to see that referendum fail miserably, not only nationwide but decisively in every state. There were many reasons for this failure, but I would argue that the National Rifle Association (NRA), which saw the Brazilian referendum as an important item on its international agenda, supported much of the negative publicity (see Goldstein 2007a). Everyone remains well armed in Brazil, and the number of deaths of young Afro-Brazilian men in gang-related violence that involves guns remains high (Goldstein 2000).

The violence of the Rio favelas of the early 1990s that I describe in *Laughter* continued and continues, albeit in different, updated forms. Governmental and nongovernmental sources have made many well-intentioned attempts to address this issue. But the problem seems at times to be beyond the grasp of the policies that are actively creating broader middle-class categories. Solving issues associated with urban violence and criminality will continue to be challenging, as they are embedded in generations of inequality. The gangs are now institutions that serve a range of desires, some of which supersede simple economic needs; they seem to embody specific historical lineages and appear both ineffable and persistent. For example, the violence in Rio during the past two decades looks cyclical in some ways, yet it is hard to know which events ought to be seen as linked and iconic. In May 2003, drug dealers sprayed a group of university students with gunfire at a coffee shop in a poor neighborhood in Rio in retaliation for the slaying by police of a local drug trafficker. In 2005, four men in a white car killed some thirty people in two working-class neighborhoods in Rio; gunfire hit random victims. Some of the dead were shot as they stood outside a car wash, while others were killed in front of a bar at a plaza called Bible Square. It is believed that the perpetrators of this violence against civilians were military police protesting the crackdown on police brutality at that time.

In 1992, prior to moving to Rio de Janeiro, I was living in São Paulo when the Carandiru prison massacre took place, an incident that began with a prisoners' revolt but ended with the deaths of 111 prisoners at the hands of the military police of the state of São Paulo. Survivors claimed that police shot at inmates who had already surrendered; many recall the incident as an important signal of the decrepit state of human rights and prison conditions in Brazil. It also seems to have led to the formation of a criminal gang called the Primeiro Comando da Capital (PCC, or First Command of the Capital), which has been able to bring São Paulo to its knees—attacking police stations, banks, buses, and businesses since 2006.[6] Recently the attacks by the gang have focused on members of the military police, particularly when they are off duty.

When Luís Inácio Lula da Silva took office as president in 2003, he appointed a well-known public intellectual—a cultural anthropologist named Luis Eduardo Soares—to head up the federal Office of Public Security, a man who had begun addressing urban violence and marginalization issues while leading the state of Rio de Janeiro's Department of Public Security. At the federal level, Soares overhauled police institutions and addressed police corruption and human rights abuses, all of which had been taboo topics for the left and the right of the political spectrum for many years. Many citizens predict and hope that the World Cup and Olympics bids have given a renewed impetus to tackling public security and human rights problems. It is hard to know where to start analyzing the recent set of policies that are meant to partially address these issues, including the program that has received the glowing attention of global news media and is known in Rio as the Pacification Program.

Most sources point to Dona Marta in 2008 as the first time of many that a favela received the Pacification Program, created and implemented by the state public security secretary of great fame José Mariano Beltrame, with the backing of Rio governor Sérgio Cabral, who in 2013 is serving his second term (2011–14). The goal of Rio's state government is to install forty Pacifying Police Units (UPPs, using the Portuguese initials) by 2014. The idea behind the UPP has always been to combine law enforcement and social service delivery, with the hope of winning the hearts and minds of *moradores* (favela residents) through good deeds; that is, to turn police presence from something violent, negative, and oppressive into something positive that will help bring these communities back into the fold of the state. But the Pacifying Police Units have produced many unintended consequences. The October 2012 issue of *National Geographic* begins with the following, by Antonio Regalado: " 'We are guinea pigs,' declares Fabio do Amaral, a drug-gang killer turned evangelical minister. Brother Fabio preaches at a church in Santa Marta, one of Rio de Janeiro's favelas. What he means is that the citizenry of Santa Marta is part of a plan to clean up the hill-side slums for the 2016 Olympics." What pacification will mean over the long term is difficult to know, but the violence of liberal utopia and neoliberalism's differential treatment of distinct kinds of citizens will surely be on display.

The Pacifying Police Units are assigned to favelas that criminal gangs have traditionally controlled. The first order of business is then to send in the BOPEs (Batalhões de Operações Policiais Especiais, or Special Police Operations Battalions) to clear out the drug-trafficking gangs, together with their caches of heavy weaponry. This paves the way for an UPP to enter the community, create links with its residents, and prevent the return of the traffickers. But what has become clear is that criminals who are swept out of one area must go somewhere, and it is believed that they have migrated to areas in the Zona Norte—where Felicidade Eterna is located—the Baixada Fluminense, and also Niterói, just across the bay. Most Cariocas are wondering whether this migration will be a temporary or a permanent one. What will happen when the World Cup and the Olympic games are over? Will these criminals return? And what will happen to the communities occupied by UPPs in the meantime?

After the initial police invasion in November of 2011, both Rocinha and its neighbor Vidigal had Pacification Programs installed. I had vis-ited Vidigal many times in the 1990s, accompanying Glória and her children, all of whom had strong links there, as well as in Rocinha. Glória had grown up in these now-infamous communities, but because of her son's connections to drug trafficking, she had been forced to leave by the time I met her. But her roots were still strong in these favelas, and I understood that her childhood connection to this part of Rio was meaningful. Still, she had made the decision to move and felt it was safer to live in an unknown, peripheral favela where the gang activity was less intense. But even when I lived with Glória and her family in Felicidade Eterna, we all witnessed the shifting and sometimes unpre-dictable dynamics of gang activity and its effects on residents.

Jason B. Scott, an anthropology graduate student working with me, arrived in Vidigal in July 2011 and stayed a year. He was one of many other—by that time—middle-class Brazilians and foreign visitors who had fallen in love with the community and taken up residence there. Arriving just in time to witness first invasion, then pacification, and finally a kind of incipient gentrification process, Jason described what happened to Vidigal that year from a newcomer anthropologist's perspective.[7] What he witnessed is still very much in process, and we cannot know with certainty where it will lead. As he describes it, a BOPE came in, the gangs left, and the value of properties began to rise, as did interest from wealthy outsiders.

Vidigal was invaded on November 13, 2011. The police had announced about two weeks earlier that they were coming in. Most of the gringos left, and the longer-term Pacification Plan made many male residents nervous, as they would become targets of suspicion. The traffickers threw one last all-night rap and *baile funk* (funk dance) party shortly before leaving, and they used the microphones for a last round of commentary, shouting, "*Vou matar todos*" (I will kill everyone) and "*Vamos ficar aqui*" (We are staying here). In the next few days they put their equipment into plastic bags and then into fifty-gallon drums, taped them up, transported them out, and then left. The police arrived on Sunday morning and brought more than one hundred armed Choque (similar to BOPE) forces, two tanks, two helicopters, and a gaggle of journalists. They searched several hundred homes in Vidigal but did not arrest anyone at first. Later in the month, many men were arrested for alleged associations with drug dealers. The Choque unit was quite intimidating, especially in its approach of constant searches. By January 2012, the UPP came in with horses, Tasers, and friendly smiles for the residents. The UPP chief in Vidigal was a native of the community, which seemed to smooth out some of the awkward relations. In contrast, in Rocinha next door, violence returned quickly, and it is not clear if the pacification process there is permanent or temporary. Jason reports that drugs were never completely gone from Vidigal but that postpacification, there were fewer people carrying guns.

What happened too was that Vidigal was made safe, it seems, for a new round of gentrification, which had started much earlier, in the 1980s and 1990s, with the construction and habitation of middle-class high-rise apartment buildings that had been built at the favela's entry point. In the months after pacification, all property values rose enormously—the Associated Press noted a 50 percent increase[8]—and this meant that residents were getting real estate offers that tempted them to leave. The anticipated gentrification could potentially change the community forever, pricing residents out of their own homes and forcing them to live farther away, in the city's growing peripheral neighborhoods. And while the prices paid for property in Vidigal would be a temporary boon to these individuals, there is no guarantee that any such one-time deal would ensure economic stability. As has happened with other museumifying (mummifying) processes in other places, Vidigal may be very capable of becoming a historical favela without *favelados*, similar to other cities, such as Rome (Herzfeld 2009), where the social arena is suffering the effects of neoliberal policies—and the violence of liberal utopias—and the traditional left has become incapable of authentically aligning itself with residents. Rio shares some of these intangible qualities with Rome. The full impact of pacification in Rio remains to be seen, but it looks like the effects will be felt far beyond the city. Some observers have suggested that the police murders that occurred late in 2012 in São Paulo and were attributed to that city's PCC may instead be a result of the pacification process in Rio.

My early fieldwork in Brazil coincided with the tail end of the democratic opening and the elections that brought Fernando Collor de Mello to the presidency. It was a time of great disappointment in and animosity toward an administration marked by a strong neoliberal turn and numerous corruption scandals, ending in Collor's impeachment. There were moments that had in fact offered some insight into what was in the future. The curfew imposed in Rio de Janeiro during Eco-Rio 1992 was memorable: the city was presented as safe to its foreign visitors while residents of its favelas were treated as criminals. It had the veneer of security, but at the expense of human rights and civility. Many people declare that Rio today has a good vibe, and I would like to embrace that thought, but I wonder what things will be like when the stadiums are completed, the games have been played, and the city returns to its new normal.

STILL MARVELOUS

Shortly after *Laughter* was published, I became a mother and felt a great deal more vulnerable about the kinds of experiences I encountered in Rio. For the most part, Rio remains a magical city, the marvelous city, full of energy, friendliness, and optimism. But during the last few weeks of a two-year stay in Brazil, I was robbed by gun in broad daylight in Copacabana and began to experience burnout. I had it in my mind that my guardian angel must have been on strike, so I decided to take a break from my work in Brazil. I allowed myself to wander both intellectually and geographically and found myself engaged in fieldwork on pharmaceutical politics in Argentina and Mexico. I turned to the exploration of research questions that were different from what I had focused on in *Laughter* and that kept me elsewhere in Latin America with the sense that I would eventually return to Brazil, perhaps with new eyes and new perspectives on its luminous presence in the region.

Having now spent significant time outside Brazil but still in that region, I find that my appreciation of Brazil is that much greater and that my extended Latin American experiences have helped me to appreciate it with a renewed comparative perspective. Certainly, when one is working in Argentina, and even in Mexico, Brazil's presence as an economic and cultural force is not imaginary. It was interesting to find Brazil to be the object of Argentine and Mexican admiration on a number of fronts, for instance its success in overcoming the patent lock of large pharmaceutical companies based in the United States and Europe to produce cheaper and more widely accessible generic HIV/AIDS medicines, a feat that neither its neighbors nor any other countries in the region have matched (Goldstein 2007b). I can only imagine that Brazil's hosting of both the World Cup and the Olympic Games will generate envy in other countries in the region and the world. Having been in Brazil while its team was playing in two World Cup games and witnessing its well-known soccer fever, I have memories of the long and tense silences in the streets during these games, interrupted by the loud shouts that accompany a significant play or *GOL!*

There is a sense that these imminent global events are providing Brazil, and Rio in particular, with an opportunity to create new infrastructure and to repair the old; in short, there is a will to embrace this form of opportunistic modernity, complete with less-regulated neoliberal forms of private investment, and then to hope for the best. This investment in the future may include additional nuclear power plants, possibly two in the northeast and two in the southeast. With the possibility that private industry may take over parts of the nuclear industry, we are left to ask what effects the shift away from government management might have on construction decisions, safety, risk, and responsibility in the case of an accident. On the other hand, with the government taking action on crime in impoverished communities with interventions such as the Pacification Program in Rio, we might also speculate on the effects of militarized government. Whatever happens, we can be sure that Brazil's experiments with differing visions of liberal utopia will produce unpredictable outcomes, not only for the poor but also for the wealthy. We can also be sure that the whole world will bear witness.

Donna M. Goldstein
May 29, 2013

POSTSCRIPT

It is now the last week in June of 2013, as the FIFA Confederations Cup Brazil 2013 approaches its conclusion. Across the country, citizens have taken peacefully to the streets to protest the apparent government attention to Olympic and World Cup infrastructure while basic social needs such as investments in health, education, and transportation still remain dismal in many places. Several weeks ago, the government angered physicians with plans to hire up to six thousand Cuban doctors to make up for alleged personnel shortages, without plans to address deeper public health issues. Dr. Ângela Maria Albuquerque, who appeared on national news in this timeframe, expressed the deep collective dissatisfaction quite clearly: "I am a doctor, and I am disgusted. I can't practice in this shithole here. I can't do anything here." Dr. Albuquerque speaks to being overworked in a public hospital lacking space and materials; she is angered that people are dying in the corridors of the hospital while government investments are geared toward infrastructure for soccer matches. People will resolve this matter in the streets, she suggests. While the street protests were meant to be peaceful, in some cities the demonstrations were taken advantage of by individuals who used the crowds to provoke violence and destroy property. The police decision to unleash tear gas, rubber bullets, and excessive force against protestors revealed what is problematic about civilian and police interactions and what may be rotten in the core of pacification. Yet it is significant that Brazilians raised serious political and social questions in the midst of soccer madness. When even soccer is no longer sacred, perhaps Brazilians have gained the wisdom to see clearly into the future.

Donna M. Goldstein
June 30, 2013

NOTES

1. In 2011, a Johnny Walker commercial depicted Brazil as an awakening giant, which of course has already been a metaphor for Brazil's economic surge. According to one analyst at *Adweek,* the advertisement went viral and received more than three hundred thousand hits on YouTube in just five days (Gianatasio 2011).

2. More than 80 percent of Brazil's power comes from hydroelectric power stations, 8.5 percent from gas, coal, and oil, and 4 percent from biomass sources (Tavener 2013).

3. Wikipedia, s.v. "Angra dos Reis," http://en.wikipedia.org/wiki/Angra_dos _Reis (accessed May 29, 2013). The phrase was not in quotes or used ironically.

4. Byrne (2012).

5. Secretariat for Social Communication (SECOM) of the Federative Republic of Brazil, "Additional Facts on Brazil's Middle Class," www.brasil.gov.br/ para/press/press-releases/august-1/additional-facts-on-brazils-middle-class (accessed March 4, 2013).

6. See Biondi (2010) for a gripping ethnography of the PCC.

7. Jason generously shared with me his written fieldnotes regarding Vidigal.

8. Associated Press, "Rio de Janeiro Slums: From 'No-Go' to Must Buy," January 13, 2013, www.foxnews.com/leisure/2013/01/13/rio-de-janeiro-slums -from-no-go-to-must-buy (accessed March 4, 2013).

Acknowledgments

I would like to first express my gratitude to the people of the shantytown Felicidade Eterna, particularly Glória, Soneca, and their neighbors and friends who—through their willingness to share with me their experiences, stories, laughter, and humor—helped form many of the interpretations made in this book. All their names have been changed, as has the name of the shantytown where they resided throughout most of the 1990s, although I have kept their version of my name, Danni. I would also like to thank the hundreds of women living in shantytowns and working in factories in Rio de Janeiro and São Paulo who spoke with me in focus groups and individual interviews.

Although the focus of my interests has shifted over time, this book originally began with a preliminary research visit to Brazil back in 1988, when I was a graduate student at the University of California–Berkeley. I have been a fortunate recipient of a number of grants and fellowships that supported early phases of this research: a UC-Berkeley Regents Fellowship; a Foreign Language Area Scholar (FLAS) Award; a Fulbright-Hays Doctoral Dissertation Research Abroad Award; an International Center for Research on Women (ICRW) research grant; summer travel grants from UC-Berkeley's Center for Latin American Studies; Lowie Funds from the Department of Anthropology at Berkeley; and UC-Berkeley's Chancellor's Dissertation Year Fellowship.

Early in the research process, Brazilian friends and colleagues generously opened their world to me. I would like to thank Regina Bustamante, Leila Cohen, Cecilia de Mello e Souza and her family and husband, Ricardo Meth, and Danielle Ardaillon.

Without the friendship and support of Sandy Bullock and Catherine Lowndes, my early fieldwork in Brazil would have been extremely difficult. Thank you both for sharing so much of your lives with me. Special thanks to Marisa Helfer as well.

I would also like to thank those who made my first period of sustained fieldwork in Brazil pleasurable and who helped me through the early AIDS research—mentioned only briefly in this work. Their collaboration taught me a great deal and eventually led me to reformulate my research project in Brazil. I would like to thank members of the Coletivo Sexualidade e Saúde in São Paulo, especially Regina Rodrigues de Morais, Rosa Dalva F. Bonciani, Melodie Venturi, and Simone G. Diniz, as well as the following individuals and institutions for their support and collaboration during that time: Cesar Behs, Lys Portella, Silvia Ramos, and Veriano Terto of Associação Brasileira Interdisciplinar de AIDS (ABIA) in Rio de Janeiro; Paulo Cesar Bonfim, Wildney Feres Contrera, and Nelson Solano Vianna of Grupo de Apoio à Prevenção ã AIDS–São Paulo (GAPA; Support Group for the Prevention of AIDS); Jorge Beloqui of Pela Vidda-São Paulo; Monica Teixeira of Ver e Ouvir productions; and Ruth Cardoso, at the time of Centro Brasileiro de Analise e Planejamento (CEBRAP).

Throughout the years, I have benefited greatly from the invaluable friendship and intellectual challenges generously offered by Guita Grin Debert. I am thankful for the ways in which she endlessly and patiently discussed and debated everything imaginable with me. She and her husband, Zelman Debert, also opened their home to me and offered their hospitality, friendship, family, and lively conversation throughout my stays in Brazil. Special thanks, as well, to Lu for her good humor, Iara and Paula, and Bila and Bernardo Sorj.

I am grateful for the friendship, collegiality, and invaluable discussions over the years with Anton Blok and Longina Jakubowska. Many thanks to the extraordinary group of fellow North American Brazilianists whose engaging insights I have benefited from over the years: Maureen O'Dougherty, Linda-Anne Rebhun, and Robin Sheriff. I would also like to especially thank Linda-Ann Rebhun and Claudia Fonseca for their detailed and generous feedback on a critical version of the book manuscript.

Many friends throughout my years spent in Berkeley aided this process by providing challenging conversations and important interventions:

Jiemin Bao, Cecilia de Mello e Souza, Ellen Hertz, Lynn Kwiatkowski, Mary Beth Mills, and Anna Werner. Special thanks to Sydney White for her supportive friendship, intellectual companionship, and warm collegiality.

Since arriving at the University of Colorado–Boulder in 1994, I have gained new insights through exchanges with an exceptional group of graduate students, who have also become important friends and colleagues. I would like to thank Susan Erikson, Joanna Mishtal, Colleen Scanlan Lyons, Angela Thieman Dino, Carol Conzelman, and Shana Harris. Joanna Mishtal and Colleen Scanlan Lyons were especially generous with their time and energy in numerous stages of the writing process, painstakingly reading through various drafts of the manuscript. I express heartfelt gratitude to both of you.

A number of friends, colleagues, and students have read drafts of individual chapters or an early version of the manuscript at critical moments or have simply offered useful ideas. In this spirit, I would like to thank Anne Allison, Sawa Becker, Guita Grin Debert, Tracy Ehlers, Wendy Fleischer, Claudia Fonseca, Kira Hall, Dan Hoffman, Janet Jacobs, Pennie Magee, Catherine Millersdaughter, Rui Murrieta, Betsy Olson, Marc Raizman, Jim Schechter, Nancy Scheper-Hughes, Robin Sheriff, Robert Shirley, Thomas Skidmore, Ivette Visbal, and Howard Winant for their generous comments and acute insights. I also thank the students in my spring 2000 and spring 2001 Anthropology of Brazil classes for offering helpful suggestions for the chapter drafts they read.

A number of grants and fellowships from the University of Colorado–Boulder enabled me to make additional field trips to Brazil in 1995 and 1998 and provided vital institutional support in recent years: a Junior Faculty Development Award; a Twentieth-Century Humanist Grant from the Department of Spanish and Portuguese; a small grant from the Council on Research and Creative Work; a small grant from the Graduate Committee on the Arts and Humanities; and a Dorothy Martin Faculty Award.

In 1998 I was fortunate to receive a full year's funding from the National Endowment for the Humanities, which enabled me to reconceptualize my research in important ways by providing an entire year of research and writing support. Special thanks, as well, to the Rockefeller Fellowship in the Humanities at the State University at Campinas (UNICAMP) in São Paulo, which allowed me to return to Brazil in 1998 and to benefit from its special program titled "Building Democracy: Citizenship, Nation and Contemporary Urban Experience."

I have been fortunate to be surrounded by supportive and generous colleagues at the University of Colorado–Boulder: I would like to express my gratitude to every one of my colleagues in the Department of Anthropology, all of whom have offered friendship, collegiality, and ongoing conversations that have sustained me throughout these years. Special thanks to Paul Shankman, Dennis McGilvray, and Bert Covert for being especially generous colleagues and friends. I am grateful to Barbara Voorhies and Darna Dufour, who during their terms as chairs in the Department of Anthropology facilitated my research in important ways. Many thanks to the department's administrative staff, especially Linda Fry, Linda Kerr-Saville, Valerie McBride, Debbie Otterstrom, Fran Snow, and Mindy Wilding.

A solid contingent of friends have, in innumerable ways—and some from great distances—provided support, friendship, and intellectual engagement over the years: Feynner Arias Godinez, Michael Ehlers, Tracy Ehlers, Wendy Fleischer, Rebecca French, Jane Garrity, Aileen Gribbin, Karen Jacobs, Joan Kruckewitt, Pierre La Ramee, Chris Leatherwood, Deborah Letourneau, Kippy Love, Beth McGilvray, Heidi Mitke, Maria Nguyen, Barbara Reale Dillingham, Antonette Rosato, Sally Shankman, Brigitte Stark-Merklein, Bill Tally, and Peggy Heide Tally.

I have been lucky throughout the years to have found a few excellent mentors. Special thanks to Patricia Garrett, who cultivated my interest in Latin America when I was an undergraduate student at Cornell University and gave me my first opportunities to work there. Aihwa Ong's intellectual rigor and scholarship have been important guides to me throughout the years. Without the energy, enthusiasm, intellectual engagement, and inspiration of Nancy Scheper-Hughes, my own project would have been difficult to accomplish. I am grateful for her friendship and guidance over the years, and for her commitment to and passion for the field of anthropology. I also appreciate her willingness to take risks. Special thanks to Philippe Bourgois for joining Nancy Scheper-Hughes in providing a foreword for this book.

I have had the amazing luck to find an editor and friend, Richard Camp, who has accompanied me through the entire writing process. I thank him for being a fine coach and teacher, for helping me to think through questions of flow and audience, and for being such a kind and patient interlocutor as well. Special thanks to Bia Yordi, who worked on Portuguese-language translations and corrections, and to Pennie Magee, who transcribed interviews in Portuguese early in this process. Many thanks to Christine G. Ward for her mapmaking skills and to Zachary Mack for generously offering his production expertise in the final stages.

Warm thanks to the extraordinary, professional staff at the University of California Press (Annie Decker, Sierra Filucci, and Suzanne Knott), to Susan Ecklund, copyeditor, and especially to my editor at the press, Naomi Schneider, for being wholly supportive of this project. Many thanks are due to Rob Borofsky, whose commitment to intellectually and publicly engaged anthropology is unwavering.

Book projects sometimes span the lifetime of more than one family arrangement. I am grateful to Gita Steiner-Khamsi and Manu Steiner, who accompanied me through some of the most difficult early periods of fieldwork. I thank them for giving themselves so completely to this project and for sharing in numerous discussions, frustrations, and discoveries during this time.

Ivette M. Visbal has been a wonderful and patient *compañera* in these last stages of writing. I am grateful for her steadiness and encouragement, as well as her willingness to plan activities that took me away from the daily grind and helped me to escape the loneliness inherent in the writing process.

I extend full appreciation to my mother and father, Renée and Alex, and to the rest of my family for their continued love and support.

Heartfelt thanks to Kira Hall for all of her loving support in the final stages of the editing process.

All these people have given me the strength to finish this project. None of them, however, is responsible for the errors in argument or interpretation I may have made in this book.

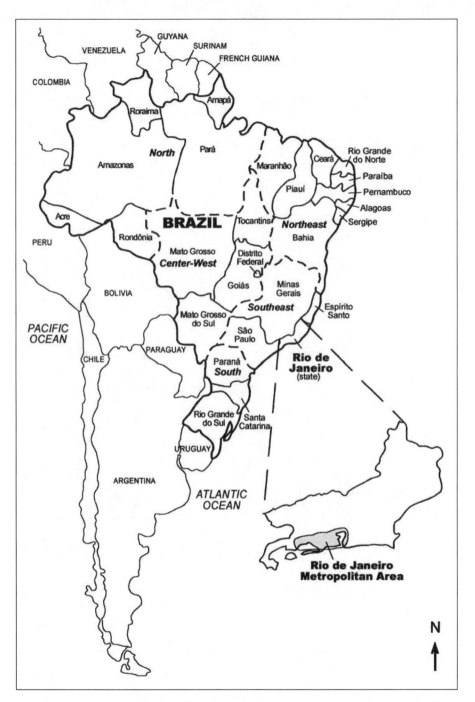

Map 1. Map of Brazil, showing location in South America, states, and regions (highlight of the state of Rio de Janeiro).

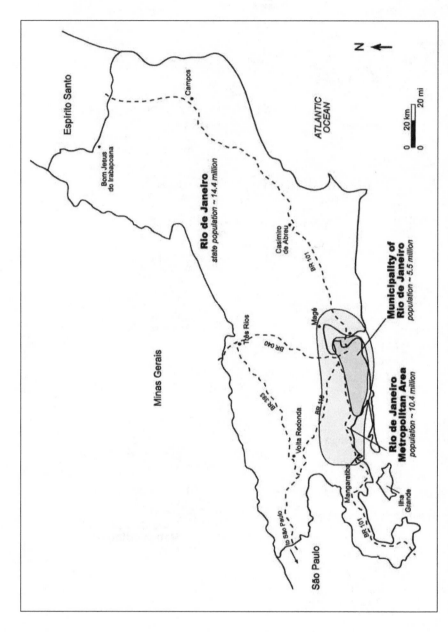

Map 2. Map of the state of Rio de Janeiro, with shaded areas depicting the municipality and the metropolitan area of Rio de Janeiro.

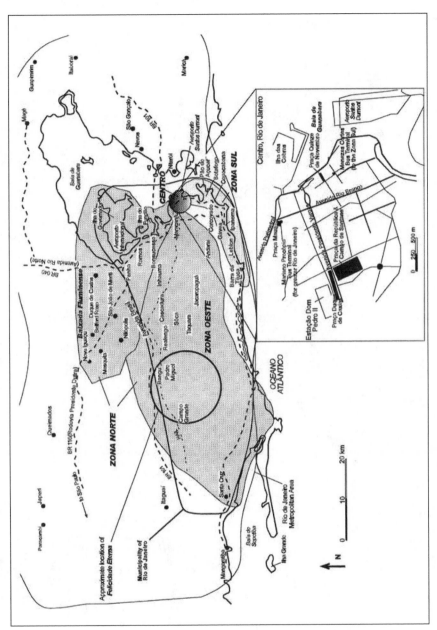

Map 3. Map of the metropolitan area and municipality (also known as the city) of Rio de Janeiro. Areas known as the Zona Norte (North Zone), Zona Oeste (West Zone), Zona Sul (South Zone), and the Centro (Center) are marked. Enlargement of the Centro at bottom right.

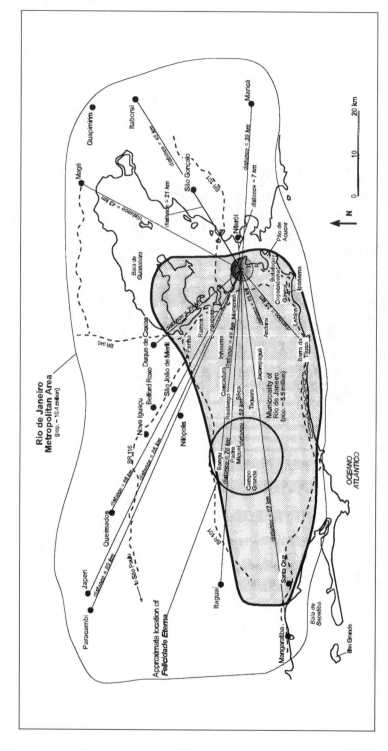

Map 4. Map of seventeen municipalities (with approximate populations noted) within the metropolitan area of Rio de Janeiro. Approximate distances to the Center of the city are noted.

TABLE I. POPULATION OF EACH OF THE MUNICIPALITIES IN THE RIO DE JANEIRO METROPOLITAN AREA

Municipality	Population
Belford Roxo	433,120
Duque de Caxias	770,858
Guapimirim	32,614
Itaboraí	187,038
Itaguaí	81,952
Japeri	83,577
Magé	205,699
Mangaratiba	24,854
Maricá	76,556
Nilópolis	153,572
Niterói	458,465
Nova Iguaçu	915,364
Paracambi	40,412
Queimados	121,681
Rio de Janeiro	5,850,544
São Gonçalo	889,828
São João de Meriti	449,562

SOURCE: IBGE Web site: www.ibge.gov.br/cidadesat/default.php.

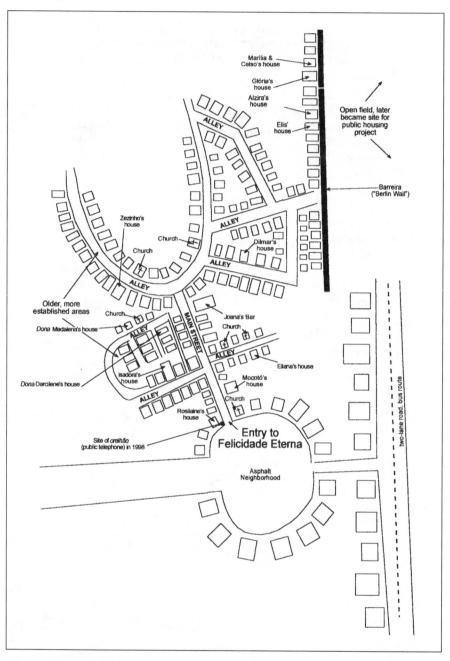

Map 5. Map of Felicidade Eterna, a favela located in the Zona Oeste, circa 1991.

Introduction

Hard Laughter

> The secret source of Humor is not joy but sorrow. There is no
> humor in heaven.
>> Mark Twain, "Pudd'nhead Wilson's New Calendar"

When I began the research that resulted in this book, I had no idea that
I would use humor as one of the consolidating themes of an ethnography seeking to chart the complex intersections among the hierarchies of
race, class, gender, and sexuality at work within poverty-stricken communities in Rio de Janeiro. I expected to write about the state and
transnational processes shouldering their way into the lives of the urban
poor—an insistent phenomenon increasingly insinuating itself into other
local contexts, both urban and rural, in Brazil and all over the globe. But
rather than locating my research in one of the institutions through which
these forces are channeled, mediated, or even challenged (a site of inquiry
that would have given me more direct access to these processes), I found
myself instead embroiled in the local life of Rio's *favelas,* or shantytowns,
performing a rather old-fashioned role as participant-observer. Here, despite their heavy and direct impact, these state and global processes often
seem detached and oddly indirect; they appear most of the time as vague,
burdensome shadows, becoming solid and "real" only through the routine and visceral engagements with the embodied effects of power: humiliating encounters with police, standing in line at the emergency room
with a deathly sick child, visiting a friend's relative in prison.

In the shantytowns, one gets the almost overwhelming sense that it is
not one's place to participate in these processes or engage in dialogue
with them. Residents feel largely divorced from these "outside" forces,
except as a generalized target of them. These forces originate elsewhere,

journey far above and beyond ordinary people, are controlled by and offer opportunity to others, only then finding their end point, their appointed destination, in the lives of the poor through the contemptuous gaze of a police officer or the dismissive gesture of a well-meaning but overworked doctor. It is hard, even for the researcher, not to feel trapped within this particular reality—an existence blinded to the larger workings of these processes that, despite their undeniable daily impact, are strangely diffuse and seemingly well beyond local influence. Indeed, it is almost impossible to escape the naturalized notion that these forces, and the power they bring to bear, simply do not belong to the poor. And on many days, throughout the course of my fieldwork, I felt the same way—that these processes did not belong to me either, even as objects of inquiry. I saw the effects of power everywhere. Its fallout was all around me. Yet I sometimes felt I had come to study the forest, only to get lost in the trees.

Because the residents of these impoverished communities are indeed embedded in structures of power that are often unpredictable and beyond their immediate control, I have been careful to conceal their collective identity through the fictional renaming of their community and by intentionally imprecise reference to the location of the community both on the provided maps and in the text. Additionally, I have masked all individual identities through the use of pseudonyms and the digital alteration of all identifiable faces appearing in the photographs. While all of the people I came to know were enthusiastic about the prospect of having their photographs appear in a published book, I have chosen to fog their expressive and aesthetically pleasing faces to ensure their personal security.

Despite the fact that I was caught up in a community where life was all too clearly hard, everywhere I turned I seemed to hear laughter. I gradually came to realize, first in my gut, later in my head, that there was much more behind the humor than I first realized. This humor was a kind of running commentary about the political and economic structures that made up the context within which the people of Rio's shantytowns made their lives—an indirect dialogue, sometimes critical, often ambivalent, always (at least partially) hidden, about the contradictions of poverty in the midst of late capitalism. It offered an intriguingly subtle window onto the forces that I many times feared I had lost sight of.

The shape of this humor, its resonance, felt oddly familiar to me. It was similar—although not identical—to an aesthetic I had experienced before, an echo from long ago. My parents, second-generation immigrants from Russia, began their married lives together in a run-down public housing project in Brooklyn, New York. Many of my childhood recollections include our immediate neighbors and friends who were also Jewish immigrants from Eastern Europe, some of whom had survived the horrors of the Holocaust. I know that many of them were tough-skinned, touched as they were so indelibly by the direct hand of evil. Yet I remember their dinner parties as particularly loud and boisterous affairs, unabashedly celebratory, their insistent laughter always overpowering those cramped little rooms and seeping under doorways into the dim halls or flowing from the high windows out over the noisy, bustling street. I also had the benefit of having both a father and a grandfather who saw themselves as the inheritors of a great comic tradition. Both were insatiable collectors of humorous stories and jokes, not all of which were considered to be "in good taste." Thus, my childhood was immersed in laughter. This humor, rendered darkly through the glass of their collective experience, masked a certain loss of innocence—and I took their messages about the world, however disguised, as a profound form of truth.[1]

Even now, as I finish writing this book, which I admit has taken far too long, my father cannot resist teasing me with the assertion that he is staying alive just to see the day it is published.

WORDS FLY AWAY

When you realize that you are not getting something—
a joke, a proverb, a ceremony—that is particularly
meaningful to the natives, you can see where to grasp a
foreign system of meaning in order to unravel it.
Robert Darnton, "Workers Revolt: The Great Cat
Massacre of the Rue Saint-Séverin"

The meanings embedded in humor are often elusive, hard to grasp, fugitive. Yet humor and laughter, even when they admittedly baffled me, always incited me to delve deeper.[2] Such laughter became a challenge, an interpretive method for beginning to unravel the complex ways in which people comprehend their own lives and circumstances. Perhaps at times only partially or imperfectly, I found that humor, despite its grinning, Cheshire cat–like nature, nevertheless opened up a window onto the complicated consciousness of lives that were burdened by their place within the racial, class, gender, and sexual hierarchies that inform their social world. Despite the rigidness of these hierarchies and tightly woven webs of power, they were not strong enough to contain this laughter, nor the meanings disguised within it, as it spilled over into my work.

The impoverished women in whose lives I became enmeshed—a largely nonliterate, urban, historically oppressed population—represented examples of contemporary women's popular culture, one that has few direct opportunities for self-expression. Humor provided one of the few vehicles for giving voice to this group of women who have very little access to the public sphere so exalted in theoretical writings about democratic governance.[3] And yet their culture remains elusive, much like—and for many of the same reasons as—historian Peter Burke's (1978) popular culture of early modern Europe: "Popular culture eludes the historian because he is a literate, self-conscious modern man who may find it difficult to comprehend people unlike himself, and also because the evidence for their attitudes and values, hopes and fears is so fragmentary. Much of the popular culture of this period was oral culture, and 'words fly away'" (65).

Women's popular culture in Rio is not only largely oral but also predominantly inaccessible in an obviously public form. We know very little about women's particularized perspective on the world.[4] Burke's assertion that "words fly away" suggests why detailed ethnographic studies may still provide important insights, despite the contention by some that this style of fieldwork-based ethnographic writing has been one of the great conceits of the discipline of anthropology.[5] Even though close to one million out of the ten million residents of the metropolitan region of Rio de Janeiro still live in favelas,[6] there have been very few ethnographic attempts to capture the tenor and context of daily life in these communities or the particular struggle of the women who form their backbone.

Yet, despite the rarity of cultural productions authored by women from the popular classes, Carolina Maria de Jesus, a poor black woman living in a Brazilian favela, was able, in 1960, to publish her personal diary that documented everyday life and her struggle to survive and care for her children within the context of extreme poverty. Throughout two decades, the book, *Quarto de Despejo*, served to bring the perspective of Brazil's urban poor to the outside world.[7] It became a key text in the fields linking Brazilian studies, studies of human suffering in impoverished communities, and studies based on autobiographical recording and witnessing. But while de Jesus's book has enjoyed an enduring popularity in the international arena, it held a relatively short-lived fame in Brazil itself.[8]

As a North American anthropologist and as a woman, however, I have had the opportunity to share in this perspective through the bawdy laughter of contemporary women with a rich oral tradition, one that remains relatively ignored by the elite classes. Through my experience in Brazil, I became a member, albeit temporarily, of a chorus of "laughing people" (Bakhtin 1984[1965]:474)[9]—in this case, a chorus of women and children sharing stories and making each other laugh—a privileged position that provided me an opening into understanding their particular lives, lives informed and constrained by the hierarchies in which they find themselves embedded.

This book, then, at its core, is about power relations and how they are experienced by the poor. Humor emerged as one of the organizing themes—but not the central focus—of this study because it is where a particular kind of communication and meaning-making takes place. Humor is a vehicle for expressing sentiments that are difficult to communicate publicly or that point to areas of discontent in social life. The meanings behind laughter reveal both the cracks in the system and the masked or more subtle ways that power is challenged. Humor is one of the fugitive forms of insubordination. Although I could not often see the discontent of these women directly, I found that I could hear it expressed, often meekly, sometimes boldly, through their laughter.

BITTER TRUTHS, HIDDEN TRANSCRIPTS

Rabelais, one of the wisest and most learned, as well as
the wittiest of men, put on the robe of the all-licensed
fool, that he might, like the court-jester, convey bitter
truths under the semblance of simple buffoonery.

> Thomas Love Peacock, "French Comic
> Romances," in *Memoirs of Shelley, and
> Other Essays and Reviews*

Having been raised within a family of homegrown comedians and their fellow New York accomplices, I found it no surprise, when I finally turned formally to the subject of humor, that the literature is filled with references to the place of humor within the Jewish tradition.[10] Freud's classic *Jokes and Their Relation to the Unconscious* (1963[1905]) claimed that self-critical jokes characterize Jewish popular life, and later theorists, taking this seminal work as a starting point, claimed that humor was often a survivalist response to the vicissitudes of life (Oring 1984; Koller 1988), a perspective referred to as the "Jewish" view of humor (Davis 1995).[11] While it may seem that the popular humor of the characters presented throughout this book displays a similarly survivalist perspective—after all, their humor is inspired within cruel and unusual political and economic circumstances that nevertheless allow them to make fun of the absurdity of their situation—it is also much more than that. It forms part of a shared oppositional aesthetic forged within a class-polarized context.

Countless philosophers, scholars, speculators, theorists, and their various fellow travelers—from Plato to Hegel, Baudelaire to Bergson—have contributed to the map that attempts to chart the multifold roles and difficult landscape of humor. Historian Peter Gay (1993) has pointed out that "the varieties of laughter cover so vast and varied a terrain that they all but frustrate mapping," and that "wit, humor, the comic . . . are exceedingly ambiguous in their intentions and their effects, prudent and daring, conformist and rebellious in turn" (369, 373). Yet, despite its paradoxical character, since the turn of the twentieth century (due in large part to the influence of Freud), the idea that behind the subtle and various guises of humor lies an essential aggressiveness has become commonplace.[12]

In the social science literature, this tension between the exercise and control of aggression has taken form as a debate that characterizes humor as either a conservative or a radical social force. One group of scholars describes humor as a kind of homeostatic mechanism that allows for social strains and tensions to be expressed within a group, thus leading to a kind of "escape-valve" analysis.[13] In many of these analyses, humor is perceived ultimately to reinforce the status quo. Indeed, Michael Mulkay (1988) argues that humor is basically impotent in affecting change in the real world, but its analysis is important because it reveals ambiguity, contradiction, paradox, and inconsistency while encouraging multiple interpretations of the world. For Mulkay, the humorous mode is "consistently inconsistent or inconsistently consistent" (219), thereby revealing the multiple realities of the social world more accurately than the serious mode. Mulkay is arguing, ironically, with a classic anthropological perspective set forth by British anthropologist Mary Douglas (1966), who wrote about humor as an anti-rite, seeing in it a potentially disorganizing and revolutionary force.[14]

This once-raging debate has taken a related but more subtle (although no less thorny) shape around questions of resistance within the contemporary discourse. Echoing Douglas's assertion of humor as anti-rite, James Scott (1985), for example, has suggested that humor might be one of the "weapons of the weak." Building on the ideas of E. P. Thompson and Pierre Bourdieu, Scott argued that elites perform various acts of public domination and that these displays of public power contrast with the disguised forms of protest and insubordination—folktales, millennial visions, gossip, rumors, grumbling, or humor—carried out by subordinate groups. These offstage protests are the "hidden transcripts" of resistance, those that can easily be missed or dismissed because they are not public. These acts are in opposition to the dominating rituals of the ruling classes—a "counter-theatre," to use Thompson's term[15]—through which those classes exhibit their authority and exact deference from the poor. The upper classes, by virtue of their position, can deploy their weapons directly (in the form of economic and political control, for example). The poor, by contrast, are forced to express their resistance behind the backs of power.

Both Thompson and Scott have been interested in how public rituals are used in displays of domination and how the dominated classes, meekly or boldly, meet those displays through their own ritual forces. Their analyses suggest that laughter may be a powerful, though fugitive, act of insubordination, "a sly assertion of dignity" (Gay 1993:370). Indeed, humor can be a productive site from which to read less public forms of cultural production, to explore "the relation between aesthetic forms, material conditions, and ideological conceptions" (Williams 1987:93).

This leads us beyond the arguments over whether humor functions essentially as a conservative or a disorganizing force to reveal the idea that humor, through its aggressive impulse, is a form of power: "Using the materials of its culture, humor offers splendid openings for the exercise—and the control—of aggression" (Gay 1993:368). Scott suggests that whereas the power of the ruling classes allows them to publicly deploy their rituals and theater, the hidden transcripts of the powerless are disguised forms of resistance that "insinuate" a critique of power (1990:xiii). Humor can indeed, as Scott and Thompson argue, function as a weapon of the weak. But it is important to remember that laughter also falls within the arsenal of the powerful. In other words, humor, as an expression and deployment of (class) power, is potentially both conservative and liberatory.

Certainly not all forms of protest are revolutionary; but neither are they all flaccid or irrelevant. Everyday forms of "resistance" are admittedly largely fleeting, but, I believe, they are important nonetheless. As expressions of power, such dissent reveals the fault lines within society. As a deployment of power, however weak or limited, dissent challenges the status quo. If laughter often does not live up to its radical potential, it nonetheless echoes Rabelais and speaks bitter "truths to power."[16] Perhaps this is laughter's most fundamental and revolutionary role. As Gay reminds us, at its most basic, "humor is a very human way of putting such [hidden] truths on record" (1993:373).

RESISTING RESISTANCE: SAHLINS (STILL) WAITING FOR FOUCAULT

The binary division between resistance and non-resistance is an unreal one. The existence of those who seem not to rebel is a warren of minute, individual, autonomous tactics and strategies which counter and inflect the visible facts of overall domination, and whose purposes and calculations, desires and choices resist any simple division into the political and apolitical. . . . There are no good subjects of resistance.

> Colin Gordon writing on the work of Michel
> Foucault, "Afterword," in *Power/Knowledge:*
> *Selected Interviews and Other Writings,*
> *1972–1977*

Being called upon to provide after-dinner entertainment to the Fourth Decennial Conference of the Association of Social Anthropologists of the Commonwealth, held in Oxford on July 29, 1993, North American anthropologist Marshall Sahlins (1999[1993]) took the podium and proceeded to render into dry satire the latest "postmodern" trends in the field for his esteemed, and doubtlessly delighted, colleagues:

> Power, power everywhere,
> And how the signs do shrink.
> Power, power everywhere,
> And nothing else to think. (23)

These few evocative words provide an introduction of sorts to Sahlins's tongue-in-cheek commentary that evening.[17] I was not lucky enough to have been present, but I can imagine the scene. Sahlins is perhaps the perfect trickster among what I imagine to be our discipline's more staid and proper British academic counterparts. It was a brief, humorous, but telling moment in the history of anthropology. On the one hand, his commentaries were a facetious and whimsical bit of entertainment. On the other hand, the "hidden transcript" of his often clever and biting wit reveals a stern and rather serious critique of the state of theory in the social sciences regarding hegemony and the (according to Sahlins, perhaps overemphasized) influence of Foucauldian constructions of power. "Quite wondrous, then, is the variety of things anthropologists can now explain by power and resistance, hegemony and counter-hegemony. I say 'explain' because the argument consists entirely of categorizing the cultural form at issue in terms of domination, as if that accounts for it" (Sahlins 1999[1993]:23). The droll lesson of the evening seemed to be Sahlins's version of Freud's proclamation that "sometimes a cigar is just a cigar."[18] Cloaked in humor, his is a stern admonition to be wary of the trivialities overinvested with meaning by many of today's researchers who have, according to Sahlins, become swept up in foolish faddishness.

So, while we might be tempted to dismiss Sahlins's barely buried critique because it is embedded in humor, this would be a mistake. Sahlins certainly is just "joking" about the excesses in the discipline, but the old master Freud would be the first to point out that there is seldom such a thing as "just" joking. For Freud, jokes are as powerful a window into the trials and tribulations of the psyche as dreams. (Freud was talking about the individual psyche, but we could extend this to the social psyche as well.)

In a more earnest venue, Sahlins (1999) has indeed more seriously questioned the tendency in recent ethnographic writings to claim that "all culture is power," or that everything is explicable in terms of domination and resistance. We are warned that we should not be tempted into spinning certain trivialities into material that is political, a point that I want to heed to some extent. I have taken some of Sahlins's commentary seriously and subsequently have tried to resist as much as is possible the seductiveness of seeing resistance everywhere I turn. While it is true that an act cannot be termed resistance merely because it took place in the context of domination, it is important to recognize that every act is mitigated through class position and is implicitly a class act, ultimately political in the sense that every act, as well as the analytical practices we employ to understand these practices, reflects, reinforces, and enacts class relations. It is important to remember that hegemony (Gramsci 1971)—that predominance of ruling-class interests and of the acceptance of those interests as commonsense by those subordinated to those interests—is, quite literally, "habit forming" (Lock 1993:384).[19]

Just as I do not want to fall victim to a too-easy functionalism, neither do I want to back away from an ethnography that examines the complex and ambiguous discourses, emotions, and sentiments of real people. Rather, I hope to occasionally sort the "winks from twitches" (Geertz 1973:16). "Good-enough" ethnography, to use Nancy Scheper-Hughes's (1992:28) term, champions the imperfect work of unraveling and representing how domination works, a task strengthened by including as subjects and agents those who are dominated.

BLACK HUMOR, CLASS, AND CARNIVALESQUE LAUGHTER

Frequent and loud laughter is the characteristic of folly
and ill manners; it is the manner in which the mob express their silly joy at silly things, and they call it being
merry. In my mind there is nothing so illiberal and so
ill-bred as audible laughter.

Lord Chesterfield, *Letters*, March 9, 1748,
quoted in John Bartlett, *Familiar Quotations*

While the humor of the poor may not necessarily lead directly to rebellions and political revolutions, it does open up a discursive space within which it becomes possible to speak about matters that are otherwise naturalized, unquestioned, or silenced. Further, because humor is connected to the sensibilities of a particular group, it is intimately connected to one's position within the class structure. As Gay notes, "Humor is Janus-faced; in marshaling a momentary community of laughers, it ingratiates the teller with a chosen audience, but at the same time and by the same means stigmatizes others as outsiders to be disliked or despised" (1993:370). The humor of particular classes plays an important role in boundary formation and the reinforcement of class positions, hierarchies, and structures. Through laughter—one's own as well as that of others—one's naturalized and proper "place" within the social structure is outlined and reinforced, as well as contested. In humor, "characteristic expressions of individual minds, class habits, and cultural styles" (369) are embedded.

As Henri Bergson put it, "Laughter is always the laughter of a group" (1956[1911]:64). That said, it can also be used to upset those same group boundaries.[20] The black humor I came to know in the Brazilian shantytowns was a discourse created by the poor and used against the wealthier classes.[21] Brazilian anthropologist Roberto Da Matta (1994), writing on the characteristics of popular culture in Brazil, relates popular culture to that which is not official culture, to what is often referred to in Brazil as *o povo*, a word that can invoke everything from the folk or the people to the majority or masses of the population belonging to the subordinated classes. While it was once common to think that elite culture always moved downward toward the masses and that the masses merely mimicked the elite, there is now greater interest in tracing the effects of elite and popular culture on one another.[22] Bakhtin (1984[1965]) employs this notion of circularity, an idea that refers to the interactions between popular and elite cultures, and perhaps more accurately describes the processes involved. His work on the popular culture of the Middle Ages offers a vision of this culture as one with a focus on bodily orifices and bodily functions—a kind of "grotesque realism"—that has been difficult for social historians to capture: "We cannot understand cultural and literary life and the struggle of mankind's historic past if we ignore that peculiar folk humor that always existed and was never merged with the official culture of the ruling classes. While analyzing past ages we are too often obliged to "take each epoch at its word," that is, to believe its official ideologists. We do not hear the voice of the people and cannot find and decipher its pure unmixed expression" (Bakhtin 1984:474). From the point of view of the official culture, these popular aesthetic forms—including those of o povo in the Brazilian context—represent a form of "bad taste" and, because of this distinction, are more difficult to read as part of official history. Bakhtin pointed to the ways in which the folk would play with the body in its "low" form—fart, defecate, and pick their noses—in a manner that reinscribed the body as a source of comedy. Similarly, David B. Morris (1991), in his fascinating study of the history and culture of pain, positions the body as a fundamental source and object of human laughter: "Comedy needs the body in the same way the sonnet needs fourteen lines and unrequited love. The life of the body—which most philosophers can afford to ignore or dismiss as trivial—is almost a formal requirement of comic practice" (82). Within a Bakhtinian world, a world that celebrates the rituals of the folk such as Carnival, it must be noted that bad taste is embraced. Carnival is a time when popular culture is permitted to broadcast its commentary, mustering all its power through lowness or bad taste.

Film critic and Brazilianist Robert Stam (1989) applies Bakhtinian categories to his analysis of a number of productions—twentieth-century music, theater, dance, and film—and finds that the carnivalesque aesthetic permeates Brazil. It is not merely cornered within the popular

classes; rather, it provides convincing evidence of Bakhtin's notion of circularity, of the interactions and exchanges between popular and elite cultural aesthetics.

Forms of humor can be conceptualized within this framework. For
example, black humor, as it appears throughout this book, is comprehensible across a broad range of classes. I would argue, however, that it
is borne within the material and ideological circumstances of the people
whose lives I portray here. Accordingly, I must warn the reader of his or
her own possible reactions to this particular aesthetic. Whereas an artistic production can elevate what is officially considered bad taste to the
realm of art, the day-to-day carnivalesque aesthetics of the popular
classes are often viewed by middle-class and elite culture, both in Brazil
and elsewhere, as inappropriate or out of place. In fact, the themes, language, and general storytelling of the women in the pages that follow reflect a culture and a sense of humor that are, in many respects, distinct
from the official culture of the dominant classes. The humor of these
classes is at least partially traceable to the suffering they experience in
everyday life. Nevertheless, Brazil produces its own form of black comedy, but this body of work is partially a product of a "trickling up" of a
popular aesthetic form. One might be incited to ask, then, how are the
forms of elite humor in Brazil different from the humor of the popular
classes? The difference is a subtle, although palpable, one. The elite
classes exhibit a similar sense of black humor, and their stories reflect a
knowledge of misery in their midst, but it is usually a distanced misery.
It is not that their commentary is in any way inauthentic or invalid.
Rather, their suffering has different roots and different consequences. It
is within the context of everyday lives and interactions that the stories
presented here gain distinction. These protagonists live in the same communities where stray bullets from police and gangs are flying and where
gangs and churches jointly vie for their allegiance. There is a direct relationship between the materiality of the misery and the aesthetic form,
whereas among the middle and elite classes who dominate through their
position in the social structure, it is a second-order aesthetic. Here, one
can ground Bakhtin. Here, the lives that produce black humor are lives
that are themselves plagued by particular kinds of tragedy and suffering,
caused in large part by their material conditions. These are not the same
problems lived by the middle and upper classes.

And so it is in these ways that laughter and humor play a significant
role in power relations. The black-humored commentaries of the subordinated classes are windows into the sense of injustice oppressed peoples

feel about their conditions. While those with power act out a theater of majesty, wealth, and domination, those with less power act out a "counter-theatre" of objection, defiance, and absurdity.

This body of humor, taken together, makes me believe that its practitioners understand the futility of certain forms of protest (the ones we expect to see and thus tend to look for) but nevertheless are acutely conscious of the situation they face. For those of us who are on the sidelines attempting to analyze these situations, we are troubled by the implications of what our underestimation or overestimation of the effects of their protest will mean. Rather than too easy and quiet, I have come to see their laughter as hard and loud, in a way different from the more expected forms of protest, which only rarely find expression in their lives and thus in these pages. Their laughter contains a sense of the absurdity of the world they inhabit. This connection—between absurdity and laughter—is one that the people portrayed on these pages may not articulate spontaneously, but they would doubtless recognize it. Others, too, will understand this connection, much like the architect John Donald Tuttle,[23] who playfully inscribed a quotation from Rafael Sabatini[24] above a doorway in the Hall of Graduate Studies at Yale University: "Born with the gift of laughter and the sense that the world was mad."[25]

WHISTLING PAST THE GRAVEYARD OF THE COLD WAR OF CLASS

I believe that the notion of a hidden transcript helps us
understand those rare moments of political electricity
when, often for the first time in memory, the hidden
transcript is spoken directly and publicly in the teeth of
power.

> James C. Scott,
> *Domination and the Arts of Resistance*

Brazilians have always prided themselves as a nation in being (relatively) bloodless during major moments of historical upheaval. This self-image is of course partially a revision, history tidied up to make these actors more appealing to themselves and to the world at large. But while Brazil did, for example, move from colony to kingdom, kingdom to empire, and empire to republic without extensive bloodshed, as well as abolish slavery without a civil war, there was indeed violence. The Paraguayan War (1865–70), the decimation of Canudos (1890s), and the military dictatorship's successful suppression of political dissent (1964–85) provide historical counterexamples. Moreover, one could name Brazil as that place where the extremities of radical inequality seem to effortlessly remain in place, exhibiting almost none of the strain often seen blatantly cracking the surface of other places where similar inequality is evidenced. Given the flagrant nature of Brazilian inequality, one would most likely have never predicted that Brazil would have been able to avoid the appearance of a large-scale, class-based revolutionary movement. Nevertheless, despite its sometimes misleadingly celebrated harmony, I attempt to attend ethnographically to the distinct forms of class hegemony and the muted forms of resistance against it, searching both within and beyond the distinct communicative forms people use to express dissatisfaction.

It is worth pointing out that the resistance of the population in Brazil has taken place within a number of relatively pacific and democratically oriented social movements, especially during the last twenty years. Both a strong Workers Party (Partido dos Trabalhadores [PT]) and an increasingly successful grassroots movement (Movimento dos Trabalhadores Rurais Sem Terra [MST]) made up of rural, landless workers fighting for land reform and for access to agricultural lands have enjoyed a certain measure of success. Likewise, several new social movements have emerged.[26] I tend to be slightly less optimistic—but still supportive—about these movements because, in many cases, they tend to be thick with committed and well-intentioned middle- and upper-class activists but sometimes thin on representatives of the populations they hope to represent. However, it must be recognized that they have been successful, both in professionalizing their movements in the context of nongovernmental organization formation and in making real political gains through both local and global protest networks. The women's movement, the black consciousness movement, and even the relatively newer AIDS social movement provide examples of such groups; each can point to important gains made over time, and their efforts are to be lauded. But it is important to note that the women I worked with and whose lives I speak about here are emphatically not members of these groups, nor do they have much information about such organizations. I mention this to point out that part of the problem these women face is that they do not even have access to these collective political organizations. Their only weapons of resistance are their fierce wits and sharp tongues.

The protagonists in this ethnography find themselves at the bottom of a number of complex and interacting hierarchies, a situation that makes it difficult, if not impossible, to find their way out from under these oppressive structures in any straightforward manner. They experience simultaneous and multiple forms of domination, including criminalization by the police forces and the society at large; intimidation by the local gangs whose web of activities seduce their youth and entangle many who want to remain neutral; the narrowing of public space, in terms of being made to feel ill at ease, illustrated in such examples as strict policing during periods of international attention;[27] a sense of ambiguity regarding their own evaluations of the color of their skin, hair type, and facial features; and frustration in their relationships with men who can transgress sexual boundaries as part of an acceptable cultural script. These women are, throughout their everyday lives, almost wholly devoted to surviving. They have not had the privilege of becoming a well-organized or a highly politicized social movement. At least, not yet.

The women introduced here are so far removed from the economic transformations taking place in Brazil that their particular favela has not yet even been visited by global corporations attempting to harness cheap home labor in the production of toys or sweaters or electronic goods, as has been found by some of my colleagues in other similarly impoverished communities just beyond the center of Rio de Janeiro.[28] The vast majority of the women studied here belong to a lineage of domestic workers whose daughters now are attempting to break from this tradition and are experiencing limited success in locating satisfactory alternative forms of employment. Yet these women communicate in an oppositional aesthetic style—a constant flow of spontaneous black humor—that seems to belie their everyday struggles. This black humor, one of the many offshoots described by Freud as intimately related to the human aggressive impulse and defined by Breton as the ability to find laughter in human tragedy, is significant because it is perhaps one of the few ways of escaping pain and human suffering. As Morris writes: "We tend to emphasize Freud's well-known theory that laughter expresses sublimated aggression, where the relation between comedy and pain is quite explicit. It is useful to recall, however, that Freud also sees a much more subtle and disguised relation linking comedy and pain. In a late essay, for example, he describes humor as a crucial means for *evading* the compulsion to suffer that he elsewhere finds endemic to human mental life" (1991:89). This more subtle link between pain and humor has long been known: "Even in laughter the heart is sorrowful" (Prov. 14:13),[29] or, as the comedian Jerry Lewis once remarked, "Funny had better be sad somewhere."[30] The women described on these pages seem to be laughing in spite of their suffering. Or because of it. Or, perhaps more accurately, it is a combination of both. Humor is one way of bearing witness to the tragic realities of life and an expression of discontent—the oppositional act, to turn Scott's phrase, of laughing directly into the teeth of suffering.

Is this laughter of resistance an example of what Scott (1985) has termed the "small arms fire in the class war" (1)? The ambivalence and ambiguity of fugitive forms of resistance elude interpretation. Perhaps it is the verbal equivalent of throwing stones. Revolutions have been started with less, and often it is hard for us to know when those moments are upon us. I happened to be in Rio de Janeiro during the *arrastões* (beach sweeps) of 1992, when gang youths from poor neighborhoods swept across the beaches populated by middle- and upper-class bathers.[31] I wondered whether such actions signaled the possibility of the cold war over class beginning to heat up. But waiting or hoping for the revolution is tricky business, as Scott himself points out: "For all their importance when they do occur, peasant rebellions—let alone revolutions—are few and far between. The vast majority are crushed unceremoniously. When, more rarely, they do succeed, it is a melancholy fact that the consequences are seldom what the peasantry had in mind" (xv–xvi). It is to court a hard bargain to wish for such a revolutionary moment, because we all too often know beforehand who will suffer the greatest losses.

In my own experiences in Brazil, laughter seems to fall short of a direct weapon of rebellion; humor is a much more discursive form of resistance. Humorous stories about class circulate freely and frequently on both sides of the class divide. I have heard many stories, for example, from middle- and upper-class friends who are perplexed by the laughter of a domestic worker. They have watched the same evening soap opera, but rather than being moved to tears like her employer, the domestic worker is inspired to laughter. Because of such "laughter out of place," these workers and their popular culture may be seen as a kind of "alien within" by these more powerful classes.

Thus, a Brazilian reader from any class would need much less explanation of the humor spelled out here than would the North American reader, who needs more of a guide to the context, the daily struggles, and the inequalities and hierarchies within which the humor of this unfamiliar culture takes place. Brazilians of all classes, however, will recognize this humor as part of their own because they know their own context and by now accept the circularity of this popular form. Despite this, there are moments of misrecognition wherein even elite Brazilian readers may experience a newfound identification through a close reading of this text.

Regardless of the audience, and despite my own rather ambivalent feelings regarding the radical potential of humor, I nevertheless humbly join Walter Benjamin (1978a) here in suggesting, "There is no better start for thinking than laughter" (235).

CHAPTER I

Laughter "Out of Place"

Laughter alone remained uninfected by lies.

Bakhtin, *The Dialogic Imagination*

When I returned to Felicidade Eterna in May 1995, after having been away for almost three years, I arrived at Glória's shack unannounced, hoping to surprise her and her family. Upon entering, I noticed that only Glória's children were there. It happened to be Mother's Day, and Glória had not gone to the affluent Zona Sul to work. Instead, she was seated at Joana's *botequim*, her favorite bar in Felicidade Eterna, getting on with a plan to inebriate. Everyone, including myself, had grown older in the years between visits, and there was indeed surprise and delight all around as we tried to connect the present with the images we had retained of one another from the past.

Glória's youngest daughter, Soneca, still the best storyteller in a talented group, quickly filled me in on the key events that had transpired since my last extended stay in 1992.

"Do you remember Zeca?" she asked impishly.

"Yes," I answered, smiling. "Of course I do."

She held out the index finger of her right hand and drew a line across her neck while sticking out her tongue, throwing an eye-popping glance at the low ceiling.

"*Morreu e fedeu,*" she declared. "He's dead and decayed."

I was taken aback, momentarily struck speechless, as if I had been physically slapped. She laughed teasingly, despite her recognition of my own deeply felt shock and sadness.

"I never liked him anyway," she continued. "He was a runt and a tat-

Figure 1. Zona Sul, Rio de Janeiro, with Pão de Açucar in the background.
Photograph by author.

tletale, and our mother always protected him because he was sick. I don't
miss him at all."

This was my abrupt and unsettling reinitiation into a manner of everyday interaction that, in the past, I had often experienced as harsh and
cold-blooded but over time had become comfortable with—another sort
of emotional home. Even at that moment, after I had been away for so
long and was still recovering from the unexpectedness of Zeca's death,
it felt strangely familiar.

It had been nearly three years since I last saw Zeca, Soneca, Glória,
and the rest of Glória's family and friends whom I had come to know intimately in 1992. The favela had changed in many ways over those years,
and I was busy registering those changes as I tried to digest the news that
Zeca had died.

I still had a bit of adjusting to do, since I had only landed in Rio a day earlier. I was lucky enough to still have a few middle-class friends living in the Zona Sul whom I could count on, and so I was able to procure a first-class ride out to Felicidade Eterna—rather than brave the bus—through my friend Katy (pronounced Kay-chee in Brazilian Portuguese), a British biologist working at the Oswaldo Cruz Foundation.[1] So we set out for the Zona Oeste (West Zone) of the city following Avenida Brasil in her forever reliable but rusty Volkswagen Beetle. Driving out through the city center, we passed the early-twentieth-century Opera House, the building meticulously modeled after the one in Paris and so clearly evocative of an earlier Europhile grandeur. We made our way out the bus route to the west, past the swarming bus terminal, and into the heavy industrial and trucking zone, all the while watching the endless procession of crowded buses delivering the throngs of predominantly dark-skinned service workers to their homes on the outskirts of the city.

Eventually, away from the center of the city, the highway becomes wider, and we caught a glimpse of the beautiful, lush tropical hillsides, many of which are still without houses. Factories, car dealerships, and McDonald's restaurants slipped by in the heat as we continued north and west until the landscape flattened out and began to sprawl as the poor neighborhoods of the West Zone spilled around the far edges of the city, marching sloppily, endlessly, toward the horizon.

I felt extremely fortunate to have been able to arrive in this way with Katy in her car; I had usually made the trip by bus, and through the crowds of bodies had to keep watch for my mental landmark—a particular motel that marked the entrance to Felicidade Eterna—squeeze my way to the front of the bus, and then, once out of the bus, figure out how to cross over the lanes of swiftly moving traffic to the other side.

The main entrance into Felicidade Eterna looked pretty much the same in 1995 as it had at the end of 1992. Katy and I were able to leave the car at the entrance and find the opening—a dirt path that stood between a church on one side and Rosilaine's simple cement house and yard on the left. I took note of a second church that had sprung up next to the first one, adding to the six already in place for a number of years. The streets remained unpaved, and just inside the narrow opening was a wide dirt road leading up a slight incline of about a half mile. Mocotó, a woman in her midforties whose nickname refers to a soup made from a cow's foot, was seated in a sturdy chair just past the entrance. She was missing one leg, thus the nickname. She was, as usual, selling candy and little, almost worthless, plastic toys, whatever her Clube dos Paraplégicos (Paraplegic Club) happened to be peddling that week. The club, a church-based charity, aided people with disabilities by giving them cheap, colorful trinkets and toys to sell.

Within Felicidade Eterna, two or three families owned cars, and as usual, a group of young men was working on one of these aging machines at the entrance, just in view of Mocotó. I almost never actually saw any of these cars running or transporting people. Just a few feet past Mocotó and to the left was the wide street where Isadora and her husband, Zuco, lived. Her street was a bit narrower than the main drag, and there were always children playing there, sheltered somewhat from the noise and activity of the main thoroughfare. Once on that street, one became swallowed by the favela; the homes here were some of the most established ones. Built next to one another, typically sharing a wall on one side, they by now had two stories and towered over the narrow, dusty track.

From here, one could take an even narrower alleyway and find the homes of other familiar people. Isadora's mother lived down this alley. I always dreaded walking this route because this semicircular alley never got much light, and garbage, plastic bags, and other debris were often strewn about. Once I had been startled by rats rummaging through some waste there. Unfortunately, I had to brave the route often because Zezinho's house was also on this path alongside that of his ex-mother-in-law, Dona Madalena.

Leaving this particular maze of alleyways going back out past Isadora's house and on to the main drag, one could walk about two city blocks until arriving at the horseshoe, a kind of dead end of the main street of Felicidade Eterna. Just before the horseshoe, on the right, was Joana's botequim, a colorless cement structure with an open window and a ledge for clients to lean on and view the shelf inside with various alcoholic drinks and a large freezer-style refrigerator solely used for beer.

Bearing right, one passed through another series of short, muddy alleyways and arrived at the *barreira,* the "barrier" or limit to the land that made up Felicidade Eterna. The houses leading to the barreira were quite mixed; some shacks were neat, little, brightly painted bungalows with cement floors. Some were Northeast Brazil–style wattle-and-daub huts. Others were more ramshackle structures made of any combination of brick, wood, cardboard, or other found materials. The barreira was the newest part of the favela, and many of the shacks leading up to it and lining it were in various stages of construction. Compared with the homes lining the main street of Felicidade Eterna, these homes were

Figure 2. Favela, or urban shantytown, in the Zona Sul, Rio de Janeiro.
Photograph by author.

made of the least stable materials. This is where Glória and her large
family lived.

When I first visited Felicidade Eterna in late 1991, it was a small community—fewer than one hundred houses. It had remained that way up
through 1995. A few of the residents had built small extra shacks on
their tiny properties, giving up yard space to accommodate a grown child
starting his or her own family. Early on, Glória, too, had built a tiny
shack adjacent to her own—one barely large enough to shelter a single
bed—for her daughter Filomena and her boyfriend, Adilson, and their
infant son, David. In 1991, the view outside of Glória's shack just beyond the barreira was an empty field where Zeca and Félix and other
boys would fly kites and occasionally take a ride on an underfed horse

that one of the children from outside of the favela pastured there. By 1995, however, the barreira itself was transformed.

Just a few hundred feet from the houses along the barreira, the government replaced the flimsy wire fence with barbed wire because the empty lot of land adjacent to the shantytown was now to be used for the construction of low-income housing. A series of small, attached two-room cement bungalows in six lines were being constructed and were within perfect view of Glória's rickety shack.

Glória's network of friends in Felicidade Eterna spanned the economic spectrum from the poorest to the wealthiest. Isadora, who lived near the entrance to the shantytown and had a lucrative bar and store inside her two-story brick home, was one of Glória's closest friends and the *comadre* (godmother) to one of Glória's children.[2] Although their homes were separated by only a few blocks, their economic situations represented the two extremes in Felicidade Eterna. Glória and her immediate family represent—not only to outsiders but also to her neighbors—the poorest end of the working classes. In this position, Glória often had to rely on Isadora for help in times of trouble. I learned that over the course of many years this inequality placed an enormous strain on their relationship, eventually causing a lasting rift in their long-established friendship.

Despite the economic stress felt by almost everyone in Felicidade Eterna, every household had some kind of television and radio—varying in age, quality, and state of disrepair. Glória's rabbit-eared, unreliable black-and-white television sat atop a flimsy wooden shelf. It was necessary to pound its top with a closed fist in order to get a clear picture. Glória's shack was not equipped with a proper antenna, an item sported by the rooftops of some of her more affluent neighbors. Isadora, for example, owned a relatively large and well-performing color television set with perfect reception—an advantage, I suppose, of living in one of the tallest buildings in the neighborhood. In the evenings—and often during the day—one could hear boisterous voices and perceive the dull blue flicker of television light bleeding out of open doorways and windows. Many people seemed to enjoy having the television or radio on as a kind of background noise, even during the day when they were busy. When a good *telenovela* (television soap opera) was playing in the evening, more focused attention was directed toward the screen.

When I first met Glória in late 1991, she had charge of fourteen children. Of her own children, beginning with her youngest, there was Félix,

Figure 3. View from Glória's shack: barreira and low-income housing units before they were occupied. Photograph by author.

Zeca, Tiago, Soneca, Filomena, and Anita.[3] Additionally, she had taken in Lucas, Marta, Cláudia, Alexandro, and Roberto, the children of her sister Celina. Celina had died in 1985, and Glória made a concerted effort to track down each of her nieces and nephews, who had been sent to live separately among a constellation of godparents and assorted relatives. By 1990, she had collected all of them. In addition to these nieces and nephews, she had also taken in three of her former lover's children, who, even after the couple parted ways, preferred to remain with Glória rather than with their father.

As I stood with Soneca, still reeling from the news of Zeca's death and at the same time strangely comforted by Soneca's Aesopian laughter,[4] I found myself doing an all-too-common arithmetic—mentally running through all the faces of Glória's cobbled-together family and subtracting Zeca's face from the picture. Without Zeca, there were now only thirteen children sleeping in Glória's shack.

FIRST ARRIVAL

I arrived in Brazil to begin my dissertation research at the very end of 1990, just in time for the New Year's celebration that takes place every year on the beaches of Rio's Zona Sul. It is a major festival, perhaps second only to Carnival. The first day of January is devoted to the Afro-Brazilian *orixá* (African divinity) or the goddess Iemanjá. The night before, scattered along the beach, were members of the numerous Afro-Brazilian religious groups—Umbanda, Candomblé, Kardecists—all camped in clusters according to their *terreiro* (temple or congregation).[5] Rich and poor, people came that evening to offer flowers, fruits, and drinks to Iemanjá, the goddess of the sea. Every year the city is transformed during the weeks leading up to this ritual. Giant loudspeakers are set up along the beach walkway, and music—*samba, fricote, funk, forró*—is always blaring. Bursting into dance during this time is common. Mobile trucks with live bands (called *trios elétricos*) on top of them roam around the city animating the crowds. These traveling parties are a Carnival import from Salvador. Wherever these trucks slowed down, clots of passersby would begin to dance in the street. Occasionally, even drivers caught in traffic would take advantage of the opportunity and dance next to their gridlocked cars.

During the afternoon of the day of the event, I was instructed by my friends—upper-middle-class Brazilian intellectuals—to dress in white and to buy new underwear. Tradition demands that everyone do so, and the underwear should be either white or pink—pink for love, I was told. Later in the evening at the beach, I was instructed to let the waves break over my feet seven times. I was also given twelve grapes to eat and told to save the seeds. When asked, none of my friends could tell me why— it is just something you do, they explained.

This massive gathering seemed like a fortuitous occasion to mark the beginning of my official fieldwork in Brazil. The mixture of individuals from various social classes and every conceivable religious group all enjoying this warm evening together along the beach is especially memorable. It became, for me, a marker of my entrée into Brazil. It especially serves as a reminder of one image I hold of Rio that speaks to its harmonious and peaceful side. That night, thousands of people enjoyed the New Year's celebration in a moment of what at the time seemed near-perfect *communitas*.[6] Despite the contradictions of class, violence, race, and gender that I later came to understand over the course of my fieldwork, this peaceful, composite image of untroubled fellowship remains with me to this day. But what initially appeared as a good omen to me— the diversity, sensuality, and harmony of this sweeping collection of people on the beach that night—I also quickly came to recognize as only a partial picture of Rio.

There is an undeniable allure to this romantic and somewhat naive but nonetheless "real" vision of Brazil. This story, played out on the beach that night and celebrated on a much grander scale every year at Carnival, stands alongside another story just as visible, but somehow subdued. Even as I basked in the celebration that night, I could not help but notice the number of mostly dark-skinned women and children begging among the revelers on the beach, or the hardworking vendors burdened by heavy loads peddling ice cream and other foods to the mass of people crowding the sand. I had seen poverty before during my years in Latin America, but I had never experienced it so blatantly as I did in Rio. The contrast of affluence shoulder to shoulder with poverty was starkly visible.

Early on, the disquiet these scenes provoked in me hindered my own enjoyment of the city with my middle-class friends. It was hard for me to appreciate simple things like a midnight snack at Cervantes, the famed Copacabana sandwich shop, because I knew that just outside the door there would be the same crew of ragged children waiting to relieve me of whatever crumb I could not finish. At about that same time, I remember, there was always a woman with three or four children and a baby in her arms who would stand at the corner of my residence. I could not really ignore her because after a few days, she, too, recognized me and had a seemingly uncanny sense of my schedule. My Carioca friends (natives of Rio de Janeiro) were also disturbed by such scenes, but it was a world they knew and had come to expect. For me, it was agonizing.

Rio has long been known as a city of contrasts. Poverty, inequality, racism, and violence are everywhere, so pervasive that they are sometimes hard to see. Such contrasting images and experiences obviously complicated my own picture of the *cidade maravilhosa*, the "marvelous city."[7] Despite the insistent shout of the romantic story of Brazil, the alternative is as Brazilian as the first. It is not that the first story is a lie and the second truth. It is not that simple. These two stories are not alternate visions of the truth to be debated over. That they are both part of a multifaceted reality is the telling tale here. The difficulty, and indeed the attraction, lies in the intriguing and baffling fact that it is tremendously hard to read these stories together; almost impossible to grasp which is the doppelgänger of the other.

In this regard, Rio is a truly remarkable place—in fact, the harmony of the beach scene and the violence and poverty of those who are left to beg on the streets are two images that make Rio (in)famous. Romance tinged with palpable danger and a sense that anything is truly possible is one source of Rio's seductiveness. The warmth and friendliness of the people, the Afro-Brazilian aspects of culture that persist, the beach culture, the exuberance and sex appeal of the yearly Carnival celebration, along with the violence and messy, exaggerated inequality that characterizes a great deal of social life have led some to comment that "Rio is a [movie] trailer for Brazil."[8] It is one of Brazil's—and the world's—most unequal cities, and, for better or worse, it remains quintessentially Brazil.

SCHOLAR IN TRAINING

Before becoming interested in Brazil specifically, I had been a Latin Americanist scholar in training. In 1980, as a sophomore undergraduate student at Cornell University, I spent my first summer in Mexico as a research assistant working for two professors, one of whom was a rural sociologist, the other an agricultural ecologist. I interviewed peasant farmers in the rural areas of Tabasco, Oaxaca, and Michoacán and then returned for a longer period of fieldwork in Tabasco the following spring, documenting the effects of a development project (a large regional dam) and the programmed collectivization on what was referred to then as the "status of women." I was a wide-eyed sociology undergraduate major working toward the completion of an honors thesis.

As an undergraduate student, I became absorbed in the political activism and solidarity movements of the early 1980s at Cornell University. My political awakening concerning the nature of U.S.-Latin American relations took place during perhaps one of the more blatant moments of U.S. imperialism and bullying in the region, spanning the Reagan and Bush years. It was an era marked by anticommunist, anti-Russian, and anti-Cuban rhetoric signaling the cold war politics of the time. I became active with the Committee on U.S.-Latin American Relations (CUSLAR), a campus-based student activist group that tracked the thin and often jingoistic portrayals in the mass media of events taking place in Central America, especially El Salvador and Nicaragua. CUSLAR attempted to (re)educate the university community and general public by presenting a more critical account of U.S. involvement in the region.

But my interests extended beyond exposing North American imperialism. After my all-too-brief experience in Mexico, I wanted another chance to get closer to the lives of people on whom the politics and economics of capitalism impinged. When I was offered a research position in rural Ecuador in 1982, I jumped at the opportunity to work in the Andes and to conduct research among peasant farmers. I spent two and a half years in Ecuador, working in a northern rural area not far from the Colombian border, interviewing small-scale bean producers from three different class and ethnic origins in three distinct ecological zones.[9] This was the research style of that time, and it made for a neat package for all kinds of comparisons.

My colleagues and friends in Ecuador were, for the most part, exiled intellectuals from the Cono Sur[10]—Argentines and Chileans.[11] These friends helped broaden my political and intellectual interests in a southerly direction and piqued my curiosity about Brazil. For them, Brazil was an exceptional place in all sorts of ways. They loved the music—especially the protest music of Chico Buarque, Gilberto Gil, and Caetano Veloso[12]—and the sound of the Portuguese language. They were familiar with the ecstasy of Carnival. One of my friends, a Paraguayan intellectual, had visited Rio de Janeiro as a child and had remained impressed by the prevailing dress code. Coming from Paraguay of the 1960s and 1970s, she considered Rio's scantily clad beachgoers the sexiest and most liberated people on earth. In some ways, these Latin Americans spoke of Brazil as if it were a completely distinct Latin America.

Spurred on by this contagious enthusiasm, I spent three months of

1988 in Brazil on an exploratory summer research expedition. By that time, I was an anthropology graduate student at the University of California–Berkeley. I traveled widely throughout the country on a Brazilian air pass, visiting Rio, São Paulo, Brasília, Salvador, Recife, Fortaleza, Belém, and many small towns and villages. During this time, I found myself harkening back to those conversations I had had with friends in Ecuador, still trying to put my finger on what exactly was so fascinating about Brazil, even for those Cono Sur intellectuals who were, in charming ways, proudly nationalist with regard to their own countries of origin.

I was still unsure of the focus of my studies and needed to get a sense of the regional differences within the country. I had vowed at that time that I would not be seduced by Rio de Janeiro. So many who had been there had already warned me of its charms and of how difficult it would be to resist them. After all, I thought, Brazil is a large, diverse country, so I should attempt to work in an area that has been less studied. In the end, as it turned out, I was not strong enough to overcome the allure of Rio.

During the intervening years as a graduate student, I developed a number of research proposals for potential projects that were of interest to me. Indeed, I became obsessed with this process, understanding that I would ultimately be wedded to any project I chose for many years. Perhaps because of that realization, I kept finding reasons to reject a great number of possibilities. Finally, after much frustration, I settled on and developed a solid research proposal based in the former capital and slave-trading center of Brazil—Salvador, Bahia. I applied for and received funding. Fulbright in hand, I flew to Brazil in the final days of 1990, my point of entry being Rio de Janeiro.

As I stood in the sand early on that first morning of 1991, watching the water rush over my feet and then slip back out to sea, my plan was to study class relations and religious affiliation in Salvador, Bahia. I intended to focus on the changing relationships between domestic workers and their *patrões* (bosses) in the midst of the vast constitutional reforms.[13] But I had arrived in the country during a unique moment. There was a growing awareness both internationally and within Brazil itself of the enormity of the AIDS epidemic; coinciding with this, an expansive AIDS activist and solidarity network was forming in Rio and São Paulo. As so often happens, I was inspired by the politics of the time, informed both by events and changes within Brazil itself and by the growing influence of the transnational networks that spidered the globe, linking Brazil and Latin America with North American and Western European governments and inspiring the formation of both locally and internationally oriented nongovernmental organizations (NGOs). I decided to shift my research focus to analyzing the effects of the AIDS epidemic on low-income women. I then spent a year working with two teams of AIDS prevention and education workers, one in Rio de Janeiro (from the organization Associação Brasileira Interdisciplinar de AIDS [ABIA]) and one in São Paulo (from Coletivo Feminista Sexualidade e Saúde). During that first year in Brazil, I spent most of my time conducting interviews with low-income women living in favelas and other impoverished neighborhoods in Rio de Janeiro and São Paulo.[14] The interviews focused on women's sexual lives and histories and on their relationships with men.[15]

Despite the fact that I spent so much time working in poor communities, my friends, collaborators, and close contacts were for the most part intellectuals and activists, both in the women's movement and in the AIDS movement. Like myself, they were generally from middle- or upper-class families, university-educated, and cosmopolitan in outlook. What I came to understand during this collaborative research endeavor was that while my activist friends had a great appreciation for popular culture and a genuine and profound concern for the plight of the poor in their own country, they also maintained a crucial distance from the people we interviewed. I admired then, and continue to admire today, the work these colleagues manage to do under frustrating and sometimes quite difficult circumstances. They are devoted to social change in their country and, because of the structuring of academic and intellectual life in Brazil (decidedly more similar to France or Germany than to the United States),[16] they are closer to being able to seize opportunities that promise to bring about political change in their country. The combination of class privilege and activist engagement often enables particular individuals to impact public policy in ways that North Americans are rarely able to achieve. I was envious (and perhaps still am, in a manner blunted somewhat now by experience and less tinged with the more naive aspects of my—admittedly youthful—idealism of the time) of the opening that calls upon them to be active public intellectuals. On the other hand, there are aspects of their taken-for-granted privilege with which I, as an outsider, have never been entirely comfortable. My friends—both male and female—very seldom, if ever, have to address the division of labor within their own households because even the more modest earners among them purchase the labor of a domestic worker to cook, clean, and help take care of their children. While these arrangements all vary to some degree, I have rarely met a middle-class or elite Brazilian woman or man who cooks and cleans for her or his own family on a regular basis. Rather, their lives are significantly marked by the pleasure and the nuisance of these domestic relations.[17] They are, in fact, constantly cared for by others, usually women, who perform the onerous tasks of daily life for them, freeing time for creative activities, including professional advancement, hobbies, and an active social life. Engaged intellectuals are therefore able to both work hard and be gracious hosts and hostesses, qualities I have benefited from and for which I am entirely grateful. Nevertheless, I was perhaps inspired to believe that fieldwork among the very poorest women was a worthy project in part because I could sense that even my middle- and upper-class activist friends in Brazil did not seem to have a very grounded sense of the lives of the poor, despite their good politics and good works.

CARNIVAL: THE EPHEMERALITY
OF LAUGHTER AND FORGETTING

In 1991 I had been given a copy of Alma Guillermoprieto's book *Samba* (1990), a moving, close-up journalistic account of the Mangueira *escola de samba,* or samba school, composed of *favelados* (shantytown dwellers) living in one of the notoriously steep hillside shantytowns inside the Zona Sul.[18] During the early part of the twentieth century, these samba schools were the centerpieces of community organization for the favelas of Rio, and their strength and continuity into the present are reminders of the Afro-Brazilian and popular roots of contemporary Carnival, the main festival of Rio's poor.

Inspired by Guillermoprieto and by anthropologists attempting to forge a more politicized anthropology through a focus on disenfranchised populations, I sustained a curiosity about people living in shantytowns, and women in particular. Many earn less than livable wages as domestic workers and yet, through their employment, have intimate access to the lives of the wealthier classes. It seemed to me that given the almost obscene disparities of wealth, Rio ought to be more violent. When I compared the lives of workers with those of their counterparts in the United States, I sensed a certain volatility and rawness to the Rio situation, where opulence and misery confronted one another on a daily basis. I admired Guillermoprieto's ability to get inside many aspects of this particular popular culture, but I also craved more knowledge of what Rio was like beyond the days of Carnival.

Anthropologists and others have long argued that Carnival is central to Brazilian consciousness. One early interpretation of Carnival was set

forth by Brazilian anthropologist Roberto Da Matta,[19] who, building on
Victor Turner's (1995[1969]) analysis, has interpreted Carnival as a ritual of inversion, where the poor and marginalized—and their accompanying aesthetic forms—temporarily take center stage and allow a critique
of standard elite culture. It is a time when the world of the *casa* (home)
and that of the *rua* (street) are inverted and members of the poorer
classes don *fantasias* (costumes) of nobility while those in the wealthier
classes parade in the streets without regard for bourgeois morality. It is
a time when the rules and realities of the everyday world are forgotten
and transgressed.

Carnival is a celebration that is not unique to Brazil. It takes place in
other parts of Latin America, as well as in the United States (Mardi
Gras), southern Europe, and West Africa. Brazil, however, seems to have
taken Carnival further, transforming it from religious ritual to national
metaphor. Indeed, Carnival, according to anthropologist Richard Parker
(1991), forms the core of *brasilidade,* or essential "Brazilianness": "*Carnaval* would be the clearest example in contemporary Brazilian life of
those peculiar moments when a hidden tradition comes out of hiding and
an entire society discovers and reinvents itself—when for a few brief
days, myths of origin take shape in cultural performance, the past in-
vades the present, and the sensuality of the body defies sin. It is a time
when everything is permitted, when anything is possible" (139). Carnival is more than a ritual of last indulgence and licentious behavior before the austerity and self-denial of Lent. It is more than those few, all-
too-brief days when class hierarchies are turned upside down and the
strictures governing sexuality are momentarily suspended. It is more,
too, than the spectacle offered by the tourist brochures, an exotic experience to be purchased and consumed. Carnival is a looking glass image
through which Brazilians define themselves and by which they present
themselves to the world.

Robert Stam (1997) argues that Da Matta's account falls short because it fails to theorize the political ambiguities of Carnival. Stam suggests that Da Matta's emphasis on the inversions of social roles and the
sense that Carnival is a moment "out of time," when social rules are broken, has led many to place too much emphasis on its liberatory possibilities. Those who tend to examine Carnival from the perspective of particular subcultures, however, are generally less sanguine about these
possibilities, highlighting instead its more contradictory, ephemeral qualities. After all, Carnival is only four days and five nights out of an entire
year, and one's place in society is more likely determined by one's gender,

class, race, and sexuality than it is by one's experience of Carnival. This latter perspective does not place much political hope in the liberatory aspects of Carnival, instead perceiving it as more politically ambiguous.

It is perhaps best to note that each of these stories about Carnival is a partial truth—true for some populations some of the time. Carnival, much like humor and laughter, is neither entirely conservative nor entirely liberatory. Rather, it exists and shifts between these polarities. Even so, I am skeptical of those who too easily and broadly celebrate its liberatory features—Da Matta on inversions of hierarchies and Parker on transgression. In the case of Da Matta, I recall a point that Scheper-Hughes (1992) notes in her description of the Carnival of the poor in Bom Jesus: "If Brazilian *carnaval* creates a privileged space of forgetting and a dream world where anything is possible, the marginals' *carnaval* of Bom Jesus also provides a space for *remembering* and is as much a ritual of intensification as a ritual of inversion" (482). Anyone who attempts to be wholly negative about Carnival risks the accusation that he or she does not understand Brazil or, worse, the essence of brasilidade, and Scheper-Hughes's analysis probably did not win her any friends in Brazil. But it showed how nothing really changed for the poor as a result of Carnival. There was still no water or decent health care, and the class structure remained rigid. While I agree in many respects with Parker's characterization of Carnival as a moment of lived transgression, I would argue that men have a much wider degree of freedom to transgress than women do. Again, Carnival is not the same experience for all populations.[20]

Carnival's meanings are multiple and shifting with regard to community and historical context. Indeed, Carnival can ultimately serve as a conservative ritual that reinforces class positions and gender and sexual hierarchies. As Scheper-Hughes notes, "There would be no need for *carnaval* in the first place if there were not monstrous things that needed to be banished and forgotten" (480).

Despite the widespread identification with brasilidade across classes, for the poor, Carnival is not just a time of laughter and forgetting. It can also be, as Scheper-Hughes notes, a time of remembering, a profoundly ambivalent and ambiguous event. I learned that Glória, for example, had once been a great lover of Carnival during her youth, but over the years she had become less enthusiastic about the festival, suffering from a kind of burnout. Certainly, many people in Felicidade Eterna played Carnival, but none of Glória's close friends on the barreira were able to afford the elaborate costumes required for participation in the culminating Sambódromo event during the years I was there.[21] When it came down to "the truth" as Glória and her friends saw it, they felt that my everyday experiences in the shantytown, rather than Carnival, were the "real" story, the one they imagined people on the outside would not believe. So, in effect, my choice of research was, for better or worse, not to look at Carnival—that ephemeral yet partial truth—but rather to look at everyday life. When I was considering a number of titles for this book, my friends in Felicidade Eterna very much wanted me to call it "It's All True."[22]

Recognizing the transformative limits of Carnival, Stam (1989) suggests that other aspects of Brazilian culture—embedded in art, literature, and film, as well as everyday life—nevertheless exhibit carnivalesque aesthetic forms. The everyday humor of Glória and her friends and family is in many ways carnivalesque. It makes fun of the wealthy, but it also pokes fun at the miserable circumstances in which they find themselves. It mocks the world and its madness and seems to be an unconscious masking of deep personal feelings that are too painful to deal with directly. It makes fun of dead, sexualized, and grotesque bodies and of the death of poor bodies.

This extension of Carnival into the carnivalesque raises some old and some new questions. It could be argued that Carnival may well reinforce the dominant social structure simply because the inversions that take place during that week are temporary and ultimately take place only with elite approval. Rio's Carnival, for example, has moved in stages historically from being a street Carnival to being a commercialized competition between samba schools held in the Sambódromo. On the other hand, the carnivalesque aesthetics that permeate everyday life—rather than a week during the year—may provide a fruitful opening for witnessing the more durable forms of resistance existing the other fifty-one weeks of the year. My interest in and exploration of black humor provide a point of entry for getting behind the mask of Carnival.

The impulse behind this desire, at least in part, stemmed from my growing dissatisfaction with the limitations of my early survey research—despite the many positive outcomes of the AIDS and sexuality survey research I conducted. It did lead to an awareness among the activist community of how much empowerment work with women was still needed around issues of sexuality, but at the end of this project I still felt unsettled. I was disturbed about what we could understand about women's sexuality through short-term, decontextualized survey-style research. Moreover, I felt disconsolate about what activists and researchers from middle- and upper-class backgrounds could understand about people living in abject conditions of poverty through only this kind of short-term contact. I recognized that our intervention was incomplete. The AIDS prevention and education programs of the moment addressed women's empowerment issues in the realm of sexuality, but they lacked a broader vision of the economic and gender hierarchies within which women are embedded.[23] Survey research can capture and help one to make sense of a large amount of information, thereby providing a sense of the big picture, but it does not seek beyond surface meanings to achieve the kind of thickness and complexity that ethnographic research can offer.[24] Survey research by design is distanced and broad rather than deep. I wanted to go further and get closer; to begin to better understand these lives of which I had only begun to scratch the surface. I wanted to find out how the working poor experienced living within the social apartheid that characterized Rio, how they understood it, tolerated it, and even, at times, made fun of it. I sensed that because of the rigid and highly naturalized hierarchies that structured the lives of shantytown residents, their responses had to take place in a form not generally recognized.

HABITS OF CLASS AND DOMINATION

I took it for granted that certain "popular" aesthetic forms are delegitimized and others elevated as part of the process of class reproduction. When I stumbled upon the black humor of Glória and her friends, I sensed that I had located a subtle form of popular expression that warranted translation and contextualization not only to a North American audience but also to privileged Brazilian audiences. Unable to revolt, they use their laughter to oppose official Brazilian racial, class, and gender ideology. Laughter reveals the fault lines in social relations.

The carnivalesque laughter—the black humor—of Glória and her friends may appear to the reader as just another example of "bad taste." What can be more distasteful than somebody making fun of the death of a family member or a rape? Such humor begs for some kind of analysis, an understanding that can be achieved only by knowing intimately what the lives of people in these classes look like from their own perspectives.

I had long been convinced of the applicability to Brazil of Pierre Bourdieu's (1984) analysis of class and culture in France, especially of how concentrations of economic and cultural capital lead to unequal levels of political capital and, ultimately, through an elaborate symbolic struggle between classes, to a legitimation of social differences. In *Distinction: A Social Critique of the Judgement of Taste* (1984), Bourdieu argues that the struggle between classes over the appropriation of economic and cultural goods also becomes a symbolic struggle to appropriate distinctive signs. Certain aesthetic tastes and goods become legitimized, while others are delegitimized. In this way "taste" becomes a kind of literacy, a feature that one acquires at home and at school, which ultimately legitimizes social difference and one's social orientation or "sense of place" in the world. Since taste is in fact arbitrary, it is best seen as the mechanism by which certain classes or groups gain and maintain power within the social order. Bourdieu (1977) has described habitus—a historically structured, reproducing, and durable ordering that refers to the maintenance of a class-divided social structure. The concept is useful because it captures more than just an economic dimension of difference. In Bourdieu's scheme, taste is one of the mechanisms through which inequality, difference, and privilege are structured and embedded in one's habitus, naturalizing schemes of perception. All individuals in a similar group or class acquire the same habitus. Ultimately, Bourdieu is interested in how relations of domination are legitimized and how the dominated become accomplices in their own domination. So, while tastes may change or shift according to historical context, the relationship between classes is maintained through this constant reproduction of taste-based distinctions.

Scholars who employ the idea of cultural hegemony share a number of qualities with those who consider Bourdieu's ideas regarding class, domination, and habitus. Indeed, many anthropologists—such as Sherry Ortner and Jean and John Comaroff—often breathe Bourdieu and Gramsci together, linking them with Marx and de Certeau. These theoretical perspectives seek to go beyond economic determinism and to understand the cultural forces that construct and limit class domination. Gramsci's (1971) idea of cultural hegemony refers to the system of attitudes, beliefs, and values that—through ideological control of the dominated classes, that is, through their manufactured consent—supports ruling-class domination. Hegemony, in a manner similar to habitus, hides or naturalizes the dominance of one economic class over another.

John and Jean Comaroff (1992), citing and extending Bourdieu, offer a productive clarification of the relationship between power, hegemony, and ideology, arguing that power is not above or outside of culture and history but rather is implicated in their construction:

> We take hegemony to refer to that order of signs and material practices, drawn from a specific cultural field, that come to be taken for granted as the natural, universal, and true shape of social being—although its infusion into local worlds, always liable to challenge by the logic of prevailing cultural forms, is never automatic. It consists of things that go without saying: things that, being axiomatic, are not normally the subject of explication or argument (cf. Bourdieu 1977:94). This is why its power seems to be independent of human agency, to lie in what it silences, what it puts beyond the limits of the thinkable. It follows that it is seldom contested openly. Indeed, the moment that any set of values, meanings, and material forms comes to be explicitly negotiable, its hegemony is threatened; at that moment it becomes the subject of ideology or counterideology. (28–29)

It is therefore understood that where hegemony is realized, coercion is unnecessary. It is only when subordinated groups force hegemony into ideology that the possibility for resistance becomes evident.

Although it may seem that humor is one of those depoliticized projects that cannot possibly link up to a broader political landscape, it is in fact a window that is key to understanding how people experience their lives; it shows how the downtrodden perceive the hierarchies in which they are embedded. The black humor that appears throughout this book as a kind of discursive playfulness among Glória and her network of friends and family may appear to many readers to be in "bad taste." But taste, again following Bourdieu, is a form of cultural and class capital that is hard to measure or describe. And yet taste is fundamentally political because it is really only the capacity to discern aesthetic values. Embedded in taste is the essence of power relations between classes that are then naturalized and constituted as meaningful. "Taste" actually serves to cloak the real agenda, which is power.[25] Black humor as an emotional aesthetic emerges out of the difficult circumstances of everyday life. It is a living example of the interconnectedness between comedy, on the one hand, and suffering and tragedy, on the other.

RETURN TO LAUGHTER

Over time, the Rio that became most familiar to me was the one associated with Soneca's laughter—a laughter that was genuine enough but that both masked and revealed the anger and sorrow at the kinds of everyday violence experienced by people like Glória and her family. In fact, as I later learned, Zeca's death was just another poor person's death in a poor person's hospital, with doctors trapped in a system inade-

Figure 4. Hospital for the poor on the outskirts of Rio de Janeiro. Photograph by author.

quately built for attending the poverty-stricken masses. It was a perfect example of what Scheper-Hughes has called "bad faith" medicine, and sadly, nobody was fooled by the situation.[26]

Zeca's story, as told by Soneca, echoes a Bakhtinian or Rabelaisian version of life, where one sweats, farts, shits, and laughs his way to death.[27] His story is marked by spasms—orgasm and death, lacking only the third, birth—that Bakhtin claimed to give life to the grotesque body. Zeca's tragic death lent itself to countless jokes, parodies, obscene gestures (including bulging eyes that go blind), stiff bodies and stiff sexual organs, doctors claiming their medical and class authority, chatting and smoking while a child dies. For the outsider, the story is not so funny, but it seems that the humor found in the story gave people the strength to deal with it.

Zeca was so sick in the hours before his death that he was not able to make it to the bathroom in the tiny shack. Instead, he dirtied himself with his own feces, collapsing at the door of the shack. The children were able to get help from neighbors and managed to transport him to the hospital. Glória, who had been working in the Zona Sul that day, only made it to the hospital several hours after Zeca had been interned. Soon after announcing Zeca's death to Katy and me, Soneca described the treatment in the local hospital emergency room. The doctors threw him on a metal cot, put a thermometer underneath his arm, and prohibited his siblings—Soneca, Anita, and Tiago—from giving him water. Next they put him in a chair and covered him with a blanket wet with alcohol. Zeca was losing his eyesight during this procedure, and his siblings were attempting to reason with the doctors, explaining that Zeca had *anemia falciforme* (sickle-cell anemia), and had been treated in the past at a hospital in the Zona Sul, where the doctors understood his particular condition. One of the doctors responded, "Who is the doctor here, you or me?" He preferred to enter into a power play with these young, desperate children rather than explain what was happening. Finally, at the end, Zeca lost his tactile senses. When he was finally dying, the doctors put him on top of a bed and gave him shock treatments. They were not able to revive him. According to Soneca, the most bizarre part was that after his death, the doctors placed Zeca in a freezer, "similar to the giant refrigerators in a butcher's shop, next to another guy who had gunshot wounds." These details were both tragic and funny at the same time, and Soneca made sure to feature the absurd elements in each telling. According to the children who observed this horrific scene, Zeca suffered from nine in the morning until two in the afternoon, and the doctors did nothing but smoke cigarettes and watch as he died.

After Zeca died, the family had to pull itself together to dress him for the burial, but it was difficult to do so because his body was so stiff. The final, even more grotesque aspect of the story was that Zeca had a little "hard-on," a detail that during each telling of the story brought laughter to those who listened and remembered one more time the details of this tragic story. For Soneca and the others who witnessed his death, there was nothing left to do but laugh. This laughter was mad and absurd, similar to the conditions under which they lived.

During my initiation into Glória's world, I learned to laugh along with the others, even though I did not initially find the stories funny. Glória had spent the eve of her sister's death with her, accompanying her on a hospital visit for what appeared to be the beginning of a difficult pregnancy. Celina had been Glória's favorite sister. Glória loved to tell the black-humored story of how, at the time of Celina's death, her husband, Cícero, misunderstood the news of the death as being *only* that of the baby, rather than the death of his wife and her as yet unborn child. Thinking that only the baby had died, Cícero naively declared, "One less to eat my *angu* [corn-meal mush]"—a line that threw Glória and her family into a collective fit of laughter. Just like Soneca, Cícero had been trying to lighten up about the death of his child, making fun of the fact that one fewer child alive would mean one fewer mouth to feed.

Throughout my years of getting to know the people of Felicidade Eterna and sharing in their lives, I began to share in their emotional aesthetic of their humor. I learned, at least partially, to get the joke.[28]

REDISCOVERING RIO DE JANEIRO

Glória, the central character in the work that follows, was employed by many of the same AIDS activists in Rio de Janeiro with whom I worked in the early 1990s. I first met Glória in the home of friends, two women who had an incredibly active social life and who absolutely depended on Glória's cooking and cleaning. I happened to be working with one of these friends on the AIDS survey research work in Rio and arrived at her apartment one morning knowing that she had hosted a big party the night before. Glória was already in the apartment, making order out of the chaos of dirty glasses, abandoned dishes, and overflowing ashtrays scattered about. At the same time, she was cooking up a little *fubá* (maize flour cooked into a kind of couscous) and eggs for breakfast. Later I saw her leave and then return with five or six plastic sacks of food to prepare. She worked three days a week in my friends' apartment and usually made a few days' worth of dinners during each visit, leaving everything neatly organized in the refrigerator. Glória was the kind of person who engaged with people immediately. She caught my attention as well because of the way she joked and laughed with my middle-class friends. She was also a perfectionist, frequently and painstakingly waxing and polishing the wooden floors on her hands and knees, sorting delicate and everyday clothes into bundles for either hand laundry or machine wash, and endlessly washing dishes. She left my friends' apartment completely transformed in the process.

In early 1992, I began sharing an apartment with a young university student in Santa Teresa, a bohemian neighborhood perched on a lush, tropical hillside halfway up the road to Rio's famous Corcovado and overlooking the sun-drenched beachfront communities of the Zona Sul.[29] Over time, I realized that my relationship with my apartment-mate was in serious danger because of our differing standards of cleanliness. I asked Glória if she had a free day in her schedule to travel up to Santa Teresa and work in our apartment. Glória agreed, which thankfully diffused the tension between me and my apartment-mate. I soon began to look forward to her visits, listening for her footsteps just outside the door. Because I usually remained home writing on the days she would come, and because I did not maintain an "appropriate" distance from her, since she was the first domestic worker I had ever employed, our exchanges grew longer. A friendship blossomed within a context that was strange to me but ordinary for Brazilians. I think Glória found my unfamiliarity with the rules and boundaries of this relationship quite amusing. Small gestures—such as my preparing lunch and setting the table for both of us to sit together and eat—would tickle her. I would often share with her some of my research findings from the AIDS research project about women's attitudes concerning their relationships with men, and Glória, in turn, would share with me how she saw those same issues, most often complicating, but also deepening some of the findings from our survey research. Glória often suggested that I accompany her home to her shack in Felicidade Eterna to see how *a gente* (meaning "we," but also literally meaning "the people") really live and think. Eventually, I accepted her invitation, and not long after I became a regular visitor to her house, eventually spending a few nights a week there and gradually getting to know her network of friends, neighbors, and family. In this process, she "adopted" me into her family as if I were another daughter. Soon after, she stopped working in my apartment in Santa Teresa. Neither of us felt comfortable continuing an *empregada-patroa* (domestic worker–employer) relationship once we had crossed certain boundaries and our friendship, ambiguous and uncertain at first, solidified. From this point on, Glória would teasingly introduce me to everyone she knew as her *filha branca* (white daughter), watching to see if anyone would challenge the possibility that she could have produced a child with skin as white as mine. I, in turn, teased her about being my *mãe preta* (black mother), a characterization that invoked its own particularly charged double meaning, one that at once mocked and acknowledged the echoes of Brazil's lengthy entanglement with slavery, which still strongly colored contemporary race relations.

Even as we had both quite easily freed ourselves from our brief empregada-patroa relationship and founded what would turn out to be a lasting friendship, we now quickly entered into that even more complicated relationship of anthropologist and primary "informant."[30] Power relations, of course, infuse themselves into all such relationships, and there is no adequate response to those who critique the dilemmas of this kind of research. I can simply assert that Glória is not the kind of person who would let anyone take advantage of her.

My first visit to Felicidade Eterna with Glória left me in shock. Fourteen children were packed into her dirt-floored, leaky, unstable, ten-by-fifteen-foot shack with a minuscule kitchen and an even smaller bathroom. The kitchen had an old stove with two functional burners and a small wooden table for food preparation. From the bathroom, which contained a toilet, a bucket, and a water faucet that inconsistently supplied water, one could trace the meandering path of plastic tubing that led out into the barreira's outdoor sewage system. The bucket collected the water from the tubing and provided the only source from which to dole out water for bathing purposes, as well as a sufficient amount to dump into the toilet basin to send off bodily waste. The contrast between how Glória lived and how my middle-class friends and I were living not far away was revolting. It was clear from my first visit that Glória faced a great deal of hardship in her life and that somehow, in the midst of the many tragedies that marked her struggle in this world, she managed to retain the capacity to laugh.

WRITING ETHNOGRAPHY, WRITING POVERTY

By the time I began my fieldwork, anthropologists had produced and subsequently renounced an abundance of work known as the "culture of poverty," a body of literature associated with the anthropologist Oscar Lewis, who wrote about slums in Mexico and New York City.[31] When I mentioned to my Brazilian colleagues that I wanted to work in a favela, they dismissed that sort of work as passé and poorly conceived—work that had already been done, and done poorly at that. To others, however, it was merely uncomfortable fieldwork, dangerous and difficult. I was not convinced. Thus, at the end of 1991, soon after completing the AIDS research, and despite reactions that ranged from negative to tepid from my Brazilian friends and colleagues, I began my work as a more traditional participant-observer in a shantytown I pseudonymously name Felicidade Eterna. My choice reflected a combination of youthful idealism and naïveté, combined with privileged guilt and an abundance of anthropological curiosity. I was at the same time armed with and burdened by all the doubts and tentative (but still exciting) possibilities that the "crisis of representation" presented to the generation of graduate students educated in the late 1980s.[32] And today, I remain committed to understanding the motivations and sensibilities that emerge in these settings, and what the possibilities and constraints are for resistance among citizens in a newly consolidating democracy.

Many cultural anthropologists are, to greater or lesser degrees, still struggling with this legacy, still attempting to define the parameters of what makes for a reasonable or even legitimate intellectual project. While I am entirely sympathetic to the poststructuralist critiques of colonialist anthropology, especially their pursuit of unmasking the power relations embedded in knowledge-producing systems, I am skeptical about criticisms that suggest we (anthropologists) give up attempting to "give voice" to others—that, indeed, it is pure arrogance and conceit that drives us to attempt such projects. Ortner (1995:180) notes that poststructuralist and other critiques of the culture concept have been well accepted because they have pointed out problems—the assumptions of timelessness, homogeneity, uncontested sharedness—that have demanded rehistoricizing and repoliticizing. But Ortner also notes that it seems as if we can hardly do without it. Despite its acknowledged representational dangers, I would hate for all of us to abandon our work with less privileged groups and, in the spurious hope of avoiding the pitfalls of writing about those groups, devote ourselves only to the study of elites, or cosmopolitan intellectuals, or transnational social movements. This would lead to an intellectual narrowing of the field, a form of "ethnographic refusal," in Ortner's (1995:176) terms, and a condition that would fail to provide density to our representations, would sanitize politics, and would produce a thin version of culture with a set of dissolving actors.

I believe that it is still possible to capture something distinct about the lives of others and to represent those lives in a respectful and careful manner so that in the cases where there is less chance for groups of people to speak and be heard, somebody might act as a scribe or witness. This notion may ring hollow or seem old-fashioned or trite. Such witnessing, bearing the burden of simply seeing and acknowledging and writing about whatever it is you have seen, is a profoundly political and important act. Perhaps only "youthful" anthropologists (read "naive" by their more staid elders) are reckless enough to continue to take up such idealistic projects (although many of them will now do so in a multisited fashion); regardless of whether this is viewed as a strength or a weakness, doing away with them completely would be a mistake.

Scheper-Hughes's (1992) ethnographic masterpiece *Death without Weeping* begins to chart a problematic territory, sometimes referred to as a kind of political economy of the emotions. She unblinkingly maps out the context of extreme poverty and everyday violence that structures the lives of sugarcane workers in Northeast Brazil. In this work, Scheper-

Hughes analyzes the cruel and unusual political and economic context within which women of the Alto do Cruzeiro are able to "let go" of their infants whom they believe are not strong enough to survive (362). It is a consummately "thick" work, highly praised but also criticized because its "thickness" has been read as an echo of the long-defunct culture of poverty school.[33] Lassalle and O'Dougherty (1997), for example, suggest that the "intense scrutiny that local-level practices receive" (244) in the book causes the author to miss the structural bases of poverty.[34] Yet Scheper-Hughes struggles with and succeeds in putting a human face on large-scale processes that would otherwise seem inaccessible. Nevertheless, I would agree that there is a difference between examining how lives are lived within these structures versus addressing the abstract structures themselves. However, speaking about political and economic structures in the abstract detaches the collective reality of the process from the fact that such structures and processes are produced and reproduced, enacted and resisted by the lived experience of real people. To come to a better understanding of these structures and processes, thick description is still quite useful and is one of anthropology's greatest strengths.

It seems that contemporary ethnographic endeavors must still walk a tightrope between what Ortner calls the risks of "ethnographic thinness" (1995) and our desire to address political and economic structures, along with our growing fears concerning representational practices. In addressing humor, embedded as it is in thick ethnographic contexts, I choose not so much to explain why something is funny but instead to provide more and more ethnographic context to the reader. It is in and through the ethnographic context that meanings will become clear. The Berlin humorist Adolf Glassbrenner noted in 1844, "An explanation is the death of a joke," a thought captured equally well by Wordsworth in his critique of the analytic spirit: "We murder to dissect."[35]

My own approach has been to work against sacrificing depth and therefore understanding, attempting instead to combine thickness with a sense of both political economy and the historical underpinnings of contemporary, ethnographically observed practice. Ortner (1995), too, warns that studies of resistance can be especially thin because of our failure to question the internal politics of dominated groups and our fears about what our powers of representation and subjectification do. We become tentative about showing internalized oppression, false consciousness, or the ways in which dominated groups play into domination because we are afraid of replicating the errors of the culture of poverty school, of blaming the victim. I am not sure there is any straightforward way to get around this dilemma. And even as many of us become tongue-tied or get writer's block as a result, I believe we must not stop trying.

Just as Scheper-Hughes argues that certain political and economic contexts create situations that provoke "death without weeping," I would argue that a sense of humor developed and displayed under cruel and unusual circumstances provokes what I would call "laughter out of place." While Scheper-Hughes, for the most part, focuses on the straight commentary of her characters, my own work explores their humorous, dark, and ironic commentaries in similarly perverse circumstances. The cruel and unusual context of the lives of these characters must be considered in both the narration and the reading of these humorous stories, because at times they jolt our own particular moral vision and sense of moral reasoning, one that we often mistake as universal. Scheper-Hughes (1992:355) asserts that anthropologists begin their analysis from a respectful assumption of difference and face those areas of discomfort that challenge our notions of the normal and the ethical.

The women I knew often joked and laughed about child death, rape, and murder in ways that made me feel and may make the reader feel ill at ease. These jokes and accompanying laughter create a seemingly paradoxical emotional aesthetic that calls for contextualization. Grasping this different emotional aesthetic requires entering the world of Brazil's urban poor and feeling the sense of frustration and anomie that accompanies their often desperate political and economic situation. I hope, however, that I am not mistaken for a mere revivalist of the culture of poverty school. Rather, my goal is to give the reader a sense of the context within which a few quite distinct individuals—limited by an interlocking series of hierarchies—live and understand their lives, taking up Ortner's challenge to go beyond the deconstruction of public discourse: "We must always go beyond the deconstruction of public discourse and attend ethnographically to the ways in which discourses enter into people's lives, both invading them in a Bourdieuan, even Foucauldian, sense and being implicitly or explicitly challenged by them in the course of practices that always go beyond discursive constraints" (1998:14).

"REAL PEOPLE IN REAL CONTEXT": HISTORY, POLITICAL ECONOMY, AND CLASS RELATIONS IN BRAZIL

Much of this book is admittedly an ethnographic snapshot of contemporary class relations in urban Rio de Janeiro. Without a sense of Brazil's particular historical, political, and economic framework, it would be impossible to fully understand the situation that I describe. Contemporary hierarchies of class, race, gender, violence, and sexuality are a product of history. One cannot comprehend the enormity of inequality in Brazil without having a sense of how capitalist expansion and imperialism have worked in historically patterned ways.

The legacy of Karl Marx permeates so much anthropological work that it seems redundant to point to his importance directly in an ethnographic work of this kind.[36] My own work positions itself alongside that of a broad and far-ranging group of scholars who have found intellectual inspiration in what anthropologist William Roseberry (1988), quoting Raymond Firth (1975), called "gut Marxism." Gut Marxists are anthropologists and other scholars who generally feel deeply about the world situation and hold that it conforms broadly to Marx's theories of political economy and class conflict. In my own case, I still find a Marxist perspective good to think with.

Both dependency theory and world systems theory offer Marxist explanations of historical development in Latin America. To do this, they have examined the critical institutions of the nineteenth century—the balance of power in the global system, the international gold standard, the self-regulating market, and the formation of liberal states. A contentious issue in this literature concerned the relationship between nation-based class structures and their external relationship with the world capitalist system. One of the landmark books on the subject, *Dependency and Development in Latin America* (1979), was written by a now-famous Brazilian scholar (who was in exile at the time)—the president of Brazil between 1994 and 2002—Fernando Henrique Cardoso and his coauthor Enzo Faletto. The study focused on political struggles of distinct groups and classes and, in turn, each of these class's complicated relationships to the history of both internal and external structures of domination. One of the great strengths of this work is that it managed to avoid two fallacies that were common to early versions of dependency theory as well as the world systems literature. It avoided positing that solely external forms of domination mechanically condition the internal or national sociopolitical situation. It also avoided the argument that everything is due to historical destiny (Cardoso and Faletto 1979:173).

Cardoso and Faletto (1979) show how the dominating classes—as well as others—are limited by the structure of the world capitalist system. This perspective is important to keep in mind because it helps to relax what may seem an implication throughout the rest of this book, namely, the idea that the dominating classes, because of their cultural, political, and economic power, can make history just as they would want.[37] It is in this way that a political economy perspective can remind us about how the broader constraints of the system limit both the desires and the agency of the dominating classes.

It is necessary, therefore, to give some account of global political economy and class formation within Brazil's particular history, much as Eric Wolf urged anthropologists to do in his insightful *Europe and the People without History* (1982). (Wolf laments the excision of Marx, political economy, and class from the social sciences, because this change left these disciplines without a meaningful language with which to talk about the nature of production, class, and power, and argues for their reinsertion.) Another influential book, Sidney Mintz's *Sweetness and Power: The Place of Sugar in Modern History* (1985), explores the role that sugar played as a commodity traded in the world system since the late fifteenth century. Sugar's history is connected to the transformation of social behavior both in the metropolis, those countries and their centers that exercised imperial control such as Amsterdam, London, Paris, Madrid, and other European and North American centers of world power, as well as in the colonies—regions such as the Caribbean and countries such as Brazil. These countries provided tropical products such as sugar, coffee, and tobacco for the metropolis. Mintz points out that when it comes to meaning-making, no classes have perfect agency. He argues, differentiating himself from Geertz in this instance, that individuals reside not only in their own individual webs of signification but also in other webs of immense scale "surpassing single lives in time and space" (158). Scholarship that fails to address issues of class and history are therefore flawed. Without reference to class, one would assume that meanings are shared across classes. Without reference to history, one would not be able to see how relationships developed over time (180). Both Wolf's and Mintz's versions of history as political economy have been acerbically criticized for their attention to commodities and fragmented sense of particular histories.[38] Nevertheless, they served as a necessary corrective to the North American ahistorical, nonpolitical, and noneconomic versions of culture theory that dominated a generation. The approach was warmly welcomed by a new generation of anthropologists because it enabled them to place "anthropological subjects within larger historical, political, and economic movements" (Roseberry 1988:169).

The theoretical directions that these books invited into the North American scene were already part of a taken-for-granted discourse among Latin American intellectuals and among North American scholars of Latin America. A broad scholarly literature produced during the 1970s and 1980s offered a comprehensive historical explanation based on the political economic relations of the world global economy established between unequal partners since the beginning of world trade. Scholars from the United Nations Economic Commission for Latin America (ECLA) powerfully critiqued the theories of modernization that had been considered sacred up until that point.[39] They offered an alternative historical explanation, one that emphasized how the terms of international trade worked against Latin American countries.[40]

Building on this work, André Gunder Frank's *Capitalism and Underdevelopment in Latin America: Historical Studies of Chile and Brazil* (1967) and Immanuel Wallerstein's *Modern World System: Capitalist Agriculture and the Origins of the European World-Economy in the Sixteenth Century* (1974) suggested that the world capitalist system simultaneously generated development and wealth in some countries and misery and underdevelopment in others. Frank's thesis was that world capitalism maintained an essential structure—the contradiction of continuity within change—based on the expropriation of economic surplus from the "satellite" (regions that were underdeveloped) to the "metropolis" (regions that were developed). A continuous chain of exploitative relations generates underdevelopment. Wallerstein's work, using the language of "core" and "periphery" to describe the world system, reaches similar conclusions. These two works and others that followed influenced how Latin Americanist scholars interpreted particular histories and necessarily influence the rendition I provide here.

The insights of all these scholars point to the potential of a political economy approach, one built on a solid foundation of historical contextualization and political economic analysis. In my own attempts to develop this potential here, I seek—although quite briefly—to guide the reader through the kinds of larger webs that people like Glória and her network of friends and family are caught in. Additionally, I try to mark historically some salient aspects of class relations in Brazil and Rio so that the reader may connect the historical context with the contemporary relations of domination prevalent in urban Rio today and can establish, in a general sense, how these relations have taken on their particular characteristics over time.

This is an ethnography of the ways in which class is experienced by women living in shantytowns during the last decade of the twentieth

century. As E. P. Thompson (1963) has noted, the only way to understand class is to see how class relations work themselves out over a
considerable historical period. Ethnographers who work in the realm
of thick description but who share Thompson's sense of the importance of history have drawn inspiration from his work. By injecting a
historical prerequisite into class domination, Thompson rejects the
idea of class as a structure or even a category. Rather, he argues that
class relationships must always be embodied "in real people in a real
context" (9). Similarly, without at least some perspective on Brazil's
political economy, the interactions in this book would be impossible
to comprehend.

A BRIEF HISTORY OF BRAZIL

When Pedro Alvares Cabral sailed from Portugal to Brazil in 1500,
Brazil was believed to be the home to between two and four million Native American inhabitants.[41] Cabral arrived with thirteen ships and
twelve hundred men. Until the early 1530s, the Portuguese presence in
Brazil was impermanent—a series of rudimentary trading posts rather
than an established colony. With increasing competition from the French
and Spanish in the New World, the Portuguese crown began apportion-
ing huge parcels of land extending from the coast inland; these became
known as captaincies, or hereditary land grants—a system similar in
spirit to the feudal system in place in Europe. Although only two of the
captaincies were financially successful, these first families and the early
institutions they inspired became powerful as intermediaries between the
Portuguese king and his Brazilian subjects. Large estates were further
parceled out in the form of *sesmarias* (large estates) or *fazendas* (large
farms). During this period, Brazil established itself as a sugar producer.

Brazil became the largest slave economy in the world. Over three centuries, beginning with the arrival of the first slave ship to Brazil in 1538,
more than 3.5 million Africans were imported. In a triangular trade
route, African slaves were brought to Brazil, Brazilian sugar went to Europe, and European products went to Africa. Enormous plantations dot-
ted the landscape and set the stage for Brazil to become the world's leading sugar exporter by the early 1800s. Sugar—its growth on large-scale
plantations, refining in *engenhos* (mills), and its export—was emblematic of the social life described as tropical feudalism by the social historian Gilberto Freyre in *The Masters and the Slaves* (1986[1933]) and *The*

Mansions and the Shanties (1986[1936]). During the sixteenth and seventeenth centuries, cattle raising grew in importance to become sugar's counterpart. In the early 1700s, Brazil also became a world leader in gold and diamond production. As with sugar production, the gold and diamond mines were dependent on African slave labor.

Brazil never developed a diversified economy, remaining export-oriented with a firmly intact feudal landowning system. By 1807, Brazil was furnishing 61 percent of the exports that earned Portugal its trade surplus, enabling the Portuguese crown to pay off a series of debts it had incurred with England. When Napoleon's army invaded the Iberian Peninsula (1807), it forced the Portuguese monarchy and ten thousand members of the royal court to flee Europe and establish a direct presence in Rio de Janeiro. The Braganza dynasty from Portugal thereby became a presence in the New World. This unique event—a European dynasty in exile in the New World—led the prince regent, Dom João VI, to declare the Estado do Brasil an equal partner with the United Kingdom of Portugal in 1815. When Dom João himself returned to Lisbon following the defeat of Napoleon in 1821, he left his son, Dom Pedro I, in Brazil. The following year, Dom Pedro I declared Brazil's independence from Portugal, in what is recognized as an event that truly sets Brazil apart from its Latin American neighbors. No former colony in Latin America has ever embraced as its monarch a member of the ruling family from the very country it was rebelling against. In declaring himself Emperor Pedro I, Dom Pedro I declared Brazil's independence from Portugal, as well as his own independence from his father. As Skidmore (1999:39) notes, the combination of monarchy and slavery led to an atmosphere of deference that was powerfully transmitted to the non-elites of the time. The newly independent Brazilian empire was still subject to the political and economic doctrines of the elites of the time. Known as Manchester liberalism, it was an economic ideology by which each country was encouraged to produce what it could produce best and to trade with other countries for items it could buy more cheaply than produce. This doctrine kept Brazil from industrializing and kept it exporting primary goods while importing finished products. In 1831, Dom Pedro I decided to return to his native Portugal, leaving his young five-year-old son in Brazil to later assume the throne.

The years 1830–70 have become known as an important period during which the Brazilian elite was divided about the basic principles by which Brazil should be governed. Essentially, three political groups held different opinions. The absolutists, drawing support from Portuguese merchants and from coastal cities such as Rio, were in favor of a united empire of Brazil and Portugal; they favored the return of Pedro I. The moderate liberals were supporters of the Brazilian monarchy, but they supported Pedro II and believed that Brazil should remain an empire totally independent of Portugal. The *exaltados* favored a republic and greater provincial autonomy, some even going so far as to promote independence.[42] Eventually, the absolutists lost their momentum when Pedro I died. The pro-regional group then became the Liberal Party, while the pro-empire group became the Conservative Party, with the country being held together by the reign of the monarch Dom Pedro II.

The centrality of slavery to Brazil's economy gradually diminished with the ending of the slave trade in 1853. In 1865, Brazil became embroiled in a war with Paraguay and depended on slaves to carry out the bulk of the fighting, an event that hastened Brazil's incrementalist approach to the final abolition of slavery. The Law of the Free Womb, enacted in 1871, freed children of slave women upon reaching the age of twenty-one. Brazil was the last of all colonies to officially abolish slavery, finally doing so in 1888, with the passage of the Golden Law. The following year, Dom Pedro II was dethroned by the army, and the Brazilian Republic was established.

The key author of the constitution (1891) of the new Brazilian Republic was Rui Barbosa, a devoted abolitionist. The most important feature of this document was its advocacy of a radical decentralization. Additionally, Barbosa ordered the burning of all documentation related to the slave trade, thereby erasing what he considered to be a shameful chapter of Brazil's history but also destroying many important historical archives. Only 2 percent of the population voted during the first election for civilian president held in 1894. The turn of the century thereby brought about a consolidation of the elite, who managed to form a republic without significant bloodshed and who survived abolition without undergoing a major land reform.

Between 1880 and 1890, Brazil became a leader in coffee production and simultaneously experienced a wave of immigration from Italy. Italian immigrants arrived just as slavery was about to end. Brazil's colonial and agrarian structure served to foster social inequity within the country and turned Brazil into a dependent economy whose profits ultimately financed English industrialization. Rio and São Paulo themselves experienced end-of-the-century industrialization quite differently: São Paulo received the bulk of European and Japanese immigrants, many of whom came to work the coffee fields or to labor in São Paulo's newly industri-

alizing areas. By the 1930s, São Paulo emerged as one of the most economically advanced regions in the country. By the 1940s, the state of São
Paulo became one of the "most impressive manufacturing capabilities of
anywhere in Latin America" (Wood and Carvalho 1988:55). In part, this
success was related to coffee production, which had led to infrastructure
development such as railroads and other roads, as well as to a more diversified industry. In Rio, however, coffee production began to decline in
the 1890s. Although the number of industrial establishments grew between 1889 and 1920,[43] after 1900 Rio became Brazil's principal im-
porter of foreign manufactured goods (Owensby 1999:27), and Rio's
new role became that of supplier of civil servants, white-collar salary-
men. Between 1872 and 1920, the number of federal civil servants in
Brazil quadrupled to forty thousand. Fully 40 percent of those positions
were in Rio de Janeiro, turning it primarily into a distributor of imported
goods, a consumer market, and a hub of government rather than an industrial powerhouse like São Paulo (Owensby 1999:27).

Rio de Janeiro, which had been the capital since 1763, was the place
where the elites first began to develop a distinct sense of public space;
they enacted this vision through segregating practices that forced Afro-
Brazilians, many of whom were recently freed slaves, to slums outside of
the city's center (Needell 1987, 1995b). According to historian Jeffrey
Needell, these segregating and excluding practices were part and parcel
of the elite's submission to a form of neocolonial domination, one where
their own identity and legitimacy were dependent on the mimicry of foreign, particularly French and English, norms.

Another key feature of the early 1900s was immigration from Europe,
notably Italy, Portugal, Spain, and Germany, as well as from Japan. Organized labor was minimal in 1910, and most of these workers, immigrants to the urban centers of São Paulo and Rio de Janeiro, worked in
the service or informal sectors rather than in industry. Historian George
Reid Andrews's (1991) convincing study of the formation of an agricultural and urban working class in São Paulo in the aftermath of slavery
traced the ways in which state policies and everyday racial discrimination hindered black entry into the desirable employment positions. Having joined World War I on the side of the Allies, Brazil was in a good position after the war to industrialize, using its export earnings to finance
the importation of necessary materials. This occurred despite the fact
that a large portion of the political elite up through 1930 did not necessarily believe that industrialization represented Brazil's only possible future. Between 1924 and 1927, a military column led by Luiz Carlos

Prestes marched twenty-four thousand kilometers through the backlands of Brazil, attempting to ignite a popular revolution. While much of the world was experiencing the Great Depression, Brazil experienced the founding and growth of its Communist Party.

By 1930, the Brazilian military installed Getúlio Vargas, an individual whose influence in Brazilian politics is legendary because of the varied types of Brazilian governments he led throughout his lifetime. Skidmore (1999:93) describes Vargas's ruling strategy at this time as corporatist,[44] referring to his approach of building a labor movement with the state acting as arbiter between employers and workers. But the Vargas legacy lasted twenty years in Brazil, and his political strategies shifted over time and circumstance; he was elected by Congress in 1934, and between 1937 and 1945 he again ruled as dictator in what has become known as the Estado Novo (New State) years in Brazil. Vargas ruled through a combination of demagoguery, populism,[45] nationalism, and social reform, while banning political parties, imprisoning political opponents, and censoring the press. In 1950, Vargas was legitimately elected as president, returning on a nationalist and populist platform, favoring state intervention in the economy. Then, in 1954, he committed suicide in the presidential palace after losing several important political battles with the conservative party of the time (whose members were liberal constitutionalists), the União Democrática Nacional (UDN; National Democratic Union).[46]

Juscelino Kubitschek was elected president following Vargas's death. He became widely known for his electoral promise to bring "fifty years of progress" within five years, symbolized by the building the new capital, Brasília, as a draw to bring development to the interior of the country. Kubitschek is credited with attracting foreign capital and the automotive industry to Brazil but also with initiating a long-term foreign debt problem—an unanticipated outcome of his interest in "progress" and "modernization."

In 1961, after elected candidate Jânio Quadros resigned from the office of the president, João Goulart, who had a reputation as a leftist labor minister under Vargas and had been elected as vice president in the Quadros election, was about to take over as president.[47] As a result, Brazilian politics became polarized between right and left factions. Goulart's ascendancy to office, which was perceived by many as illegitimate in the wake of Quadros's mysterious resignation, brought political divisiveness to a head. On the left were radical elements of the Catholic Church, the Communist Party, a new (Maoist) Communist Party of

Brazil, and the Workers Party of Brazil. On the right were the National Democratic Union, with support from large landowners and industrialists, as well as some of the military, who favored orthodox economic liberalism. Until 1963, the compromise solution was to permit Goulart to remain in power by resorting to a parliamentary regime, thus forcing him to share power with a prime minister and a cabinet. But in 1964 the military, backed by the UDN, staged a coup and cast Goulart from the government. This move earned congratulatory remarks from the United States, which at the time was growing increasingly alarmed about Communism and the effect of Castro's Cuba on the politics of the rest of Latin America.

During the next twenty-one years, Brazilian politics was dominated by a series of military dictators, some of whom were moderates contemplating an eventual return to democratic government and others who were hard-liners, in no hurry to oversee a democratic transition. At this time, the military made an alliance with the UDN and under the presidency of Castello Branco institutionalized a group of conservative economists, termed the "technocrats," who reshaped Brazil's economic policy under the mantle of military power (Skidmore 1999:161).

The following regime, that of General Costa e Silva, was marked by increased levels of political repression, including torture and the murder of political opponents, as well as censorship of major media. A dozen guerrilla groups emerged around 1969, most of whom were young members from the elite classes. Many members of the Left, including intellectuals, artists, politicians, and academics, exited the country rather than resort to armed resistance. They sought asylum in a variety of places, including France, Cuba, Chile, and the countries of Eastern Europe. It is estimated that there were as few as five hundred combatants in urban areas, with even smaller pockets of support from the rural areas. By 1974, this armed opposition was completely liquidated (Skidmore 1999:66). This unique situation—of a military government using repressive measures against youthful members of the middle and upper classes, as well as the lessons learned by the latter while in exile abroad— contributes to a picture of Brazilian social change as exhibiting certain rather "exceptional" aspects.[48]

When the Brazilian elite of the guerrilla movement came into contact with the security forces, they were shocked by the methods used. Torture, for example, had often been applied to common criminals, but previously its use on members of the middle and upper classes had been unheard of.[49] Their confrontation with these forces put them in contact with what ordinary Brazilians of the lower classes had been subjected to throughout their history.[50]

Strangely enough, during the 1970s and concurrent with a repressive military dictatorship, Brazil appeared to be experiencing a kind of economic miracle. With financial aid from the United States and diversification in agro-industry, a series of standard economic indicators pointed to absolute economic growth. There was also a concomitant rise in inequality, as other economic indicators seemed to imply. While the absolute income had improved overall, the distribution of income for the economically active population had grown more unequal.[51] The interpretation of these economic data themselves became a political issue. Toward the end of the 1970s, it became clear that there would be a slow, but eventual, return to political democracy. In 1974, General Ernesto Geisel, a military moderate, was indirectly elected by Congress and eventually relaxed censorship and political surveillance. His moderate faction in the military was not like its hard-line ideologues; it was willing to turn the country back over to civilian rule, believing that democratic elections represented Brazil's only legitimate future. By the end of his regime in 1979, this transition to democratic rule seemed to be in the cards, and the next military leader, João Batista Figueiredo, inherited an acute debt crisis built up during the years of the economic miracle and a new generation of army officers who were anxious to shed their image as torturers. This process of looking toward a gradual return to civilian rule was called the *abertura* ([political] opening). It reached its climax in 1985 with the election of Tancredo Neves, known as a centrist and recognized as the only politician capable of uniting a variety of parties in opposition to the government candidate. Tragically, Neves died before being inaugurated, and his less popular running mate, José Sarney, became president in the midst of uncontrollable inflation and growing economic problems.

Sarney took over just as Brazil became infamous for its soaring inflation (1038 percent in 1988),[52] a factor that may have moved the military to finally give up the reins of power. In this transition, however, Brazil never actually drafted a realistic program for agrarian reform, a lack that is often recognized as one of the many pillars of Brazil's unique version of inequality.

In 1988, Brazil drafted one of the most advanced and sophisticated constitutions in the world, but, as Daphne Patai (1991) points out, the law "provides a framework for understanding both the possible and the actual" (556). So, while the new constitution declares fundamental rights—such as the right to not be subjected to torture, as well as the right of women to be equal to men under the law—these same rights are all dependent on what the law looks like in everyday practice. The constitution is a fundamental step toward providing protection for citizens in a number of areas, but in the face of the unequal application of the rule of law, it loses its ability to deliver on its promises.

During the elections of 1989, once again the country was poised between two sharply distinct programs for the future. One program has been set out by Luís Inácio Lula da Silva (known as "Lula"), a Workers Party candidate who had entered politics through labor union activism and whose party was (and still is) an interesting amalgam of European social democratic–style politicians and more radical militants willing to confront both national and international institutions of global capitalism.[53] The competing program was set out by Fernando Collor de Mello, son of a wealthy ex-senator and landowner from Alagoas in Northeast Brazil, who emerged as the choice of the rightist parties. Collor de Mello won the election but was later forced to resign from office in humiliation before an impending vote of impeachment for his role in a widespread government corruption scandal. When his vice president, Itamar Franco, entered office following Collor's resignation, he hired Fernando Henrique Cardoso as the minister of the economy. Cardoso was already a senator from São Paulo, but his reputation was that of an academic sociologist and leading public intellectual who had written some of the original treatises on dependency theory in the early 1970s while in exile from Brazil's dictatorship. Cardoso instituted the Plano Real (Real Plan), an economic program whose goal was to stabilize the Brazilian currency and control inflation. Many claim that this plan's success encouraged Cardoso to become a candidate in the presidential elections of 1994 and ushered him into the presidential palace. During his candidacy for president, the leftist parties in Brazil rejected Cardoso's offer to form a coalition with his centrist party; in response, Cardoso formed a coalition with rightist free-trade parties. Ironically, the Marxist intellectual who in the 1970s had built his career on his incisive critique of imperialism and on an original analysis of how internationalization within the domestic market led to the collaboration of the domestic bourgeoisie with international capital became in the 1990s firmly politically aligned with neoliberal and free-trade ideologues promoting forms of globalization that are anathema to his early writings.[54]

One of Cardoso's contemporary critics, Cristovam Buarque, former director of the University of Brasília and former governor of the Federal

District calls for a radical rethinking of the Left's political agenda.[55] Buarque vexes the Left with a particular reading of its own history in a thoroughly provocative call for action titled *A Revolução na Esquerda e a Invenção do Brasil* (which roughly translates as *The Revolution on the Left and the Invention of Brazil*). Buarque argues that the political elite in Brazil has shown enormous competence for continuing in power without reducing any of its privileges and through all kinds of governments, including military governments, political openings, and direct and indirect elections. Furthermore, it has never lost power and never ceded privilege, rights, habit, or advantage (Buarque 1992:53–54). More important, he accuses the Left of having been compliant with the political elite. And, even more damning, Buarque charges that intellectuals are part of the elite, one whose characteristics include isolation from the people and making claims of leftist politics, "in the name of the people but without the people" (70). According to Buarque, the majority of leftist militants have worked in factories, public administration, and universities but have never set foot in a favela, have never spoken with street children, and have never taken into consideration the lives of those who live miserably (87). Buarque also accuses the military governments of 1964–85 of having institutionalized a system of favor and influence swapping that has led to the consolidation of privilege in a way that has benefited consumers rather than the masses of people who do not have the resources to consume. Additionally, world events—the relationship between the United States and Cuba, for example, and the failure of socialism in the East—have made any kind of leftist thinking in Latin America problematic. Buarque contends that this malaise has converted many former revolutionary thinkers into apologists for neoliberal capitalism (41). Finally, Buarque suggests that Brazil is currently living a form of social apartheid and that the nation needs, ultimately, to reinvent itself in order to surpass its unique history of inequality and injustice.

CHAPTER 2

The Aesthetics of Domination

Class, Culture, and the Lives of Domestic Workers

And we do not yet know whether cultural life can survive the
disappearance of domestic servants.

Alain Besançon, *Etre russe au XIXe siècle*

One afternoon in May 1995, during a return visit to Rio de Janeiro, I
found myself with Glória and her daughter Soneca in the kitchen of her
new employer, "Dona Beth," a fiftyish, middle-class woman for whom
Glória had begun working a year earlier.[1] Beth's kitchen was typical of
the older apartment buildings in the Zona Sul that had been built earlier
in the century: small, with enough room for just one person to move
about comfortably, but with all the modern amenities. Beth's well-
stocked cabinets contained many international products acquired during
trips to Europe and the United States or bought in the fine foods section
of certain chic Rio groceries. These were items with which Glória, who
knew how to prepare a wide range of Brazilian food products, was unfamiliar. She would usually ask Soneca, if she were accompanying her, to
help her read some of the preparation instructions. A few of the packages
were in English, and so I was put to good use that day, helping Glória and
Soneca take stock of all the ingredients stored in the cabinets. While I was
explaining the instructions for preparing a falafel mixture, it suddenly
occurred to Glória that her two helpers could be put to much greater use.
Glória commented that Dona Beth had looked rather disturbed before
leaving for work that morning, and she felt it was due to the contents of
a letter Dona Beth had recently received and over which she still seemed
preoccupied. Glória, worried about the emotional state of her patroa,[2]
abruptly moved toward the desk where she had seen Dona Beth place the
letter. She pulled out the letter and asked Soneca to read it out loud. De-

Figure 5. Soneca and Glória at work in Dona Beth's kitchen. Photograph by author.

spite my protests concerning the personal nature of other people's mail, Glória was quick to convince us that her knowing what was upsetting Dona Beth would ultimately be beneficial to everyone. Glória had already become an important confidante of Dona Beth, and her confidence in this role overruled any of my concerns about privacy.

The letter, from Beth's daughter, a woman in her early twenties who was attending university abroad, read as a typical middle- or upper-class girl's coming-of-age note; here was a daughter relating to her mother how excited she was about her studies abroad and how, at the same time, she realized that being far away from her mother and family was liberating in terms of her personal and professional development. At one point in the letter, Beth's daughter stated that, in short, she loves her mother but would like more independence from her.

It was at this point in Soneca's reading of the letter that Glória waved at her to stop and entered into one of her hearty, uncontrollable bouts of laughter—which are indeed contagious. After I had joined Glória in her fit of laughter that left us all at the point of tears, I finally ascertained that Glória (and Soneca) found the letter to be extremely funny because *she* (Glória) wants to be independent from her *own* daughters, and yet she sees the irony in Dona Beth being upset by this declaration from her own child. Glória often felt as if she wanted to escape the endless responsibility of supporting so many children, most of whom were not fully convinced of the importance of school—they instead felt the pressure to work and earn money. I know that some of Glória's daughters found it extremely difficult to secure decent working-class jobs with adequate pay because of their observable racial and class characteristics, a combination that worked against them. Glória's daughters suffered doubly in an economy that rewards Afro-Brazilian women the lowest pay within the highly skewed and unequal Brazilian economy (Lovell 2000).[3] Domestic work, one of the few employment opportunities readily accessible to them, is distinguished by the fact that it is both one of the lowest-paying jobs available and is filled disproportionately by Afro-Brazilian women. Many jobs required a *boa aparência,* which literally means a "good appearance" but more often is a thinly disguised discriminatory phrase placed or implied in job advertisements and meant to discourage dark-skinned people from applying.

Only recently, Glória had gone "solo"; she left her own shack with her young teenage and pre-teen children still living there and had moved a few miles away, in with her lover at the time, Mauro. Despite the fact that Glória had raised several older children who now had independent lives, she still had several others who depended on her. And even though this dependence was not as great as it once was—she was able to leave her own shack to move in with Mauro—she was still the sole provider for these children. Glória joked about her own situation as one where she, the mother, was "running away from home," running away from the responsibilities of having so many children to care for. Glória still strongly ruled her own household from afar and spent all her hard-earned money to sustain her family, but she had removed herself from tasks such as cooking, laundry, and daily cleaning. By moving out, she forced the children, especially the young girls, to do those things for themselves and the other younger children still at home. Unlike Dona Beth, who would have liked to keep her daughter near her for as long as possible, Glória imagined herself as that person who would have liked to witness her children becoming independent. All this made Glória and Soneca laugh at the absurdity of Dona Beth's tears shed earlier that same day.

THE STRUGGLE TO EARN A LIVING WAGE

Dona Beth offered to pay Glória approximately five minimum wages per month for a six-day workweek if Glória would agree to work as her exclusive *empregada* (domestic worker).[4] After Glória accepted Beth's extraordinary offer—most domestic workers earned only one minimum salary—her life and that of her children had been transformed. By 1995, she was in a much stronger financial situation than when I had originally met her back in 1991. Glória's life in the early 1990s could best be characterized as having been a slave to feeding both her own and her adopted children.[5] She woke up every day at five-thirty or so and ordered one of the younger boys to go out to the bakery and pick up some soft white bread, baguette style. In the meantime, she would get up and start making a large pot of heavily sweetened coffee for everyone to share. She gathered up the bedding and placed it outside on the clothesline to air out, folded up the pieces of foam used for mattresses and placed them in a corner, and did a quick sweep of the shack. By the time the bread arrived, Glória was passing out half-full glasses of hot, sweet coffee, and each child was allowed to politely pull off a piece of bread for him- or herself. Glória often was out the door at about this time, running to the bus stop even before the morning breakfast ritual was completed. She worked fourteen- or fifteen-hour days and spent one or two hours every day traveling, often changing buses two or three times to reach each employer's home.

In the early 1990s, Glória would travel each day of the week to a different employer's home and do the heavy-duty cleaning (cleaning the entire apartment, changing bedding, and doing laundry), as well as a fair amount of cooking. This arrangement is known as that of a *faxineira* (heavy-duty day cleaner). Because she preferred to live at home and work for a variety of clients in this manner, nobody signed her *carteira de trabalho* (work card).[6]

I accompanied Glória on many of these fourteen-hour work days and was impressed by her efficiency and competence. Each household presented an exhausting and strenuous array of tasks. She would arrive at the employer's home and immediately change into her comfortable cleaning clothes. Then she would clean the bathrooms and the kitchen, including the usual large pile of dishes left from several days' worth of meals. She would change the bedding, gather up dirty laundry, get a wash going, then begin sweeping or vacuuming the rooms of the apartment. If the floors needed waxing, she would get on her hands and knees to apply the strong-smelling wax, allowing the greasy circles to dry into a thick filmy layer and later returning to remove it by buffing the floor by hand with a dry cloth. She would take a break by looking into the refrigerator and the freezer for what was available to cook with, then descend to the markets on the street to buy any ingredients that might be lacking. Usually, the entire afternoon was devoted to cooking three or four main dishes and an equal number of side dishes, and then, finally, to ironing and folding clothes. By the time Glória left an apartment, every piece of glass and silver was shining, clothes were cleaned and ironed and put back in their closets, floors were slippery from their new coat of wax, and the refrigerator was filled with cooked foods, meals that would last for a number of days.

Glória often did not leave her employer's home until six or seven in the evening; she would then make her way downtown to the bus terminal—a ride of a short distance that could easily take longer than an hour during Rio's rush-hour traffic. Sometimes, before leaving the Zona Sul and partially as a strategy to avoid extreme crowding on the buses during peak hours, she would meet a friend to have a few beers in a neighborhood bar before getting on the bus. But usually she got a bus to the terminal and then waited to catch another bus back to Felicidade Eterna, a ride that often required her to stand for hours until the bus finally reached her stop. Glória rarely arrived home before nine or ten in the evening. Transportation time and costs ate into her earnings. Often she attempted to scrimp by traveling on the slower, less comfortable, but also less expensive, buses to and from the Zona Sul, and what she lost in precious time, she gained in disposable income that could be used to buy more food for her family or an occasional beer for herself. At one point in 1992, the express bus cost five *cruzeiros*,[7] while the slower and more meandering bus cost only two. After this grueling ride home, Glória often had to clean up around her own house. Late at night, exhausted and hungry, she would sometimes fry a fish or two and drink a beer before settling in to go to sleep.

Figure 6. Glória at work in Dona Beth's bathroom. Photograph by author.

From Glória's perspective, there had been some distinct advantages to this work routine, where payment was made on a daily basis by each employer. Glória's tight economic situation—with so many mouths to feed—was highly compatible with this arrangement. Each day provided just enough money for her to shop in small amounts and to provide for her household directly from that day's work. If she missed a day of work because of some emergency at home, she could make up the time by doing two apartments in a day, working from early in the morning until late in the evening, combining two days of work into one long one.

In 1992, I calculated that Glória was earning about six dollars a day.[8] Approximately one dollar was spent on the round-trip transport, so that, by the end of the day, she came home with an average of five dollars. This amount barely provided enough to sustain all the children who depended on her. Glória's clients at this time were paying her the average rate or better for daily faxineira work, and many (although not all) of them belonged to a large network of AIDS activists, many of whom were gay men and lesbian women. Glória often humorously reminisced about this colorful period of her life—which lasted many years—as the time when she worked almost entirely for *viados e sapatões* (fags and dykes).[9] These words are often used derogatorily, but Glória employed them similarly to how they were used by her patrons, many of whom had embraced these words in their own everyday usage as a way of taking control of their meaning, much as "queer" has been adopted in the North American context.[10] The relationships she had within each of the households she worked in were amicable, and Glória was quite fond of many of her employers. In each household, there were different sorts of flexible arrangements that enabled Glória to solicit help in times of need. Glória was, in part, willing to put up with her often hefty workload in each household because of the benefits she received from these multiple patron-client relationships. When her son Zeca became very ill, for example, one of her clients sped her in a car to the hospital near Felicidade Eterna where he was interned and later died. Another employer, who was a medical doctor, offered to perform a thyroid operation Glória needed without charge. Many of her clients would also lend Glória money in times of trouble. Even though this kind of extra help from her employers proved vitally important, Glória was unable to substantially change the amount she was paid in a daily wage—until she started working for Dona Beth.

The pay Glória earned as a faxineira during these years was more attractive than that generally offered to live-in domestic workers. She had

already done much of that in her youth and had given it up. Many domestic workers who live and work in a single household can command
only one minimum wage, even under stringent legal protections.[11] Glória
earned substantially more in her position as a faxineira, but there were
some disadvantages to this arrangement as well. Often her employers,
many of whom were middle-class and could not afford full-time service,
would leave two or three days' worth of complete chaos for Glória to
clean up. Over the years Glória grew tired of this routine, despite the
congeniality and the *bom papo* (good conversation) she enjoyed with
many of her employers.

Beth had employed Glória as a faxineira throughout the early 1990s
and had come to greatly appreciate her work. To hire Glória full-time,
she was willing to pay a living wage of five salaries per month, an amount
considered extraordinarily generous by Glória's network of friends, as
well as by most middle-class standards. In part this generosity stemmed
from the fact that Beth could afford it; her husband was a highly paid in-
dustrialist, and if they were not in the country's elite sector, they were definitively in the upper reaches of the middle class.[12] But Beth herself
worked as a social worker at Fundação Nacional do Bem-Estar do
Menor (FUNABEM; National Foundation for the Well-Being of the
Minor), an institution that was home to "street children"; she was conscious of the importance of women's labor, and she made a deliberate effort to pay Glória beyond what most ordinary employers were willing to
pay domestic workers in the free marketplace. She also paid Glória extra
for the transportation costs she incurred. Beth was trying to make an impact in her own way, but also, I believe she was willing to pay for the stability of having a highly competent, loyal worker stay with her over the
coming years. She also agreed to sign Glória's carteira in return for
Glória's commitment. Both of them felt lucky to have found such a sympathetic situation.

Both Glória and Dona Beth understood their roles with respect to one
another, although not in an entirely typical sense. There is always a par-
ticularity to the way any two individuals will negotiate a patroa-
empregada relationship, and in this particular one the feelings between
Beth and Glória were indeed good enough to keep the work relationship
strong and to foster a complicated set of ambiguous affections. For example, according to Glória, Dona Beth was flexible and did not *esquenta
a cabeça* (get hot-headed) about the days Glória missed because of problems in her own home that needed resolving as long as there was enough
food prepared to cover the days of Glória's absence. On a day that Glória

had matters to attend to in Felicidade Eterna—such as taking a sick family member to a clinic—she would send one of her young children down to the *orelhão* (literally "big ear," meaning a public telephone) near the bakery, instructing the child to call Dona Beth and inform her that Glória would not be coming to work that day.[13] Glória was especially good at anticipating these kinds of problems, and she would often cook four or five meals at a time and then freeze them, so that all Beth needed to do in the evenings was to pull the prepared foods out of the refrigerator or freezer and heat them up.

Their relationship also included some quite typical traditional elements of paternalism. When Glória's ex-husband Zezinho died suddenly, Dona Beth lent Glória the money to travel with Soneca to Minas Gerais, a state north of Rio, to track down Zezinho's mother so that she could pay for his proper burial. And, as I discuss later in this chapter, when Soneca, after a difficult pregnancy and birth, needed a calm place for herself and her newborn daughter to spend their first few precarious months, Beth allowed them to live in the tiny empregada room in her apartment.[14]

Glória is just one worker in an economy characterized by ever-increasing numbers of workers in the lowest-paid sectors (this is the demographics of Brazil); in this setting, there is not enough expansion of the formal sector to absorb these workers. It took Glória until well into her late forties to garner a position with a wage high enough to raise her out of the lowest economic category and into the working class, and most of her friends saw her situation as exceptional, indeed, anomalous. If she had not found Beth, Glória would have continued earning one to two minimum wages per month in her faxineira position. Much like in the United States, the minimum salary designation is not really a living wage; it is a subsistence wage. The market rate for all domestic work is disproportionately low compared with what is needed for a worker's proper sustenance. These wages are also disproportionately low if they are calculated as a proportion of the income of the middle- and upper-class clients who desire these services. Middle-class wages vary greatly, but even the lowest wage for a single middle-class person would hover at approximately five to ten salaries per month. Another way to view this situation is to understand that the system demands that domestic work be the lowest paid, affordable to even the lowest ranks of the middle classes, since it is in and of itself a distinguishing feature of middle-class life.

For the middle class in Rio de Janeiro, employing a domestic worker is not only perceived as a necessity; it is also a class marker, a form of identity in the deepest sense. While for the elite, the very top of the upper classes, having servants is a class marker as well, they are not obsessed with the same fear of slipping back into that dreaded pool of the population that must supply manual labor to others—a fear that plagues middle-class families.

Everyone in the middle class expects to be able to afford a person to cook and clean for them. Because this is a defining feature of middle-class life, I suspect it will be the last luxury to be forfeited in times of economic stress. As Brian Owensby (1999) points out, Brazilian middle-classness is a *state of mind* "oriented to a dynamic social and economic arena" (8). In other words, middle-classness is a historical identity construction in process and more than a mere economic enumeration. Owensby describes how this process operated in the 1930s in Copacabana:

> Servants stood as a second difference between typical middle-class and working-class budgets. Working-class families rarely had maids. In respectable collar-and-tie families at least one servant appears to have been de rigueur. This was more than just a matter of having someone to clean the house. It meant that middle-class men and women could project to the world the fact that they were free, at least symbolically, of the most degrading manual labor involved in running a household. Moreover, for a majority of middle-class men the presence of a servant meant that however much they were subject to bosses, or social superiors outside the home, they could at least return at the end of the day to a situation of dominance over a (sexual, class, and often racial) inferior who owed them even more deference than their wives. In the case of middle-class women the presence of a maid served to reinforce traditional lines of authority and social privilege, according to which certain people could employ others to do the heaviest and most undesirable work around the house. (107–8)

This state of mind is a historically constituted one in the sense that it is simply anathema for the middle class to take an interest in the kinds of manual labor that are required to manage a household properly. Middle-class identity was historically conditioned to be dependent on having others do the work. Being a member of the middle class, in this sense, signifies that one is not a member of the serving class.

Middle-classness is nevertheless an ambiguous position. On the one hand, the middle class is supposed to make things happen economically and politically within the country; on the other hand, it is not supposed to be burdened with the stigma of manual labor. Thus, the site of employer and domestic worker relations is really a site of class formation and differentiation. The middle class is defined by its ability to pay somebody else to do its manual labor; in this sense it lives much like the upper class, although members of the upper class have a wider variety of these services available to them. The members of the middle and upper classes who have domestic workers and have always had them do not really know how to do basic chores for themselves—clean, cook, or wash clothes. Yet this dependence on somebody else—this very helplessness—has become a positive form of status and prestige for these classes. The following comments from a forty-year-old university professor illustrate this point well:

> I always had a domestic worker before I left Brazil. When I faced the situation where I did not have a domestic worker, I began to ask, where did food come from? How do you buy it? How do you cook it? Food had been a "God-given gift." Til then I couldn't see the value of these chores. I could dirty things up or throw food out; everything was a "God-given gift." People who take care of themselves, feed themselves and wash their clothes, become aware of the situation. One is closer to reality than when somebody takes care of you. (Quoted in Pereira de Melo 1989:263)

This cultivated incompetence is an important sign of class. In this sense, domestic workers are a good example of cultural capital objectified as a kind of good or service.[15] One cannot belong to the elite classes without utilizing these services. In this case, the place of domestic workers in the lives of Cariocas is like any other good consumed by the middle and upper classes. The more workers a person employs—divided by tasks, such as *babá* (nanny), chauffeur, empregada, *cozinheira* (cook)—the more economic and social prestige he or she exhibits. In some households, for example, a domestic worker cooks and does the everyday cleaning, but in addition, a faxineira will be hired on a weekly basis to do the heavy work. In other households, usually with fewer resources, a worker will come two or three times a week. Sometimes, Dona Beth gave Glória a break by hiring Glória's neighbor Marília to do the ironing, a task Glória hated. Having or not having such workers, as well as how many of these employees one can afford, determines one's social place. It is through this work that the identity of the classes becomes fixed.[16]

The desire or need for domestic help is not limited to the middle and upper classes, however. Ironically—although perhaps logically—such services are at the top of the list of services that low-income women like Glória say they would procure immediately for themselves if they could afford it. It is rare to find within any of the classes anyone expressing the notion that domestic work ought to be shared by household members. Rather, it is seen as a "natural" and desirable service, one coveted even by those currently performing such duties for others.

In addition to giving poor women like Glória a concrete symbol of "making it" to grasp on to, these relations serve to create and sustain among the poor a vision of themselves as inferior. Most domestic work is carried out by women, and a high proportion of them are Afro-Brazilian; thus the profession reflects, in many ways, the most disadvantaged workers, those who find themselves at the very bottom of a series of interlocking economic and social hierarchies.

Although Glória and many of the women in her generation have spent much of their youth and their adult lives working in the homes of wealthy people, the relationship between domestic workers like Glória and their employers is anything but straightforward. This relationship has been described as an affectively ambiguous one, and its ideological and cultural subtleties have been noted in the literature pertaining to Brazil.[17] Glória, for example, is one individual in a growing workforce of live-out domestic workers, a kind of work regime that has steadily gained adherents over time.[18] Domestic workers desire physical separation from their employers, and many employers find that live-in domestic workers take away from their own freedom (Pereira de Melo 1989:252). In the years Glória worked as a faxineira before committing exclusively to Dona Beth, her situation exemplified the precarious situation of workers in this profession. As the sole earner in a large household, she worked hard and yet could barely keep everyone clothed and fed properly. Glória is just one individual among a large class of working poor, but her situation captures an essential aspect of Brazilian class relations.

POVERTY IN BRAZIL AND RIO DE JANEIRO

Located about four hundred kilometers north of São Paulo, Brazil's most prosperous city, Rio is the country's second-largest city and its second most important port. Rio's economy has been in decline for many years; it is generally accepted that the city has definitively lost out in the struggle with São Paulo for commercial and industrial dominance. This is reflected in a number of economic statistics. In 1985, São Paulo accounted for 26 percent of the country's manufacturing production, while Rio accounted for only 7 percent. Many of Rio's leading banks, industries, and research and development headquarters relocated to São Paulo during the 1980s. In 1988, average household earnings per capita were 22 percent higher in São Paulo than in Rio, and between 1976 and 1988 real earnings in Rio de Janeiro fell by 29 percent (Tolosa 1996). Rio's population throughout the 1980s thus became poorer both in absolute terms and relative to São Paulo in the period just before my fieldwork began.[19] As Tolosa notes, "By 1989, Rio had the most unequal distribution of income of any metropolitan area in Brazil; during the 1980s it had displaced even the cities of the north-east from first place" (6).[20] Gross poverty directly alongside incredible showcases of wealth—people of all ages begging for money and food outside chic restaurants and clothing boutiques—distinguishes Rio as a city of extremes. The low-paying service economy that seems to keep the city afloat gives the impression of a predominantly two-class system with only a very thin middle class, the latter a sign that distinguishes Rio from São Paulo.[21]

One of the more dramatic changes in Rio's demographics has been the increasing feminization of its workforce and the growing participation of children in the economy.[22] Migration to the city has been a significant factor in Rio's growth since early in the twentieth century. According to the Instituto Brasileiro de Geografia e Estatística (National Institute of Brazilian Geography and Statistics) (IBGE 1996), migrants to the Rio metropolitan area make up approximately 22 percent of the total population. These migrants have come mostly from the economically impoverished states to the north: Minas Gerais, Paraiba, Pernambuco, Espírito Santo, and Ceará. Needless to say, a large proportion of poor women who have ended up in Rio, either as recent migrants or the daughters of older migrants, find domestic work—work without regular benefits or health care—one of the very few employment opportunities available to them.[23]

CLASS, CULTURE, AND THE EFFECTS OF DOMINATION

I note these statistical trends to lay the foundation for capturing the aesthetics of domination inside of Rio. But these numbers, while helping to shape some of the analysis that follows, cannot substitute for a more subtle analysis of the effects of domination in a city marked by such extreme forms of inequality. The studies that have addressed domestic service in Brazil have mainly approached the dynamics of this relationship from an economic perspective—an exchange of labor for wages—noting the typically low wages paid these workers and the entrapment of these women in an economy that cannot absorb them into other sectors.[24] Research that has extended beyond the strictly economic has often separated public and private domains of power relations, reserving the study of the "political" to public spheres of power, thus largely ignoring the more subtle forms of domination present here. The domestic worker–employer relationship merits closer attention precisely because it is one of the rare places where relations of intimacy take place despite the class gap that characterizes Brazil's "social apartheid" (Buarque 1992). Because the experiences of the working classes, specifically the domestic workers who are at the economic bottom of the working-class pay scale, are so removed from the life experiences of the middle- and upper-class families for whom they work, the social apartheid Buarque speaks of is a division of both class and everyday culture.

Through my initiation into Glória's world, I was able to grasp the intimate ways in which she and many of her associates in Felicidade Eterna had become involved in the lives of the elites they worked for in the Zona Sul—and contrastingly, how relatively little these same employers knew of their lives.

FROM SLAVERY TO SERVITUDE

I was born in the middle of the woods. A little house, a shack of co-gongrass. A board to cover the floor with and sleep on. Three of my siblings were born in Minas. At one time, we passed through a lot of hardship, hunger. We were seven at that time. I stayed at home, cooking. With wood. . . . All of the pans were cleaned with soap that we made at home. My mother made soap at home. She did everything. Everything was early. Dinner at three and lunch at ten. There was no toilet paper, no newspaper. . . . We wiped ourselves with branches, leaves of trees, or with corn cob. We ate the corn from the cob, dried it in the sun and later cleaned ourselves with this. It [the corn cob] hurts because it is dry. It itched alot. We ate lots of yam and *angu* [corn or manioc mush]. White *inhame* [yam] makes your throat itch. There were no streets, only little trails. I had to walk a lot. Always. There were snakes out there. We conserved meat for the entire year. We would salt and can it. It was dipped in lemon, to sit there, then a fire and a yew and we fried it all and put it in a can. Not one chemical in it. . . . Yam soup and angu. If I could eat angu every day . . . I could every day. I love it still today. How our asses itched. And our throats.
(Glória, forty-six, Felicidade Eterna, Rio de Janeiro, taped interview, 1992)

Glória recalls spending part of her childhood in the interior state of Minas Gerais, in a town called Bom Jesus de Moreira, working as a servant on a large farm, or *fazenda*, where her family suffered a great deal of hardship. One of her earliest memories is of herself cooking with wood in a hut where her family lived. Her mother planted coffee on the fazenda and gathered *capim*, a coarse grass used as cattle fodder. At the age of nine, Glória began working in the kitchen of the

farm owners. She remembers how the head cook had to make her a little stepladder so that she could reach the sink and stove in order to
work. She gave all her money to her mother, who, like many, longed
to escape the exploitative labor relations of rural farmwork. Eventually, the family made their way to Rio de Janeiro, migrating in the
1950s to a *barraco* (shack) in Rocinha, now the largest favela in Latin
America, with over one hundred fifty thousand inhabitants, but at the
time still relatively small. There her mother began laboring as a domestic worker.[25]

Glória had remained good friends over the years with Eliana, a
woman she worked with as a child. Now neighbors in Felicidade Eterna,
Glória and Eliana often got together to reminisce about this earlier period in their lives, speaking of it as if it were a completely different era,
a time still mired in the era "before Princess Isabel had abolished slavery." They had worked for two sisters who spent the weekends together
at their family estate in Petrópolis, a resort city for wealthy Cariocas just
a short drive outside of Rio de Janeiro. These weekend get-togethers
from their past drew Glória and Eliana together into a lifelong friendship. Glória had started working in the kitchen of one of the sisters at the
age of fourteen, later becoming a nanny, like Eliana, who began working for the other sister at the age of eleven. They each worked for their
respective employers for more than a decade, yet both of them eventually left these homes without much more than what little they had arrived with. Although they were not outwardly bitter about this time period, their reminiscing, often tinged with their characteristic black
humor, betrayed a certain sense of injustice. So, while Glória and Eliana
jokingly referred to their childhood as having happened in some distant
and mythic past—a time of slaves and "princesses"—they were also
aware that they themselves had experienced childhood in a role most
similar to slaves.

One of their specific and often repeated complaints about that period
was that they were not given the same food as that which was served to
their employers. The reference to food—to not being able to eat the same
amount and kind of food as their employers—is something that both employers and domestic workers now point to as a sign of how times have
changed. Glória and Eliana triumphantly note that in their later work experiences, they were able to eat whatever they desired. Similarly, employers often insisted on telling me—with a great deal of pride—that they
feed their domestic help exactly the same foods that they themselves eat.

It is easy to calculate that Glória's childhood was not too far removed from slavery; indeed, her grandparents lived their youths during the final years of slavery. And while Glória's mother's generation and her own did not experience slavery directly, its echoes have affected how both see themselves and their world.

COLONIAL RIO DE JANEIRO

The history of Rio de Janeiro has been intimately connected to the lives of slaves, ex-slaves, and domestic workers since the beginning of the colonial period, making the domestic worker setting there an ideal context for viewing the practices of both class and cultural domination over time. Relations between domestic workers and their employers are a perfect site within which to explore how cultural practices are produced and reproduced, and what effects are created through this form of domination. In the domestic worker–employer relationship, the extremities of the class divide are exhibited and performed—and a racial dimension is always present. The domestic worker, no matter what her skin color, is symbolically associated with the dirty work to be done in a household. Palpable in the racial commentaries across classes is a recognizable discourse that associates domestic work with dark skin, and dark skin with slavery, dirt, ugliness, and low social standing. This association, however, does not preclude lighter-skinned women from working as domestic workers. In fact, many domestic workers are white or light-skinned migrants from the most impoverished regions in Northeast Brazil. Still, the association of dark skin color with slavery, and slavery with unpleasant tasks and with dirt, is strong, influencing how even the lightest-skinned domestic worker is perceived. Despite these negative associations, the same domestic worker is often fondly venerated, even cherished, in the households of the middle and upper classes, appreciated for her caretaking activities. These relationships of servitude stemming from Brazil's period of slavery, their racialized aspects, and the discourses they inspire work in the current context to solidify a particular form of domination by the middle and upper classes.

Quite commonly, one hears middle- and upper-class Cariocas of all ages wax nostalgic about their favorite nanny or their favorite domestic worker. To the outsider, the non-Brazilian, these comments may fall on cynical ears. Yet these words of affection form part of a telling class discourse that is inappropriately nostalgic for the pampering of a lost colonial era.

Gilberto Freyre, a Brazilian social historian who wrote in the 1930s,

discussed the special place of the slave woman in the sexual life in colonial Brazil, both as mistress of the planters and as sexual initiator of their
white sons. In colonial-era expressions of tenderness such as *meu nego*
and *minha nega* (literally, "my Negro"), we can recognize that these
terms were meant as terms of endearment for slaves.[26] These terms originated (according to Freyre) out of the feelings of intimacy and engaging
affections that whites held toward their slaves. Freyre's work, of course,
has been interpreted as proposing an easygoing and humanized relationship between masters and slaves, but scholars began debating—and
continue to disagree on—his specific propositions soon after they were
first written.[27] While I generally reject the position that considers Brazil's
version of slavery "soft,"[28] I would agree that certain peculiarities were
present within these relationships, and that contemporary expressions of
this relationship reveal profound ambiguities.

Even after the legal abolition of slavery, domestic servants were expected to provide sexual services to masters and their sons, and nurturing services to younger children as "milk nannies," thus reproducing almost entirely the full range of slave relationships within the context of
paid domestic work (Freyre 1986[1933]:378). We know from scholars
of late-nineteenth-century Rio de Janeiro that servant women—either as
slaves or as free women—were the largest single occupational group of
women up through the early 1900s and that servants worked and lived
under conditions similar to those of slaves. Historian Sandra Lauderdale
Graham (1995[1988]) notes that at slavery's end, relationships between
patrões and servants still remained outside the realm of public regula-
tion and instead was viewed as "a matter of private negotiation and personal control" (130). This feature of the postslavery period meant that
the treatment and abuse of domestic workers were not to be regulated
by the law.

What also becomes a clear feature of this moment of transition is that
elites were consciously attempting to show the rest of the world that they
belonged to the group of civilized nations, those that had embraced a
modernity beyond slavery. The laudatory writings of Freyre that emphasize Brazilian exceptionalism with regard to race can be partially explained by this desire to be accepted by the rest of the "civilized" world.
The elite (and later middle-class) desire to be modern can perhaps also
help explain some of the ambiguities visible in the contemporary domestic worker–employer relationship. While this relationship is common
in other Western countries as well, in Brazil the ambiguity engendered by
its particular historical legacy and the so-called mixing of the races pre-

sented a particular challenge. On the one hand, manual labor was despised, and so the transition from slavery to servanthood needed to preserve the ability of the upper class to hire others to perform these tasks. On the other hand, the desire to disassociate themselves from the backwardness of slavery left the elite of the time in an awkward position vis-à-vis their European counterparts. This uneasiness is still readily apparent in contemporary Rio society. Even today, there is an almost automatic reliance on "the economy" as an explanation used by the middle and upper classes as part of a tortured defense regarding the "naturalness" of domestic work and the inability of the economy to absorb the lower-class population in any other productive manner. Domestic workers are part of an emotionally explosive area of social relations, on the one hand, providing a sense of identity to both middle and upper classes, and on the other, filling them with guilt and self-doubt about their status in the civilized world.

Indeed, progressive members of these classes know that there is something wrong with this relationship—that it still reeks of their colonial and seigneurial past—but they are themselves stuck in it. It has by now become so culturally expected and naturalized that they cannot begin to think about giving it up, which is why they have had to come up with explanations for why it is a necessary evil: that there is an abundance of labor, and therefore labor is cheap, and therefore they are doing a good thing by helping the employment situation in their country. At some level, this logic is completely anachronistic because members of these classes delude themselves, attempting to hide their own shame and guilt about robbing another person of a fuller, more equable life, and instead pointing to the ambiguous fact that, indeed, many such "grateful" workers remain with them over the course of a lifetime.

PARA INGLÊS VER, OR FOR THE ENGLISH TO SEE

The visit of King Albert and Queen Elisabeth of Belgium to Rio de Janeiro in September 1920 represents a telling historical moment when Brazilians (here, of the elite classes) attempted to make a particular presentation of themselves in order to show a positive picture of their city to the visiting European monarchs.[29] The visit and the preparations highlight certain aspects of the crisis affecting the city's elites at that moment. While the government attempted to prepare the city "for the king to see," that is, highlighting certain aspects and hiding others, there was a sense among some intellectuals and artists at the time that by hiding the city's poverty and the authentically Brazilian aspects of the city, the elites were actually opening up the country to ridicule and contempt by the European powers.[30] This debate about what King Albert should or should not see culminated in a later more powerful statement by the Brazilian modernists,[31] but what was at stake in both cases were fundamental questions of identity. Brazilian elites wanted to be accepted as citizens of modernity, and such acceptance, it seemed, could be validated only by Europe's postcolonial gaze.

Historian Thomas Skidmore (1993[1974]) addresses the question of how Brazilian elites thought about race and national identity in the years immediately preceding and following the abolition of slavery, approximately the period between 1870 and 1940. As Skidmore points out, the Brazilian elites, before the end of slavery and before the declaration of the First Republic in 1889, were very much concerned about the image they conveyed to their North American and western European trade partners. There was a certain amount of shame attached to their long history of slavery, as well as to the large Afro-Brazilian and mixed-race population that was to become Brazil's trademark, a characteristic often noted by famous travel writers, diplomats, and visitors to the country at the time.

Brazilian elites grappled with the latest European conventions regarding race, specifically the idea of scientific racism that was taken as common sense in the late 1800s and early turn of the century. This formal racism held that biological and racial differences were causative and reflective of different progressive stages of "civilization." Brazilians, recognizing their own racialized history, struggled with this European ideology by proposing a "whitening" of the population. Part of what the Brazilian elite worried about was the sheer numbers of dark-skinned and mixed-race people who had, to different degrees, successfully integrated into their society. In practical terms, this led to an open-door policy with regard to white European immigration.

This tension about race was played out in postemancipation urban and architectural design, which physically reinforced the separation of the privileged classes from the nonprivileged classes. The historian Jeffrey Needell (1995b) writes about the elites' conceptions of public space in Rio just after Brazil became a republic and throughout the first half of the twentieth century. He describes an elite class that constructed public spaces for themselves and for foreign tourists, diplomats, and businessmen as part of their desire to belong to the great "civilized" capitals of Europe, Paris in particular. In the process of designing a Paris in Rio, Brazilian elites made public spaces into private ones by defining the public space and consciousness of their concern along lines restricted by wealth and Europhile culture. The great mass of their country-men were simply excluded. It was not that they were ignored; rather, they were pushed aside or even attacked. In Rio, for example, poor people were often forced out of the repaired or newly constructed thoroughfares in the old City because much of their housing was demolished, police increased their harassment, and shabby commerce or Afro-Brazilian culture was for-bidden there. The poor people interfered with the elite's fantasy of civiliza-tion and so had to be hidden away in the Afro-Brazilian slums near the docks and on the hills. (Needell 1995b:538)

The elite in Rio often looked to certain areas of the city—those that con-tained the poor masses of Afro-Brazilians who had migrated there in the years following slavery—in much the same way that Europeans viewed their colonies, as areas "obstructed by an inferior race and culture" (Needell 1987:50). These areas were not so much physical threats as they were psychological reminders of their mixed-race past:

> For, if the reforms meant that Cariocas were achieving Civilization by be-coming more European, they also meant, necessarily, a negation, an ending, of much that was very Brazilian indeed. The embrace of Civilization was also the leaving-behind of what many of the Carioca elite saw as a back-ward, colonial past and the condemnation of the racial and cultural aspects of Carioca reality that the elite associated with that past. (Needell 1987:48)

This structuring of exclusion enabled national elites to legitimize themselves internationally, but ultimately the architecture and planning reveal the forms of neocolonial domination to which these elites had wholeheartedly succumbed. Needell's reading of Rio's elites offers a fun-damental framing for how we might also apprehend the transition from slavery to domestic work—from the perspective of an elite group desir-ing legitimation—at this turn-of-the-century moment:

> The word neo-colonial expresses the contradictory nature of the phenome-non to which it refers. It suggests both the new and old bonds of colonial-ism. It also refers to the kind of colonialism typical in the third world in the era after post-colonialism, a dependency and control between metropolis and colonies in which no formal (that is, political) domination is present be-cause it has been overthrown and less straightforward forms of domination (economic, cultural, ideological, military) have taken its place.
>   Something of neo-colonialism's contradictory, less straightforward na-ture often seems to touch all of the complex relations which it subsumes. Cultural neo-colonialism is perhaps the most slippery. (Needell 1995b:539–40)

Rio's elites traveled to Paris, read French, and admired Paris as an example of what a "civilized" city should look like. Planners during this period, looking to remake Rio into a "modern" city, adopted explicitly Haussmannist (named for the city planner Baron Georges Eugene Haussmann) proposals, a type of urban planning that had turned Paris of the nineteenth century into a European showcase through the planned exclusion of the poor from public spaces. Haussmannist strategies to city planning in Rio entailed the reform of public and private spaces so that the working classes, Afro-Brazilian culture, and shabby commerce were pushed either into the Zona Norte (North Zone) or onto hillside favelas, while simultaneously giving the elite of the Zona Sul easy access to a newly sanitized city center. In fact, Needell argues that in this imitation of foreign cities, Brazilian elites turned public spaces into private spaces "by defining the public space and consciousness of their concern along lines restricted by wealth and Europhile culture" (1995b:538).

Until the Modernist movement in Brazil,[32] the elites were caught up in a kind of neocolonial imitation in which they weighed their own identity in relation to the Old World, struggling with a sense of insecurity about their racially mixed population. After World War I, Brazilian elites began to develop a nationalist consciousness, an awareness of themselves as different from the people of Europe and North America. In 1922, this nationalist sentiment combined with a progressive modernist art and literary movement, beginning with a Modern Art Week festival in São Paulo, financed by Paulo Prado, a wealthy scion of a coffee family. Prado had published an important book examining the elite's crisis of identity, *Retrato do Brasil: Ensaio Sôbre a Tristeza Brasileira* (*Portrait of Brazil: An Essay on Brazilian Sadness;* 1972[1928]). This text has been interpreted as an ambivalent one: on the one hand, it contains a rather pessimistic reading of Brazil's past—and particularly its lascivious past. Prado names the "mixture of three races" as a "source of that peculiar sadness," one characteristic of the Brazilian soul (Parker 1991:20). On the other hand, Prado's text is also a treatise on "whitening," an optimistic look at the possibilities of the future regarding race in Brazil (Skidmore 1974:205).

The Modern Art Week itself stands out not only as a significant artistic event but also as a moment when the ideas of "whitening" and the belief in scientific racism were in the process of transformation. The festival also coincided with the publication of the initial writings that led to Freyre's book *The Masters and the Slaves* (1986[1933]), a work that ultimately helped both solidify the reorientation of Brazilians toward race that was occurring during this time frame and set out a new doctrine from which to build a revised Brazilian national identity. Indeed, *The Masters and the Slaves,* a social history and ethnography of plantation life in the sixteenth and seventeenth centuries, is credited with extending the Boasian convention of substituting "culture" for "race," thereby alleviating the ambivalence of the predominantly white Brazilian elite toward a historically mixed-race population. This ideological shift was embraced by Brazilian elites because it allowed them to reject biological and scientifically racist doctrines that naturalized racial inferiority. It enabled them to celebrate their origins and to recognize the mixing of European, African, and Indian cultures in the formation of a "new world in the tropics."

Although Freyre's thesis was still positioned within the framework of the "whitening" ideal, it moved Brazilians much farther and much faster away from the racist ideologies of Europe and North America prevalent at the time, and his ideas became the basis of a national ideology celebrating Brazil as a racial democracy. Brazil came to see itself not as an inferior nation among the white civilized world but instead as a proud mixed-race civilized nation, an image that became the essence of brasilidade.[33]

The new orientation provided by the modernists and Freyre allowed for a rupture in Brazil's neocolonial relationship with Europe. The modernists, in a playful parody of cannibalism—represented in Oswald de Andrade's "Manifesto Antropófago" ("Anthropophagist Manifesto"; 1970[1928])—suggested that rather than imitate foreign models, Brazilians ought to cannibalize those models and turn them into something new and uniquely Brazilian. This movement served as a radical awakening for the Brazilian elites and began a process that opened up discussions about the tendency toward imitation, as well as their own particular history of exploitation by the European powers.

PRIVATE AND PUBLIC SPACES

James Holston (1989), in describing a more contemporary example of urban and architectural planning (Brasília, from its early stages in the 1950s through the 1980s), has outlined the conventional organization of the Brazilian middle-class apartment as one that is divided into three functionally independent zones: the social area, the intimate area, and the service area, all planned specifically to separate the classes from one another:

> In both design and use, this service area appeals to the most atavistic of
> middle-class values: the apartment kitchen is still the kitchen of the *casa-
> grande* at a remove from the living space of the *patrão;* it is the domain of
> servants, rarely of the mistress of the house; the maid is still a slave of un-
> welcome presence in the family areas; and her little room with its door
> opening onto the wash basin in the service corridor is still the *senzala,* the
> slave shanty. (178–79)

These carefully planned architectural details characterize the contemporary empregada quarters in even the wealthiest homes and apartments to
this day. The domestic worker's room, once meant for a live-in arrangement but now more often for daily use, cannot fit much more than a
small single bed. The bathroom facilities are also revealing. These
cramped areas have barely enough room for a shower and a toilet basin.
In many that I have seen, the toilet bowl is bereft of a seat, and the architecture itself is such that when the shower runs, it soaks the entire
room. It is difficult, if not impossible, to make these spaces appear clean
and tidy. The consistency, size, and cramped nature of this space across
diverse middle- and upper-class apartments and houses belie a structure
far beyond liberal-conservative politics or the affective ambiguities of
slave and postslave relations in Brazil. As Holston (1989:178–80) points
out, even the communist architect of Brasília, Oscar Niemeyer, had to
adhere to certain Brazilian conventions regarding the spatial dimensions
of an ossified class division. Holston found that architects working in
Brazil claimed that Brazilian architecture—even for apartment buildings—exhibited the unique characteristic of two completely independent
circulation systems: one for masters and one for servants. Holston notes
that although Niemeyer's plans for Brasília altered spatial separations
between masters and servants in significant ways, the final design created
apartments with servant quarters and service elevators.

   While the line that runs from slavery through to Glória's generation
is a complicated one, the signs of this bondage have become incorporated
not only in the local architecture but also in the body itself. Complex
signs of bondage became internalized in classed and racialized ways, even
by members of the lower classes themselves. Glória's work in Beth's
household included occasional cooking for Beth's newly married son,
whose wife, Nilda, had never learned how to cook. Glória accepted the
terms of this arrangement, but she did not sweeten her comments about
Beth's daughter-in-law to friends. Glória perceived Nilda to be a woman
from a background similar to her own—*"gente como nós"* (people like

us), she would say—and so was unforgiving about her inability to cook properly for Beth's son. From Glória's perspective, "people like us" ought to know how to cook. After all, even Glória's youngest girls knew how to prepare basic foods. Her perception of Nilda as someone like herself made it unbearable for her to treat Nilda as she would the other members of Beth's family. Her protest registered in distinct moments, such as refusing to work at events that were to take place at Nilda's house. Further, she could barely make herself address Nilda with the usual *Dona*, part of the polite and deferential language she used commonly in addressing Beth and the other members of Beth's family. Glória seemed capable of "knowing her place" with Beth and her immediate family, but she found it considerably more difficult to perform as an empregada for somebody she perceived to be too much like herself. This was the rule, it seems, for those of Glória's generation. She preferred working for people who were comfortably stationed in the Zona Sul—not in some peripheral or noncentral neighborhood—and who, for the most part, were white-skinned and from a long-standing lineage of privilege.

Glória recognized Nilda as someone from a class and family who were themselves manual laborers or domestic workers but who could now—through the economic support of Beth—afford the services of a domestic worker. Nilda's success at having made it out of a lower-class background—through marriage—seems to have been a sore spot for Glória, who perhaps preferred to see privilege as something inherent, or white, or perhaps something that a person like her can never acquire.

This is perhaps a good example of Bourdieu's (1991) notion of historical embodiment, with the body being a site of incorporated history. Here is a juncture—perhaps a break—in the naturalized routine of service. Whereas one's habitus would usually provide a sense of how to act in the course of one's daily life, there are also moments, such as these between Glória and Nilda, of conflict and rupture. Nilda's presence brought some of the naturalized forms of deference to the surface, rendering them questionable. Nilda was much darker-skinned than Beth's white European family; her manner of speaking and her body language were easily recognizable to Glória as similar to her own, and this brought out resentment and resistance in a person who otherwise worked within the hierarchies constructing her life with a great deal of grace and good humor. Nilda had accomplished the (almost impossible) dream held by Glória and many of her contemporaries; she had married well and now was able to afford an occasional empregada. But Glória's implicit understanding of the class dimensions of domestic work framed Nilda as one not worthy of the deference embedded within the domestic worker–employer relationship.

I highlight this example because it places in relief the ways in which these relations embody much more than mere economic exchanges. They are relationships in which notions of inferiority and superiority based on class, race, and gender are enacted and reproduced. When the obvious signs of class distinction and racial hierarchy are "off"—as in the case of Nilda—the relations of deference seem to fall apart, and an opportunity for resistance is registered. Sadly, some of the resistance in this particular case is enabled by the confusion of class and racial signs that someone like Nilda inspires. Glória's own analysis of the situation rested on grounds that Nilda, unlike the rest of Beth's family, did not know how to treat her correctly. She insisted that Nilda did not know how to speak to her properly and was awkward in asking for things. In part, at least, Glória recognized that Nilda was not used to asking another person to perform various tasks for her. More to the point, Glória had trouble "performing" with deference toward a person she perceived as a social equal, a situation that certainly suggests at least some level of internalized racism on Glória's part, and perhaps on Nilda's as well. Nilda was, in sum, perceived as a "fraud" rather than as a potential class or racial ally.

AMBIGUOUS AFFECTIONS

Glória's close relationship with Dona Beth extended in specific ways to her daughter Soneca. When Glória first started working as a faxineira for Beth, Soneca, just a child at the time, would occasionally accompany her mother to Beth's to work—the purpose being not to earn more money but to learn how to do the job and to help her mother finish her job in less time. Although Soneca was for the most part compliant in these situations—recognizing her mother's need for help in supporting the family—she also made it clear that she would not follow in her mother's footsteps as a domestic worker. Soneca had been an exemplary student, completing her first years of school with near-perfect marks, and she could read and write at a reasonably competent level. In 1992, before leaving Brazil, it became clear to me that Soneca was serious about continuing her studies toward a profession outside of the realm of domestic work. She had expressed some interest in secretarial work, and so I put aside some money for her to begin schooling at a computer institute, where she was to be trained in basic typing and computer skills and then helped to find placement in a permanent job. Later, I found out that it was quite impossible for her to complete this course: at the time, there were still too many younger children at home who needed attention. Since Soneca was the most responsible of the girls, she was the most likely person to be able to care for the younger children still left in the household, and when Glória exited to live with Mauro, Soneca was left at home to take on the lion's share of household chores. Additionally, Soneca admitted to me later that she ultimately lost interest in the course because of its fast pace and a set of expectations she felt she could not possibly fulfill. In the end, Soneca, an inveterate romantic, fell in love with Sílvio, a light-skinned boy and gang member who lived in a house on an asphalt-paved street just a short walk from the entrance of Felicidade Eterna,[34] and soon after she became pregnant with his child.

Glória was outraged when she discovered Soneca's pregnancy, declaring loudly that "she wasn't going to support a child *and* a grandchild!" Soneca had been forewarned by those around her that Sílvio was not going to marry her, nor was he likely to provide much support for their child. She found herself in a bind because Glória was unwilling to tolerate even one more mouth to feed in her house, despite her usual generosity in such matters. Glória had often proclaimed that the pot that feeds a few can feed many, but she was exasperated with what she felt was Soneca's lack of responsibility in this case. Soneca thus found herself wanting to have a child but not having any financial support. Dona Beth, who had gotten to know Soneca from her occasional visits, was updated on Soneca's drama through Glória's telling. Beth took pity on Soneca, perhaps because she worked with many teenagers in a similar situation, and allowed Soneca and her tiny daughter, Diana, to live in her maid's room behind the kitchen of her apartment for almost a year. Further, she even served as a grandmother figure to Soneca's firstborn. She made sure that Soneca ate properly and provided her with baby clothes and toys. According to Glória, without Dona Beth's support, Soneca would not have been able to support herself and her child. Over time, however, Glória made it clear that she was annoyed that her own hard work was not being directly rewarded to her but instead was being recognized in the form of Dona Beth's generosity toward Soneca.

Both Beth and I were caught in situations where we wanted somehow to help the people we cared about, yet neither of us could provide more than a very temporary "solution." In the end, Glória was annoyed that Soneca had squandered her chances for training at the computer institute with the money I had provided, but she also recognized that she needed Soneca's help at home to take care of the younger children. I think Glória would have ultimately preferred that I had left *her* any money I could for the purposes of helping their situation rather than attempt, as I did, to invest directly in the wage earnings of the next generation. I came to this tentative conclusion after realizing that Glória was annoyed with Beth for taking Soneca into her home and caring for her granddaughter rather than simply rewarding Glória's own hard work more directly. Both Beth and I had become involved in exchanges that were more than economic. Beth had attempted to make a difference by offering shelter and food to Soneca and her daughter during a vulnerable period. I had attempted to invest in the training and education of one of Glória's children with the hope that a skilled laborer could eventually bring in more wage earnings, thereby relieving the economic stress in Glória's household. Of course, both of these attempts were complicated by the affective relations involved: Beth was Glória's employer and was extending her own patronage to Glória's daughter. In my case, Glória was my principal informant and friend, and I was looking for creative ways of compensating her and her family for being willing to work with me.

These ambiguities and complications are so ingrained and embodied throughout the stream of daily social relations that everyone, regardless of their good intentions, gets entangled in similar situations. Both Dona Beth and I were forced to walk a fine line between wanting to help and recognizing the limits to what was possible or expected. In Beth's case, she opened her home to Soneca, but there were still internal spatial limits that were enforced naturally, without any specific rules being mentioned. I never, for example, found Glória or Soneca lounging in Beth's living room; they remained in the kitchen and laundry area. These physical boundaries are marked from both ends. Despite the ambiguous affections involved, patroa and empregada both know their place.

The historical constitution of these relations has always been somewhat ambiguous:

> House servants experienced most sharply the profound tensions that characterized the relationship of master and servant as one personal and proximate, perhaps long-lasting, but never one between trusted equals. The closeness allowed for the tender recollections of wet-nurses, but also for the suspicion or resentment with which patrons viewed servants. For masters the ties with servants were necessarily unstable, because mistrust, even con-

tempt, for those on whom they relied for the maintenance of family and household resonated with ambivalence, requiring repeated confirmations from servants of reliability and loyalty. The bond that linked family and servants surely held a different meaning when servants lived in their own housing or worked for a family only sporadically. A family could not expect the same loyal and devoted service, nor a servant the same favor that a closer relationship or one of longer standing merited. Even the weaker bond, though, required that both patrões and servants meet their reciprocal obligations at least minimally. (Graham 1995[1988]:107)

As Graham further points out, the elites themselves also experienced this relationship as problematic:

The conduct of domestic life was awkwardly personal. Countless daily exchanges between patrões and servants within the narrow confines of city houses accentuated the perceived tensions between family and non-family. Where neither could stay entirely aloof from the other's near-constant presence, their mutual but unequal dependence became compellingly immediate. By relying on women that maintained their households and made privilege concrete, patrões rendered themselves continuously vulnerable. (91)

Many middle- and upper-class Brazilians talk about their domestic workers with a mixture of love and appreciation. They express familial-like affections or a fondness for that special domestic worker who lived with their family for many years and devoted her life to serving the family, or the nanny they had as a child, who pampered them in special ways, such as by cooking their favorite foods or comforting them in times of sorrow. Certainly, these sentiments are common enough, but these same affections also reveal a sense of uncertainty and distance, often about the very same people.

A middle-class friend once shared with me a story about another friend who had recently experienced what she called a *cura baiana* (Bahian cure). My friend's friend was a psychoanalyst from a prominent family but had married a much younger man from a lower class background. Eventually, he left his psychoanalyst wife for a younger woman, rendering my friend's friend emotionally devastated and depressed, partly, at least, because her own transgressions of class, gender, and age rules had made this tragic outcome predictable. Her loyal empregada administered the cura baiana, which consisted of the domestic worker's preparation of special foods, such as fresh orange juice, delivered directly to her in bed. We also know from this narrative that the servant is privy to the intimacy of her employer's private life and on an emotional level is capable of comprehending the loss of a loved one as well as administering psychological comfort. Of course, this story was related to me with a certain amount of self-awareness and irony, which I am sure may have even been shared by the actual recipient of the cura. Many progressive-minded Brazilians possess a certain self-consciousness concerning the complicated and perverse aspects of these relationships. Here, for example, is a psychoanalyst receiving a psychological cure from her own domestic worker. The goal of my friend's narrative was not only to illustrate the intimacy of the patron-client relationship but also to laugh about how the relationship is likely to become its own peculiar burden over time.

I recall the case of Renata, a middle-class professional living in the Zona Sul whose family had a long, complex relationship with their live-in empregada, Cida. Cida was brought into the household—into the "family"—as a live-in domestic worker at the same time the family's three daughters were about to leave home. Their father had recently passed away, and the girls wanted to hire an empregada as a kind of surrogate daughter, someone who would stay at home and care for their aging mother. Renata, one of the daughters—a woman in her early forties at the time of this interview—described the relationship between her mother and Cida as complicated, a mixture of love and hate:

> The relationship with my mother is complicated. Cida is now the daughter that you abuse, because she [my mother] can't do that to the others. A type of stepdaughter that you can abuse. It is very ambiguous. A love-hate relationship. She loves my mother like a mother because my mother has done a lot for her. But she hates her because she's not her daughter and she doesn't treat her like her child and she keeps bossing Cida around . . . so it's difficult. . . . None of the daughters want to have the responsibility of their aging mother, so they want to have Cida living there. They don't want her to leave. (Renata, taped interview, 1989)

Thus, while Cida was not really treated like a daughter, she was expected to carry out filial duties. She was alternatively spoken of by the family to others with a great deal of love and affection, as well as described as an uncouth and uneducated creature, one in need of special training:

> She has been in my mother's house for fourteen years or so by now. She came to my mother at about the age of nineteen. Cida came through family connections. Someone knew her cousin, a Nordestino[35] who was gay and

from a poor class, working in the house of a family friend as a *copeiro* [domestic worker with waiter duties]. She had just come from the Northeast. She spoke completely wrong. For example, she would say "*istambre*" instead of "*estômago*" [stomach]. She spoke wrong because she had heard the words but she couldn't read or write, so she didn't know the correct word. Many everyday words she needed to be taught. My mother had to teach her. Mentor her. (Renata, taped interview, 1989)

Stalleybrass and White (1986) discuss the class dimensions of carnivalesque activity and point to the purpose of maintaining a proximate "low Other" as an object within view of the bourgeois high-culture gaze. The intimate presence of the service worker perhaps carries out a similar function in contemporary Brazilian households. The presence of this "low Other" reminds the middle and upper classes of what it is they strive not to be. Stuart Hall (1991b) makes a similar point about identity: "When you know what everybody else is, then you are what they are not. Identity is always, in that sense, a structured representation which only achieves its positives through the narrow eye of the negative. It has to go through the eye of the needle of the other before it can construct itself. It produces a very Manichean set of opposites" (21). The middle and upper classes need this "low Other" in order to know who they are. On the other hand, the very same presence may feed their fears about being stuck in an abysmal premodern slot that identifies these labor relations as indicative of a backward "third world" status. Without an internal critique of what is wrong with the system, they are left in their own kind of blindness, unable to extricate themselves from their own incorporated history.

One of the most commonly mentioned characteristics of domestic workers is how they "talk differently," and Cida was obviously not exempt from this type of commentary. Stories about the linguistic limitations and the inarticulateness of empregadas are part of the commentary that the middle and upper classes engage in when exchanging stories about domestic workers. It is sometimes even the source of a smug, deprecating humor. According to Renata, "[Cida] is a bit stupid. She is not intelligent. There is something—I don't know how to say it. She doesn't know how to report anything, how to '*relatar uma história*' [tell a story]. For example, if you ask her what happened in the *novela* [soap opera], she says something like, 'Maria got tired of Pedro, and, well, I forgot. I don't know how to tell, I don't know.'" The idea that these workers are a bit stupid because they cannot "tell a story" or are not very articulate, or speak *errado* (wrong) is so common that I came to expect these comments in my conversations with middle- and upper-class Cariocas. The "innate" inability of the working classes to function in what is considered to be everyday, ordinary, middle-class society is a common theme among them, a complicated discourse in which their class privilege is implicitly protected as "natural."

THE EUPHEMIZATION OF POWER RELATIONS

The protection of class privilege is highly visible in everyday interactions not only inside domestic space but outside as well. Endless physical signs reinforce the sense for the *povo,* or the masses, that they are less—that is, somehow less civilized, less worthy as citizens, less human, than those belonging to the privileged classes. Brazil has an incredibly vibrant consumer culture that caters to the middle and upper classes, and the mass media encourage consumption habits that the majority cannot possibly adhere to. I have described the Europhile tendencies that led to the redivision of public space in Rio de Janeiro—poor neighborhoods and favelas were pushed out onto hillsides and to the outer edges of the city. The elites thereby reinforced the sense that the poor ought to remain out of sight except when they are performing their roles as service workers. Ultimately, over time, these impoverished neighborhoods came to be perceived as eyesores by the wealthier classes. The continued segregation of architectural forms—such as the division between service and public entrances to middle- and upper-class apartment buildings—reinforces a sense of inferiority among the poor and working classes. The stories the elites have told themselves about Brazil being a racial democracy are not necessarily wholeheartedly embraced, but they still serve as a euphemization of the official transcript. I have to agree with Scott (1990) that these relationships need to be euphemized because otherwise there would be revolutions in the making.

Scott borrows Bourdieu's (1977) idea of euphemization to express this aspect of domination: "The imposition of euphemisms on the public transcript plays a similar role in masking the many nasty facts of domination and giving them a harmless or sanitized aspect" (Scott 1989:157). Scott illustrates euphemization by describing how, in the antebellum American South, paternalism substituted as an official story that argued that slavery was in the best interest of the slaves because it kept them properly fed, clothed, and the like. Similarly, contemporary Brazilian elites use a specific form of paternalism to explain their case. They claim that poorly paid service work is the outcome of the country's third world status and point out that domestic workers are actually better off as workers in their homes—where there is adequate food, shelter, and protection—rather than living a "typical" lower-class life. This paternalism comes in the form of charity, little gifts, and other favors—such as the case of Dona Beth inviting Soneca to live in her service quarters—that highlight the benevolence of the individual, emphasizing the interpersonal aspects of the relationship and downplaying its structural constraints. Euphemization, the cleaning up of the official or public transcript, thus serves to hide domination. It can, as I have struggled to point out, even be done with good intentions.

The effect of these euphemizing discourses is that the privileged classes manage to convince themselves that their patronage is healthier for their servants than the lives available to them "on the outside." It is common to hear how the empregada was "better fed" or "appeared much younger" before she went off and married a man of her own class. For example, Renata spoke in tragic terms of her own domestic worker, Lia, who left Renata's household when she married:

> Generally, when women of that class get married, they are on their way to getting worn out. . . . In Lia's case, I hadn't seen her in two or three years (we were away in England). I was shocked. She had been a beautiful woman. She had [given birth to] two children and had lost a front tooth and the other ones had blackened. Only three years. The guy wasn't too bad and they had gotten together in a factory. He would administrate and she would sew. She was still a slave, but they had other employees. They produced clothes for the other people like themselves [meaning clothes of low quality]. (Renata, taped interview, 1989)

In another typical and thoroughly naturalized discourse, patrons often point to the longevity of their relationship with their domestic workers, using the number of years spent employing a particular worker as an indicator not only of the health of the relationship but also implicitly of the health of the entire system. It is as if to say that if a worker spends twenty years in one household, then the conditions cannot be too bad, right?

Another upper-class Carioca in her late fifties, herself originally a migrant from Salvador, Bahia, told me a series of stories about a male domestic worker who had worked for her family in various capacities for more than thirty years and had relocated with her family when they left Salvador for Rio. Despite her fond feelings for him, she nevertheless sprinkled her story with references to his "low" intelligence, as if this somehow explained his life of servitude to her family:

> He is ignorant. He can't express himself well. Even today, he can't read well. He speaks very little. He doesn't comment on things, only if I push him to comment on things. For example, he is treated much better here than in Salvador. People in Salvador don't know how to treat workers. . . . In Rio, things are different. There is respect. . . . When I push him [to talk about the differences between Rio and Salvador], he says, "*Oxente*,[36] things are different here." But only if I push him. (Marcela, taped interview, 1989)

After hearing these kinds of narratives repeated in interview after interview, I found myself beginning to focus almost exclusively on the archetypal character they portrayed, letting the little details of each telling float quietly away. Soon, even my awareness of this discourse as a naturalization of privilege melted away, and I was left with an unexpected, yet sharp, poignant sense of the underlying, quietly desperate need buried in these stories that the elites have for their servants to acknowledge how much better they—their patrons—make their lives. Ultimately, these elites desire that their workers express a proper appreciation for them; when it is not forthcoming, it is explained away as proof of a worker's ignorance.

Just how successful the euphemization of power relations is may be illustrated by the postscript in Graham's book regarding the national meeting of the Young Domestic Servants, who had convened in Rio de Janeiro in 1961 to create a manifesto. This manifesto, published more than forty years ago (but also, notably, more than seventy years after slavery's end), provides an important reminder of the difficult and lengthy efforts necessary for de-euphemizing social relations:

> In 1961 a national meeting of The Young Domestic Servants convened in Rio de Janeiro with the aim of forming an association, the first step in becoming a legally recognized labor union. The meeting issued a "Manifesto às Patroas" in which they stated both their rights and duties, as they, the domestics, intended them to be understood. As the first of those rights, they expected to be considered with "love, respect and understanding within the houses in which we work, being considered members of the family. . . . " In return, among the duties they named, they pledged to "guard the secrets of the families of which we are considered members." (Graham 1995[1988]: 137)

A GAME OF SIGNS: CULTURAL CAPITAL AND THE REPRODUCTION OF CLASS

Cida was, in the scheme of things, treated "well" and given a flexible enough schedule by her employers so that she could attend secondary school at night.

Cida always studied. When she arrived, she couldn't read correctly. Cida
did secondary school twice. She went through the whole thing twice. Twice
freshman, sophomore, junior, senior. She keeps reenrolling. . . . She wants
to have beautiful handwriting; it is almost more important than writing itself. [Cida knows] handwriting tells where you come from immediately.
You glance at handwriting and you can tell everything. She knew this.
Handwriting can do this. I can tell what social class somebody is from just
from their handwriting. (Renata, taped interview, 1989)

Renata recognizes that the academic credentialing system does not really lend itself to social mobility, especially in Brazil's highly class-
segregated school system. Renata appreciates Cida's concerted efforts to
move forward, but she also understands the numerous obstacles Cida
faces. A good deal of class membership is embedded in codes that would
ultimately prevent a person like Cida from attaining social mobility, even
under ideal circumstances.

For Bourdieu, hegemonically constructed forms of cultural capital are
a possession of the dominant classes and are acquired through the
process of class production and reproduction. Handwriting is a good example of where such capital becomes visible. Similarly, bodily movements and ways of behaving are easily marked and distinguished as part
of one's general cultural capital and indeed give one away as being a
member of one class or another. In Cida's case, there is a tragic element
to her concern with her handwriting. Cida seems to believe that if she can
just improve her handwriting, she may have a chance at social mobility;
what she does not understand is that handwriting is only one of the physical signs of an entire set of skills connected to cultural capital. Her impulse is correct, however. She recognizes class as a game of signs.

Renata told another story about Lia, her own domestic worker, who
had been "given to her" by her husband's aunt, herself the patroa of Lia's
aunt. It is still somewhat common for families to speak in this way, regarding domestic workers as pieces of property to be passed down from
generation to generation. Lia was thought to be an "ideal match" for this
newlywed couple because she was about the same age as Renata and thus
could potentially work for Renata over the course of a lifetime. But, as
mentioned earlier, soon after starting work for Renata, Lia herself became engaged to be married. Renata and her husband were the *padrin-
hos* (godparents) of the wedding, and they wanted to get something special for the newlyweds. Renata and her husband thought it would be nice
to get the couple an upscale "honeymoon weekend suite" in a motel on
the beach in Barra de Tijuca, a little taste of a better life.[37] But as the de-

tails unfolded, Renata realized how complicated this choice of gift actually was:

> To get to this motel in Barra, you need a car—or you can go by bus—but nobody would ever do that. Nobody in the poor class has a car . . . so they don't know how it [the motel] looks or what it is like. No access at all. So we went with them in the car. . . . They never had gone to a place like this. They didn't know how to behave in the door of the motel. They didn't have the courage to go alone to this motel. What they were lacking was the knowledge to have the power to know that this is the place where you belong. So my husband and I went with them to check them in. It was the most paternalistic thing you have ever seen. (Renata, taped interview, 1989)

Renata's comments point to her own recognition of the kind of class knowledge that Lia and her husband were lacking. Of course, to some extent the liberal class acknowledges the paternalistic nature of the relationship and even recognizes how the extremities of the class division in Rio contribute to an exaggerated class distance such that the working poor do not always know how to act "appropriately" in many of the naturalized public spaces belonging to the middle and upper classes. One might expect such recognition to lead to outrage, as it often does among poor male youths. But there is a much greater discussion about how public space for the wealthy is becoming more limited because of crime; the outrage is about their own class privileges being eclipsed rather than about the perversity of class differences. The middle and upper classes seem to have become obsessed with crime and the shrinking of public space,[38] yet if one considers the exclusionary practices outlined by Needell (1995b) in his analysis of fin de siècle Rio, it is the working classes that in distinct ways continue to be barred from important dimensions of public life. The chic stores and restaurants that define public space in the Zona Sul are not welcoming of people in working-class attire. The elite's fantasy of civilization in fin de siècle Rio had defined areas of the city as neighborhoods by and for the elite, and even today, there are entire areas of the Zona Sul where people like Glória are uncomfortable entering public establishments.

Once I spent the day with some of Glória's children at Copacabana beach in the Zona Sul, afterward inviting them to a restaurant to eat. Feeling uncomfortable with the idea of going into an establishment to which they had never before had access, they immediately became shy and "didn't know how to behave." As it turned out, they had never seen a menu before, had never dealt with a waiter. Glória, too, I discovered, was extremely uncomfortable in such situations. In short, Glória and her family—in a way not too dissimilar to Dona Beth's daughter-in-law Nilda—simply did not know how to be served. Things that I had completely taken for granted were foreign to them, and yet, because I knew that they had seen and been in contact with middle-class people all their lives, I had wrongly assumed that they would know more. All these things were within their purview but not of their particular world. Thus, I could see behind the stories of those in the middle and upper classes who were "shocked" at what their empregadas did not know and could recognize the naturalization of class privilege that was at work here. So, while Glória's children understand how to behave in places such as Dona Beth's apartment, they are exceedingly uncomfortable in a great number of public spaces in the wealthy Zona Sul. Another example of this discomfort became apparent to me when they immediately jumped out of a swimming pool of an apartment building in the Zona Sul where we were guests when a uniformed armed policeman strolled by the poolside. They "knew"—even though our invitation to be there was clear—they did not belong there. There is thus collusion at the societal, household, and individual level in creating both external signs and internalized notions of where one naturally "places" in the world, where one properly belongs.

THE LIMITATIONS OF ACADEMIC CAPITAL

Renata also recalls friends of hers from Salvador, Bahia, a couple who, being simultaneously "millionaires and socialists," provided private schooling (the same as for their own children) for two of their young empregadas. These young women eventually graduated and now constitute the rare Pygmalionesque "success" story; one became a doctor and the other, a lawyer. According to Renata, "They were able to do this because they are millionaires. It doesn't generally work. Generally, the superrich are reactionaries—they are not going to send the empregadas to the same school as their children. They simply won't do it." Implicit in Renata's commentary is her recognition of the bifurcated public and private school system in Brazil, a topic I will address briefly in the following section, since it helps to underline some of the additional elements that limit social mobility and ensure a rigid social class hierarchy. Bourdieu's (1984) understanding of educational capital and how corollarially schools actually serve to reproduce the cultural and class divisions in any society in both visible and invisible ways is a useful point of reference.

In Brazil there is an even clearer limitation to educational capital than there is in the United States, or even in France. Perhaps this is because in Brazil educational capital is already so closely tied to cultural capital, and cultural capital so closely parallels historical privilege. The liberal notion that education will bring social mobility is one that must necessarily be restricted because of the other factors that constitute the makeup of the system. The school system in Brazil is "classed" from the very start, with a public school system that functions (rather poorly) for the masses and differing levels of private school education that cater exclusively to the middle and upper classes.

While living in Felicidade Eterna, I had the opportunity to visit the nearby grade school with Félix, who was constantly nagged by Glória to attend and perform well in school. By the time he was twelve, Félix had been held back in school three different years and became the object of much teasing by his siblings. I understood quickly why Félix never cared much for school after visiting his classes with him a number of times. Although Glória worked hard to keep his uniform clean and ready for use on a daily basis, he had only two changes of shorts and shirts, and it was a struggle for Glória and Soneca, who helped do the laundry, to do this. Sometimes Félix simply had to miss school because his clothes were not ready. The school itself was a short walk from Felicidade Eterna in a typical public school building. Each class held well over thirty students, and teachers did not have even the most basic school supplies to work with. The concrete walls reached only three-quarters of the way to the ceiling, and, depending on where one sat in the room, it was often easier to hear what was going on in the next classroom than in one's own. The teachers had to shout just to be heard. Although this design may have been a wise architectural decision in terms of allowing for the better distribution of the hot, muggy tropical air, it was not practical in terms of maintaining focus in a classroom.

Félix enjoyed the social aspects of school, and under better circumstances—different forms of encouragement at home, such as help with homework rather than unmitigated teasing, or a sense of what education might help him do—he might have performed better. He was making his way through the system but was barely learning to read and write.

In Felicidade Eterna children are expected to be productive and to work from a very young age. By the age of five or six, children participate in chores such as cleaning, washing clothes and dishes, sweeping, and taking care of younger brothers and sisters. By the age of nine or ten, girls are often the primary caretakers of their baby siblings. Girls, especially, are often sent out as domestic workers or as wageless helpers to their mothers. All this adds up to the fact that even when an individual does have access to education, it is often impossible to make it a high priority.

In contrast, the children of the wealthier classes are usually prohibited from even entering the kitchen in their own homes. There is absolutely no encouragement for or value placed on learning to clean or cook, since these tasks are carried out by the domestic help. The children of the wealthy are therefore able to focus on their studies and the other creative pursuits of childhood, whereas the children of the poor, if they go to school at all, enter a second-class educational system perfectly suited to reproducing second-class citizens. Therefore, although public education is paid for through government funding, it rarely functions as the great equalizer that many liberals desire it to be. To enter the institutions of higher education, students must pass a highly competitive *vestibular* (admissions examination). After attending second-rate primary public schools, very few individuals in the poorest sectors of the population are able to pass this rigorous exam. Young people who have attended private school, on the other hand, are well prepared for the examination, as well as for the demands of advanced study.[39]

Yet perhaps what is most telling about the educational system in Brazil is the precarious position of the middle class. Middle-class parents know that the public school system is, at best, mediocre, and they worry about being able to provide for their young children the necessary resources to attend expensive primary and secondary private schools. The middle classes, perhaps because of their precarious position between the rich and the poor, recognize the inequality within this bifurcated education most fully, knowing that their own class reproduction is dependent on their uncertain access to private schools.

While education and class position are highly associated in Brazil, the educational structure is even more tightly restricted than the social structure of Brazil at large, as José Pastore points out in his book *Inequality and Social Mobility in Brazil* (1982). Pastore suggests that Afro-Brazilians, locked into the lowest earning sectors in the economy, face a challenge that is doubly hard; they first must enter and succeed in the labor market before even entertaining the hope of gaining access to institutions of higher learning. Pastore's study is now somewhat dated, but his conclusions are still worth noting because they indicate that the liberal solution that proposes education alone as a realistic route to social mobility is deeply flawed.[40]

"MUCHACHAS NO MORE"

In contemporary Rio de Janeiro, one can see signs of the bonds of patronage, dependency, and deference exhibited in many aspects of the domestic worker–patron relationship.[41] Domestic workers still use the service entrance and the separate service elevators of the luxurious apartment buildings in the wealthy Zona Sul. They still usually address their patrons with the polite and deferential forms, including *Dona* and *Seu,* while they themselves are usually addressed by simple first names. There is, often visibly, a deference in the body language of this serving class, as well as other signs of social origin; these markings are often so clear that most middle- and upper-class members of society readily admit being able to discern social class instantly by a person's walk, style of dress, or simply an utterance.

But all is not entirely quiet. There are signs of resistance and a growing backlash against the most blatant holdovers of the kinds of relations associated with slavery. Indeed, not all women living in Felicidade Eterna work as domestic laborers, and there is a growing rebellion against such work. Unlike most of the women I met who were in Glória's generation—in their middle to late forties and older—women in their late teens and early twenties no longer wanted to work as domestic workers but were more willing, it seems, to take their chances in the factories of Rio's industrial suburbs. Domestic work was viewed as honest hard work, but it was also seen as being at the absolute bottom of the occupational and pay-scale ladder and as being associated with slavelike relations of labor. Young women are instead choosing to work in the industrial areas nearby, in most cases, for not much better pay. While such jobs were not seen as ideal, for they rarely pay more than one to two minimum wages, they were viewed more positively by this generation than the prospect of domestic work.

Filomena, for example, could easily have found work as a domestic laborer because her childhood with Glória had given her many of the necessary skills. By the time she was a young teenager, she had already become a talented cook and cleaner, but she worked hard to find an alternative to domestic employment. Filomena considered domestic work too claustrophobic—she hated being indoors all day long, and she detested the long bus rides to and from the Zona Sul. But the job she found herself in during 1998 was not exactly her ideal job either. Filomena worked for thirty *reais* per week (close to thirty dollars in U.S. currency at the time) packing cooking charcoal into bags in a cramped, dangerous storage area in Duque de Caxias (also known as Caxias), a city in the vast Zona Norte. In two large rooms, employees stuffed charcoal into bags that were then stacked to the ceiling. Filomena lived in fear of the teetering piles of charcoal someday falling on her, a fate that had happened to another employee, who was seriously injured only weeks before Filomena began her job. Filomena's other three colleagues at work were single mothers, and none of them were getting their carteiras signed or receiving any other benefits. They were simple day laborers, barely earning a subsistence wage. If for some reason they had to miss a day of work, they were short of the immediate cash needed to supply food to their household that day. They were all afraid to protest their situation, however, because they could easily lose their jobs for merely complaining.

While the refusal to enter domestic work may seem like only a small bit of resistance to the bondage associated with domestic work, it is significant that at least some members of this generation are no longer willing to play into some of the more subtle, ambiguous, and deferential relations of the domestic worker–employer relationship. Indeed, as Hall (1991a) points out, the process of resistance is a slow one:

> Hegemony is not the disappearance or destruction of difference. It is the construction of a collective will through difference. It is the articulation of differences which do not disappear. The subaltern class does not mistake itself for people who were born with silver spoons in their mouths. They know they are still second on the ladder, somewhere near the bottom. People are not cultural dopes. They are not waiting for the moment when, like an overnight conversion, false consciousness will fall from their eyes, the scales will fall away, and they will suddenly discover who they are.
>
> They know something about who they are. If they engage in another project it is because it has interpolated them, hailed them, and established some point of identification with them. (58–59)

In his work on the street culture of young male Puerto Rican immigrants in the East Harlem drug economy, Philippe Bourgois puts his finger on a process that is highly relevant to the discussion here. Bourgois, adopting what has become known as cultural production theory,[42] attempts to solve the classic structure versus agency problem in the social sciences by arguing that political economy does constrain the choices these young men make, but that they—as individuals belonging to a particular subculture—are also agents of their own futures.

The ethnography used as a guidepost by Bourgois, and most often referred to as the consummate example of how this theory works in practice, is Paul Willis's book *Learning to Labor: How Working Class Kids Get Working Class Jobs* (1977). Willis argues that working-class boys practice their resistance through their denigration of mental work, highlighting the emasculating aspects of white-collar jobs. In this process, they end up in manual working-class jobs, the very target of their refusal. Their resistance and oppositional culture contain the very elements of their own destruction. Bourgois makes a similar argument about young men involved in crack dealing in East Harlem. In their search for dignity and respect and in their rejection of racism and subjugation, their own street culture winds up aiding and abetting their self-destruction, as well as the destruction of the communities they belong to (Bourgois 1995:9). Ultimately, this oppositional culture is self-destructive because in seeking to unmask and lay bare the ideology that oppresses them, these agents wind up being unable to occupy the positions of their oppressors. By working against the dominant ideology, they are then unable to fulfill the requirements that would be needed to occupy any other class position. It seems ironic, but it makes sense. As Willis points out more concretely in the case of the working-class "lads," it is in their making fun of white-collar culture and in their pranks with one another that they encourage the formation of particular masculine identities, ones that discourage them from seeking success through imitation. In this manner, they seal their own fate and end up perpetuating their membership in the manual labor force.

Similar to Willis's working-class lads and Bourgois's young crack dealers, many male youths of the lower classes in Brazil have become "unruly" in their behavior, many of them choosing to join violent gangs that promise them status and respect in their own local contexts but that also define them as criminals in the broader society. It is not mere chance, I would argue, that young men from the poorest segments of the working classes in Brazil, rather than choosing to enter into timeworn relations of deference, are instead choosing other more resistant and more violent futures for themselves.

Most observers discount the possibility of armed revolution in Brazil, but there are many instances of resistance that fall somewhere between passivity and complete upheaval. Oppositional culture, for example, is resistance, and it is subtle, unorganized, diffuse, and spontaneous. It is registered in humor and laughter and in approaches to living that seem to be burdened with their own dangers. Revolutions are more organized, sustained, and, ideologically speaking, much more focused.[43]

Oppositional culture, however, can still be viewed as an authentic response to domination, moving social scientists beyond the problem of "false consciousness" and other theoretical directions that blame the victim. The resistance in such cases is anything but false; rather, despite its authenticity and logic, it makes sense that it would backfire. In Brazil, there is the added component that there are very few high-status males of black or mixed-race heritage who have risen out of the lowest classes—very few success stories other than soccer players and musicians. Thus, it makes sense on a number of levels that the dream of so many young favela boys is to become a great soccer player.[44] But because members of this generation have so little hope of social mobility in mainstream culture, the gang leaders often become their folk heroes and more realistic role models. The gang leaders become significant in the young men's search to redefine their place in the world—one apart from the denigrating, deference-demanding positions that have typically been accessible to them.

Similarly, I would argue, women have their own distinct forms of resistance. Darlene, a dear friend of Glória's who often teases her about the number of hours she spends at Beth's house, decided years ago that working a few hours a day as a sex worker was far more rewarding—in financial terms as well as in the effort expended—than low-paid domestic work. Darlene, a light-skinned thirty-five-year-old Afro-Brazilian woman, was of the generation between those of Glória and Filomena. Darlene once was a domestic worker in a household in the Zona Sul, but over time she came to prefer sex work as a means of providing a livelihood for her family. Because Glória found Darlene's perspective on life refreshing, she had always wanted me to meet her, and I finally had the opportunity in 1995.

Glória and Darlene met when Darlene was only seventeen years old. At that time, Glória was going out with a large, heavyset man named Ignácio who played music with a *pagode* (popular samba form) band and was living in Duque de Caxias. In 1995, Darlene was caring for five of her own children and one niece. According to Darlene, Glória used to drink and *zoava* (get rowdy) quite a bit, but despite her occasional outrageousness, they formed a friendship. Many years later, they still leaned on one another in times of trouble to *desabafar* (let out feelings) and receive advice and comfort. In 1995, Darlene sought out Glória's advice about what to do about her suspecting husband, Antonio, who doubted whether Darlene was doing the domestic work she was claiming to do. He insisted that she labor as a domestic worker, and though she periodically tried, she could not commit herself to this kind of job. Mostly, she claimed, this was because nobody wanted to pay her what she considered a fair wage. So, instead, she packed her "working clothes" into a plastic bag and went off every day for just a few hours to one of central Rio's prostitution zones, returning home in the evening and pretending that she had worked a full day in a patroa's house. She worried that her husband would some day find out and kill her, and she solicited Glória's help to keep her secret from being known. Sometimes Darlene even borrowed stories from Glória's repertoire of patroa stories so that she could repeat them to Antonio and the rest of her family in the evenings. She often jokingly declared that the right amount of money would take her out of "the life"; otherwise, by her calculations, it was not worth it. "For my part, I have children to feed. I can't do that for one [minimum] salary," she explained. On the street, Darlene could earn up to five *reais* per customer,[45] making sex work a much more lucrative position for her than domestic work or the other limited options available to her. Darlene was keenly aware of the fact that women of her generation and schooling were supposed to be employed as domestic workers, and her suspicious husband kept her constantly conscious of this fact. She and Glória would tease one another about their different choices and, through their humor, would point out the absurdity of attempting to support a family on one or two minimum salaries. Darlene's choice, in some ways, foreshadowed the feelings of the younger generation, who would rather do almost anything other than work as a domestic worker.

Darlene's choice of sex work over domestic servitude can be read as one example of what I am referring to as women's oppositional culture.[46] As pointed out throughout this chapter, the wages for most domestic workers are just about the lowest of any profession—set slightly above one minimum salary and rarely rising above five—and the work hours are long and both physically and emotionally exhausting. Darlene discovered that by working independently in the center of Rio de Janeiro and taking in just a few clients a week, she could earn as much as she would in a domestic service position. With much less effort than full-time domestic work, and on her own terms, she found she could earn the money she needed to support her family.

THE LAUGHTER OF A COMMUNITY

During the years I spent among Glória and her network of friends and family, I became an avid fan of the Brazilian telenovela. A number of either daytime or evening programs had captured the attention of my friends, and I soon overcame my own initial aversion to these programs and tried to understand what was so appealing about them. So many of these programs were devoted to the lives of the wealthy that watching them together with people in Felicidade Eterna itself became an interesting fieldwork experience.[47] The telenovelas, in many respects, reinforced my friends' perceptions of the life of *os bacanas,* or the "good life people," gained through their own experiences as domestic workers. As a genre, it transported them into the lives and problems of people distant from their own lives and problems.

While watching television in Felicidade Eterna, which was always a group activity, there would often be a scene that any other audience would perceive as tragic. Yet here, among a collection of people who live in absurd conditions, the tragedies of the elites depicted in the telenovelas tended to fall on deaf ears. These scenes were much more often poked fun at rather than wept about, much like Glória's laughter over Dona Beth's distress at her daughter's "breaking away." Perhaps we should not try to separate this distinct laughter from its context. Such "laughter out of place" does not go unnoticed by the middle and upper classes, though it is often summarily dismissed. Renata gave the following description of Cida: "Sometimes we'll see her laughing at the most tragic part of the *novela*—it's like something between cynicism and *bondade* [goodness, kindness]. Everyone is sitting in front of the novela and crying and my sister will come over to me and say, 'Watch Cida,' and she will be dying of laughter and nobody knows why." To Renata, Cida's behavior in front of the television is not simply a case of inarticulateness and lack of education; it is also a case of inappropriateness of affect, the inability to function well in the public realm. Yet Cida is firmly installed in Renata's mother's household in a quasi-sister arrangement, and her laughter, to some extent, provides evidence of her difference from Renata and the rest of Renata's family. In a broader, more fully symbolic sense, it is Cida's presence and place as a low Other, embodied in her misplaced (or misunderstood) laughter, that elevate and psychologically sustain these families in their positions, further solidifying economic conditions into more enduring class and cultural distinctions.

Color-Blind Erotic Democracies, Black Consciousness Politics, and the Black Cinderellas of Felicidade Eterna

With reference to Brazil, as an old saying has it: "White woman for marriage, mulatto woman for f——, Negro woman for work," a saying in which, alongside the social convention of the superiority of the white woman and the inferiority of the black, is to be discerned a sexual preference for the mulatto.

Gilberto Freyre, *The Masters and the Slaves*

Eliana, one of Glória's best friends from childhood, is a dark-skinned black woman whose eighteen-year-old daughter, Elzineia, also dark-skinned, became pregnant by a white boy from an economically more prosperous family living just outside the borders of Felicidade Eterna. Because the boy had not taken any steps toward acknowledging his relationship with Elzineia, nor his imminent paternity, Eliana worked with her daughter to try to abort the child. They tried every poison imaginable, but nothing worked.[1]

Eliana's grandchild, Fausto, turned out to be very light-skinned. When Eliana appears in public with Fausto—shopping, taking a stroll, or carrying on some other grandmotherly activity—she often is perceived by others to be his babá, an occupation she held for many years in her youth. Eliana laughs about her fate to once again be (mistaken as) a babá in the public eye, although she is retired from her job as a domestic worker and spends most of her time taking care of her own house, children, and grandchildren. The links between color and class are particularly clear in the case of Eliana and her grandson Fausto. Color—hers and Fausto's taken together—is "naturally" perceived as an indicator of a class relationship. The irony of the story is that even with her own grandson—because he is so much "whiter" than she is—Eliana cannot escape the automatic assumptions about their relationship. It is not so much that it is assumed that she is not related to the child; Brazil's multicolored expression of diversity is a matter of national pride. Rather, their presence together suggests a racialized class relationship: that of lower-class (black) nanny and upper-class (white) child. Eliana's friends smile when they see them out on the street together; grandmother and grandchild together play a visual joke on the world, and those who understand their "true" relationship get the joke and laugh.

RACE AND CLASS IN BRAZIL AND THE UNITED STATES

It is almost a cliché to propose that in the United States people generally do not think about, or through, class relations, partly because of a number of foundational myths having to do with meritocratic routes to success, and partly because of the ideological bias against speaking in any rhetorical forms that resemble Marxist language.[2] North Americans generally like to think of themselves as part of the middle class and often do not think in terms of class-based forms of power.

Indeed, North Americans seem far more comfortable talking about race, and this has led to some interesting outcomes. On the one hand, North Americans readily engage in debates about forms of race-based affirmative action but rarely engage in debates about the possibility of class-based affirmative action. On the other hand, poverty is more easily spoken of in terms of race than in terms of class, leading to a number of fallacious perceptions, including the idea that most welfare mothers in the United States are African American, when in fact there are far greater numbers of whites on welfare.[3]

In Brazil, it is race and racism that people are generally uncomfortable speaking about. Brazil never had an all-out civil rights movement where a black power or black pride movement captured the public imagination. A series of powerful historical events enabled Brazilians to embrace *mestiçagem,* the reputed historical blending of indigenous American, Iberian, and African peoples into a single national identity. Whereas in the United States race is often used to suggest utterly separate human

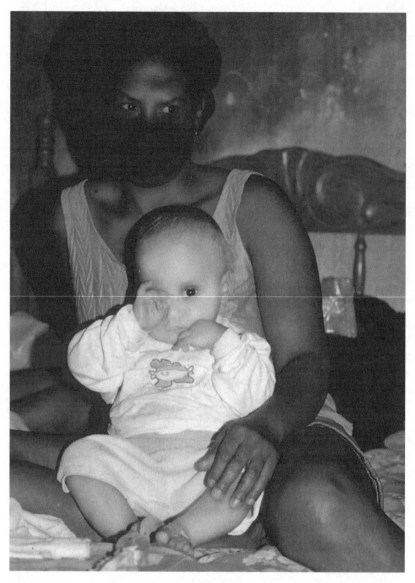

Figure 7. Grandmother and grandchild: Eliana and Fausto. Photograph by author.

types, in Brazil this was never the case. Additionally, Brazil did not develop a structure of legal supports to racism, and perhaps because racism in Brazil was less codified and more subtly manifest in social rather than in legal relations, it could not be challenged directly in the courts and became difficult to address. The lack of a Brazilian race-based civil rights movement provides a stark contrast to events in North America, where racism was indeed codified and then challenged, both in a widely supported social movement and within the legal system. When something African-derived emerged as part of national tradition in Brazil, it was eventually adopted and absorbed into the broader definition of Brazilian identity (Ortiz 1986). Many of the Afro-Brazilian religious traditions, but especially Umbanda, which is sometimes referred to as the national religion of Brazil, as well as musical traditions such as samba provide examples of this kind of appropriation and de-Africanization.

In Brazil, those cultural elements that remained purely African or too closely associated with slavery were denigrated. In spite of the absorption of some elements, which sometimes legitimated and elevated previously denigrated African traditions, blackness—dark skin color and African racial features—continue to be associated with slavery and are considered ugly. Despite the economic legacy of slavery, poverty in Brazil is conceptualized as a class problem rather than a race problem. While this perspective does have some advantages, such an interpretation ignores historically structured, race-based oppression in ways that make it almost impossible to address institutionally. In concrete terms, this means there never has been and there currently is no race-based affirmative action in Brazil.

"Brazil is different" not only is the popular Brazilian view but also seems to be the refrain of many contemporary scholarly analyses that deal with race relations. This claim is especially true for many scholars who are cautious about the kinds of comparisons they make between Brazil and the United States.[4] Brazil, however, is closer to other parts of Latin America and the Caribbean in terms of its construction of race. It is "different" only when compared with the United States. Despite the explosive nature of this kind of comparison, this exercise yields a number of useful grounding points.[5]

Although there is no legally sanctioned racism in Brazil, the structures of racism are present in everyday experiences. Because their existence and significance are often conveyed through indirect forms of communication—black-humored jokes and coded silences—they are much more difficult to describe and challenge. For this reason, ethnographic approaches to race—ones that set out to capture how the discourses of color, race, racism, racial prejudice, and racialization permeate everyday life—are sorely needed. Race is embodied in everyday valuations of sexual attractiveness, and this attractiveness is gendered, racialized, and class-oriented in ways that commodify black female bodies and white male economic, racial, and class privilege.

Since the 1950s, most Brazilianists have agreed on the following interpretation of the construction of race in the two countries: Brazilians evaluate race primarily according to appearance, offering a plethora of fluid and ambiguous categories,[6] whereas North Americans have, until relatively recently, tended to follow a "one-drop-of-blood" rule and a comparatively bipolarized (black and white) vision of race. In the United States, one is legally either black or white, although this dichotomy is undergoing serious challenge and revision as a result of the rise of identity politics and multiculturalism.[7]

In Brazil, where one can place oneself or be placed by others along a color spectrum that shifts in relation to who is speaking and to whom one is speaking, as well as other aspects of context, such as the signs of class perceptible in language, social manners, and style of dress, this has never been so.[8] Color terms in Brazil are complicated and elided with words used to refer to "racial identities." The words include black (preto, negro), white (branco), brown or mixed (moreno, mulato), dark (escuro), light (claro), closed (fechado), freckled (sarará), and others, making both color and race ambiguous to insiders and outsiders alike. Marvin Harris's (1964a) classic article on race in Brazil, in which he suggested that the attribution of a racial category may be influenced by a person's class and argued that the old Brazilian adage "money whitens," may still be relevant.[9]

The everyday interactions of Glória and her network of friends and family illustrate the ways in which such valuations of color and the possibilities—either real or imaginary—of social mobility play out in everyday discourses and relationships. Their situation may also lend new insight into why they, and others living under similar socioeconomic conditions, have not become enthusiastic supporters of the Movimento Negro, the current black consciousness movement in Brazil.

In the historical development of Brazil, the whitening ideology of the turn of the century, one that called for the gradual whitening of the African population through miscegenation, was sufficiently strong in both social and psychological ways that have made it extremely difficult for black organizing around the question of racial identity to take place in Brazil. Afro-Brazilians are wary of taking pride in and declaring their blackness. Blackness was—and still is—associated with slavery, dirty work, and ugliness. Only highly politicized people can speak openly about their race without feeling the shame attached to blackness.

ANA FLÁVIA PEÇANHA AZEREDO: A BLACK CINDERELLA?

In 1993, Veja, Brazil's popular weekly newsmagazine, reported the case of Ana Flávia Peçanha Azeredo, a black woman who was physically assaulted for delaying an elevator in a middle-class apartment building.[10] Because of her skin color, she was "mistaken" by her white assailants as a person not worthy of making others wait. In other words, she was assumed to be merely *preta e pobre* (black and poor) by her assailants, who assaulted her both verbally and physically. As it turned out, she was the nineteen-year-old daughter of the governor of the state of Espírito Santo, and she filed a racial discrimination suit against her attackers.

It is interesting that the Veja article described Ana Flávia as the "black Cinderella." Why Cinderella? Perhaps her attackers felt that they were rightfully throwing an imposter out of the ball (because in Brazil you would have to be a fairy-tale character to be both a governor's daughter and black).[11] The fact that their perceptions of her race made them unable to see that she actually belonged at the ball, so to speak, again highlights the systemic relation between race and class in Brazil.

In his article "Black Cinderella? Race and the Public Sphere in Brazil" (1994a), political scientist Michael Hanchard interprets this case as a "nail in the coffin" of the myth of racial democracy in Brazil. After all, here was a clear case of everyday racial discrimination and the perfect opportunity for a person with power to expose it. Hanchard (1994a) uses this episode to suggest the development of an evolving racial polarization in Brazil, one that is beginning to make a clear-cut political distinction between black and white:

> Her [Ana Flávia's] blackness in the eyes of her assailants implies a broadening of the category of negro/a in Brazil and more importantly an increasing polarization of racial categories. Her beating may signal that the mark of blackness has come to include Brazilians who are perceived as people of African descent, whether from Brazil or not. Unlike the distinctions between African- and Brazilian-born slaves in the previous century, Africanness—the parent symbol for blackness—no longer marks a place; it now marks a people. (178)

Anthropologist Peter Fry, in a series of publications (1995, 1995/1996), critiques Hanchard's (1994b) earlier work on the black consciousness movement and his interpretation (1994a) of the Ana Flávia case. Fry argues that race and color casting in Brazil is highly situational and that racial bipolarization is more a desire of the politically correct North Americans and elite Brazilian classes and less a reality among the poorer segments of Brazilian society. Fry interprets Hanchard's work as subtly evolutionary in suggesting that an Americanized vision of race will lead to a more satisfactory form of race relations in Brazil. Fry instead maps out what he calls the "multiple mode" of everyday racial discourse in Brazil[12]—a discourse that appears to suggest that Brazilians conceptualize race as composed of multiple categories rather than as a simple dichotomy between black and white. He also suggests that the leaders of the Brazilian black consciousness movement are out of touch with the majority of the population, which still thinks about and experiences race situationally, with an eye for class differences.[13]

Fry's critique of Hanchard is based on the familiar Brazilianist notion that "Brazil is different" (i.e., not racist) because Brazilians celebrate a "color-blind" sexuality. The logic of Fry's scholarly argument is also repeated in the everyday discourses of low-income Brazilians,[14] a discourse easily misread as a liberal attitude toward race and sexuality. Moreover, Brazilian women living in shantytowns seem to be in touch with the notion of Brazilian exceptionalism in a concrete way. They point to interracial unions in their communities as proof of their freedom from racism; conversely, they point to the comparative lack of such unions in the North American context as an indictment of race relations there. Sexual unions across the color line speak loudly and seem to provide proof of Brazil's racial democracy, but they may also get in the way of perspectives that seek to lay bare the patterned forms of inequality embedded in or enacted through certain forms of racialized eroticism.

THE "TREASURE CHEST COUP": FEMALE FANTASIES OF SEDUCING THE *COROA*

Living in a favela is automatically a class marker in Rio de Janeiro. Those who are lighter-skinned or who have "whiter" characteristics are believed to have better chances of succeeding in life, including greater job opportunities and even greater possibilities for leaving the poorest shantytowns and moving into neighborhoods that qualify as poor but respectable. Despite research findings that show little difference in social mobility between darker- and lighter-skinned mixed-race people,[15] the belief in color as a determining factor of one's chances in life seems to persist and frames many of the everyday commentaries on race and color that I heard in Felicidade Eterna. Many of the women I came to know through Glória believed that one of their best opportunities for "getting ahead"[16] was their ability to seduce older, richer, whiter men, whom they referred to as *coroas*.[17] A coroa, in this context, is distinguished first by age and wealth or class, and is only by implication white. An older, richer, black person *could* be a coroa, but the general connotation among these particular women is that the coroa is also whiter than they are.

Parables of upward mobility constitute a genre told by women among themselves. In these stories, the woman actively plots and pursues her goal, whether it be to simply obtain a favor from a coroa or, in its more complete form, to procure long-term economic sustenance from the relationship. The most successful woman carries out a *golpe do baú* (treasure chest coup).[18] The happy ending of the more extreme story is that the woman moves into the apartment of the coroa in a neighborhood that is not a favela and becomes comfortable or even wealthy.

This fantasy is dependent on a coroa who is willing to be seduced, and it is recognized as a realistic and legitimate, albeit rare, form of social mobility. It also serves to confuse the race issue because it is interpreted in fairy-tale terms: a poor, clever, and seductive dark-skinned woman finds her rich, old, and white "prince." Gender, class, sexuality, and race, as well as beauty and age, are all intertwined in one story. Given the barriers preventing upward social mobility in Brazil, the promise of this fairy tale, with its magical solution, holds great appeal. The women I came to know in Felicidade Eterna would not easily give up this fantasy.

In 1991, Glória told me that her friend Janaína, who lived in a favela near Felicidade Eterna, was on her way out of the favela, that she had found herself a coroa, a man in whose house she had been employed for a number of years as a domestic worker. Over time, he developed a special affection for Janaína, and in the sunset of his life, he wanted to offer her access to a better life for herself and her children. For Glória and her friends, such cross-class and cross-color cases provide evidence that white men who prefer dark-skinned women are "logically" not racist because they sexually desire dark-skinned women.[19] It did not seem to matter that Janaína's partner-to-be was an elderly widowed man with grown children, one of whom was close in age to Janaína. And even though they would be able to tease Janaína mercilessly—working from the ageist assumption that an old man cannot satisfy a young sexual appetite—Glória and her friends regarded her story as a legitimation of Brazil's racial and erotic paradise.

This version of the coroa parable is similar to a black Cinderella story: both include seducing an economically more stable man, and both female protagonists experience social mobility as a result. The fantasy is not entirely serious, however, since it is often mixed with humorous commentary related to the likely age of the prince. The ageist assumption that an old man will not be able to satisfy the passions of the younger morena seductress is often embedded in the black Cinderella story. Although at first glance the mixed-race and black women I refer to here seem easily, in both fantasy and occasionally in reality, to cross racial and class boundaries, on closer inspection they are also ambivalent, making fun of the trade-off they would potentially be forced to make: receiving "whiteness" and wealth, but missing out on a certain level of sexuality and romantic passion.[20]

As a method of escaping from poverty, however, marrying or seducing a coroa is based on gendered and racialized values of attractiveness in an erotic market. Hence, men and women bring with them different sorts of capital to such potential sexual encounters. Men's attractiveness is related to their economic well-being (although racial calculation is also important), and women's attractiveness is related to their beauty and sex appeal. It is important to highlight here that a coroa's money is a polysemic symbol embodying a culture of wealth. It refers to upper-class norms of behavior, including being well-mannered (e.g., not using crude language in public) and "educated," the latter often implying what women living in the shantytown perceive as the less macho attitudes of some elderly men, especially those from the middle and upper classes. The symbolic meaning of the coroa's money is important because low-income women's fantasies of being crowned are not confined to the wish of escaping poverty but are more broadly constructed as a means—should they be realized— of attaining a better life. Hence, the desire of low-income black women to seduce a richer, lighter-skinned coroa cannot simplistically be equated with "false consciousness"; rather, it is based on mutual attractiveness, no matter how different and unequal the criteria for attractiveness are.

In the coroa story, the women themselves have inverted the historical master-slave relationship and have opted—at least in fantasy, and sometimes in reality—to pursue the coroa. Importantly, they have made this myth their own. At the level of popular culture, the imagery of the seductress—the sexualized mulata—has been absorbed by black and mixed-race women themselves. This internalization, in turn, has both empowered and disempowered them in interesting ways. They seem to have taken the seductive imagery of the mulata, troubled as it is by the legacy of Brazil's slaveholding past, and claimed it as their own, partly as a response to increasing economic immiseration but also as a way of resisting the widespread notion that equates blackness with ugliness. Being a successful seducer enables them to negate this oppressive equation.

REPRESENTATIONS AND COMMODIFICATIONS
OF BLACK BODIES

The late-nineteenth-century novel *O Cortiço* (published in English in 2000 as *The Slum*), written in 1890, just after abolition, by Aluísio Azevedo, connects eroticism, race relations, and social mobility in Brazil. The narrative traces the fortunes of three Portuguese immigrants after their arrival in Brazil. One of these immigrants, Jerônimo, ends up falling in love with Rita Bahiana, a beautiful mulatta woman: "He saw Rita Bahiana go inside and return in a skirt and sleeveless blouse, ready to dance. The moon emerged from behind a cloud at that moment, enveloping her in its silvery light, accentuating the sinuous movement of her body, full of irresistible grace, simple, primitive, a mixture of heaven and hell, serpentine and womanly" (Azevedo 2000[1890]:60). Soon after this scene, the steady, hardworking Portuguese immigrant begins his process of transformation into a carefree, but lazy, Brazilian:

> Weeks went by. Jerônimo now drank a big mug of coffee every morning, just like Rita, along with a shot of rum "to get the chill out of his bones."
> Day by day, hour by hour, a slow but profound change was transforming him, altering his body and sharpening his senses as silently and mysteriously as a butterfly growing in its cocoon. His energy drained away, he became contemplative and easygoing. He found life in the Americas and Brazil's landscapes exciting and seductive; he forgot his earlier ambitions and began to enjoy new, pungent, strong sensations. He was more generous and less concerned about tomorrow, quicker to spend than to save. . . .
> And so, little by little, all the sober habits of a Portuguese peasant were transformed, and Jerônimo became a Brazilian. (75–76)

Here Azevedo's novel provides a foundational vision of the mulata seductress and her symbolic linkage with everything tropical, sensual, untamed, and Brazilian. She is simultaneously beautiful and dangerous.

Both in postcolonial writings about race and sexuality[21] and in black feminist writings on slavery in the North American context, scholars have amply deconstructed colonial representations of black female sexuality. Sander Gilman (1985), for example, has pointed out how the perception of the prostitute in the late nineteenth century was merged with the perception of the black body in art, literature, and science and how representations of the black body, in such forms as the Hottentot Venus, came to define black sexuality as something Other, exotic, yet at the same time pathological. Patricia Hill Collins (1990) describes four American stereotypes of black women that similarly pathologize black women by linking them to specific forms of sexuality. These four images—the Mammy, the Matriarch, the Welfare Mother, the Jezebel—are both racially and sexually charged. In her analysis of the Jezebel image, she shows how the black woman, reduced to her sexuality and portrayed as sexually aggressive, provided the rationale for sexual assaults by white men (Collins 1990:77).[22]

In contrast, Brazilian images of black women, and particularly representations of the sexually "hot" mulata, have largely remained unexamined, particularly in the public space of Brazilian popular culture. While these images are surely addressed in scholarly writings, the mainstream use of this kind of imagery is not the target of an organized cultural critique. Because the mulata is so much a product of a national ideology about both race and sexuality, it forms a particular set of images that is much more protected and even exalted as a positive reading of national identity, and not one that is criticized as an overly exoticized or overly sexualized image of black women.

In the Brazilian context, the sexualized mulata is not the negative or tragic figure portrayed in the North American construction. Despite the negative features portrayed by Azevedo in his character Rita Bahiana, the mulata figure is in fact recognized as a positive image of the citizen, an embodiment of mixed-race creativity, beauty, and sensuality. The mulata is, among other things, the embodiment of Carnival. Yet, in spite of these positive readings, Brazilian television rarely features anyone but white actors. This paradoxical absence and yet exoticization of sexualized blackness still serves to privilege whiteness and "imaginary"[23] rather than actual blackness.[24]

Some recent attempts to deconstruct the historical and contemporary imagery of the mulata in Brazil are available in the work of Sonia Maria Giacomini (1988), a Brazilian anthropologist who explores the representations of the mulata image in the writings of Brazilian intellectuals, including Gilberto Freyre. Giacomini argues that while the colonial *senhora's* (white married female's) sexuality was regulated by rigid religious and moral conceptions, slave women escaped the determinations of the dominant classes. The female slave's sexuality was not in the service of procreation nor of the ideological reproduction of the white family. To be beyond these limits appeared, from the perspective of the white master, as being free from the ties of any order, religious or moral; thus the slave was appropriated solely as a sexual object. Giacomini talks about the *mãe preta* in Brazilian imagery, literally, the "black mother," who is, like the Mammy of Collins's scheme, an example of a caretaker, a desexualized slave, or a domestic worker. There is also the *ama de leite,* or milk mother, who is hired to supply milk to a white child but not necessarily her own. As in Collins's scheme, there is also the representation of the slave as a sexual object to be used at the whim of the master.

According to Giacomini (1988:66), this representation of the exalted and cultivated sexuality of the mulata served as an ideological justification for sexual attacks on slaves, a finding that is comparable to Collins's analysis of the Jezebel image in the American South. She also claims that the images and occupational realities of black women in contemporary Brazil can be traced and made sense of through a historical analysis. The restrictions upon the rights of procreation and of an autonomous private life characteristic of Brazil's slave period are still present in some contemporary labor arrangements in Brazil. Proof is visible in the abundance of black women who serve as nannies and domestic servants, and in the perpetuation of the sexualized mulata imagery. What ultimately separates Collins's (1990) and Gilman's (1985) analysis from Giacomini's (1988) is the novelty of Giacomini's work; within the Brazilian context, there has been relatively little sustained critical examination of these representations of black and mixed-race women.[25] Nobody is protesting in the streets about such representations, and in social science scholarship, this topic seems to be relatively recent. Giacomini's work is one of the first to start questioning this representation of the mulata. What is notable is the fixity of the sexualized nature of this representation: the mulata is forever exalted as an erotic Other.

These representations have real-life consequences. In pursuing her interest in the sexualized imagery of the mulata, Giacomini (1990) also carried out a contemporary study of mulata dancers—professionals of the tourist industry associated with Rio's nightclubs, Carnival, and traveling shows that promote the city of Rio de Janeiro. She examined the gender and color determinants implied in the category of mulata dancers and found that there are some prerequisites about color, but that they were not rigid. Mulatas were expected to have some kind of black ancestry, but they were also expected to represent a mixture with whiteness. They needed to possess the *dom do samba,* the knowledge of how to dance the samba, and had to have a certain body type. The size and shape of the *bunda* (buttocks) was key, that is, its preferred form was large and shapely. These mulatas were supposed to be seductive, but Giacomini found that this expectation created difficulties because the young women continually needed to develop a defensive dialogue about their sexuality so that they were not confused with prostitutes. This last point is noteworthy: their titling as professional dancers did not manage to shield them from the coupling of black or mixed-race female bodies with sexual availability.

Angela Gilliam (1998), writing about this mulata imagery in the context of an emerging global economy, summarizes the problem these representations create for poor Brazilian women: "Poor Brazilian women have become increasingly identified as elements in a growing sex trade on a global scale, in part due to the tradition of romanticizing and 'not talking' about predatory patriarchy. The extension of the *mestiçagem* narrative into the twentieth century disembodies women's capacities for power and authority over their lives" (63).

While thinking about these representations of Brazilian mixed-race and black women, I decided to search the Internet. I entered the keywords "Brazil" and "mulata" into the search engines on my computer and was immediately placed into sites that offered "Brasilian [sic] amateur babe," which, in turn, were linked to porn sites, many of them in Brazil. It was amazing how tightly connected the keyword "mulata" was with the vast array of pornographic sites. Many of the "Brazilian babes" featured in these sites were positioned with their bundas taking up most of the screen. Many had their eyes covered. There is no need to get into a lengthy discussion of pornography here, but my brief exploration of the Web convinced me that "mulata" is synonymous with eroticized black and mixed-race female sexuality. This very contemporary Internet gaze clearly echoes the historical gaze, identified by Collins (1990) in the North American context, one that began at the slave auction block and continued forward in postabolition representations of black women: "One key feature about the treatment of Black women in the nineteenth century was how their bodies were objects of display. In the antebellum South white men did not have to look at pornographic pictures of women because they could become voyeurs of Black women on the auction block" (168). Collins explains that slavery early on installed a specific kind of pornographic gaze of white males upon black female bodies, one she associates with the Jezebel image. The Jezebel is an aggressive and dangerous (amoral) whore, an image both racially and sexually charged that reduces black women to an essential, primal sexuality (78).

But in Brazil, the construction of this relationship and its representation has not been problematized. While in the North American case this master-slave relationship was early on perceived as rape, historians and the lineage of Brazilian intellectuals have not constructed this relationship in the same way. Giacomini recognizes that because slave women were outside of the rigid moral and religious orders surrounding white women, they were perceived as outside the ties of the moral order. In an analysis similar to that of Collins, Giacomini suggests that the cult of sensuality built up around the mulata has actually served—in varying historical circumstances, and perhaps in the contemporary case as well—as a justification for sexual attacks on black and mixed-race women.

BRAZILIAN SEXUALITY:
HISTORY, REPRESENTATION, AND SCHOLARSHIP

Brazil's "erotic paradise" has been celebrated in the historiography of colonialism and slavery, as well as throughout much of the more recent academic literature on sexuality in the 1980s and 1990s. It is also celebrated during Carnival and in the tourist brochures that present Brazil to the outside world. This celebration of Brazilian sexuality is intricately connected to the question of race because the primary icon of "hot" sexuality in Brazil is the mulata. Conversely, Brazilian understandings about race and color are intimately connected with Brazilians' representations of their own sexual history.

Gilberto Freyre, the extremely influential but controversial anthropologist and social historian trained at Columbia University under the guidance of Franz Boas, began writing about Brazilian race relations in the 1930s. Freyre described miscegenation between white male colonialists and indigenous females in the early days of Brazil's colonization, presenting this unequal "love affair" as a celebration of interracial sexuality as well as an argument for how Brazil was different from and, indeed, morally superior to other New World countries such as the United States. It is difficult, indeed, to separate Freyre the anthropologist and social historian from Freyre the intellectual ideologue.

Anthropologist Ann Stoler's (1989, 1995) writings on bourgeois European perspectives on race and sexuality in the colonies help to fashion a productive way to think about Freyre's ideas. Stoler's work points to the necessity of considering how colonial sexuality was represented in European writings, both during the period in question and in the years of historical rewritings that followed. The colonies were represented at the time as places that embodied the primitive. They were considered racially uncivilized places of chaos and sexual and moral abandon. The colonies became places that the Europeans feared and worked hard to define their own societies against.

Stoler (1997) also notes that in the process of rewriting the histories of racism, scholars have often taken on a redemptive tone, constantly repositioning themselves in relation to past histories of racism, thereby marking their own particular positions as participant-observers in a political field of power and knowledge. Her observation reminds us that it is not only what Freyre wrote that is worthy of consideration but also how contemporary writers—both Brazilian scholars and others—position themselves in relation to Freyre.

It was in the early colonial context, Freyre (1986[1933]) claims, that European men and "Indian" women began the widespread "mixing of the races":

> No sooner had the European leaped ashore than he found his feet slipping among the naked Indian women, and the very fathers of the Society of Jesus had to take care not to sink into the carnal mire; for many of the clergy did permit themselves to become contaminated with licentiousness. The women were the first to offer themselves to the whites, the more ardent ones going to rub themselves against the legs of these beings whom they supposed to be gods. They would give themselves to the European for a comb or a broken mirror. (85)

His titillating imagery, in which lascivious women of color "offer themselves to the whites," set the tone not only for national ideology but also for the underlying defense of *democracia racial* (racial democracy). For Freyre, the Portuguese colonizers' inclination to idealize, in sexual terms, the dark-skinned woman (partly, it is widely believed, as a result of the Moorish occupation of Portugal) fueled miscegenation and contributed to a lack of racial prejudice (at least compared with North American and European societies and other colonies at that time). This attitude later extended toward slaves and, according to Freyre, created a less violent form of slavery in Brazil than in other parts of the Americas.

In the heart of the Brazilian plantation, or so Freyre's writings propose, the master was able to live out his sexual fantasies with either black slaves or mulatas.[26] Freyre's vision of slavery and race relations has been difficult to deconstruct not only because contradictory passages have led scholars to different conclusions about Freyre as an individual but also because his writings captured and reflected back to Brazilians the prevailing notions of the elites of that time.[27] Freyre enabled elites to form a cohesive national identity, one that was on a more equal footing with that of their European counterparts. Freyre's publications may, in fact, have been taken beyond his authorial intentions.

Historian Thomas Skidmore (1993[1974]:192) recognizes that while Freyre could be interpreted as a more progressive thinker on race, his ideas were in fact harnessed by Brazilian elites at the time to promote the "whitening" ideal—the belief in and desire for a gradual racial purification process that would "whiten" the population and lead to the triumph of white culture. Thus, although Brazil was the last country on earth to abolish slavery, it was redeemed in some sense because, as a nation, it forged a tentative identity that accepted and even celebrated its racial mixture, and thus diverged somewhat from standard European narratives of the time that glorified their own whiteness and homogeneity. Since Freyre accomplished this in an era when biological theories of racism were fashionable, his writings were in their own time considered quite progressive, despite the absence of a critique of unequal power relations between the gendered, sexualized, and racialized subjects of his work.[28] In this process of identity construction, the imagery of a fun-loving population, of free and unhindered sexuality, and of tropical sensuality was summarized and celebrated in the representation of the sexy mulata.

Freyre never emphasized rape as a central component of miscegenation between white plantation owners and slaves, instead suggesting a level of mutuality underlying Brazilian sensuality, what seemed to be a belief in a uniquely Brazilian color-blind erotic democracy. Mutuality is coded throughout Freyre's writings. Skidmore (1988) implicitly recognizes the benefit to Brazil of producing an intellectual who was able to articulate an opposition to scientific racism, and the Freyrean refutation of such racism early in the twentieth century does seem to set Brazil apart in many ways. While I readily sympathize with Skidmore's reading of Freyre,[29] I appreciate historian Jeffrey Needell's (1995a) alternate interpretation. Needell argues that Freyre embodied a perspective of "seigneurial heterosexuality" toward women of color and that, ultimately, Freyre returned these women to their place in the hierarchy by not seeing their sexuality in the context of violence and rape. Needell's position seems to get to the heart of the matter, but I find it severe to hold Freyre to late-twentieth-century understandings of gender and sexuality.

Freyre's concept of racial democracy has been debunked in various ways by numerous scholars,[30] but his image of the sexualized slave, a seductress who is sexually insatiable and who uses her sexuality to enslave

men, has found continued embodiment in everyday discourses, literature, and mass media that idealize the image of the mulata.[31] Freyre's depiction of a racial democracy, with its suggestion that "Brazil is different," is based on his uncritical, and by now dated, vision of master-slave
sexuality. Brazilian elites in the postslavery era had to carve out their position on modernity at the same time that they were taking a position on
race and racial politics. Freyre's vision of master-slave interracial sexuality has played a key role in codifying the idea of Brazil as both a racial
democracy and a color-blind erotic democracy. This is important because
the fantasy and practice of "interracial" sex (uncritically envisioned as a
color-blind erotic democracy) distorts both popular and elite perceptions
of contemporary race relations in Brazil.[32]

Few Brazilians can see themselves as racist in a highly conventional-
ized political economy of interracial desire. Mixed-race or black women
(or idealized representations of such women) with certain "whitened"
characteristics are appreciated for their beauty and sensuality, while the
majority of low-income mixed-race and black women are barred from
economic and social mobility. They are trapped at the bottom of several
hierarchies at once—including that of race/color and class, even while
they are exalted as hot, sexual mulatas. The construction of colonial "desire" in Brazil was between white landowners and their female slaves.
Black and mixed-race men are also trapped at the bottom of a number
or hierarchies, but they are not exalted for their sexual appeal in the same
ways as women.

The contrast with the literature on racial mixture in the United States
during Freyre's time frame provides an interesting foil here. At about
the same time that Freyre was writing about Brazilian plantations in the
colonial period and articulating a set of representations that led to the
formulation of the mulata figure, social scientists in the United States,
such as Robert Park, were writing about the male mulatto as a tragic figure, the illegitimate offspring and descendant of the female slave and
white master. Whereas in the United States, the male mulatto was perceived as a tragic figure or a "marginal man,"[33] in Brazil, it was the figure of the mulata that gained recognition and attention.

Of course, there is another strand to this story, namely, how Brazilian
elites at this time began to think about themselves in comparison with
the rest of the world, particularly in relation to Europe and the United
States. Brazilian elites were concerned with the idea of "progress and civilization" and wanted very much to be accepted into the fold of "mod-

ern" nations. Their colonial history had been different, however. Slavery had been abolished in stages in Brazil, and interracial partnerships, marriages, and rape all contributed to the existence of a large mixed-race population. When Freyre helped to turn this history into something positive and transformative of this young nation, nobody came along and pointed out that domination, coercion, and rape were perhaps the more accurate depiction of Brazilian miscegenation.

Indeed, much of Brazilian exceptionalism hinges on this construction of the mulata, because the mulata is the positive sexualized product, the celebration of miscegenation—a representation that Brazilians recognized and embraced, and which other countries denied. It is precisely this embracing of racial mixture that has enabled many Brazilian intellectuals to still argue that the "Brazil is different" claim is a valid one. While placing the mulata at the center of national ideology was a historically radical step in some ways, it was also problematic.

The mulata was represented as having emerged out of the black African slave cultures—polygamous sinners with large sexual appetites who left the colonials defenseless. And Freyre's foundational myth that Native Americans (read also Africans brought as slaves) in Brazil were shameless, lusting women who would trade "a comb or a broken mirror" for sex was just the beginning of this representation. Perhaps the contemporary end point of this representation is best illustrated by the Web sites that offer "mulata babes" as part of the standard tourist package to global business partners of Brazil.

Stallybrass and White (1986), writing about the formation of social hierarchies, the relationship between "high and low" culture in Europe between the seventeenth and twentieth centuries, find a recurrent pattern: "The 'top' attempts to reject and eliminate the 'bottom' for reasons of prestige and status, only to discover, not only that it is in some way frequently dependent upon that low Other (in the classic way that Hegel describes in the master-slave section of the *Phenomenology*), but also that the top includes that low symbolically, as a primary eroticized constituent of its own fantasy life" (5). The "low Other" is associated with the subordinate classes, those discursively connected with crime, dirt, the city, the fair, and even the carnivalesque. This figure becomes, for the dominant, "a primary eroticized constituent of its own fantasy life" (5), which perhaps provides another complementary response to the question of why in Brazil the mulata has become so closely aligned to an *eroticized* fantasy; it is the racialized outcome of the formulation of the "low Other."

DISCOURSES (AND SILENCES) ON RACE

After Freyre, the coupling of race and sexuality all but disappeared from scholarly work concerning Brazilian sexuality, as if the topics, taken together, are just too difficult to address. Even though in the last twenty years there has been much groundbreaking work on sexuality in Brazil,[34] discussions of race are conspicuously absent from this scholarship.[35]

A similar situation exists concerning the literature on race. For a long time, writing about the politics of race was taboo. In his revised preface to *Black into White: Race and Nationality in Brazilian Thought* (1993[1974]), Skidmore writes, "Brazilian scholars, especially from the established academic institutions, continue for the most part to avoid the subject of race, in virtually all its aspects, at least for the twentieth century. Indeed, Brazilians often regard non-Brazilians who pursue the subject as having misunderstood it" (xi). If race alone is a troublesome topic, writing about race in the same breath as sexuality in the Brazilian context becomes doubly troublesome. As is evidenced by the work of Gilman (1985), Stoler (1989, 1995), JanMohamed (1990), and others,[36] it is clear that this taboo against joining discussions of race and sexuality has increasingly been broken down in other colonial and postcolonial contexts, yet this theoretical and topical move has barely been applied to Brazil.[37]

One reason it is difficult to talk directly about race and sexuality together is because of the ambiguities involved in the sexualization of racialized bodies. As we have seen, the powerful imagery surrounding the Brazilian mulata, for example, is tied up with the spirit of celebration, of national identity, sensuality, and exotic color difference. Another reason is because the two topics touch on an intimate area of social life. Despite the abundance of discourses about certain aspects of sex, many women's discourses on sexuality are silenced by a prevailing *sexo é bom* (sex is good) discourse.[38] Anthropologist Robin Sheriff (2000), who studied racial discourses in a shantytown in Rio de Janeiro, suggests that the silence surrounding discussions of race and racism in Brazil constitutes a form of cultural censorship.[39]

In the cases of sexuality and race, anthropologists are finding that because of the difficulty of addressing these topics, people resort not only to silence but also to jokes, stories, and innuendo that form a hidden discourse within daily interactions. These fugitive communications are extremely difficult to describe and analyze other than through the observation of daily interactions, but they are important because they reveal ruptures in the naturalized silences around such difficult topics as sexuality and race.

HIERARCHIES OF BEAUTY AND SOCIAL MOBILITY

In Felicidade Eterna, being a mixed-race or black female is not sufficient for being considered a hot, sexual mulata. The women in Glória's network rose in social status among their peers only when they proved that they could successfully seduce a coroa. A woman might thus be able to "overcome" her negatively valued dark skin or African characteristics by performing as a seductress. Given the low value these same women are apportioned in their everyday work situations, it is not surprising that they would value the art of seduction among themselves. To some extent, these women appear to adopt the dominant elite ideology of Brazil as a racial democracy and erotic paradise and, as best they can, play with the various possibilities offered within their world. They know that Brazil is not a racial democracy,[40] but they toy with the idea of an erotic democracy. The generally accepted equation is that a particular combination of white and black characteristics creates mulata beauty, but white characteristics alone can also qualify in another (higher) category of beauty. Purely African characteristics with no mixture of white characteristics are considered ugly. These categories defining beauty and ugliness turn sexual attractiveness into a racial matter.

When Glória and Isadora, her white comadre,[41] are sitting around having a beer or drinking a bit of *café*,[42] they often exchange stories about their hopes for their children. In these conversations, there are recognized areas of agreement between friends. Black or African characteristics, such as kinky hair and flat noses, are considered ugly. These are also considered characteristics that one can poke fun at by juxtaposing them with the characteristics of slaves or those in contemporary situations of servitude. For example, Félix, Glória's darkest-skinned child, was often taunted about his dark, bluish-black skin color. Sometimes, after playing outside and getting dirty just like any other child, he would be teased and called an *urubu* (black vulture), and when he failed to do well in school, he was reminded that he would later "only be fit to clean up the mess of white people." Of course, all these statements are said in jest, and in the context of a mother or a sister attempting to coax a child into more disciplined behavior, but the taken-for-granted message is that Félix's skin color is already a liability and can easily set him up for failure. Black is made beautiful in this context only by the addition of white features. But whiteness, unsurprisingly, has a high value by itself. None of this is said directly, though.

Isadora wanted her two youngest daughters from her second marriage, Katryny and Priscila, who are white, to go to the Xuxa modeling school in Botafogo (a neighborhood in the Zona Sul). The school is owned by Xuxa, one of Brazil's television icons and a symbol of beauty, who has blonde hair and blue eyes. During the last ten years, she has hosted the most popular children's show in Brazil.[43]

Although Glória and Isadora both live in Felicidade Eterna, these two friends were not exactly equals. Isadora was married to a white man who worked as a long-distance truck driver and sent home enough money each month to keep Isadora's botequim—an open window with a ledge serving as a counter—stocked with food and liquor, and with enough liquidity to give everyone in Felicidade Eterna credit until payday. During the course of an evening conversation over beer, Glória and Isadora found themselves in an awkward discussion about the possibilities of sending their young daughters to the Xuxa modeling school. Glória encouraged Isadora to send her daughters to the school, but Isadora remained silent about the possibility of this option for Glória. They implicitly acknowledged to one another that whiteness registers as beauty in this context, that is, with regard to the categories established by the Xuxa modeling school. Although the defining characteristic of their everyday discourses on race and color could be described as multiple and ambiguous, in specific situations such as this one, degrees of blackness and whiteness were recognized as part of an accepted scale of beauty, with black at the ugly end of the scale. In the context of the Xuxa modeling school, whiteness was "naturally" recognized as more valuable. Glória's children could never enter the school, regardless of financial issues and regardless of the beauty of her own daughters; they were simply too black. This well-understood limitation, however, was never openly discussed. It provides a good example of Sheriff's (2000) observation of cultural censorship around racial issues.

THE COROA AND THE IDEOLOGY OF WHITENING

In an astute psychological account of internalized racism in Brazil titled *Tornar-se Negro ou as Vicissitudes da Identidade do Negro Brasileiro em Ascensão Social* (*To Become Black or the Vicissitudes of Identity in Upwardly Mobile Black Brazilians*, 1983), black female mental health activist Neusa Santos Souza explores the emotional costs of social mobility on black identity. Many of the individual case studies in the book present upwardly mobile Afro-Brazilians' contradictory feelings toward their bodies and sexuality: on the one hand, experiencing themselves and experiencing being seen by others as more sensual and exotic because of their blackness and, on the other hand, feeling inferior and ugly in a world that values whiteness. For the women in Felicidade Eterna, the seduction of a lighter-skinned man may actually also serve to empower them in a culturally meaningful way, since the seduction requires a self-representation that emphasizes the heightened erotic powers of black sensuality. It is their mulata bodies, whose parts can also be described negatively in the context of African characteristics, that they believe allow them the possibility, however remote, of capturing an opportunity for social mobility.

Frantz Fanon (1925–61), the Martinique-born author and psychiatrist who wrote about anticolonialism, black consciousness movements, and African struggles for liberation, provides some useful analyses for thinking through some of the long-term political implications of assimilationist and whitening ideologies. In the second chapter (titled "The Woman of Color and the White Man") of his classic study of black identity, *Black Skin White Masks,* Fanon (1967[1952]) describes the negative psychological consequences of black admiration, including romantic desire for whiteness—and all it symbolizes—on the black psyche. He begins his analysis by examining the autobiographical book *Je Suis Martinquaise* (*I Am a Martinican Woman,* 1997) by Mayotte Capécia. Capécia describes her own admiration for whiteness and the desire to be with a white man, in part simply *because* he is white: "All I know is that he had blue eyes, blond hair, and a light skin, and that I loved him" (quoted in Fanon 1967[1952]:42). Fanon concludes that in this sort of hierarchically racialized world, being with a white man serves to extract that person from the category of slave and enable her to enter into the world of the master. Women of color, Fanon thus argued, are enslaved by their feelings of inferiority and their aspirations of being admitted into the white world. Within this social structure, women of color, both black and mixed-race, desire to either become white or avoid "slipping back," and for this reason, "love is beyond the reach of the Mayotte Capécias of all nations" (44).

There is an obvious parallel between Fanon's analysis of the "Mayotte Capécias of all nations" and the women living in Felicidade Eterna who understand and play within the parameters of the coroa fantasy. Carl Degler (1971) proposed the theory of the "mulatto escape hatch" in his book *Neither Black nor White: Slavery and Race Relations in Brazil and the United States.* He suggested that because Brazil had afforded blacks the possibility of social mobility through whitening, racial polarization had been avoided. Subsequent critiques of Degler's work have challenged his original hypothesis[44] by pointing out how his notion of the escape hatch does not really pan out in terms of social mobility because blacks and browns do not have significantly different profiles in terms of quality-of-life indicators (Silva 1985; Hasenbalg and Silva 1988). But subsequent work has suggested that there are indeed distinct gender differences involved in perceptions of racism and discrimination (Sheriff 2001; Twine 1998), many of which emerge in the context of interracial romance (Twine 1996). France Winddance Twine (1996) finds that rural, upwardly mobile Afro-Brazilian women are less likely than their male counterparts to perceive racism in their everyday lives, one of the reasons being their belief that they are romantically and sexually appealing to whiter men. Sheriff (2001:100) suggests that women are more reluctant to interpret others' behavior as racist than are men because they tend to encounter racism in intimate contexts that are charged with ambivalent emotions, such as the domestic worker situation. The coroa example provides further gendered evidence of the reasoning behind Afro-Brazilian women's reluctance to interpret certain kinds of interactions as racist. Interpretations of racism within these contexts would necessarily preclude the possibility for seduction, and in some cases, that would endanger one of the major hopes of these same women for economic and social mobility.

The manner in which the coroa fantasy plays with the ideology of whitening illustrates a perfectly ambiguous romantic relationship in which women expect to gain materially while they play out the sexualized role of the seductive mulata. And while these gains may never register substantially on any measure of economic well-being, the approach exists as one of a number of survival strategies that women pursue. Degler's mulatto escape hatch may not be wholly realistic, but it may capture some of the popular sentiment behind the coroa fantasy.

This is not to suggest that all women seek social mobility through a sexual partnership with their employers, nor that all dark-skinned women seek out whiter partners. In fact, endogamous racial unions are still the most common throughout all regions in Brazil.[45] There is even an overall pattern of darker-skinned men with lighter-skinned women rather than the opposite.[46] The widespread discussion about the possibility of seducing a coroa illustrates a number of conceptions about race and social mobility held by women in the most oppressed segments of Brazilian society. It is exactly their situation that seems to drive Fanon to despair with regard to the limitation he perceives in the possibilities for racial consciousness, in this case among a black middle class: "I know a great number of girls from Martinique, students in France, who admitted to me with complete candor—completely white candor—that they would find it impossible to marry black men. (Get out of that and then deliberately go back to it? Thank you, no.) Besides, they added it is not that we deny that blacks have any good qualities, but you know it is so much better to be white" (Fanon 1967[1952]:47–48).

The story of the coroa is interesting to consider in the context of age, class, sexuality, and gender, although it is actually race that is being socially weighed and sexually valorized. The coroa's whiteness, wealth, and class can make him attractive in spite of his age, and the seductress's darkness can make her attractive in spite of her race and poverty. Black female sexuality is valorized and considered erotic because it is suspended in a web of power relations that make it available in a particular way.[47] Blackness becomes valuable only in specific situations where sexual commodification is the operational framework. Thus, the coroa story, in addition to reflecting an element of unequal gender exchange, also seems to reflect unequal racialized patterns of sexual exchange.[48]

In some sense, the coroa story is just one narrative genre illustrating a broader thematic subject among this group. For example, the women in Felicidade Eterna were quite open about the kinds of expectations they had of their partners and how they had to use their bodies as part of a broad strategy of economic survival.[49] Glória's twenty-three-year-old neighbor, Marília, depicts some of the taken-for-granted meanings embedded in the coroa relation when she describes how she had to deceive a coroa into believing that he would receive sexual favors in return for his assistance (which he was able to provide because of his economic status) when her daughter Jessica was interned in a hospital:

> My baby got sick and began to vomit—had a fever. My sister-in-law, who was spending a few days there, said, "Marília, tomorrow we will take her to the doctor." My sister-in-law had a coroa who was giving her money. She phoned him and told him to come. When he got there he paid a private doctor to look at her. He got there and paid the bill and the doctor said, "Look, she has pneumonia and she has to be interned." And I was crying and everything. She was one year and two months old. He [the doctor] put her on intravenous, but didn't let us do anything. We could only come on visiting day. The coroa who was with my sister-in-law was interested in helping. He was well-off and every day he would call there saying that he was the father of the girl—and asking how she was. . . . I told my husband

that my brother had given me the money, but it was a lie, it was the coroa
who gave me the money to pay [for the hospital]. I was deceiving the coroa.
I would speak with him and every day mark a time and that time would ar-
rive and I would excuse myself saying I couldn't. He gave me all the money.
Money to buy things. I rented a house with the money he gave me.
(Marília, taped interview, 1995)

It is perhaps no surprise that women with extremely low incomes who
have difficulty paying for medical care and negligible chances of structured economic mobility would consider trading their bodies for money,
and that they would even pride themselves on their ability to survive by
attracting partners with economic resources. This particular theme is not
unique to these women but is rather part of the mainstream; economic
mobility through marriage and/or sexual seduction is a favorite theme
in Brazilian telenovelas, and it transcends any reference to race. In these
television programs, the class-based motivation for seduction of a
wealthy patron is a familiar scenario,[50] but the role of race is usually left
unmarked, since white actors are used in all roles. Pragmatic calculations
of wealth certainly influence the survivalist sexual strategies of low-
income women, and given the real economic and social status of whiteness, it, too, figures as one variable that is considered in evaluating a potential partnership.

Rational economic calculation intersects with sexual desire in complex ways in communities like Felicidade Eterna, where families are
struggling with day-to-day survival. Here, the coroa story translates into
a story of a "black Cinderella" in some provocative ways. First, it provides a grounded example of how an elite ideology celebrating Brazil's
color-blind erotic democracy correlates with a popular ideology visible
in the fantasies of low-income women. It also provides an explanation
of how blackness and black characteristics, which are considered ugly in
most situations, can in the context of commodified sexuality be eroticized and valorized. Further, this eroticization and valorization still lead
many Brazilians to conclude that since interracial sexuality has never
been regarded as taboo, then certainly Brazil cannot have the same sorts
of racial problems as those that occur elsewhere. In its more extreme
form, this relationship between race and sexuality provides the basis for
the belief that Brazil is hardly racist at all. A reading of the latter kind ignores how sexuality (acts and fantasies) is constructed through the
prism of power, masking the inequalities associated with race, gender,
and class.

The story of the coroa—as told by Glória and her friends—is a story of hope told among low-income women. It has multiple meanings: one is that the way out of the favela is through seduction of a coroa; the other, a more subtle meaning that I want to emphasize, is that the coroa desires his domestic servant and *therefore* is not racist. In this discourse, the intimacy of sexual relations and the willingness to take the low-income dark-skinned woman as a companion are thought to neutralize the class exploitation and racism that exist in actual practice. The morena is said to use all her sexual potency and innate sensuality to intoxicate the coroa. The seduction of the coroa is clearly a gendered, racialized, and sexualized popular vision of social mobility, but it is also a story of mistresshood and potential abuse.[51] The tendency is to interpret the sexual desire of these men as a signal of a liberal, even enlightened, racial worldview and not as part of a racially and economically skewed system. The fantasy creates a context in which these women participate in their own sexual commodification. In Brazil, it is widely believed that miscegenation and racism are contradictory, yet it is precisely their superficially uncomplicated coexistence that is part of Brazil's uniqueness.

TWO KISSES

In 1991, I accompanied Glória on a visit to one of her employers—white, male, and over sixty years old—whom she characterized as a coroa. He was an elite gentleman, recently widowed, who lived in the Zona Sul. Janaína, Glória's friend from Felicidade Eterna who already had her own ongoing romance with a coroa, also came along to help Glória complete her duties in the man's apartment on this particular day. When we arrived, he greeted me with two kisses, one on each cheek, the traditional Carioca greeting. I noticed that he barely said hello to Janaína and neglected to greet either Janaína or Glória with the customary two kisses. When we left his apartment, he gave me two more courteous kisses. His neglect of Glória and Janaína did not mean anything to me, since I had interpreted the greeting and good-bye kisses as part of a ritual of introduction. It did not occur to me at the time that my whiteness was the important factor in this interaction. I was introduced as Glória's "white daughter," but he most likely assumed I was another of Glória's employers. For Glória and Janaína, however, not being kissed took on a significance that is important to consider in light of the context within which they live: the absence of two kisses inspired Glória and Janaína to speak directly about racism—something they seldom did. I followed up on their reactions in later conversations, attempting to understand why this incident provoked such strong sentiments, while other more racially charged occurrences that had appeared more severe to me were dismissed as "not meaning anything."

Glória is greatly respected and regarded as a tough woman in Felicidade Eterna, yet she rides a separate elevator in her employers' buildings, dresses in a separate room, uses a separate bathroom, and eats apart from those for whom she cooks and cleans, all seemingly without complaint. Glória abides by the segregating practices applied across race and class; somehow those practices are normalized while the evaded kisses are not. Why?

Glória often referred to this episode—the two kisses—as an example of racism among middle- and upper-class people. Her experience of racism seemed to be profoundly felt in this particular moment of physical rejection. She viewed her employer's aversion to the two kisses (for her, an aversion to physical intimacy) as racist. Conversely, she viewed interracial physical contact, including sexuality, as proof of a nonracist attitude. Glória was able to bear the fact that her employer paid her a subsistence wage and subjected her to various forms of segregation, but she was seriously upset by the tangible physical distance that he emphasized when he refused to say good-bye properly.[52]

INTERNALIZED RACISM AND SOCIAL MOBILITY

> *Glória*: Roberto, my son, what does a black pregnant
>   woman have in common with a car that has
>   a flat tire?[53]
>
> *Roberto*: I don't know, auntie, what?
>
> *Glória*: They are both waiting for a monkey *[macaco]*.

With great élan, Glória told me of this exchange with her favorite nephew, Roberto, as a way of explaining why she and Roberto were no longer on good terms. "It was only a joke," related Glória. "But he didn't like the joke."

Roberto, who is a young, dark-skinned moreno,[54] had impregnated a morena named Geni in Felicidade Eterna. Glória did not like this girl very much and especially did not like the fact that the girl was so dark-skinned—as dark as Roberto. Roberto did not end up living with the girl, but he made considerable contributions to the child's welfare on a monthly basis, taking economic responsibility for the child even though the relationship with the mother had never really stabilized. Glória had very high hopes of social mobility for Roberto and never liked the fact that he was courting Geni—a girl whom she felt was not good enough for her nephew.

Roberto had completed his yearlong military service and soon after began working in a Rio-based grocery store chain.[55] In some ways, his story is somewhat anomalous in that he is a dark-skinned black man from an extremely poor family who barely completed primary school. His professional attitude toward his military training, combined with his gentle leadership skills, enabled him to rise quickly within the company. Glória was extremely proud of him but was also a bit hurt that he had fallen out of contact with her during his career ascension. She felt she was owed better treatment, since she had taken Roberto into her family after the death of his mother, Celina, Glória's sister. Glória always liked Roberto because he provided a positive male role model for her own children. He was a hard worker, and he purposefully stayed out of trouble, especially with the gangs in Felicidade Eterna and elsewhere. Glória never said so directly, but her joke to Roberto expressed her disappointment that he had chosen somebody she considered too common and too dark-skinned, a girl Glória considered far beneath him in terms of his potential for social mobility.

When I challenged Glória because of what I assumed to be her own form of internalized racism toward Geni, she retorted that she had been *brincando* (joking) with Roberto when she told him the macaco joke. *Macaco,* meaning simultaneously "monkey" and "monkey wrench" in Portuguese, is also a racial epithet and can be considered extremely insulting. Here, it seemed, I had stumbled upon a great example of the aggressive impulse behind jokes that Freud (1963[1905]) had long ago identified. Here was a joke that got its punch precisely by expressing a perspective that would otherwise be inexpressible. Statements made in the process of "only joking" can often provide a window into deeply held and troubling feelings, such as those that deal with race. Glória's teasing about the macaco was meant to warn Roberto about getting tangled up with somebody who might prevent him from attaining his long-term goals. Glória viewed herself as wanting to protect the best interests of her favorite nephew. Her discourse on "whitening" (Twine 1998; Shapiro 1996) consisted of a persistent discouragement—in the form of constant teasing and joking—of Roberto from pursuing his romantic (and sexual) interest in Geni. The embedded message in the joke would probably never be addressed in a serious conversation between her and

Roberto because speaking directly about race is often considered impolite or even shameful.[56]

Buried inside of Glória's joke was a codification of sentiments concerning both sexuality and race. Geni, from Glória's perspective, was not worthy of serious attention from Roberto because she was too dark-skinned. Similarly, underlying the complex positions on democracia racial that have challenged Brazilianist scholars since the 1950s is a codification of race inscribed into aesthetic valuations of sexual attractiveness that has nurtured both popular and elite visions of race in Brazil but has not been addressed in the scholarly literature.

Similarly, Glória's joke registers her disapproval of Roberto's choice of a sexual (potential marriage) partner without making it necessary to directly announce her objections to Geni's color. Geni's color and poverty make her an inappropriate choice for Roberto, an upwardly mobile black man, because in Glória's reading of the situation, Geni has nothing to offer Roberto.

CONCLUSIONS: BLACK CINDERELLA AND BLACK CONSCIOUSNESS POLITICS

The construction of race in Brazil, both among members of a broad popular culture and among elite academics, has been influenced to some extent by the idea of racial democracy set forth by Gilberto Freyre early in the twentieth century. The particular relationship between race and sexuality—how it has been interpreted by scholars, as well as how it is lived by the popular classes themselves—has been considered here as a window into an understanding of why some of the poorest segments of the Afro-Brazilian urban population have not enthusiastically joined the current black consciousness movement in Brazil, despite their own clear recognition of racial discrimination. While I agree with Hanchard's argument that racial hegemony prevents mobilization in Brazil, I would add that we still lack fine-tuned ethnographic data that illustrate how racial hegemony works. In Felicidade Eterna, the idea of seducing or marrying a coroa presents itself in the everyday lives of women as a possible form of social mobility. To some extent, when entering the realm of romance and sexuality, they adhere to the belief that they live in a color-blind erotic democracy. It is in this arena, too, that African characteristics that are normally devalued in a general aesthetic of beauty can be harnessed for the purposes of seduction and, in the process, made beautiful.

Simultaneously, women like Glória and her friends interpret the actions of those who enter into interracial liaisons as not racist, as in her reading of Janaína's relationship with her former employer as an example of nonracist behavior. Glória and her network of friends and family see forms of Brazilian exceptionalism in exactly such situations. Yet we must not forget that Glória's joke about the macaco to her nephew Roberto was also a signal of her attitudes about race, namely, that a dark-skinned woman has nothing to offer an upwardly mobile, dark-skinned man.

In fine-tuning Hanchard's (1994b) claim of racial hegemony in Brazil, I must add that the people represented here are well aware of Brazilian racism but are inhibited from expressing their discontent openly—that is, in direct verbal statements or in active political support of the black movement. Along with Sheriff (2000), I would suggest, rather, that there is much about their discontent that is silenced. Moreover, I would also suggest that much of their commentary about race is expressed in jokes, teasing, and other forms of humor, such as in the stories Eliana imagines are being told about her and her grandson as they stroll through the streets, or in the stories about coroas who are tricked into providing needed services and who might be humorously portrayed as sexually impotent. These coded genres come close to Scott's (1989, 1990) notion of a hidden transcript, Aesopian forms of communication that take place offstage and are more muted, informal forms of protest.

Scholars Hasenbalg[57] and Silva[58] have together and separately over the years written numerous articles and books defining and measuring the parameters of racial inequality in Brazil. In a recent summary article (Hasenbalg and Silva 1999), they lay out some of the broad dimensions of the racial problem in contemporary Brazil. One of their conclusions is that in Brazil, one still finds strong evidence of the continuation of the myth or ideology of racial democracy, despite the black movement's ongoing public denunciation of racism. They also call for research that would help black movement activists understand why there have been difficulties building a broader constituency within the black consciousness movement.

In his book *Orpheus and Power: The Movimento Negro of Rio de Janeiro and São Paulo, Brazil, 1945–1988*, Hanchard (1994b:102) analyzes the history of racial politics in Brazil and points out that the repression and denial of Afro-Brazilian protest have been characteristic of both military and civilian regimes, and to some extent of both left and right political regimes as well. As mentioned earlier, racial ideologies such as the Freyrean notion of racial democracy were part of the equation, thereby hindering racial consciousness movements. Early race-based organizations, such as the Teatro Experimental do Negro (TEN), founded in 1944 and led by Abdias do Nascimento, were primarily theatrical companies made up of white and black elites, but they provided the foundations for the later, more formally political groups that would follow.[59] Hanchard notes that a characteristic of these pre-1970s groups was that they seem to have worked within the dominant whitening ideology of the time. When a black movement emerged in the early 1970s, after a long period of authoritarian rule, it rejected "whitening" and favored a "back-to-our-roots" orientation, an adherence to negritude, and a revalorization of African origins (Hasenbalg and Silva 1999:164). Nevertheless, with this orientation, the differences between the small group of activists and the vast majority of the poor, poorly educated black population who were to be represented by their efforts were and still are enormous. Hasenbalg and Silva (1999) recently lament the fact that most academic studies have not understood the "general public's attitudes on matters of race relations" (165–66). They cite a classic study of racial attitudes, "Collective Identities and Democratization: The 1986 Elections in São Paulo,"[60] based on interviews from a sample of 573 residents of the city of São Paulo, eighteen years of age and older. The study found a strong rejection of the idea that a collective movement should be restricted to those being discriminated against (Hasenbalg and Silva 1999:167). The preferred solution proposed by the majority of both whites and nonwhites is that of a movement that incorporates both whites and nonwhites into its activities. Hasenbalg and Silva conclude that "harmony and the avoidance of racial confrontation seem to be the translation, or natural expression, of the racial ideology in Brazil" (167–74). Hanchard (1994b:137) notes that such movements have faced many impediments, including resource deprivation, racial hegemony, and culturalism, as well as the historical problem of the low level of racial identification as black. To some extent, this gap between current black movement activists and their desired constituents has only grown over the years, thus creating a movement with a valid cause but with the attendant problem of seemingly being unable to convince its constituents of the value of becoming active participants.[61]

The Movimento Negro has attempted to bring attention to racial discrimination in Brazil, as well as to promote the positive aspects of Afro-Brazilian history and culture (Hanchard 1994b). To accomplish this, it has had to advocate for an identification among its constituents for a form of racial exclusivity and racial pride that is somewhat anathema to the everyday practices that nefariously yet silently reproduce the hierarchies of beauty that denote black characteristics as ugly and white characteristics as beautiful. In the desperately impoverished situation in which so much of the Afro-Brazilian population currently is trapped, it comes as no surprise that the Movimento Negro has experienced mostly middle-class and elite success. Any movement that would attempt to push for a stronger version of racial affiliation or for the exclusivity of the black experience would have to call into question the romantic and sexual appeal of whiteness, upon which the coroa fantasy is built. It would also necessarily call for a decommodification of the black female body in a context where black women have already had to self-commodify in order to survive.

This chapter has examined one particular fantasy of interracial sexuality among low-income, dark-skinned women living in shantytowns in Rio. In doing so, I would hope to link this constituency to the groups that seek to represent them. I have argued that sexuality and race are intimately connected and ought to be analyzed together. In Brazil's carnivalization of desire, the ideal representation of the mulata is eroticized, exoticized, and celebrated, while real women of color are kept from mainstream economic advancement. Contemporary scholars of sexuality have avoided the connection between race and sexuality, thus preserving the notion that Brazilian sexuality guarantees an implicitly color-blind erotic democracy.

Glória and her friends fantasize and tease one another about seducing older, richer, whiter men known as coroas. In the process, they racialize their own bodies, approximating in certain ways the images of the hot, sexual mulata that form part of Brazil's self-representation as a racial democracy. Sexual discourses about black or mixed-race women are in this manner appropriated and reproduced by the women themselves. However, both in the rare discussion of racism by Glória initiated by her employer's physical avoidance of her and in the more mundane conversations among her friends concerning the taken-for-granted nature of black ugliness and white beauty, as well as in the everyday experiences of both interracial love and racism, evidence suggests that the underlying belief and thorough investment in the idea of a color-blind erotic democracy in Brazil actually contributes to the preservation of the myth of racial democracy among low-income black and mixed-race women. It prevents them, consequently, from joining a mass movement that would challenge the racializing practices that reproduce racism in Brazil.

By making this analysis, I do not mean to say that this is a permanent condition or that black consciousness politics are destined to fail. Nor do I mean to say that there is no hope in organized resistance or even in commodified approaches to bringing race into a position of national prominence and public dialogue. In 1996, the first black magazine to feature black models appeared on Brazilian newsstands, representing another positive step in the process of calling attention to race in the Brazilian context.[62]

As part of the Movimento Negro, GELEDÉS, the Black Women's Institute founded in 1990 in São Paulo, for example, has worked hard specifically to raise the consciousness of black women but has experienced problems similar to those faced by the broader black consciousness movement.[63] It and other race-based organizations have focused on issues that are truly of significance to Afro-Brazilian women, such as domestic and sexual violence, youth self-esteem, reproductive rights, and labor market discrimination. Yet many of their potential constituents, such as the women in Felicidade Eterna, have very little knowledge of or access to these groups and seemingly find the discourses of such groups quite alien. According to Sheriff (2001:214), black activists and people living in favelas are isolated by cultural censorship and by the class distinctions that divide and differentiate Brazilian social arrangements more generally.

There is also evidence of continuing widespread defense of the myth of racial democracy by broad segments of the population, including contemporary scholars such as Fry. Underlying this optimistic sense of racial democracy in Brazil, however, is an uncritical and inaccurate (Freyrean) vision of interracial sexuality. Although the practices associated with interracial sex may be consensual in a legal sense, they are anything but egalitarian. It will be a challenge to black movement activists to speak to the issues of interracial sex and marriage.

When the statistics concerning the "failure" of the black consciousness movement are read, they seem consistent with what Fry (1995) refers to as a "still highly assimilationist Brazil." Fry (1995) cites a 1986 survey on attitudes of the population toward activism in São Paulo:[64] "When asked what blacks and mulattos should do to defend their rights, 75.3 percent of the black and mulatto respondents and 83.1 percent of whites replied that they would prefer to see the formation of a movement composed of whites, mulattos, and blacks. Less than 10 percent of each category thought that the problem should be addressed either individually or by an exclusively black movement" (7). Fry argues that facts such as these make Brazil "different," a point that attractively negates the possibility of reducing Brazilian race relations to a blueprint comparable to that in the United States. However, such an argument is also reminiscent of what Hanchard terms "Brazilian exceptionalism" with regard to race, an argument that he sees as having contributed to the racial hegemony that exists in contemporary Brazil. I must agree with Hanchard's assessment. Embedded in the "Brazil is different" argument is a dated celebration of Brazilian miscegenation that uncritically supports the notion of a Brazilian color-blind erotic democracy.

The fantasy of seducing a coroa held by low-income mixed-race women provides evidence of a pattern of erotic calculation that is neither democratic, nor egalitarian, nor idiosyncratic; it is instead tied to the economic correlations of blackness in Brazil. The black Cinderellas of Felicidade Eterna were not interested in embracing a black consciousness movement, in part, at least, because of their investment in the beliefs related to black female sexual allure and a color-blind erotic democracy.

It is time to bring a deeper understanding to the nature of eroticized racism, rather than simply declare that "Brazil is different." It is time to suggest that scholars explore race and sexuality together. In Brazil, racialized sexuality occurs in specifically gendered and commodified patterns that are almost entirely taken for granted. Unless we understand these constructions and recognize the prominent roles of class, gender, and sexual power differentials, we tend to either underestimate the significance of racism in Brazil (Fry) or overestimate the significance of the emergence of a black consciousness movement there (Hanchard). Many mixed-race and black women who might otherwise feel, and scrutinize, the pangs of everyday racism in their lives and enthusiastically enter into racial identity politics are instead caught at the edge of economic survival, tethered to ambivalent fantasies of social, and in a sense racial, mobility.

The idea that Brazil is a color-blind erotic democracy—that the power associated with gender, race, and class plays no role in sexual partnerships—helps to mask and normalize everyday racism and internalized racism in Brazil.

CHAPTER 4

No Time for Childhood

In the early evening, along the beachfront in a city in North-east Brazil, people are out strolling. A well-dressed white man of the upper class and his son, probably about the age of seven or eight, decide to stop and have their shoes shined by a dark-skinned boy, shoeless, and not more than seven or eight years old himself. I was close enough to hear the father instructing his son how to speak to the other boy, how to demand a certain polish to be done in a certain way at a certain price. The father insisted that the job, both the shine and the orchestration of behavior between his son and the shoe-shine boy, be done to perfection. The shoe-shine boy was keen to show off his dexterity and did not need any instruction about what to do. At the end of the shine, the young son paid the shoe-shine boy with his father's money, and the shoe-shine boy, happy to have earned a few coins, walked off down the beach in search of new customers. The man and his son continued strolling along.

Author's fieldnotes, 1988

One evening in 1995, after completing her day of work at Dona Beth's, Glória was waiting for her bus near the pyramid fountain at the Praça XV de Novembro (Plaza XV of November) in downtown Rio and ran into one of her ex-partners.[1] It was Gérson, a man she had lived with for five years as a young teenage girl in Rocinha and with whom she became pregnant with Pedro Paulo, her firstborn, and then later with Fernanda, her oldest daughter. According to Glória, Gérson was looking as if life had been treating him fairly well. He was in what appeared to be his own car, sipping a Coke from a fast-food cup, and sitting next to a well-dressed woman, three signs that to Glória meant he had moved far beyond the kind of poverty that she still inhabited. Inevitably, after they verified that indeed they were speaking to the right parties, Glória asked Gérson if he had by chance heard about Pedro Paulo's death in Rocinha. He had not heard about his death, nor did he know that his son had grown up to be one of the leaders of the Comando Vermelho (Red Command), one of the imperialist drug-trafficking gangs in Rocinha.[2] Notably, Glória told this story to me as one that she found to be funny, and she assured me that soon "I would laugh about it, too." What she found surprising and hilarious was the fact that Gérson began to weep on the spot after digesting the news that his son had died. Glória, who many years earlier had distanced herself from her oldest son because of his criminal activities, had told me that when she learned of his death in a shoot-out in Rocinha, she was "tired of shedding tears over him" and by that time had no more left to shed. Gérson, her ex-partner, had never paid any attention to Pedro Paulo even when the boy was young; he never once helped Glória financially with the costs of raising their son, and she found it ironic that he cried over Pedro Paulo—a virtual stranger to him—while she, the mother who had single-handedly raised the boy and seen him gone astray, could not muster a single tear at the time of his death. With this realization, Glória abruptly ended their brief encounter, telling Gérson that "tears were not going to bring him back."

A VISIT WITH PEDRO PAULO AT ILHA GRANDE PRISON

I had the opportunity to spend a couple of days with Pedro Paulo in Ilha Grande (Big Island) Prison (also known as the Devil's Cauldron) in September 1992 while I was living with Glória and her family in Felicidade Eterna.[3] Glória planned a weekend trip, during which Zezinho, Zeca, Félix, and I would accompany her to the prison where Pedro Paulo was serving a fifteen-year sentence for the armed robbery of two apartments on the Lagoa (the Lake neighborhood in the Zona Sul) in Rio. We started our trek from Felicidade Eterna at about four o'clock in the morning. We had cooked pots of food throughout the previous night, and all of us fell asleep on the bus. As a result, we slept through our point of exit in Mangaratiba, where we needed to catch the ferryboat to the island, and so we had to backtrack to the correct stop. Eventually, we found our way to the docking area and paid for our voyage on the boat that makes the trip between the mainland and the island. When we docked on the island, it was about nine o'clock in the morning, and a female security guard employed by the prison was waiting at the pier to greet us. At that hour, most of the passengers on the boat were coming to the island to visit loved ones, but there were also a few tourists and residents. There on the pier, in full public view, the security guard began to match her list—the prisoners—with those of us who had come as their visitors. After she marched us briskly to a security headquarters especially for visitors and divided the men from the women, I found myself waiting with Glória and about thirty other women for the next eight hours. Zezinho and the boys had been placed in a separate room for men. Everyone in our room was placing towels or small blankets they had brought with them on the floor, attempting to claim precious space for lounging and a possible nap. They all seemed to know the routine and were prepared for the long day of waiting. One woman, who saw me standing and waiting patiently for the process to begin, called out to me, "Ohh, Neguinha [Little Blackie; term of endearment],[4] sit down," in a kind attempt to let me know that it would be a lot more comfortable to claim a space to sit down on for the day than to have to stand. There were a few chuckles when she called me "Neguinha" because I was one of only two or three whiter-skinned women in the room, and I definitely stood out. One by one we were called into a tiny office, where we were asked to strip naked. Then flashlights were beamed on all our private parts to make sure we had not smuggled in a prohibited object, such as a knife. Glória was not the only one who had brought gifts and pots of food; the inspection of everything we all had brought with us took hours, and I was forced to leave my camera and tape recorder in the security area. Finally, at about five o'clock, a minivan from the prison came rumbling down the long dirt hill to pick us up, and we all piled in, exhausted by a long day of waiting and anticipating the reunion with loved ones. The climb to the prison seemed long—more than a half hour—through thick tropical vegetation. The curves on the road were sharp and dangerous.

Upon arriving at the prison, we were led to what was known as the *área de lazer* (recreation area) and served a sweet drink similar to Kool-Aid. Pedro Paulo had not been certain that we were coming, and he had to be summoned to the area, which was actually a long, narrow hallway with twenty to twenty-five rooms spread out along two sides. Iron bars were welded onto the padded doors of the rooms, but the doors were left swinging open at this time of the day, and one could peek in and see that some of the rooms were quite spruced up, with television sets and throw rugs on the floor. Unfortunately, we were issued one of the worst cubicles, one that was quite dirty and had years' worth of tropical fungus growing in every corner. There was a set of bunk beds, a sink, and a little cooking area where we were able to set our pots to warm.

In our room that night was Amélia, another guest at the prison, a young woman who was there on her birthday to visit her long-lost brother, Adhmar. She claimed that she had not seen him since they were children of three or four years of age, more than two decades ago. According to Amélia, she and Adhmar were separated as children when she was given to one family, and he, to another, after the death of their mother. Adhmar was a heavyset, soft-spoken man who grew up on the streets and was now serving a long-term prison sentence. I never asked what his crime had been; it would have gone against the prevailing etiquette. Amélia reminded me of a young nun; she appeared innocent to an extreme, almost otherworldly. I doubted that she actually was Adhmar's sister. I had heard about women who became involved with men who were in prison from women in Felicidade Eterna who knew of such cases. Soneca and Anita believed that a certain kind of woman— and they even hinted that it might especially be common among women who had recently become *crentes* (literally, believers, religious converts)—hoped, through their faith, to help redeem another person from a criminal life. Likewise, I had read popular articles about the religious conversion of prisoners in Rio's prisons. Thus, I wondered whether Amélia was really related to Adhmar or whether perhaps she was one of the women who made themselves emotionally and/or sexually available to prisoners in an almost martyr-like way. She kept repeating clichéd phrases such as "When a woman loves, she really loves, and it is one person." I did not believe that they were siblings, but this was a story I would not be able to confirm either way. In any case, Amélia's optimism and faith in the goodness of human nature, as well as her religious approach to the world, made an interesting contrast that night to the combined cynicism of Pedro Paulo and Adhmar.

Having been informed at the last minute that he had visitors, Pedro Paulo arrived at the recreation area from the bowels of the prison. Finally, I was able to greet Glória's firstborn son. He was a young man of about thirty, extremely tall and muscular, and the most articulate of her children. She introduced me to him as her *filha branca* (white daughter), and this confused him for a moment and made him pause, I believe because he was wondering whether it was possible that Glória actually gave birth to someone as white as me. Perhaps because he had been out of touch with her for so many years, he thought anything was possible. After letting him wonder for a bit, Glória laughed loudly and explained that I was like a daughter to her, and that I was an anthropologist writing a book about women in the shantytowns of Rio de Janeiro. Pedro

Paulo immediately understood my presence as a chance for him to be remembered and perhaps even immortalized in my book. Pedro Paulo seemed like a young man who was used to being listened to, and he had much to say. Unfortunately, we were all exhausted. None of us had eaten more than a few salty crackers during the entire day, and I felt dizzy with hunger. The children, Zeca and Félix, were even too tired to wait for the beans and rice to be heated, and they opted for bed before dinner. They were all too used to days like this, when one's body becomes tired and ultimately disinterested with what often turned into an all too long and familiar wait between meals.

Pedro Paulo was a fan of reggae music, and one of the first things he requested from me was to find him a Jamaican-colored *boné*, or cap, similar to the one Bob Marley wore. He seemed to have an affinity not only for the music but also for the politics that reggae music represents. Compared with the many other friends I had in the shantytown of Pedro Paulo's generation, he seemed far more politicized and aware of the absurd nature of the poverty in Rio. One could see in his body language and hear in his monologues that Pedro Paulo was a young and energetic man, filled with anger. He had recently learned that his "woman" in Rocinha, Josilene, was pregnant with his child and was considering having an abortion. Pedro Paulo threatened that if she aborted his child, the first thing he would do upon leaving prison would be to kill her: *"Ela matou o meu filho. Agora vou ter que matar ela."* ("She killed my child. Now, I am going to have to kill her.") He felt that when a woman has sex with a man, she ought to know the consequences, a comment that forced the women in the room out of their listening mode and into verbal battle. Glória and Amélia countered that men ought to take part in birth control as well—that it should not only be the domain of women. Soon, however, Pedro Paulo launched into another long harangue, this time about Comando Vermelho of Rocinha and how it does many things to preserve "family values." Pedro Paulo connected his own personal position on abortion to his sense that Red Command, as a group sharing a set of core values, promoted his particular sense of right and wrong. Pedro Paulo told us he hated abortion and equally despised women who were not monogamous. For Pedro Paulo, the job of "the man" is to put the food on the table for his family, and as long as this is taken care of, it is fine for him to have as many women as he wants—as long as they "don't lack anything,"[5] of course. I was surprised by how well he was able to articulate the male double standard on fidelity, making it sound as if it were a unique, well-developed doctrine emanating from Red

Command rather than a more generalized cultural norm. According to Pedro Paulo, all his prison inmates at Ilha Grande were members of Red Command. The other prisoners, who were collectively called Alemães (Germans), were separated out and placed in a different prison. Pedro Paulo did mention how he wound up in prison this time. He had bungled a major armed robbery—cash and cameras worth over 70,000 *cruzados* (which we figured at the time of the robbery was close to about $10,000 U.S.)—and his only regret was that he wished he had known how to invest the cash so he would not have been as broke as he currently was.

At midnight, the visitors are locked into the cubicles together with the prisoners, a fate that seemed daunting after having spent the evening chatting with Pedro Paulo and Adhmar. I was forced by Glória into taking a section of the bottom bunk bed; she was concerned that her *filha branca* sleep comfortably. Meanwhile, she and Zezinho unrolled some blankets and spread themselves out on the floor. Shortly after the lights went out and as I was dozing, I noticed the smell of cigarettes close to me and felt a man attempting to place his hands on my body. It was extremely dark in the room, and I was guessing that the hands were Pedro Paulo's. I whispered to the transgressor that I was "like a sister" to him and that he should treat me with a little more respect. Finally, I threatened to wake Glória and tell her what he was doing, at which point he immediately pulled away and moved back sheepishly to the other bed. I was momentarily giddy for having thought of using Glória as a threat against Pedro Paulo, but I realized early in the morning that the intruder actually had been Adhmar! Nevertheless, I am guessing that through his friendship with Pedro Paulo, he had understood that Glória was not someone to cross, and my threat to expose him had indeed functioned almost magically. I decided, wisely, I believe, to not tell Glória about the episode until we were safely in the minivan heading back down the road from the prison, so as not to disturb the rest of our visit. Her response was what I had suspected. She would have liked to "break his face" for trying something like that with me, and she probably would have wanted to cut short our visit, or worse, she might have entered into some kind of battle in that tiny room. In any case, I was glad I did not ruin the trip, and I made her swear and promise never to mention the incident to Pedro Paulo either, since I did not want Adhmar to suffer any for his momentary transgression.

The story, however—and we all recognized this—became quite funny over the years as Glória and I repeated it as further proof of her own hard-won reputation for toughness—one that even hardened criminals feared! She was delighted that I was able to use *her* as a threat to protect myself in this situation. And, of course, everyone thought it was funny that I had mistaken Adhmar for Pedro Paulo, but that Adhmar had re-treated anyway. What I also learned from this experience was something that all my friends in Felicidade Eterna seemed to know intuitively, and which they tried to explain to me at various times: while a bad event is happening, the moment is not funny at all, but when it is over and time has passed, that same event is subject to being made the source of humor.

Upon his release from prison in 1995, Pedro Paulo went back to his gang and his old life in Rocinha.[6] Josilene, the woman Pedro Paulo had referred to as his "woman," had not followed through with the abortion, and Pedro Paulo returned to her and responsibly took over his fatherly obligations to his son, Raul, which included teaching him how to dis-tinguish between different kinds of guns. During our brief prison visit, Pedro Paulo had made it clear that he was not interested in working for slave wages as his mother had done her entire life. He openly scorned Glória's definition of "honest" work and quite articulately described the impossibility of any self-respecting man supporting a family on a Brazil-ian minimum wage. He was angry and impulsive, but I found his analy-sis of minimum-wage work to be quite accurate. In 1995, only a few months after being released from prison, he was killed in a shoot-out with police in Rocinha. Glória had no tears left to shed over Pedro Paulo, perhaps because she had tried so hard over the years to reason with him and had come to accept their different perspectives on the world.

Over the years, Glória's lament about Pedro Paulo had been constant. She tried to understand why her firstborn had turned out to be a *mar-ginal* (marginal, criminal). She considered him the most intelligent of all her children—he had completed his secondary schooling and could read and write at a relatively sophisticated level. But, according to Glória, early in life he exhibited his love for "the street," and this tendency, fi-nally, was the strongest influence on his character. In many of the life sto-ries of the women in Glória's network of friends and family, the women had worked in the homes of others, raising the children of strangers but being forced themselves to leave their own children with older sisters, a grandmother, or "the street." Glória herself was raised by her grand-mother while her mother worked in Rio de Janeiro to earn enough money to move the entire family. In reflecting on her own work-filled life, she also attributes the loss of Pedro Paulo to "the street" and its violence to the fact that she was too busy to keep track of him as much as she would have liked.

According to Glória, Pedro Paulo spent a good portion of his youth in and out of the state's child correctional institution—Fundação Nacional do Bem-Estar do Menor (FUNABEM).[7] He seemed to have emerged from that experience even angrier than when he went in, and upon finishing his time there, he quickly returned to Rocinha and became involved with the infamous Red Command. From that time on, Glória knew that his life would be a short one. She had always told her children, using Pedro Paulo as a negative role model, that *"bandido não tem amigo"* ("bandits have no friends"). Pedro Paulo was known to sleep restlessly, with a gun under his pillow in expectation of trouble.

Pedro Paulo had watched Glória and her entire generation slave away as domestic workers in the homes of the wealthy in the Zona Sul for barely subsistence wages. He was not moved either by the men he knew in Rocinha who worked at honest jobs. Men like Pedro Paulo felt they had been cheated out of their own futures. Further, Pedro Paulo had figured out early on that those of his class and background do not have a great deal of social mobility. Those whom he knew in "honest" professions—domestic workers, construction workers, security guards, and so forth—struggled their entire lives, working hard but still barely making a living for themselves and their families. My sense is that what marks Pedro Paulo's generation is the recognition, although in some ways inarticulable, of the impossibility of "the good life" for those of his race and background. In places like Rocinha, gang leaders and some "successful" gang members have built large houses for themselves and have been able to acquire a piece of "the good life" that is so central to Carioca identity. Rio de Janeiro, the marvelous city, is ultimately a city of pleasure for the wealthy, and Rocinha's position as a shantytown that borders the wealthy neighborhoods of the Zona Sul provides a stark contrast. Here, children in difficult economic circumstances see wealthy children in the newest styles of clothes and sneakers and watch them eating in restaurants, driving in cars, and being spoiled endlessly. The Italian psychoanalyst Contardo Calligaris, commenting on the treatment of children by middle- and upper-class Brazilians, described a setting in which "the child is king."[8] This observation is striking when considered alongside the rituals of childhood among the lower classes.

More than anyone else, Pedro Paulo had a sense of the riches and the good life of the bacanas, those who lived on the asphalt, the wealthy people in the Zona Sul, as he referred to them. His descriptions of apartments he had robbed were filled with details about electronic devices,

Figure 8. Children playing in an alley of Felicidade Eterna. Photograph by author.

Figure 9. Main street in Felicidade Eterna. Photograph by author.

clothes, and other elements of "the good life" that he believed these people inhabited. His anger seemed somehow justified to me because I knew of few cases of social mobility out of the favela and safely into middle-class existence. It surely did happen, but the route was treacherous and reserved for a lucky few. As an intelligent young man growing up in Rocinha, Pedro Paulo found the allure of gang life to be irresistible. It seemed to offer an alternative to backbreaking manual labor, at the same time promising a decent wage and offering instant economic improvement.

Pedro Paulo's choices form almost a classic example of male oppositional culture. Because he had grown to a position of leadership in Comando Vermelho, it was expected that there would be some jockeying for power upon his release from prison. It was practically a given—and a joke—that it would be a miracle if he were still alive the next time I returned to Brazil, so I was not shocked to learn that Pedro Paulo had been killed in the time between my visits, shortly before I arrived in 1995.

What Glória brought to her parenting after her early experience with Pedro Paulo was a profound sense of failure and loss—of having lost Pedro Paulo to the street, to FUNABEM, to the gang, and to a life that was sure to end violently. She regretted how things had gone and recognized that early on she had lost authority over her own child. She now was especially suspicious of FUNABEM, viewing it as a training ground for young criminals. After her sister's death, she rushed in to rescue her nieces and nephews from a possible fate in FUNABEM, fearing that their lives would be lost if they were to be raised within the institution. She attempted to look tougher than the peers or gang members or other influences that might corrupt her children, hoping to discourage them—sometimes quite aggressively—from getting involved in trouble, especially with the gangs.

For the most part, she succeeded, except with Lucas, Celina's son, who in 1995 decided to join up with the *bandidos* (literally, bandits, meaning the gangs or anyone carrying out criminal activities) in Rocinha just shortly before his cousin Pedro Paulo died in the shoot-out. By this time, Tiago, Glória's child, and Alexandro, Lucas's half brother, had already managed to get apprenticeships with car mechanics, and although their actual paychecks were small (less than one minimum salary), they were heading into a career of honest work. They would tease Lucas, accusing him of joining up in order to have an early funeral. And Lucas would jokingly agree, acknowledging the near certainty of this ending with his chosen refrain, *"Eu vou morrer cedo"* ("I am going to die young").

THE KILLING STREETS

Increasingly, the trend among the middle and upper classes in Brazil's major cities has been to move behind higher walls to protect themselves from what they perceive as the growing violence on the street. Teresa Caldeira (2000) refers to the social segregation and the construction of a "city of walls" in her description of São Paulo during the late 1980s and early 1990s. She argues that the discourses on and fear of crime have served to legitimize private and illegal reactions, such as the organization of death squads, which became internationally known in the early 1990s for their brutal extermination of "street children." On July 24, 1993, the front page of the *New York Times* carried a story titled "Gunmen in Police Uniforms Kill 7 Street Children in Brazil."[9] Hooded members of a death squad, who were actually off-duty police, killed seven homeless boys and wounded two others, spraying them with gunfire as they lay sleeping in front of the Candelária Church in the center of Rio de Janeiro. In May 1992, *Newsweek* ran a feature article titled

"Dead End Kids," with the subtitle elaborating that "about 200,000 Brazilian children live on their country's streets—and are in danger of being slain."[10] Brazil's "street children"[11]—their great numbers, living conditions, and extreme vulnerability to physical assault—make middle- and upper-class Brazilians feel uncomfortable about the way their society is represented by the international press, in part because of their own celebrated child-centeredness. But Brazilians have known about this enemy within long before the Candelária killings. In his book *A Guerra dos Meninos* (1990), Gilberto Dimenstein had revealed the systematic assassination of street children in Brazil by death squads and the ambivalent feelings of the middle and upper classes with regard to these children. On the one hand, the children are seen as innocent victims of their country's social and economic conditions. On the other, they are perceived as part of a growing population of irredeemable criminals. At the time of the Candelária massacre, middle- and upper-class Brazilians were once again forced to question fundamental aspects of the historical and contemporary condition of their country as the international press presented Brazil as a country that killed off its already victimized children. Whether reported in the international press or the Brazilian media, events such as the Candelária killings offer a confounding array of images that, in one breath, depict children of the poor who are out on the street as innocent victims and, in the next, depict them as dangerous criminals.[12]

HOME CHILDREN, STREET CHILDREN, AND INSTITUTIONALIZED CHILDREN

The issue of street children has for some time formed part of an awakened national consciousness for Brazilians. In 1980, Argentine-born Hector Babenco directed the provocative, internationally acclaimed feature film *Pixote,* using children who were not actors but who were residents of Brazilian favelas as the protagonists. The film depicts the violence of the streets, as well as the cruelty of the institutions (FUNABEM and FEBEM) that house these children. Babenco's film seems to be a self-conscious dialogue with Luis Buñuel's earlier *Los Olvidados* (1950), a film set in urban Mexico that explores the lives of impoverished, unrestrained, and parentless (mostly fatherless) youths. While with hindsight Buñuel's film was even more controversial in its representation of these youth as amoral psychopaths, Babenco's film did not completely succeed in avoiding a sympathetic but criminalized representation of them.

In the first scene, Babenco captures the initiation of Pixote, a scrawny, weak boy, into the state institution: Pixote watches as another boy is raped by the older, stronger boys. By the end of the film, the still tiny Pixote is carrying a gun, has pimped and trafficked drugs, and has killed three people, including one of his friends. Pixote—a "real" boy from Rocinha who was attempting to launch an acting career—was killed in 1988 in a run-in with Brazil's military police.[13] Babenco succeeded in creating a film that reflects the complex feelings of middle- and upper-class Brazilians—the film's primary audience—who sympathize with but also fear these "dangerous" children. He did not, however, adequately capture the lives and feelings of those who raise and nurture these children, nor the context of everyday violence perpetrated not only by the economic conditions of poverty but also by the criminalization of the poor both by the police and by the society at large.

Children are increasingly important in Brazilian discourse about urban violence because they are often recruited to do the dirty work of organized urban favela gangs dealing in drugs; children are often drafted for other illicit activities, since it is well known that they get off with lesser or restricted sentences.[14] These children, out on the street begging, watching cars, and looking for work in the informal labor sector, also play a vital role in the household economy of their impoverished parents.[15] More often than not, the only wage earner in their households is a single mother earning one minimum-wage salary per month, out of which she must feed and clothe herself and her oftentimes large extended family. Although they are often recruited by the favela gangs, these youths are not immune from the violence and punishment meted out by these same gangs. In November 1992, for example, a group of young "street boys" in Rio were lined up by members of a gang and shot in the knuckles. It was rumored that they had been stealing too close to one of the favelas that was under the protection of the local gang, and the latter wanted to teach them a lesson about stealing in the wrong places.[16] As the number of street children has grown, the middle and upper classes have begun to view these youths as bandits and have accommodated to the idea of urban death squads "cleansing" the streets of the most bothersome of them.[17]

Many middle- and upper-class Brazilians have a ready, well-developed, even progressive discourse about the problems in their country; they shell out a few coins at the end of their shopping sprees, agree to have their cars watched or even washed while they shop, and, in private, despair at the growing number of these youths who are most often seen as nuisances.

Each middle-class person has his or her own strategic rationale toward the problem, ranging from refusing to give any money at all, since "these coins will not solve the problem," to giving some money out of a deep-seated fear or even as a kind of magical protector, realizing that they would rather give voluntarily than be assaulted by the same child later on. My own field observations of the impact these children have on their own family income suggests that these "nuisances," earning the little money they do, often add significantly to the daily subsistence of their families, a finding supported by anthropologist Tobias Hecht's (1998) research with children living in the street.

In his brutally honest ethnography of street children in Recife, Hecht (1998) makes an interesting and apt distinction between two forms of childhood in Northeast Brazil. He describes the class difference that results in differential childhoods for the rich and poor as creating either "nurtured" children or "nurturing" children: "Nurturing children, in essence, are poor children who from an early age take on serious responsibilities; they bring in resources to their mothers and nurture the household, activities they view as moral obligations. Nurtured children, on the other hand, are the coddled progeny of middle-class families" (21). Hecht focuses on children living in the street in Recife, but his analysis also grasps, as well, the elements of struggle faced by children living within favela households. Some of these children live in home situations that may put them at risk or in unbearable conditions that eventually lead them to opt for the street, despite the dangers. Da Matta's (1991a) classic distinction between the *casa* (home) and the *rua* (street) in Brazilian cultural life applies well here. In this division, the home is the female domain; it is identified with a hierarchical and personalistic moral world, whereas the street is both more egalitarian and more individualistic. The street is a place of danger and excitement where hierarchies are suspended: the poor rob the rich, women flirt with men, the young deviate from parents' rules, and people of color disobey white people. While Da Matta's scheme holds to a certain extent, there is more to life on the streets that begs consideration. The street is also a place where unprotected women become vulnerable. It is often subject to the logic and rules, as well as the revenge cycles, of gangs.[18]

Hecht (1998:108–9) extends Da Matta's distinctions in an attempt to explain, from the perspective of the poor, the relationship between impoverished children—nurturing children—and their mothers. For the poor, children can be understood as an economic asset, and many take on the role of providers within their own homes and see this as a virtue

(Hecht 1998:81). He accurately notes that "home" and "street" are notions that also apply to these relationships. Thus, being at home can refer to being with one's mother (or mother figure), "'helping' one's mother by doing things in the home she wants done, accepting her advice and discipline, and augmenting the family income" (109), and even going to school. Street life is, from these children's perspective, a betrayal of their role in the matrifocal household (197). Being in the street can signify a number of scenarios, including actually living in the street, getting into trouble in the street with either gangs or police, or even being subjected to one of the state's institutions. Further, impoverished mothers in the favelas deeply fear that some of their children will find the street more attractive than their crowded, destitute, and sometimes contentious households. These women often initiate harsh forms of discipline in the hopes of keeping their children in line and off the street.

MIRELLI'S STORY

I had heard about Mirelli from Glória for many years but was able to meet her only in 1998, when Glória and I spent a few days at her house during the final games of the World Cup soccer tournament. Mirelli, Glória's favorite goddaughter and cousin, had been born in Rocinha but had spent much of her youth in FUNABEM. She now lived a few hours from the Zona Sul in a colony of people afflicted by Hansen's disease and their families in Itaboraí (a suburb of Niterói, on the outskirts of Rio; see maps 3 and 4).[19] Mirelli was living with a man whose parents had Hansen's disease and who, as the only son, had inherited (while they were still alive) their pretty little house and yard. In the *colônia* (colony), as it was affectionately called, there were research facilities and a hospital, as well as a small community of modest, well-kept houses. They were similar in size to many of the houses in Felicidade Eterna, but they were all sturdily built, with cement walls and floors, and each had a sizable backyard with enough room for fruit trees and a little garden, giving the place a decidedly more rural feel. Mirelli's life history is fascinating because it provides a sense of how the state's institutions, such as FUNABEM, functioned. But it also sheds light on FUNABEM as a tangible symbol for the poor, showing how Glória and others like her evaluate the role of the state in their own lives and the lives of their children.

Mirelli's story highlights a number of themes that run throughout this chapter and throughout the book in general. Her childhood is an example of how vulnerable anyone—whether a child or a woman—can be when they are literally placed out "on the street" and of how female children in particular, whether in unstable family situations or actually out on the street, are preyed upon by men. Her story also bears witness to how cruel, at times, the state's own institutions can be.

Mirelli's story begins with the event that turned her own mother's life around. Mirelli's father "lost" her mother in a card game called *ronda* or *baralho;* this humiliating defeat meant that her mother had to sleep with the man he lost to. From that time on, she drank heavily and lived as she pleased, rotating her affections between Mirelli's father and several other men. Mirelli's father was an educated man who worked at a decent job in the Rio Prefeitura (city hall). Like his wife, however, he also had given himself over to drinking. Because both parents were alcoholics and they had no stable place to live, Mirelli and her two sisters, Josefa (who was older) and Denise (who was younger), lived mostly on the street, sometimes killing their hunger by eating leftovers from the garbage cans behind the luxury hotels in São Conrado, an area adjacent to Rocinha in the Zona Sul. When Mirelli was six years old, her mother died, and Mirelli's destiny was decided by the circumstances of her extended family. Mirelli's father was deemed incapable of taking care of the three girls on his own. One of the other two men who had been partners with Mirelli's mother was willing to raise the three girls, but Quitéria, Mirelli's maternal grandmother, stopped this from happening because she suspected that "he wanted to raise them for him," in other words, that he only wanted to raise them in order to have them (sexually) later on.

Mirelli confirmed Quitéria's suspicions later in life when she realized that this same man would come and flirt with her and her sisters when they returned to Rocinha for visits. She also remembered that one of the men who was an occasional partner of her mother's used to pass his hands all over her and her sisters while he was making love to their mother, and that her mother was usually so drunk she did not realize what was happening. Mirelli is grateful to her younger sister, Denise, for saving her and Josefa from more extreme forms of sexual abuse. Denise, an infant at the time, would always cry in bed, thus making it difficult for anything more than furtive groping to take place.

Mirelli feels that she never really experienced a childhood. During many of her early years, she and her sisters intermittently slept on the streets or with whomever their mother had found that particular evening. Mirelli believed her mother gave the men she was with the liberty to seek pleasure from her daughters as well, creating for Mirelli a sense of ambivalence at the time of her death. Her mother's occasional life on the street put Mirelli and her sisters at greater risk of physical vulnerability because of how they were perceived by others. They were seen as girls of the street—without the protection of a man or a family and thus open to sexual predation. Hecht (1998) finds that girls are more physically vulnerable than boys on the street because the street is seen as transforming girls—even very young ones—into *mulheres,* or sexually initiated women:

> I believe that, on balance, life in the street tends to be even harder for girls than for boys, not only because of their greater physical vulnerability but also because of social expectations in Brazil about girlhood and boyhood, about the street and about the home, and about the gendered nature of public and private space. Girlhood is typically more closely circumscribed, more inimical to the street, more closely allied to the home. The street is perceived as a threat to the moral values adults seek to inculcate in children, especially to those of girls, for whom contact with the street is apt to transform them from *meninas* (girls) into *mulheres* (sexually initiated women). (20)

When their mother died, Mirelli and her sisters hoped that their grandmother Quitéria would take care of them permanently, but she was still raising some of her own children (she had sixteen in all), and those who were left in her household at the time did not want her to take on the additional responsibility of caring for her grandchildren. For a time, she sent Mirelli and her sisters to the home of one of her oldest daughters, Maria Antônia. Maria Antônia had been raised in the home of a *madame* (here meaning an upper-class woman) since the age of ten and was, because of this experience, the most different of all their blood relatives. She had been given to the woman of a wealthy family as a kind of daughter—but also a servant—at a time when Quitéria could not care for all her children. Maria Antônia grew up in one of those strange in-between situations where she was not quite a full family member, but over the years she had become identified fully with this family and acquired some of the habits of the upper classes. In her house, everything had to be in its place, and there were many rules about bathing and eating. Mirelli and her sisters feared that they could never live up to her standards, and ultimately, Maria Antônia decided that she could not take on the full-time responsibility of raising three girls who had lived so many years on the street. Quitéria reluctantly had to give in to Maria Antônia's request to send them to a *colégio interno*—FUNABEM.[20]

The entrée to FUNABEM was "deceiving," according to Mirelli; during the first three months, all three sisters were placed in a temporary *triagem* (selection and sorting) area until an opening became available in one of the permanent institutions. They had to lie and say that their father had died, something that still pains Mirelli because "he was *safado* [screwed up], but he gave us more mother-love than our mother did." The triagem took place in a clean, well-equipped facility in Laranjeras in central Rio, whose grounds had a swimming pool, tennis and basketball courts, and an area for learning knitting and sewing. The dormitory rooms were clean and tidy, and the dining hall had real plates—not plastic ones—and utensils, meaning knives and forks. During these three months, the girls learned how to eat with a knife and fork, and they were taken on excursions around Rio de Janeiro. Although they were sad to be there, away from their grandmother and their familiar surroundings, they got used to it. What they did not know at the time was that this was a temporary facility and that after three months they would be transferred to a completely different institution, one that would leave them with the sense of having been permanently punished.

Mirelli and her sisters were notified that they would be transferred to a FUNABEM in the Zona Norte, an area known as Campo Grande. The facility was crowded and dirty, and everything they had learned in terms of personal cleanliness and personal space in the Laranjeras facility was undone there. There were many more girls to a room than could comfortably fit. Bedding and clothes were changed only on a monthly basis rather than weekly. In this institution, the utensils were plastic, and the girls were expected to eat everything with just one spoon. They were allowed to bathe and change their underwear only infrequently. According to Mirelli, the women in charge were punitive and authoritarian, and the girls were beaten, often for no reason, until they had large bruises on their bodies; some of the women used their position of power to abuse the girls sexually. Mirelli described the relations within the institution as similar to gang rivalries on the outside. Each of the four administrators had control over a group of girls; each had *seguranças* (girls who acted as security guards for them); each held absolute power.[21]

Inside this institution, Mirelli completed the fourth grade of *primário* (elementary school), which was as far as one could go there.[22] Although this is not a highly advanced level of education, it is for a person with Mirelli's life history. Her reading and writing abilities far surpassed those of others who have had a similar level of public schooling on the outside, and she has held better-paying, higher-status jobs as a result. But Mirelli felt that she was a prisoner during her childhood, and she hated her years in FUNABEM. When she was finally permitted to leave, she was quick to make a life for herself on the outside. She lived for a short time with Quitéria and then with Glória; by the age of fourteen, she started having her own children. In 1998, when I met her, she was in her midthirties and had a stable family life with a partner of six years with whom she was raising her five children. Even though Mirelli's story had a happy ending, she is still bitter about her experience, a bitterness that confirms for Glória her own strong sense that these state institutions are breeding grounds for criminals—as dangerous as life on the street. With both Mirelli's stories and her own experience with Pedro Paulo on her mind, she resolutely decided to rescue her nieces and nephews after her sister's death and bring them into her home.

LUCAS'S STORY

When Celina, Lucas's mother, died, the rule of thumb for how to best care for all her children was to divide them up so that each child would go to the home of his or her respective godparents. Here was a case of a death that initiated a pattern of what Claudia Fonseca (1986, 1995), working among low-income households in Porto Alegre, has termed "child circulation" or "child shifting" *(criança em circulação)*. This was an ideal solution given that none of the immediate relatives or individual godparents could afford to care for all of Celina's children together. In Lucas's case, he thus went first to his godmother, Aparecida, his father's sister. Lucas's experience proved unlucky in this household. While he was living in Aparecida's house, he lost 1,000 cruzados—a good sum of money at the time, I was told—and Aparecida's husband wanted to give him a serious beating. Aparecida helped remove Lucas far from the wrath of her husband, taking him to the house of Rosineide, her husband's sister, another aunt. But Rosineide's family lived at a level of poverty that was extreme even by Glória's standards. Rosineide's six-year-old son actually gave his baby brother away to a stranger in exchange for a package of biscuits while his mother was trying to procure rice on credit at a nearby store. This shocking story, which became legendary among members of Glória's family, followed Lucas around like a bad penny over the years. Once it was even broadcast on a radio show called "Where Are My People?" that many people in the shantytowns of Rio listened to. It seemed never to be forgotten that Lucas had lived in conditions of acute poverty, even more extreme than those of Glória and her family. It was in the midst of this desperation that Lucas's future was being decided.

The plan had been to put him in a colégio interno, only because the family could not afford to keep him. Glória, having heard about Lucas's impending fate, wanted to save him. Rather than allow Lucas to suffer in such a place, she chose to track him down and bring him to live with her. Glória found Lucas in a desperate situation:

> I arrived there, and it was difficult to find the house because that favela had no electricity or anything and the people were saying, "Don't go that way, it's really dangerous, go this other way." Finally, at nine in the evening we managed to arrive at Rosineide's house. It was sad for us to enter.
> Look, it was dark there. They didn't even have a candle for lighting. Only water in the house. When I arrived, there was a man on the bed [Rosineide's husband]. He was a pure skeleton. A skeleton in bed. I said, "Clovinho, *quem te viu, quem te vê?*[23] What's happening with you, Clóvis?" "Ahh, Glória, it was a gulp of café I drank, a prepared drink.[24] After this gulp of café I never got out of bed." Now, that was a café that they gave him from a *macumba*.[25] And he drank it. It was meant to kill him, but he didn't know it. He died [later]. . . . And I said, "So where's Lucas?" Yellow, my daughter, and without any clothes to dress him in. Lucas only had a little green or yellow shirt, so I grabbed it. I stole Lucas away.
> Lucas must have been about twelve years old, it seems. He's been with me now for more than five years. He must be eighteen, or seventeen by now. . . .
> So I brought Lucas home. I got home and the children were here. And they said, "*Mãe* [mother], where did you get this little boy?" "Where did you get this little boy?" And I said, "Ahh, my daughter, I found him in the street, poor little thing, he doesn't have a mother and he is hungry." (Glória, taped interview, 1992)

As it happened, Lucas's siblings—Cláudia and Alexandro—had already been taken in by Glória, but because they had been separated from Lucas at a young age, and because he was so badly undernourished, they could not recognize him. Glória had emphasized that in the house he was living in, there was not even any fubá (maize flour), a traditional filler food for the desperately poor. The agreement had been that each month Aparecida, Lucas's true godmother, was to bring Rosineide's family a kilo each of beans, sugar, rice, wheat, and fubá to help with the cost of keeping Lucas. But because there were already eight other children in the house, this food could not go exclusively to Lucas, and in fact it did not go very far at all. Glória was so emotionally affected by the level of poverty in Rosineide's household that, later, she got together the members of her *sindicato de cachaça* (her alcohol-loving friends whom she lovingly named "Cachaça Union") to collaborate with her and collect some items to bring. With their help she was able to put together a bundle of items, including toothpaste, toothbrushes, rice, beans, coffee, and a couple of bags of clothes.

> I took all of this to Copacabana and worked and from there I got the bus and went alone with Falecida [No. 2, Filomena] and God to Cesarão (a location in the Zona Norte). I left there at five from Copacabana to get to Cesarão. When I got there, we had a party with all of these bags of food and clothes. The kids were *doido* [crazy, mad with enthusiasm] with the food. I even brought him a three-piece suite of white linen. And he said, "Glória, as soon as I get better, don't worry, I am going to help you with the children." In that time, three *contos* was money, and I gave him three contos and I filled the house with food.[26] Milk, everything I brought. Everything, everything, I brought. Girl, he was so happy with all of that! The kids were happy. It was two or three months later that I heard that Clóvis had died. The kids were thrown all over the place. There were two who went out on the street to sniff glue, the two eldest. (Glória, taped interview, 1992)

When Glória arrived home with Lucas that first night, she purposely held off telling the other children immediately that he was their relative and, for some, a sibling:

> I said, "Do you know this little boy?" [They responded,] "Uuuueee *tia* [auntie], ohh *mãe*, didn't you say you found him on the street?" I said, "I got him. Do you know who he is? He is your brother, son of your mother." Ahh, my daughter [referring to me], everyone began to embrace and to laugh and that same beauty lasted a week, until later they started fighting. And then the fights began, with one implicating the other and another saying things like, "You were found in the garbage. My mother found you in the garbage." And then a fight would start. (Glória, taped interview, 1992)

Through these stories, it became well known to all that Lucas had come from an extremely impoverished situation. In fact, he barely survived at all, except for the tenacity of his aunt Glória, who had once dreamed that her beloved sister Celina requested that she promise to care for her children when Celina was no longer able to do so herself.

THE EVERYDAY LIFE OF CHILDREN

Most days in Felicidade Eterna were interminably long and often boring. Glória went off early in the morning, and after the children finished their breakfast of coffee and bread, they had to bathe and complete their chores before starting their day. Back in 1992, Zeca, Félix, and Soneca were still attending school—either the morning or the afternoon session. Zeca was a mediocre student but passed his classes; Félix did very poorly in school and repeated the same grade a number of times. Tiago, Alexandro, and Lucas figured out sometime before eighth grade that they did not like school very much, and they had found odd jobs as helpers in car shops. Mostly they cleaned up and ran errands in these shops for spare change, hoping that with time they would be able to become apprentices and eventually learn car mechanics. These jobs were only intermittent and were scheduled for only a few hours a day, so by the afternoon those children who were not at school would be lounging around in the shack, escaping the heat of the afternoon sun. The boys would be sent out to buy food or to borrow items such as garlic or salt from a neighbor. Soneca attended evening classes, and so she and Anita were in charge of getting the shack cleaned up after breakfast, making sure everyone had clean clothes. They were responsible for preparing the midday meal and for making sure that everyone had eaten. Soneca also watched Nelsinho for Elis while she was off at her stable, well-paid, but long-houred job as a chef. Elis usually paid Soneca in kind for her services and occasionally paid her cash. Because Nelsinho was just a toddler at that time, he was often the center of attention around Glória's shack on these days, passed around among all the children so that Soneca could get her cooking, cleaning, and washing done while still keeping an eye on him.

Zezinho, Glória's on-again, off-again partner during this time, had been left to care for his own six children after his first wife, Lucina, ran away with Sandrão a Policião (Big Sandra the Policewoman). It was said that Zezinho was abusive toward Lucina and that he had caused his own fate. Glória's house during these years became filled with children who depended on her and her minuscule wages for their daily subsistence. By contrast, Zezinho, who worked occasionally as either a handyman or a security guard in the middle- and upper-class apartment buildings in Rio's Zona Sul, spent a good portion of his own meager wages on alcohol. When they lived solely with him, Aguinaldo and Emílio rarely attended school. They had dropped out of school when their mother left home and instead preferred to walk a mile or two to the nearest large grocery store and offer to help customers carry packages, guide them into parking spaces, or demand pay for guarding their cars while they were inside shopping. They looked like any of the "street kids" one sees in large urban centers. These marginal activities allowed them to bring some money home to Zezinho, which he often used on himself. In Zezinho's family, the children were practically the main providers. In classical psychological terms, they were "parentified" children, or, in Hecht's terms, "nurturing children." They even contributed on Zezinho's

Figure 10. Inside Glória's shack, Félix ironing his clothes for school. Photograph by author.

behalf to Glória's household, and his children continued living with Glória for more than a year after she and Zezinho split up. During all this time they spent in her household, she pleaded with them to attend school, but they were too embarrassed to go. Glória attempted to put them back in line when they came to live with her, and she bought them new school uniforms and shoes, but she often lamented that they, too, had become too accustomed to the street.

During Glória and Zezinho's often turbulent and unstable relationship, the two families would merge, eating and sleeping together, and whenever Glória and Zezinho fought or seemed to be splitting up, Zezinho's children made it clear that they wanted to stay with Glória and her family no matter what the outcome of the argument between Glória and Zezinho. They knew that there was never anything to eat in Zezinho's house and that, because of this, they were forced to beg on the streets, eat the scant refuse from the waste of restaurants, or depend on the endless goodwill of other families living in Felicidade Eterna. Glória fed them and was a "real" mother to them. The worst thing that could happen to one in the world, they would say, was to not have a mother. Glória, for her part, was willing to be a mother, but she also made demands while Zezinho's children were living in her home. Mostly, she wanted them to go to school and to help with chores around the house; she wanted them to stay out of trouble and to bathe before eating their afternoon meal. During their years with Glória, Emílio and Aguinaldo continued to work out on the street. And while Glória appreciated their contribution to her household expenses, she preferred that they go to school.

In any case, whether for pragmatic or other reasons, Glória took pity on Zezinho's boys, and although she was already responsible for eleven children at the time, she adopted Zezinho's two boys after she had split from Zezinho for good. As Glória would often say, "The same pot that feeds eleven can feed thirteen." She offered this even though in order to fit into her shack, everyone was forced to sleep head-to-toe and on their sides, huddled together like spoons. This kind of invitation was characteristic of Glória, and many in Felicidade Eterna recognized her as a person who was generous with the few resources she had. Many in the community also saw it as a big task to "educate" these children, given that they had now become used to spending so much time out on the street. Glória's own children already knew what was expected of them and were able, for the most part, to follow her house rules, although they sometimes, as I will illustrate, suffered from her strict approach to childhood discipline. All of Glória's retraining did not seem to stick, however. When

I visited in 1998, I found that Emílio had joined a newly formed local gang and was a minor drug dealer.

Aguinaldo, who in the interim had been adopted in by Mocotó, was teetering between joining his brother Emílio on the streets and staying with Mocotó. According to Soneca, Emílio had also been temporarily adopted in by Mocotó, but the situation had not worked out for him there. Mocotó, however, had better luck for a time with Aguinaldo, whom she attempted to put on what she considered a good path. She often lamented that despite her provisions for his schooling, and despite her membership in one of the evangelical churches, Aguinaldo still seemed to find the street attractive. Aguinaldo could not seem to completely abandon his brother, and Emílio's life on the street often drew his attention.

Glória was a hard taskmaster and drill sergeant, I discovered over the years. Indeed, she was considered by many people in Felicidade Eterna to be rather "strict," and some even considered her abusive.

THROWING OUT ONTO THE STREETS

Glória was just as likely to throw a child out onto the streets as she was to adopt one in. During my stay at Glória's home, I witnessed an episode in which Glória, in the end, expelled one of her own young daughters (aged fifteen) onto the street, thereby exposing her to a series of dangers and hardships. The events that led up to the expulsion were simple enough. While Glória was drinking at Joana's Bar in Felicidade Eterna, the children got into an argument in the shack, and Filomena, Glória's fifteen-year-old daughter, threw a high-heeled shoe at Alexandro (Celina's son), causing a gash in his head. Alexandro, holding a T-shirt filled with blood and accompanied by Tiago, Glória's son, and Roberto, Alexandro's brother and a tough, muscular youth, found Glória at the bar and told her what had happened. Roberto warned that if Glória did not "break Filomena's face," he was going to do it himself out on the street. "Nobody sheds the blood of my brother," he kept repeating. He told me, "She can't make my brother bleed and have nothing happen to her." "But," I interjected, "isn't she sort of a sister to you, too?" He answered, "No, she is only my cousin. Alexandro is my brother." I was surprised by the importance this detail represented both to Roberto and, later, to Glória, and how it influenced the manner in which Glória chose to deal with this conflict.

When Glória arrived back at the shack, Filomena had a blank look on her face and sat immobile on the bottom of the bunk bed. Filomena had been hit by a car earlier in the week, and one of her legs and one of her arms were in plaster casts. Glória rushed to grab the cutting board from the kitchen and came in with the board lifted above her head, ready to strike. She started to scold Filomena, waving the cutting board above her head, while Filomena watched her, sitting and staring blankly, practically lifeless on the bed. At one point Filomena muttered, *"Eu nunca gostei de você"* ("I never liked *you*"), and it was this phrase, especially the use of the disrespectful pronoun *você*, that seemed to push Glória, still slightly drunk, over the edge.[27] Glória, meanwhile, kept repeating the phrase, "Nobody makes blood flow in my house." Only by pleading with her were Elis, Glória's neighbor, and I able to get Filomena out of the house without her being severely beaten. After that night, Filomena was referred to humorously as "A Falecida Dois" (The Second Deceased), and she was not allowed to return to the house.

Obviously, many events and personalities preceded this episode, and there are a variety of possible explanations for what happened on this particular night. Filomena was not the first to be thrown out, and she probably would not be the last. "A Falecida Um" (The First Deceased) was Fernanda, the daughter Glória had thrown out of the house years earlier because Glória caught her sending love notes to Glória's lover at the time. When I met Glória, Fernanda's name was practically taboo in her home, and Glória thought Fernanda was working as a prostitute in Copacabana. Glória, however, regretted her own early mistakes with Fernanda. When Fernanda was a young girl, Glória had sent her off to live with an aunt—Glória was young and destitute and focused on caring for her younger children and decided to let somebody else help raise Fernanda. Fernanda spent her youth drifting between different households, finding her way back to Glória's home for brief periods. She never stayed long, and when she was caught flirting with Glória's boyfriend, she was banished permanently from the household. When Fernanda finally reunited with Glória and the rest of her half siblings years later, she was already an angry *(revoltada)* young woman who felt she had been cast away. While Glória believed that Fernanda was living as a high-class prostitute in Copacabana, Soneca and Anita, who maintained more contact with Fernanda, interpreted her situation as one where "she has a few white kids and is living with a *gringo* [foreigner, white person] in Copacabana."

Unlike her decision with Fernanda, Glória's choice to expel Filomena from the house was an impulsive one. Years earlier, Glória had briefly thrown Filomena out of the house, and Filomena sought refuge in the house of her aunt Andira, who lived in Rocinha. There was an almost tacit agreement between Glória and Andira at that time to perform this role for one another. In turn, Glória later allowed Andira's child (Glória's nephew) to hide out in her shack during one of the many gang wars in Rocinha. Essentially, Filomena found protection from Glória's temper in the same way that Glória's nephew found refuge from the violent gang wars. This time, however, Filomena was not allowed to return to her Aunt Andira's house and wound up at the home of her boyfriend, Adilson.

Preexisting relationships play a very important role in understanding the motivations that led this mother to send one of her teenage daughters out onto the street. What I understood from this experience was that in order to keep the "larger peace" within this singularly impoverished and tiny space, Glória was forced to run her home strictly and with little room for disobedience. When at various times I tried to plead on Filomena's behalf that she not be banned from the house permanently, attempting to reason with Glória that "Filomena was just a child," Glória made it clear to me that, in her mind, Filomena was *not* a child. Filomena had broken the rules by bringing the violence of the street into the home, and Glória was not willing to tolerate this behavior, at least not from Filomena, who, at fifteen, was considered by Glória to be an adult, responsible for her own actions and able to take care of herself. People in the favela who knew Glória and her family understood that she worked hard to feed her family; thus, they were reluctant to judge or criticize her actions. Many neighbors felt that at some point Glória could have forgiven Filomena and permitted her to return to the house, but Glória chose not to do so for well over a year. Given that Filomena had only a few people outside of her home on whom she could rely, including her boyfriend, Adilson, and her Aunt Andira, it was possible that she would spend much of her time "on the streets," with all the danger this entails. Later, Filomena told me that a male relative of Adilson's approached her sexually soon after she had been kicked out of Glória's house and while she was temporarily stationed at Adilson's home. The man later explained to her that he assumed she was the type of woman who was accustomed to this sort of advance—that she was *da rua* (of the street).

Glória needed to leave her children by themselves for sixteen or seventeen hours a day, and, as she repeated many times, she did not want to come home one day and find some of them dead. Also, she was forced, it seems, to prove to the children who were not fully her "blood" that she was willing to defend them even from one of her own children. What can we possibly learn from the cruel and potentially dangerous punishment that Glória meted out to her daughter?

In this case, the perpetrator was given the worst punishment of all— banishment from the household and exposure to the dangers of the street. In Glória's eyes, Filomena was no longer a child, and therefore her "sentence" remained unmitigated. Glória's reasoning regarding Filomena was devoid of the therapeutic discourse that characterizes North American and upper-class Brazilian notions of childhood. The concept of adolescence and adolescent rebellion as we know it in the United States is missing from Glória's understanding of Filomena. There are, instead, other contemporary influences that serve to maintain the habits and punishments that, while not necessarily representative, fall within a broad spectrum of acceptability.

In contrast to the survivalist strategies of the working classes, the Brazilian middle and upper classes are quite enamored of psychoanalysis and appear, in some respects, more like their French counterparts than their own impoverished compatriots, who have never heard of psychoanalysis. While certain segments of the middle and upper classes are known to be highly therapeutic and psychologizing in their approach to social life, those in the poorer classes do not share in this approach.[28] Instead, these impoverished working classes focus on how to survive in a harsh world. This survivalist ethos leads, in turn, to some rather harsh forms of discipline and punishment. To Glória, Filomena was already an adult acting irresponsibly, and her bad behavior was judged in this manner. In referring to Filomena as "The Second Deceased" rather than by her name, Glória was emphasizing that Filomena was no longer a child, and that she had profoundly transgressed Glória's rules for belonging to her household.

Another example of Glória's survivalist ethos is illustrated by the case of Marta. The last one of Celina's children to be found and then taken in by Glória, Marta was rescued from her pitiful situation in 1992, during a time I happened to be living with the family in Felicidade Eterna. Marta, aged sixteen, had actually already been a street child and beggar for years, according to Glória. She had somehow been separated and completely cut off from her other siblings (Lucas, Alexandro, Roberto, and Cláudia) at the time of her mother's death. Glória was determined, however, to unite *all* her sister's children in her own household. Shortly after Marta's rescue, Glória began complaining that the girl was going to be a difficult project to take on because she was so accustomed to living on the streets. Even Glória's generosity was sobered at times by the realization that Marta would be difficult "to train":

> Marta was a beggar, she was a street kid. She slept on the street. She slept on the street and asked people for food. . . . After so many years, she still wanted to come and live here with us. . . . She is really a good kid, but she isn't in the rhythm, you know. She never had any person caring for her. She was a beggar on the street and never had that kind of care. She didn't have a roof over her head, not even a plate of food to eat. Now she does. But whose head do you think she fell on? In the hands of Glória. Now she has a house. What is mine is theirs too. She knows now that she is together with her blood. (Glória, taped interview, 1992)

Glória felt that taking Marta in off the streets was the right thing to do. In 1992, during the Christmas holidays, and shortly after Marta moved in with the rest of the family, Glória found Marta a temporary job as a domestic worker and babá in the house of one of her clients in the Zona Sul. Marta cried because she would have to spend the holidays away from her recently rediscovered family. Glória stood firm, however, and insisted that Marta go because this client had children who had to be taken care of properly. When I asked about their ages, I found that Marta was going to prepare food and care for children who were approximately her own age, a detail I found to be both ironic and tragic.

Glória reasoned that Marta needed to be learning how to earn a living, and Glória herself was already working in the home of another client during the holidays. What Marta perceived as a kind of punishment, Glória considered part of a necessary training and initiation into a work ethic that she felt Marta needed to counter the influence of so many years on the streets. Her intention, of course, was to teach Marta how to survive and to earn a living for herself, but I could not help being sorrowful about the fact that rather than get to spend her first Christmas with her recently reunited family, Marta would instead be expected to care for the children of the wealthy.

Pierre Bourdieu (1984) highlights the influence of a therapeutic discourse, particularly psychoanalysis, in creating a particular ethos toward child rearing, one that is common among the French middle and upper classes. This therapeutic ethos, "with its psychobabble of 'liberationist' commonplaces ('father figure,' 'Peter Pan complex,' etc.), credits the child with a good nature which must be accepted as such, with its legitimate pleasure needs (for attention, affection, maternal care)" (368). Brian Owensby (1999) makes a series of accurate observations about middle-class Cariocas and Paulistanos (natives or residents of São Paulo) up to the 1950s, capturing the position of this class within the developing national political scene. Owensby found that despite being the beneficiaries of modernization, the middle class found itself unable to articulate its power within the political scene.[29] Owensby points out that having given up on the idea of class conflict, these middle-class citizens instead seemed to turn inward, emphasizing individual striving at work and at home and attaining satisfaction in these arenas rather than pouring themselves into what seemed like a political abyss. Likewise, it would not be too much of a leap to notice that throughout the late 1970s and 1980s, when the economic crisis was acute in Brazil, this same middle class, disappointed by the political system but still seeking inclusion in some version of Brazilian modernity, may have found refuge in individualistic forms of help such as psychotherapy and other psychological forms of intervention. Owensby hints at this process himself in the closing pages of his book.[30] This inward turn is just one characteristic that seems to have solidified and become a sustaining aspect of middle-classness throughout the 1990s. In Rio de Janeiro at least, one sign of this development is the middle class's fascination with a range of spiritualities, as well as a range of psychotherapeutic practices (see Figueira 1985). One only has to look on the Web sites related to psychotherapy in Rio de Janeiro to get a sense of how deeply professionalized a wide range of therapeutic options and practices has become.[31] Another way to think about this class-linked penchant for psychoanalysis and other psychotherapeutic discourses is in terms of Foucault's (1980[1978]) reflections on the processes of professionalization as they occurred in Europe in the late 1800s, and how the most rigorous forms of repression were actually applied to the privileged and politically dominant classes, rather than the laboring classes. It is not that the lower classes are not subjected to medicolegal institutions (witness the institutions for street children, for example); rather, particular forms of psychotherapeutic treatment are purely middle- and upper-class habits, something indeed foreign—in both language and logic—to my friends in Felicidade Eterna.

Scientific psychology[32] and therapeutic discourse,[33] as they are currently practiced by the middle and elite classes, presently have little impact on the lives of individuals in Felicidade Eterna. Despite Glória's daily contact with the ethos of the middle and upper classes, she adheres to her own form of justice and her own expectations of her children. Her discipline is speedy, extreme, and nonnegotiable, and it is interpretable as part of a broader ethics of care that Glória feels she needs to provide to ensure that her children survive within their present context. In Marta's case, Glória felt that she needed to put her in the "rhythm," meaning getting her used to a life of hard labor, feeling that this was the only way that Marta's training on the street could be undone. Glória's own strategies are not so different from those of many of the charitable institutions and nongovernmental organizations (NGOs) that Hecht (1998:174–87) describes, whose mission is to transform the lives of street youths through hard work. The discourses of salvation and recuperation with regard to these particular youths are strikingly similar. These discourses promote the idea that through strict discipline and hard work, everything can be accomplished. Gloria, too, believed that she could transform the future of her children through discipline and hard work.

EATING SHIT IN A FAVELA

Glória's children would sometimes share their humorous stories—which were also thinly disguised complaints—about Glória with me while she was out working and there were no other adults around. As with many of the stories I was privy to in the shantytown, these often had an edge to them; they were told while laughing, but could also have easily been told while crying. Telling "funny stories" about pain and tragedy was part of the shared emotional aesthetic of black humor that I now fully participated in. So whenever the children began to speak of their earlier years, I would brace myself because I knew Glória had been a tough taskmaster.

The children told me stories about Glória and her past lovers and of the various punishments they had received from these outsider adults. These stories were told not only to amuse me but also to make some declarations about Glória. The children were eager to communicate how the situation I was witnessing in the early 1990s was different from the lives they led when they were younger, and how time had mellowed Glória. Soneca told me of the time that Lucas, shortly after being rescued from Rosineide's house, defecated in the bed at an age Glória considered beyond "normal," and how Glória made him eat his own excrement when he awoke the next day. But the punch line of Soneca's joke was not that Lucas was made to eat the excrement; the punch line was that he was made to lick his lips and say "Mmmm" out loud—as if it tasted good.

Then there was the case of Tiago, who, passing through a late childhood phase of bed-wetting, was once made to parade around the neighborhood with a wet, urine-stained bedsheet around him, sucking on it. Glória had indeed mellowed considerably by the time I met her, but she still defended some of her harsh disciplinary measures (now in the distant past), explaining that certain behaviors from an older child were simply unacceptable and meant many hours of cleaning and work—labor she did not welcome given her already daunting work schedule. It meant hand washing in cold water in a tiny basin and hanging out to dry the sheets and foam pieces they all slept on, causing disruption and discomfort for everyone else in the crowded shack.

When I confronted Glória with the recollections of her past behavior and methods of punishment as remembered by her children, she tried to explain her frustration at the time at being what she considered the only civilizing force in the household. She wanted to teach her children that they were not animals and that to survive they would have to learn to behave in human and adult ways. There was not much time to be a child. She wanted to teach her children how to survive and, more important, how to be *gente* (people). By doing this, she was also taking care of them, preparing them for the world at large.

I heard other stories about Glória's disciplinary extremes. One told how Glória once purposely burned Alexandro's hand on the stove after discovering that he had stolen money that had been set aside for a wedding gift. In later years, Glória punished a household thief in what her children considered a more humane manner. After Emílio had stolen some money, the other children reasoned with Glória and convinced her that she should punish him by making him pay it back, rather than by beating him up. Glória agreed, and so Emílio had to go out and work, guarding the cars of shoppers for days until he earned enough coins to replace the stolen money.

Glória attempted to keep close tabs on all her children and tried to keep them near home or within familiar territory where they would be safely removed from the trouble on the streets. Glória always worried that one of her male children would be in the wrong place at the wrong time—or simply done away with by police or *os capuzados* (the hooded ones), a commonly used term for off-duty police who functioned as death squads. Her children sometimes went out in clothes that were tattered or dirty from play, and Glória worried that they could easily be mistaken for "street children." Her children, in turn, were terrified of being picked up by the police because, as they had discovered themselves, even when no crime had been committed, police interrogations were frightening and usually punctuated by both verbal and physical abuse. The following experience of Tiago and a few of his friends was commonplace. They were once picked up for no reason and taken to the police station, where they were questioned in a threatening manner and verbally abused. They were released within a few hours, but in the process the police robbed one of Tiago's friends of his boom box.

When Félix began to look more like a young man, Glória asked if I would accompany her to the necessary administrative offices to obtain a *carteira de identidade* (identity card) for him so that if he ever were stopped on the street, he would have documentation proving that he was under eighteen and a legitimate member of a household. Félix had always been a bit sloppy with his dress, and also tall and very thin; most important, he was very dark-skinned, a characteristic that made him particularly vulnerable. Glória understood the code very well; Félix had the look—from the perspective of the police (and therefore to some extent the middle and upper classes)—of a young *malandro* (scoundrel, thief), someone who might be up to no good. Glória continually worried about his fate, and she hoped he would never be in a situation of mistaken identity.

Over a period of a couple of days in August 1998, I thus found myself with Glória and Félix waiting in an interminable line in a documentation office located in the Zona Sul to obtain Félix's identity card. We learned the first day, after standing in line for more than four hours, that we did not have some of the documents required to issue the identity card, so we had to come back a day later and wait all over again. We eventually emerged from that office with Félix's identity card, and right away, Glória began instilling in him the idea that he needed to carry it with him at all times—that it could save his life.

THE "PROTECTION" OF CHILDREN

Glória's children believe that one of the reasons their mother had mellowed since moving to Felicidade Eterna was because the chief and gang leader of the favela, Dilmar, made it known that in his territory there were to be no child beatings. To Glória's children, this mandate from the boss made him into a local hero. To Glória, however, he represented the threat of one more of her children "going bad." One of Glória's key motivations for being a harsh disciplinarian is that she believes it will keep

Figure 11. After a long wait, Glória finally obtains Félix's identity card. Photograph by author.

her children not only in line but also out of prison and alive. She also encourages them to do "honest" work, the grueling minimum-wage work of the poorest, so that they do not get involved in the gangs that represent the most obvious alternative to unemployment. Glória's world is divided into bandits and honest workers.[34] Her ultimate goal is to discipline her children—through harsh physical punishment and harsh words—into becoming honest workers. Glória constantly uses Pedro Paulo as an example of what the others should strive not to become— dead in the street.

There is a great deal of truth to Glória's fears that if she cannot keep her children "in line," some of her boys, despondent about their prospects for low-paying wage labor, may find it preferable to join the local gang and get involved in its activities. Although the favela gangs rule through violence, fear, and terror, they often provide the only economic stimulus available to poor communities. In addition, they often are perceived as protectors, especially against enemy gangs; in the particular case of Felicidade Eterna, they were often perceived as a "protector" of children, as Dilmar's antibeating command demonstrated. Glória attempted to appear more terrifying than the gang leader in the

hope of dissuading her children from disobeying her and joining this attractive but dangerous alternative, doing her best to ensure that her children went to school, and forbidding them from spending too much time
away from the shack, on the street, fraternizing with the "bad elements"
in Felicidade Eterna. Glória simply says that she wants her children to
survive, to remain alive and outside of jail; thus she demands that they
grow up fast, go to school, and find "honest" work. From her perspective, "nothing bad is intended" by her harsh disciplinary measures. In the
words of the old adage, she is "being cruel in order to be kind" in the
only way she knows.

CHILDHOOD, OPPOSITIONAL CULTURE,
AND THE IDEA OF RESISTANCE

I want to return here to Pedro Paulo's assessment of honest work. Everyone he knew who labored in honest professions, people like Glória and
Zezinho, were working in situations close to slavery. He considered this
work humiliating and repulsive, with little chance of advancement. As an
intelligent young man with access to the mass media and to the lives of
os bacanas, those living the good life in the Zona Sul, Pedro Paulo
wanted to grasp some of that good life for himself. In some ways, Pedro
Paulo's preference for toting a gun and tolerating the dangers of gang life
parallel rather than contradict the middle-class disgust toward manual
labor. While I do not know whether Pedro Paulo ever held an "honest"
job, I do know that early on he felt comfortable on the street, and he was
seduced by the idea of "easy money," a concept that honest workers
often use in expressing the ethos of those whom they perceive as bandidos. In many ways, Pedro Paulo's choices also echo those of the young
Puerto Rican immigrant men described by Philippe Bourgois (1995),
who perceive the low-paid service work available to them as a form of
"slavery-ing."[35] Pedro Paulo's particular choice, whether seen as resistance or as oppositional culture, produces some unintended consequences. Young men growing up in these circumstances have an extremely high mortality rate. In Rio's poor neighborhoods, homicide is the
leading cause of death for young men between the ages of fifteen and
twenty-four.

Glória's regime for "rescuing" children is distinctly the opposite of the "giving up" process that Scheper-Hughes describes in *Death without Weeping* (1992). Rather, it is an extreme and paradoxical expression of "holding on" to a child. Glória is trying to make sure that her older children have the skills, including the obedience, humility, and even the subservience necessary for a poor, dark-skinned black person to survive in urban Brazil. Whether her methods work may be questionable. Nevertheless, these hopes are embedded in her actions. In the case of Lucas, at least, she could not force him to become an "honest" worker. As with Pedro Paulo, his calling was *na rua* (on the street).

Inscribed in Glória's behavior is an attitude concerning the training that needs to take place early if children are to survive, before they grow up and become untrainable adults. Her home is a revolving door of extended family where her blood kin, fictive kin, and the hungry can find shelter and be informally adopted in and cared for. It is also the home from which one can all too easily be thrown out for a minor infraction, as in the case of Filomena.

It is not surprising that Glória's method of disciplining her children, that of "being cruel in order to be kind," while perhaps being logical and reasonable within a survivalist ethos of child rearing, may actually backfire. Glória's techniques of discipline did not entirely pan out as she intended. Pedro Paulo found a stronger calling on the street than for minimum-wage work. Fernanda, who circulated into the more economically stable household of one of her aunts, turned out to be an angry young woman, eventually seeking a vengeful satisfaction in the seduction of one of Glória's lovers. These outcomes parallel, in many ways, the unintended consequences of gang culture, which is, in itself, a powerful example of oppositional culture, with its unintended consequence being the early death of the participants. Glória's techniques may not always have worked, but most of her children chose "honest" work over gang culture. Roberto, for example, was on his way to entering a stable career in a management position, and Tiago and Alexandro were hoping eventually to move out of their mechanic apprenticeships into full-time work.

The children of the poor are not treated as children except at the youngest ages. While these children are entering the labor force, often before it is legal, and learning what it means to work hard for low wages, their counterparts in the middle and upper classes shun manual labor of all kinds and, unlike their European and North American counterparts, never work at minimum-wage or low-wage labor jobs, not even as apprentices. Middle- and upper-class youths, however, similar to their European and North American counterparts, do experience class-appropriate forms of adolescent rebellion—experimenting with drugs, sex, and alcohol, for example—none of which endanger their class privilege. In Felicidade Eterna, and in the surrounding neighborhoods of the Zona Norte and Zona Oeste, the funk dances and the violence associated with competing funk *galeras* (gangs based on funk dance membership), perhaps function as a muted form of youth rebellion.[36] But it is the youth gangs themselves, as I have referred to them here, whether in the form of the more imperialist gangs such as the Red Command or local gangs, that are an ever-increasing option—one of both crime and resistance—for angry male youths, and so they are now a problem for the middle and upper classes, as well as for mothers like Glória.

Despite everything, Glória manages to maintain a strong sense of family togetherness. The cruelty of Glória's punishments needs to be interpreted in a way that also recognizes how much she sacrifices and how hard she works to keep her family together and put food on the table. I have tried to paint a sympathetic portrait of Glória despite my own initial feelings of disgust about her methods of punishment. I wanted to offer some alternative explanations to the academic and upper-class discourse about child abuse that would blame Glória and others like her for personal failings that may be better understood as caused by broader and more complex social problems. Glória will not be able to abandon the harsh survivalist ethos that drives her to inflict cruel punishments on her children until the social and economic conditions in her life allow her to live without chronic hunger and deprivation, and until real alternatives—beyond serving the wealthy for minuscule wages or joining the favela gang—exist for her children. Glória knows well that the life of children who somehow wind up on or choose the street is a short one, as the life and death of Pedro Paulo ultimately illustrate.

In 1998, during my last return visit before completing this book, I asked Glória about how each of her children was doing. I paused before mentioning Lucas because I knew he had always looked up to Pedro Paulo and had been serious about his desire to join the gang. I feared that his life was a precarious one. Glória found my concerns appropriate but told me that Lucas was alive and well and still working as a bandido. She then added some information that contributed a new dimension to the sense of Lucas that I had developed over the years. According to Glória,

Lucas had made a not-too-serious threat on her life recently because he believed that long ago Glória took some personal financial gain from what he imagined was his *herança* (inheritance). When Glória uttered the word *herança*, we both burst out laughing because of the well-established and horrifying facts surrounding Lucas's childhood. Our laughter was a mixture of comedy and tragedy, however, since it was unpleasant to think of Lucas toting a gun. I wondered if his threats were truly idle, as Glória seemed to indicate they were. The idea of guns in the hands of angry young men was an alarming prospect, and I realized that sometimes even tough women like Glória cannot convince young people that there are other alternatives. This story also made me wonder whether Glória's approach to "childhood discipline" was doomed to fail. I doubted that her promise to repay one form of violence with another was an effective way of gaining trust, loyalty, and love.

CHAPTER 5

State Terror, Gangs, and Everyday Violence in Rio de Janeiro

Life, in short, was becoming abnormally normal, taking on at the same time certain extravagant aspects.

Euclides Da Cunha, *Rebellion in the Backlands*

Celso called me from the orelhão to let me know that there was no reason to fear coming back to Felicidade Eterna. "It was just a little accident we had here, Danni. I cleaned up all the blood and put roof tiles on top of the blood-stained areas. *Tá limpinho, tá limpinho* [It's clean, it's clean]. You can come back now." Then he laughed, knowing that what he said would strike me as a bit absurd and would do very little to calm my nerves. The day before I had been out at the favela, and everything had seemed fine—nothing out of the ordinary. Everyone I knew was still alive. But that night, Adilson, Glória's ex-son-in-law, was shot in the back of the head eight times, his blood running along the lanes beside the shacks I knew well. Celso, Adilson's compadre, pulled himself together after the murder and cleaned up the blood-stained areas before the authorities came. He and everyone else knew that the local gang had killed Adilson, but there was nothing to be done about it except to keep a *boca fechada* (literally, a closed mouth, silent). The favela's "law of silence" stood firmly in place after Adilson's murder. Talking about his death could easily provoke another one.

I begin this chapter inspired by the death of a young man—Adilson—whom I had come to know well over the years. His was but one violent death among many I heard about during my years working and living in Felicidade Eterna, but his was the closest, the one I experienced most personally and most viscerally. During my fieldwork, I had often made the observation—and seen the relevant statistics—that an inordinate number of young men came to violent ends in favelas, and like many other researchers I had wondered why. With the death of Adilson, I asked the question again, this time more personally. In this instance, I accompanied Filomena, Adilson's ex-wife, who like so many of the women I had come to know in Felicidade Eterna had asked this question out of a sense of personal loss and grief. Out of grief. *Why do so many young men in Rio's shantytowns die violent deaths?* Unfortunately, the answer is harder to come by than it might first appear.

Understanding violence within a specific population requires theorizing violence and learning about the actors who count in the neighborhoods where this particular kind of violence takes place. I begin with the obvious—the idea that violence is unequally distributed throughout Rio de Janeiro, with poor neighborhoods and shantytowns experiencing the highest levels of violence on a number of different scales. This is readily illustrated with survey research and census-type data that differentiate homicide rates by neighborhood. But exactly who the actors are in these pockets of violent activity is not immediately clear.

CRIME AND VIOLENCE IN RIO DE JANEIRO

Contemporary Rio de Janeiro is a city of extremes that provides abundant visual clues of class and racial antagonism. Rio—quintessential Brazil—is one of the most unequal cities in the world, and crime and violence in their many forms are experienced and commented upon across vast divisions of class. Rio's Zona Sul is characterized by elegant apartment buildings with security guards and a middle-class and elite population that has become increasingly obsessed with crime, violence, and fear of the street. The middle- and upper-class preoccupation with crime is apparent in the never-ending "talk of crime," which "feeds a circle in which fear is both dealt with and reproduced and in which violence is both counteracted and magnified" (Caldeira 2000:19). In her book *City of Walls: Crime, Segregation, and Citizenship in São Paulo,* Caldeira writes about crime as both a "disorganizing experience" and an "organizing symbol."[1] It would be easy to infer from this "talk of crime" heard among the middle and elite classes that they themselves are actually experiencing the most extreme forms of crime and violence. Despite their own sense of vulnerability, however, the middle and upper classes have relatively little exposure to the kind of violence experienced by the poorest. Their fear of crime is real, but the everyday structure of it is not the same, as I will illustrate.

Certainly, this talk of crime is essential in creating among the middle and upper classes both the stereotypes and the prejudices that associate residents of favelas with crime and with these classes' growing sense that their own public space is shrinking. In fact, the average middle- or upper-class Carioca who knew that I was a foreigner working in a favela was shocked to find that this kind of work was even possible. Large favelas are strikingly visible from most parts of the Zona Sul; they have a reputation of harboring petty thieves, as well as more serious criminals, including participants in the drug trade. But they are also known to be the homes of domestic workers, the cooks, day cleaners, and nannies who service the same wealthier classes. Additionally, vast North and West Zones are expanding with the growth of both lower- and middle-class neighborhoods, low-income housing developments, and squatter settlements that include both newer and older favelas, of which Felicidade Eterna is one. These settlements in the North and West Zones contain large class differences even within them, but from the perspective of those living in the elegant Zona Sul, the entire area seems unknown, dangerous, and crime-ridden.

During my first extended period of fieldwork, in the early 1990s, I experienced Felicidade Eterna as a remarkably safe place. My experience there was similar to that of Janice Perlman, whose classic work about three Rio favelas, *The Myth of Marginality: Urban Poverty and Politics in Rio de Janeiro* (1976), describes them as "internally safe and relatively free from crime and interpersonal violence" (136). As a foreign researcher, I felt safe in a small shantytown where everyone knew who I was. Nevertheless, in the years that followed (during return visits in 1995 and 1998), I realized that the peaceful moment I had experienced in Felicidade Eterna during the early 1990s was not necessarily a stable one. Felicidade Eterna experienced distinct cycles of calm and violence that were not immediately perceivable in one time period. In those later years, residents described to me a feeling they had that their situation was deteriorating, referring to what they perceived as an inability for the honest worker to remain outside of the cycles of violence that plagued these areas. Residents felt that the violence of the 1990s was becoming increasingly unpredictable, drawing in targets and victims who had nothing to do with drugs or violence.

During my return visits, I discovered that there were many sorts of relationships that had to be precariously balanced to achieve periods of peacefulness such as the one I had experienced in the early 1990s. For one thing, having a local gang that was led by a reasonable person was key to the stability and safety that residents of Felicidade Eterna experienced at that time. Later, when the boss was killed and younger, less reasonable men took over, there was less predictability and stability. These poorest working-class sectors experience levels of everyday crime and violence that are in a completely different realm from those experienced by the middle- and upper-classes. In turn, such everyday experiences of violence have compelled these populations to embrace solutions that seem paradoxical but, upon closer examination, make good sense, given the absurd situation they find themselves in (stifling poverty, profound class inequities, alarming levels of domestic violence, naturalized racism, and so forth).

Although talk about violence and crime proliferates across classes, the forms and levels of daily violence and suffering in the city are experienced differently according to class, race, gender, and location. As Anthony Pereira (1997) explains, the rule of law, so often touted as the measure of a consolidated democracy, is applied differentially in Brazil.[2] One of the reasons such a wide gap exists between the universalism of formal legality and the actual extension of citizenship rights is due to the country's hugely inequitable economy, statistically represented in its extraordinarily high Gini coefficient (0.63), which surpasses those of both South Africa and India.

Pereira (1997) dubs the differential application of the rule of law "elitist liberalism," or "the granting of the right to civil liberties on a differential basis depending on some aspect of the person's social status and identity (be it neighborhood, profession, skin color, gender, or something else)" (9). This elitist liberalism is not merely some conspiracy of the middle and upper classes against the poor to hold back the consolidation of democracy; deeply rooted (hegemonic) historical and structural factors make a transition to a more inclusive liberalism difficult to achieve.

THE LOCAL GANG AND ITS LEADER

During the early 1990s, when the favela had no more than a few hundred residents, the gang in Felicidade Eterna consisted of Dilmar and four young men. Very soon after I started visiting her in the shantytown, Glória insisted on bringing me by Dilmar's tiny shack and making the appropriate introductions. His name was often spoken in a whisper, as if to mention him at all was to ask for trouble. In his midthirties, Dilmar was tall, charming, and handsome, with olive-colored skin. He seemed to hang around the shantytown most days, making many *psssssiu* sounds signaling to passersby with whom he had business. Dilmar, like many in Felicidade Eterna, shuffled around the hardened dirt alleyways, which turned to mud during the rainy season, in his trademark yellow flip-flops. The only sign of wealth I could see was the expensive-looking watch on his wrist, and I was surprised to find that his shack was almost as bare as Glória's—it had a stove, a bed, and a slightly better television and stereo system, but not much else. If Dilmar was making money from his position as gang leader, he was not investing it in his daily life in Felicidade Eterna. Because I had seen the homes and sensed a different kind of wealth among the members of the larger, more imperialist drug-trafficking gangs in Rocinha and Vidigal—mostly members of the Comando Vermelho—I had expected him to be better off economically. His wife was younger than he was, and pregnant when I first met him, but if I had not been told that he was the *chefe* (boss), I would never have guessed it from his appearance and his home.

After introducing myself as an anthropologist and outlining, however feebly and inadequately, what anthropologists do, I explained to Dilmar that I was interested in writing about how the poorest segments of the working classes in Rio live, and that I was especially interested in the lives of women like Glória. Dilmar thought it was a fine project and gave me the names of some of the elders who had participated in the first land invasions in Felicidade Eterna and who could provide me with some "local history." He also asked that I not take pictures of him or his *turma* (group), a request I readily agreed to. From that afternoon on, I would obligatorily nod to Dilmar whenever I passed the corner of his shack. He seemed to be pleased to help me in my request to "hang out" in the favela, and because I spoke mostly with women, he was satisfied that I was not a snoop or a spy for the police.

AN OVERVIEW OF GANGS

When I started my fieldwork in Felicidade Eterna, I was naive about the role of gangs in the shantytowns; I had a somewhat general notion about them as being the local power brokers and as providing some kind of local-level protection, but I did not really understand their significance. I did not realize how and to what extent gangs intervened in all kinds of family and lovers' feuds, how they mediated relations with the local police, and how they kept other gangs from invading or from using Felicidade Eterna as a drug-selling site. Although many residents felt ambivalent about the local gang, they also recognized the importance of having one.

The danger of writing about local gangs in favela contexts is that such work could unintentionally reinforce the standard and erroneous position of middle-class and elite Cariocas who consider the favelas to be the breeding ground of all criminal activity. In response to that belief, I emphasize what most shantytown residents already know—that middle-class and elite drug consumption and the international drug trade ultimately fuel gang activity. This is not to say that gang activity would disappear if the drug trade dried up—the gangs perform functions well beyond their involvement in trafficking illegal substances.

Drug consumption among the poorer working classes is perceived and practiced differently from that among the middle and upper classes. For the poorest, such as those who make up the majority of residents in Felicidade Eterna, all drugs are viewed as problematic because their use usually signals a connection to the local gang and the drug traffickers in some form or another—through either membership, indebtedness, or addiction. Users who have no interest in other gang activities can unwittingly become involved with the gang simply to be able to supply themselves with the goods. Thus, drugs have a more dangerous feel to those among this particular population than the recreational and bohemian meanings they hold among the middle and upper classes. In this context, a person spending money or going into debt because of a drug addiction is automatically seen as *metido* (involved), unnecessarily endangering him- or herself and, possibly, his or her family as well.

The gangs have a seductive quality that goes beyond their involvement in the drug trade. For many young men, they offer a place of belonging and a sense of identity that low-paying (and sometimes humiliating) service sector employment does not provide. In Felicidade Eterna and other shantytowns I came to know, drug traffickers offer work to young, unemployed males, thereby seducing them into their gangs with the offer of comparatively decent "wages."

Among the gang members I knew, there was a distinct awareness of the inequities of the Carioca wage system. They had seen their parents, and especially their mothers, slave hard at the very bottom of the hierarchy of working-class jobs. They had watched older men work a lifetime at backbreaking jobs for low wages, and many of them had opted quite consciously for the life of a gang member. According to the U.S. Department of State summary of Brazilian government statistics, the monthly per capita income for white males is 6.3 times the minimum wage; for white women, 3.6 times the minimum wage; for black men, 2.9; and for black women, 1.7.[3] Given such statistics, I propose that, in many cases, gang members' decision to join a gang and their anger against the wealthy bacanas were based on a clearheaded analysis of the injustice of the system.

The gang's presence, in addition to being a seduction, was also a nuisance for some young men because it meant they had to watch carefully to stay out of the business of the gang. Roberto, Glória's nephew, would never leave the shack when he was home on visits from the army. He was so intent on not becoming involved that he barely let anyone else in Felicidade Eterna know that he was there. His strategy was to stay out of sight. As a young, strongly built, dark black man intent on finishing his time in the military and on securing a decent job, Roberto fastidiously avoided all contact with young people, especially young men, in Felicidade Eterna. He became identified with the forms of masculinity promoted by the military, even though he often commented on how much he resented the fact that he had to spend a good chunk of his youth there. The gangs also offer a space within which an ethos of masculinity can be enacted (see Zaluar 1994:101). In Felicidade Eterna, upon joining the gang, a member was given a gun of his own. When Lucas, Roberto's half brother, joined the gang in Rocinha, he was extremely proud of the fact that he now had access to a weapon.

DRUG-TRAFFICKING GANGS IN THE RIO CONTEXT

The presence of the drug-trafficking gangs of different organizational structures and sizes in Rio's favelas is extensive in terms of control even though most residents are not involved in the trafficking or in any other illegal pursuits.[4] The residents do, however, have to cope with the gangs' presence and with the absence of the rule of law, which is inextricably tied to the police's routine treatment of the poor as criminals. This process is cyclical. The presence of gangs in the favelas has provided legal and moral justification for the government's use of excessive force. Intermittently throughout the 1980s and 1990s, some of Rio's largest favelas could be characterized as internal war zones where the military police, as state representatives, were called upon to show their power and force as more consequential than those of the chefes, as the drug lords are called, who control the *bocas de fumo* (literally, mouths of smoke), the points of sale for distribution of marijuana and cocaine. The logic of the use of force by the state to control what appears to be a state of emergency has been normalized in everyday discourses. Favelas and other peripheral neighborhoods are seen as high-crime areas and perceived to be controlled by drug traffickers. The government, backed by popular sentiment, attempts to capture the traffickers and to return these neighborhoods to the state.[5] From the perspective of residents, however, the prospect of being returned to the state is not necessarily any more attractive than remaining under the control of the gangs.

In favelas such as Felicidade Eterna, the drug chiefs are important local figures; they are often homegrown and locally based, and, as is well known, they provide badly needed services—for example, housing and cash in times of emergency—as well as a form of employment for youths. Despite the fact that there is much more to the story than this materialist reading of the relationship between favela residents and their local gangs, it is relatively easy to explain why the gangs have a more sympathetic profile than the police.

As a result of power struggles within the local gang and challenges from outside gangs, between 1991 and 1998 the favela experienced cycles of violence and relative calm. My initial perceptions of Felicidade Eterna in 1991 as a wholly calm place were based on just a moment in one such cycle. Return visits in 1995 and 1998 altered that perspective considerably. During this brief period of seven years, a number of young men from the shantytown had died violently, primarily at the hands of other young men.

Felicidade Eterna originated as a land invasion sometime around 1978. It was said that a few strong men, some of whom had guns and most of whom were migrants from Northeast Brazil, stood guard on the grounds and protected the new residents from other invaders and from police. This piece of land was known to be owned by the municipality, and it was purposefully targeted for an invasion, the early invaders believing that since it was a public area, they would not face intense opposition. The piece of land that was to become Felicidade Eterna was also quite small, another reason given by residents who could remember for why they were ultimately allowed to stay. The few residents I found who had been present during the initial occupation remember the evenings when gunshots were exchanged, but for the most part, the invasion was peaceful.

Throughout the 1970s, many favelas were actually undergoing removal, a policy promoted by the authoritarian politics that had been installed beginning in 1964 with the military coup.[6] Felicidade Eterna was under construction in the late 1970s and early 1980s, just as the political climate was changing. Leonel Brizola, the populist politician from the

Figure 12. Operation Rio outside a favela in Rio's Zona Sul. Photograph by author.

Partido Democrático Trabalhista (PDT; Democratic Labor Party), was elected governor of Rio de Janeiro in 1982, and favela residents generally consider his term in office (1982–86) one that was more sympathetic to the needs of the poor. Although his political activities and his enormous popular appeal throughout his career are indeed complex, Brizola is nevertheless fondly thought of by residents of favelas, and in Felicidade Eterna his governorship rather magically is credited with having enabled the favela to stabilize and survive.

Eventually, the barreira to the favela was drawn, and the squatters were left alone to build their shacks just up to that line. On some evenings in the early 1990s, there would be stationed a single military policeman across the barreira, ensuring that the remaining vacant land was not invaded. Together with his group of four young boys from the favela, Dilmar and his gang earned, at least among some residents, the reputation of being "good bandits." Many residents perceived them as being either *vagabundos* (vagrants) or *viciados* (addicts), interested only in "easy money," but the general presence and actions of these young men were seen as normal aspects of community life. Every community had a few young men who preferred petty crime to low-wage work. Since these local gang members were boys who had grown up in the favela, residents were not necessarily too troubled by their presence. As a group, with Dilmar as their leader, they took it upon themselves to "protect" the favela from other outside invaders who might want to use it for drug dealing or gun battling—a fate that seemed common to any favela that appeared to be vulnerable or without its own security structure.

Residents generally thought it worse to have outsiders coming in to control things, a situation they had experienced during periods of instability and therefore preferred not to deal with again. The local logic on this issue dictates that protecting the favela from outsiders—intruders and bandits from other favelas—is of utmost importance (Zaluar 1994:79). In this insider-outsider dichotomy, it is the outsiders who are likely to *sujar a área* (literally, dirty the area; commit a crime).[7] The community residents believed that at least their boys would not "dirty" their own favela, and it was hoped that their mere presence might prevent others from doing so.

A CHRONOLOGY OF POLICE-BANDIT RELATIONS: LULU AND IVO

Before Dilmar's time, there had been Ivo, who was considered one of the founding fathers of the favela (and the local *dono* [literally, owner] of Fe-

licidade Eterna at the time), and his "counterpart," Lulu. Lulu was remembered long after his death as the corrupt civil police officer in charge
of the area who would charge Ivo a "protection" fee for his operations.
Even after he was dismissed from his official job, Lulu still considered the
favela his own personal territory. Lulu terrorized it throughout the
1980s, extorting money on a weekly basis from Ivo, demanding his share
of any profits derived from drug dealing and other illegal activities, and
making a theater of terror when things were not working to his satisfaction. One afternoon, Lulu came to the favela to confront Ivo, who
was late in making a payment. To show Ivo and others in Felicidade
Eterna that he was not to be crossed, he shot a dog and drank its blood
in full view of many residents. The next time Ivo was late with a payment, Lulu arrived and shot him in the face while he was brushing his
teeth. Eventually, and to the satisfaction of many, Lulu was murdered at
a nearby pagode (local popular samba club). Those who witnessed his
death remember that while he was lying in a pool of his own blood, a
number of men stepped up to urinate on his face. He was a much-hated
figure, and there was a great sense of relief in Felicidade Eterna after his
death.

Lulu, it turns out, came from an entire clan of civil police officers. His
sister, nicknamed by the residents "Katy Mahoney" after a popular
North American television police drama personality, still occasionally
appeared (at least up through 1998) in the favela. It was said that when
she arrived, everyone would scurry inside. Her "method" was to grab the
young, strong men on the street and to smell them to see if they had been
smoking marijuana or sniffing cocaine. If she found them to be guilty of
the offense, she would beat them up with whatever she had in her hand,
which was usually her gun. According to the residents, she used her *arma*
(firearm) with much greater "efficiency" than any of the male civil police officers. She would come around looking for bandidos, and they, in
turn, were all terrified of her. She was a minor character in the local authority structure but a presence nonetheless—familiar because she belonged to Lulu's family. She was respected for being a tough woman who
knew how to use force but who, despite her toughness, did not murder
anyone. In this way, her reputation was distinct from that of her brother
Lulu, whose only remembered feature was his marked corruptness.

Isadora, who was one of the founding "invader" residents of Felicidade Eterna, recalls the end of the Ivo-Lulu era (1980s) and the usher-
ing in of Braga (early 1990s), a tough but respected civil police officer
with his own distinct style of rule:

It was a marvelous year after Ivo died. Nobody took over. There were no invasions. It was a year of total peace. It was a paradise here in Felicidade Eterna. Nobody. Nothing. A year of peace. It was a very good year. This was around 1989–90. . . .

Then, they started to come, some guys who had been released from prison. They started to come here to "measure" things—to see where there were escape routes—and it started again. They were from outside. . . . At every corner in every place they were with a bag selling drugs. On bicycle or in cars, pretty girls and nice-looking boys [meaning rich people] came by in their cars. Then the boss comes and collects the money—the same as in a bank. Each one giving their part, putting it in a bag and giving it to the boss. There were those that would earn thirty, forty, fifty each day. . . . They were not from the area. It was a kind of invasion.

. . . The evangelicals were praying [to get rid of these guys]. One killed the other. It was a killing among themselves, they went on killing, killing. Between themselves. Not involving us. Without involving residents. That was it. Then the police started to come and get them. Braga came. It was the "Era of Braga." Braga cleaned up everything. He got rid of it all. . . . (Isadora, taped interview, 1998)

The consensus about Braga was that he saved Felicidade Eterna from the chaos of a complete takeover; whenever residents spoke of him, there was a sense that he cleaned up the area—in a tough yet respectable way. Apparently, Braga was promoted through the ranks in his work, and, in a soap opera–style ending, he wound up marrying Dilmar's ex-wife and caring for Dilmar's children:

Braga doesn't play to lose. He has three or four cars in his garage—all new. Today he is a sergeant. He doesn't like bandidos, nor the women of bandidos. He cleaned up the area. He would come to my shack and say, "Eu vou limpar a área de vocês." [I am going to clean up your area.] This is what he said. "Pode ficar tranqüila, Senhora." [You can be calm now, ma'am.] It is Braga who hooked up with Dilmar's woman. He lives with Dilmar's wife. Married. He even has a child with her. He takes care of all of Dilmar's children. If one of them becomes a bandido, it is because they are themselves bad because Braga is after them, ohhh (snapping two fingers together). . . . Braga only killed bandidos, minors no. . . . If you shot at him, he would go after you to kill you. . . . He moved his post to a better one, I don't know where. (Isadora, taped interview, July 1998)

This reflection on the "era of Braga" exhibits certain typical attitudes of residents of Felicidade Eterna who, given their own experiences with a wide range of police-bandit relations, feel secure within the boundaries of a certain kind of relationship. Here, the existence of outsider drug dealers invading the favela epitomizes a dangerous situation, whereas the existence of Dilmar, a "homegrown" leader, was not threatening in the same way. In fact, what made Braga a particularly good policeman in the eyes of many residents was the fact that he could distinguish between "invaders" and "the local gang," and between real bandits and children getting into trouble. Likewise, a good bandit such as Dilmar is able to nurture a certain kind of relationship with a policeman such as Braga, protecting the favela from unnecessary but commonplace police brutality. He seemed to be able to avoid serious problems with the police by paying them off appropriately and keeping his operations small enough to not be of any interest to the larger drug-trafficking gangs. It was alleged that Dilmar was so congenial and so good at smoothing out difficult relations that it was at a small party he hosted in his shack where the policeman Braga was introduced to Dilmar's ex-wife (who appeared at the party as a friend). Braga dated and eventually married her.

By the time Dilmar took over as dono of Felicidade Eterna in the early 1990s, residents understood that their own peace was correlated with that of the local gang, because when the gang did not pay enough corruption money, the police would come around looking for trouble. Whenever Dilmar needed money to pay off a particular civil police official, residents who normally tried to distance themselves from illegal activities would lend him money simply to keep things peaceful and stay on his good side. Dilmar always paid the residents back, a rule of courtesy that not all chefes necessarily abided by. Additionally, by the standards of the local population, Dilmar and his local boys were considered a decent group, consistently warning residents to take children off the street before shoot-outs began. He would, as was part of the job, offer any empty shacks to families without a place to live or would lend them materials so that they could build a shack of their own on any scrap of vacant land in the favela.

Dilmar was eventually murdered by members of his own gang because they believed he was planning to betray them. After murdering Dilmar, his four young assassins ran away temporarily, fearing that the policemen loyal to Dilmar would *marcar eles de morte* (mark them for death).

A NEW DONO

Breno, the principal planner behind Dilmar's murder in 1994, went into self-imposed exile after the murder, later landed in jail, and while he was there wound up becoming friends with a man from an adjacent favela, Vila Maria. He sent a letter to some of his friends in Felicidade Eterna, ordering them to make alliances with the gang in Vila Maria, a group widely known as Amigos dos Amigos (ADA, or Friends of Friends). But a local gang from yet another neighboring favela, which called itself Colégio das Árvores (Tree High School) after the school located in its neighborhood, had already claimed Felicidade Eterna as its territory during the lingering moments of uncertainty after Dilmar's death. Thus a low-level gang war erupted. During these battles, residents would be warned to get off the streets, and, within minutes, shooting across the rooftops would begin. These "little" wars, as they were sardonically referred to by the residents, were still taking place as late as 1998, even after Breno had completely lost control of the local gang. This was because in the wake of Dilmar's death, nobody except Breno—known to be a hotheaded adolescent—had stepped forward as the dono, thus leaving Felicidade Eterna vulnerable to outside invasions. At least, this is how people living in Felicidade Eterna explained it.

After finishing his prison term, Breno returned to Felicidade Eterna to assume his role as a dono of sorts, counting on the distant support of this outsider gang. He eventually helped consolidate ADA's power within Felicidade Eterna and then was expelled from the gang as a result of his own foul play. After stealing a car and selling it, instead of splitting his profits with the rest of the ADA gang as was expected, he bought his mother a television set and a few other household items. Although Breno was forced to leave Felicidade Eterna, his mother and the rest of his family were allowed to stay. Because it was only Breno who had crossed these gang members, no punishment of his family took place. Such was the general rule, although it did not always hold true.

Soon after Breno's expulsion from Felicidade Eterna in 1995, his younger brother, Jairo, was murdered. According to residents, one afternoon, three men dressed in jeans and claiming to be civil police officers entered the favela with *escopetas* (short rifles or carbines).[8] They began asking people who the dono was. One resident told the men that this was a favela of workers, not criminals. Another resident told the first one to "shut up," that the men "were just doing their job," and that "they knew who they were looking for." Indeed, they found Jairo, Breno's fourteen-year-old brother, who had been in the drug business only about three months, working as an *aviãozinho* (literally, little airplane, but also meaning little drug deliverer). They asked Jairo who the dono was, but he would not tell them. The men asked the other youngsters they had gathered up with him if Jairo was a *vapor* (drug delivery person), and somebody in the crowd nodded, indicating that he was.

Then they walked Jairo up behind the favela to an open field where they could not be seen; there they executed him, shooting him at close range in the head.

BANDITS, POLICE, "POLICE-BANDITS"

Residents were confused about who actually carried out this murder. When asked, nobody was sure whether the executioners were bandits, police, or "police-bandits." The term "police-bandits," as used by the residents of Felicidade Eterna, referred to their own sense of the inescapability of violence in their world. They were aware of the violence of the gangs and the normalized and routine corruption of police, but police-bandit seemed to mean something more. It seemed to refer to the possibility that both of these entities inevitably played by the rules of revenge and personal reputation, and their blurring signaled the recognition by residents of the dysfunctionality of the justice system. All three categories were used interchangeably in 1998, suggesting that the players had become hybridized to such an extent that nobody was certain who were bandits, who were police, or who were both.

Alba Zaluar (1994:32) notes that while Rio's gang culture is a form of organized crime, it lacks the centralization and organization—and therefore the connection with the state—that other historical forms, such as the Sicilian Mafia, maintained. The difference stems from a number of factors, including the fact that each local gang *(quadrilha)* has to maintain its own local base of protection and is not guaranteed protection by the larger, richer traffickers. So, while the police view the poor as criminals, the worker who is poor sees the police as colluding with criminals. When I asked residents directly why these men had killed Jairo, who obviously was a small-time player in the drug war, they offered what seemed to them to be obvious explanations. Those who believed the men were police assumed they wanted to know who the dono was, because "if they get the dono, then they get *grana boa* [good money]." "You know," I was told repeatedly, "these guys earn more from corruption money than they do from their own salaries." Those who thought the executioners were other bandits assumed that they killed Jairo because his brother, Breno, had cheated the big guys out of the money in his greedy car deal, and Jairo had been chosen to pay for his brother's sins. Those who thought the men were police-bandits implied that the latter wanted to control the drug trade in the area themselves.

The term "police-bandit" captures the sentiment that what is taken for granted about police is their absolute corruption.

REVENGE PRACTICES

In areas such as the one encompassed by Felicidade Eterna and its neighboring communities, violence and murder are used by both bandits and police in the course of ordinary business. Revenge is a stand-in for a legal system that is absent or dysfunctional. Because of the absence or corruption of the state, the gangs play a major role in providing a form of justice that many residents not necessarily involved in illegal activities themselves are willing to see administered. Cycles of revenge between gangs, between individuals in a personal conflict, and between any two partners who do not see any other justice system taking over help to explain the absurdly high death rate of young males in the poorest neighborhoods.

Intimate relations exist between police, bandits, and local small-scale drug traffickers in Felicidade Eterna. Individuals are considered good or bad bandits, good or bad police. There are police who are bandits, and bandits who are police. In this economy of revenge, both bandits and police acquire identities, reputations, and personal fame. The actions of any person or group are perceived and interpreted in local terms by whether or not the appropriate target is hit, as well as whether or not the actions serve to protect the local from other outside forces. Personal fame can be either negative or positive: if the "correct" person is punished, one is granted a kind of positive fame; if "innocents" are ruthlessly murdered, a kind of negative fame is achieved. It has become increasingly unclear to residents during any particular incident whether the violent actions were meted out by police, bandits, or "police-bandits." Examples of this blurring are already well documented by human rights organizations.

Many members of the police work during their off hours as death-squad members, settling personal vendettas or completing business that may have started during their official hours. Human Rights Watch/Americas (1997:17–18) refers to five types of police brutality in one of its recent publications; "police-bandits" would seem to parallel what they refer to as the fourth type, one that involves off-duty police killings "either to resolve personal vendettas or in response to some minor provocation or inconvenience."[9] In the local vernacular, the term "police-bandit" captures the sense of the breakdown of the rule of law in the poorest neighborhoods, making clear the corrupt nature of the police and lending credence to Guaracy Mingardi's (1998) contention that the system must have the blessings of the state if the interpenetration between police and bandits is in practice so extensive. But local populations have their own day-to-day issues that they need to solve and for which they rely on whatever local authority structure happens to be in place at that moment. The following sections describe the types of activities in which gangs are likely to become involved.

Some activities are what one would expect—protection from outsider gangs and small-scale drug trafficking—but others could be described as "private" matters. The greater the inability of the state to provide a policing and a legal system that works, the more other entities become involved in practically institutionalized ways; that is, there seems to be a tendency to seek immediate attention for a grievance, and the local gangs that are firmly embedded in communities are willing to take on these sorts of hard issues. This means, then, that in addition to carrying out the expected activities of a gang, they are also involved in resolving daily injustices in the local arena. Because the code of justice is dependent on the personalities and caprice of the leaders and gang members of the moment, there can be no true predictability or continuity to the way affairs will be solved. Often, situations are likely to be resolved by brute force or murder. And, because leadership lacks predictability and continuity, people get the sense that one can never tell what kind of justice will be administered at any particular moment.

THE SOLUTION OF "PRIVATE" MATTERS

Brazilian state and municipal authorities are particularly uninvolved in addressing an entire host of problems that people living in Felicidade Eterna must deal with on a daily basis. In countries that have social service systems, sexual abuse and violence are addressed from within the system. These are affairs that in the context of the favela border on what many people consider to be private and therefore outside of the legal system. Nevertheless, without social service institutions of the state made available to these populations, and without a reliable policing system, these kinds of problems create their own cycles of revenge and involve the gangs as on-hand substitutes. The following examples, in which local justice was meted out by the local gang, the police, or some combination of the two, shed light on the role of the gangs and on the complicated nature of police-bandit relations.

Sexual Abuse

In 1998, it was discovered that a man in Felicidade Eterna had been sexually abusing his two stepdaughters. For two years he kept them locked inside his shack, not allowing them to go outside or to attend school. His attitude, according to one of his neighbors, was that he was not going to "fatten them up for somebody else to eat *[comer]*."[10] The word *comer* is also used colloquially to mean "screw," and he meant that he was not going to support the girls financially so that some other man could have the (sexual) benefit of them. The man's wife was from the northeastern region of Brazil, and she was perceived by others in Felicidade Eterna as being too afraid to denounce him, a stereotyped vision of rural women from Northeast Brazil among Rio-born urban dwellers.[11] When word of this abuse reached the local gang, gang members went to his home and severely beat him, eventually expelling him from the favela and finally threatening him with death if he returned. In the community there was a general consensus supporting the gang's actions. Residents felt that there was no other way to get rid of a criminal of this sort, defending this point of view with statements such as *"Tarado tem que morrer mesmo"* (Rapists of children rightly have to die). If they had wanted to, or if the personalities in the leadership perhaps had been different, the gang members might have killed him with the support of the entire community.

A Case of Adultery

Adriana, a neighbor of Glória's and the common-law wife of a man named Ciro, was having an affair with a young man in Felicidade Eterna who was also in a common-law marriage. Ciro discovered Adriana's infidelity after months of suspecting it, and when he caught her lying about her whereabouts, she bluntly declared that she had fallen out of love with him. Ciro, in the heat of a cuckold's rage, sought immediate revenge and called upon the local gang to beat up Soni, Adriana's lover. It complied with his request, honoring his feelings of having been wronged, and prohibited Soni's return to the favela. Adriana chose to flee with Soni, and they left Felicidade Eterna together.

But the beating did not satisfy Ciro's desire for revenge. Later, Ciro and his mother-in-law's boyfriend entered Soni's old shack with the intention of raping and beating Soni's abandoned wife. According to their logic, they were paying Soni back by violating his ex-partner.[12] When neighboring residents became aware of what was going on, they called in the local gang (once again) to stop them. But Ciro's accomplice, perhaps even more enthusiastic with this particular plan for revenge than Ciro himself, was unwilling to "stop what he had started," and one of the gang members was forced to shoot him in the leg when he refused to stop raping Soni's ex-wife. That bullet eventually caused him to lose his leg. From then on, he, too, was prohibited from entering the favela. Later, however, to avenge the loss of his leg, he hired two men to kill the gang member who shot him, and they succeeded. Although it may seem from the outside as if such cycles of revenge are merely spiraling irrationally out of control, the actions are often moments of consensus in which the rules of the community are enforced.

Soni's ex-wife was already quite badly injured by the time the gang intervened, and she spent a long time recuperating in the hospital. She never returned to Felicidade Eterna. When residents recount these events, they universally consider the gang's behavior—of intervening on behalf of an innocent woman being raped—as perfectly justifiable. In this case, it was the same gang that initiated the punishment of a case of adultery. It did not, from the local perspective, "take sides" in the two cases: it simply pursued a sense of justice, just as the police are supposed to do. Of course, it is not the job of the justice system to punish adulterers, but among men who live in this community and who have strong feelings about being cuckolded, the matter calls for attention. The combination of a case of adultery occurring within a community and the overlap of friendships between gang and nongang members in the end enabled the gang to intervene on Ciro's behalf. A more general sense of justice enabled it to stop the rape of an innocent when the wrath of the cuckold got out of hand.

Gun Control

After Breno's brief and impetuous rule, a nonlocal gang (ADA—the same gang that Breno had cheated with his car deal)—invaded Felicidade Eterna, claiming it as its own territory. It prohibited anyone who was not part of the gang from owning a gun and were especially wary of anyone with connections to Breno. Breno's brother-in-law, Franklin, a resident, owned a gun that the new gang insisted he give up. After numerous verbal threats, members of the gang resorted to force and one evening entered his home with the goal of confiscating his gun. His wife was at home alone. They had, by then, decided to kill Franklin if he resisted. His wife was severely beaten for being either unwilling or unable to tell them where the gun was hidden. While this was taking place, Franklin arrived at the entrance to the favela, and other residents alerted him to what was happening at his home.

Because at this time the local gang was nonexistent, Franklin had no recourse but to call for the help of the police. The police arrived, and a shoot-out with the ADA gang members ensued. The gang members escaped that evening, and Franklin and his wife had just enough time to gather a few possessions before fleeing their home. They knew they could not stay; it would only be a matter of time before the gang members returned to seek revenge, and the police offered no lasting protection. Franklin's only possibility for gaining access again to his house and his possessions was to carry out a successful reinvasion of the favela by allying himself with the gang's rivals, Cólegio das Árvores. Only through this kind of alliance could Franklin possibly dislodge the occupying rival ADA gang from power. Subsequently, Franklin's alliance brought much gunfire to the favela as two rival gangs fought for the territory.

Some residents described Franklin's actions as having been caused by his disgust with this particular gang's tactics. The police ultimately could not resolve his problem with the gang and could not guarantee his safety there. The only way his security might have been guaranteed would have been if the police had managed to kill these gang members. Generally, the police themselves are reluctant to become involved in these types of internal favela struggles. Residents assume that the police themselves are fearful of being targeted in revenge killings—a popular theory that helps explain why some police have become members of masked death squads, executing their suspects while off duty and disguised.

A Case of "Petty Theft"

Isadora once recounted a story about how her grown son, Afonso, was taught a lesson by the local civil police officer, Dinho. Her attitude reveals some of the complex issues that local residents face when dealing with a local authority structure that includes both the gangs and police. It is not always the case that a civil police officer will be as present and "known" as Dinho, but this was a time when this was indeed the case. Isadora fondly remembers Dinho as "considerate," given the circumstances.

Afonso had collaborated in a theft at his own workplace—a robbery at the nearby bakery where he had been employed for a number of years. Isadora was horrified that one of her children had become involved in a crime because she views herself and her husband as honest citizens, as folks finally experiencing some social mobility after many years of hard work.[13] Thus, Isadora's perspective on her son and on the circumstances is as much about her desire to be seen as an "honest citizen" willing to see justice done—even to one's own child—as it is a detailed example of how problems are resolved at the local level. Isadora's narration of the events reveals the ways in which she experiences the possibilities available within the local justice system:

> He had a problem there in the bakery where he worked. This guy [who robbed] was from far away, and he took the things to his house where he lives, and he left Afonso [my son] a ham and a pack of cigarettes at his doorstep [thanking him for his cooperation in the robbery]. Afonso worked at the bakery. They grabbed him and beat him. My son was beaten because he deserved it. They got him because he thought he could earn easy money. Dinho, the [civil] policeman, beat him up good. It was Dinho and another policeman who beat him up, even breaking his teeth, everything. They beat him, beat him real good.
>
> Zuco [my husband and Afonso's stepfather] went over to Afonso's to try to save him. I didn't go. I just prayed to God for compassion and make it so that he survived and learned a lesson to never do something like that again. Zuco liberated him. He went there. He told the policemen, "I didn't teach him to do these things. He learned this when he was older. So, do what you need to do now, but you can let him go. He is going to take a bath and go after the things that the other guy stole. If he doesn't get everything back, my wife will go to the bank and pay everything, the bill for everything."
>
> Afonso came over to my house all bloody and I said, "Go take a bath. Change your clothes and go get those things back." Because Dinho had said that if they didn't appear with the things both of them would die. I said, "É bonito pra sua cara, né? [It's pretty on your face, isn't it?] Only now isn't the time for sermons, it's the time for action. Go and take care of your side. Get the things from the guy and return them. Because your body is the prize." He went. It was just lucky that the guy hadn't sold anything yet. Everything was still there. He had taken 150 cartons of cigarettes—not packs, but cartons. Scale. Calculator. Everything was inside in a bag.
>
> Later, I said, "Afonso, be a man for once in your life. Why did you do that?" "Ahh, because he obligated me to do that." I said, "Nobody obligates anybody without a firearm in the hand pointed at their face or chest. . . . Only a gun." He returned and delivered the stuff. I went to Dinho the policeman's house at night and delivered the things so that he would know what was delivered. Because if not, he could keep the things and later say I never delivered them. Later, he went and delivered the things [to Seu Carlo] in front of me. I said to Seu Carlo, "See if everything is there. I like things to be right. My husband, too. I asked him to pardon me. And he said, 'You don't have anything to be ashamed of.' . . . "

He didn't *sujar a carteira dele* [dirty his record]!! Everything was there. I said that he had all the reason to give a *justa causa* if he wanted to, but he didn't.[14] Afonso paid him everything. Afonso stayed at my house because he was afraid to go home. Because if it had been the bandidos, they would have killed him. It was lucky that it was a policeman that got him. Two bandidos came to my house saying to Afonso, "Look, man. You go and look for Seu Carlo's things. Because if not, you are going to fall [dead]. . . ." They said that. They wanted to protect the area. They didn't want anyone dirtying their area. (Isadora, taped interview, 1998)

Here was a case where the policeman was more gentle than the local gang. Isadora was thankful that Dinho had merely beaten Afonso instead of killing or arresting him. Within the rule of law set by the local gang at the time, Afonso could have been subjected to extremely harsh punishment because he had "dirtied his own area." The lower-middle-class merchant, Seu Carlo, relied on Dinho, the policeman, to provide him with justice in the robbery of his store. But the local gang at the time would have been much more strict, especially because Afonso was a member of its community and had broken the rules by aiding the robbery of a local merchant. In this scenario, Dinho, who did not ever actually arrest Afonso, was seen as a "hero" of sorts for solving the problem on his own and for not ruining Afonso's life by sending him to jail. He was viewed as being kind in this situation for offering Afonso a beating instead.

Solution for an Abusive and Adulterous Husband

Marília, Glória's young neighbor, experienced a period of upheaval with her husband, Celso, who was having affairs with other women and returning home to beat her—a situation she found intolerable. She was able to use the threat of her brother, appropriately nicknamed "O Criminoso" ("The Criminal"), to scare her husband into more appropriate behavior. According to Marília, her husband was cheating on her at work and then coming home to their own children without any milk or food. Eventually, because they did not pay the rent on time, Marília was forced to move. She decided to taunt Celso with the prospect of visiting her brother, a convicted criminal, in Bangu prison. She knew that Celso would be worried about her brother because his toughness was legendary and because he had spent so much time in prison, where one gets even tougher. In fact, Marília's brother wrote Celso various letters from prison, threatening to kill him if he did not treat his sister well. The threats worked, at least for a while:

> Then he started to care correctly for me because he feared my brother. He was afraid of my brother. Over there, there is a mountain of letters from my brother that my brother sent to me and to him. There is a bag full of letters. He threatened to kill him, and Celso was fearful. I had told my brother that he hadn't wanted me to visit him, and my brother swore him to death. After that, he became good. My brother left the jail. Then one day, Celsinho was lying in bed and my brother knocked at the door. Only that my brother, when he left the prison, became a crente, went to the church, you know. He wasn't robbing anyone or anything. When Celso saw my brother he got scared. My brother said, "You can stay calm since the promise I made I won't be able to keep because I joined the church and I won't be able to kill you, no, I won't. But still continue to treat her well." (Marília, taped interview, 1995)

Rape of a Child

Marília also explained to me how, oftentimes when a murder occurs, nobody is really sure about the identity of the killers, nor are the killers sure about who they are supposed to be killing. She told the story of how her own brother-in-law was mistaken for the rapist of a three-year-old girl in the neighborhood where he lived, and explained that she never found out whether the men who came to him seeking revenge were members of the local gang, a private hit squad, or off-duty police. Masked men came to the street where Marília's brother-in-law lived and threw him into a car, telling him that he had raped a three-year-old and that he was going to die. Marília's brother-in-law protested, explaining that he was not a rapist and that they had taken the wrong man. Later, another car pulled up and a man told them that Marília's brother-in-law was "the wrong guy," but that they had the right one in the other car. Then the men holding Marília's brother-in-law had to decide what to do with him. They decided "not to waste a bullet on him," but instead to throw gasoline on him and set him on fire. He managed to escape death but was severely burned. In the aftermath, he and his wife began a new life in Petrópolis, where he eventually became a manager of a fast-food restaurant. Notably, when Marília explained the case to me, she insisted that whoever had actually raped the child ought to be punished—despite such risks of mistaken identity—and that it did not matter how or by whom. By now, the populations living in these areas are willing to accept any justice; as long as it is directed at the right person, they are not concerned with who administers punishment or exacts revenge.

ALTERNATIVE JUSTICE IN THE "BROWN ZONES"

In 1997, the entire country of Brazil was able to watch a videotape of a middle-class motorist being harassed and eventually shot by a policeman who was trying to extort money for no apparent reason.[15] The scene caused a stir throughout the country. I was not in Brazil at the time, but I tried to imagine how different segments of the population might have viewed this event. Given the experiences of my friends in Felicidade Eterna with local police over the years, they must have found the broadcast to be something quite familiar. It may have shocked them, though, to see a middle-class person being treated similarly to how they are usually treated, for the unspoken rules of class have led to a situation in which the middle and upper classes do indeed experience some elements of the rule of law, however imperfect, whereas people living in areas plagued by poverty experience the rules and regulations of an alternative justice system. What was shocking about this particular event was the fragility of the rule of law, even as applied to middle-class citizens. Needless to say, the middle and upper classes were dismayed and outraged by this transgression.

It is perhaps a useful time to recall Rio's early turn-of-the-century transformation into "the marvelous city," one in which the middle and upper classes attempted to hide the impoverished neighborhoods that had formed after abolition and beyond. This was an attempt to emulate the great cities of Europe, and the planning and architecture of the reformed city led to the marginalization of the poor, who were pushed into favelas on the steep hillsides or outward into peripheral regions of the city. Over time, this segregation has led to a situation where contemporary Rio includes a great many impoverished pockets where residents live in many respects beyond the reach of the state; a distance that is indeed sometimes physical but most often is a symbolic distance rendered into practice through a narrowed access to decent health care and other forms of social services. Whereas for the middle and upper classes, some semblance of a rule of law exists, for the lower classes it has traditionally been denied. So while the broad desire of the Brazilian population after the end of military dictatorship and the abertura of the late 1980s has been for a process of democratization and democratic consolidation, the absence of a reliable rule of law in so many areas of the country has led to a crisis of confidence in this same process. One cannot help but wonder how democratic consolidation will proceed in Brazil with such large segments of the population divorced from a viable system where the rule of law applies equally and fairly across the social spectrum. As Pereira (1997) has commented:

> The ideal of the rule of law as a pyramid of universal rules applying to everyone, including those in the most powerful state offices, is in tension with social relations that are structured hierarchically. The juridical fiction of equality of citizenship rights clashes with the sociological reality of inequality, relations of dependence and deference, bossism and tutelage, and the lack of a public sphere and commitment to a common good. Democracy is rendered inoperative by the social relations and practices through which formally liberal institutions are constituted. (6)

Political scientist Guillermo O'Donnell (1993), in describing the uneven aspects of the process of democratic consolidation in countries such as Brazil and Argentina, has employed a color-coded, geographically oriented conception of democracy. He denotes "blue" zones as areas that have a high degree of state presence, effective bureaucracy, and a properly functioning legal system; "green" zones as those with a high degree of territorial penetration and a lower presence of the state in functional and class terms; and "brown zones" as those with a very low or negligible state presence in both dimensions (1359). O'Donnell is essentially representing the differential application of the rule of law. His analysis of democratization suggests that the brown zones are characterized by a number of distinct properties:

> In these areas there are elections, governors, and national and state legislators (in addition, in many cases those regions are heavily overrepresented in the national legislatures). The parties operating there, even if they are nominally members of national parties, are no more than personalistic machines anxiously dependent on the prebends they can extract from the national and local state agencies. Those parties and the local governments function on the basis of phenomena such as personalism, familism, prebendalism, clientelism, and the like. (1359)

In these brown areas, O'Donnell points out, the state is unable to enforce its legality, so while it may be possible for an individual to vote freely in elections and have one's vote counted, in these regions one cannot expect proper treatment from the police or the courts. Accordingly, these zones, which would be represented by shantytowns in urban areas or by rural areas where feudal relations predominate, offer a kind of "low-intensity citizenship" (1360). We expect that the state is unable to enforce its legality and therefore can find justification for using oppressive force against populations in these areas.

These factors add up to what Holston and Caldeira (1998:264), building on O'Donnell, refer to as a "disjunctive democracy." They identify two continuing paradoxes of Brazil's political democracy: first, that the state tolerates a corrupt and extraordinarily violent military and civil police bureaucracy; and, second, that the high levels of police violence have not been adequately protested at least in part because of popular support for policies that appear to be "tough on crime," a stance that is especially common within the working classes.

The rub here lies in the contradiction that the working classes, who are most often the victims of police violence, are also the keenest supporters (in polls, at least) of violent police actions: "The point we wish to suggest here is that the population's support for police violence indicates the existence not only of an institutional dysfunction but also of a pervasive cultural pattern that associates order and authority with the use of violence and that, in turn, contributes to the delegitimation of the justice system and of the rule of law" (Holston and Caldeira 1998:272–73). This "pervasive cultural pattern that associates order and authority with the use of violence" seems to be unidirectional, however; it appears justified only when such force is applied against the poor. The normalized absence of the rule of law in places like Felicidade Eterna is brought to the attention of the middle and upper classes only in instances of police abuse of those same classes. Given the contemporary situation—of a differential functioning of the rule of law across distinct regions—where citizenship is correlated with social class, it is important to think through the definitions and meanings implied by the term "democratic consolidation."[16] Such questions may help us to address the paradox described by Holston and Caldeira regarding the working class's support of actions that result in their own victimization. Further, we might be able to make sense of the continued high death rates of low-income, young black men despite the advances in political process over the past twenty years.

Such questions about citizenship in the context of democratic consolidation must be linked to the lived experiences of the poor. Their lives are both underdescribed and undertheorized, and thus viewed as homogeneous groupings that respond to public politics in ways that work against their own self-interest (such as the suggestion made by Holston and Caldeira that presents them as favoring military and police actions).

A closer look at how power functions in the brown zones will go a long way toward getting at a more grounded, local-level perspective on democratic consolidation and the depth of state involvement that would be required to support it.

In the brown zones of Rio de Janeiro, the local gangs provide a parallel state structure and alternative rule of law. In these zones, there is a great deal of consensus among the population that police are corrupt, but residents also agree that occasionally, as in the case of Braga and Dinho, the police carry out important functions. Similarly, local gangs are seen as necessary—they protect the favela from outsiders, they offer housing and employment and help in times of trouble, they do what the police cannot do—but they, too, are viewed with a great deal of ambivalence.

I have seen how in some communities, such as Felicidade Eterna, there seemed to be much support for individuals such as Braga, the civil police officer who "cleaned up" the favela and protected it from invasions by outside drug traffickers. Braga left the local gang alone during this time and even dated (and later married) Dilmar's ex-wife. He was selective in his choice of enemies and was supported in his actions despite the fact that he often used excessive force. In sum, he was respected. Similarly, the residents had a great deal of respect for "Katy Mahoney," Lulu's sister, the civil policewoman who arrived every now and then in Felicidade Eterna to smack around a few of the younger drug users. Dinho, a local civil policeman who lived just outside the favela, was respected and appreciated for roughing up petty thieves and insisting on the retrieval of stolen goods rather than leaving the punishment to the gang. But it is important to remember that these "good" police actions fit into the logic and rules of an alternative rule of law. Their success ultimately was based on their personal reputation, their ability to target the right person, and, most important, their ability to work outside of the justice system itself. Some police are just more respectable than others.

In the absence of a reliable state presence, the gangs fill a role beyond simple trafficking in illegal goods. They are called upon to right the wrongs of everyday life, and in this role they are tolerated and sometimes even venerated. Further, because they provide favors and help in times of emergency, they are perceived as good bandits or good criminals, as in the case of Marília's brother, "O Criminoso," whose threat to kill her husband was believed to help alter his behavior.

It is these brown zones, however, that not only lack a workable rule of law and trustworthy police but also lack a state capable of providing a fair minimum wage, decent employment, good-faith health care, and all the other amenities enjoyed by the middle and elite classes in Brazil and in other advanced industrialized nations. The low-intensity citizenship of the residents in the brown zones means that they must depend on the gangs not only to provide an alternative rule of law but also to fill in wherever else the state is absent.

POLICING IN BRAZIL AS SOCIAL CONTROL OF THE LOWER CLASSES

Many urban centers around the world are similar to Rio, in that they are areas where social and economic inequality is high, where the middle and upper classes enjoy some semblance of democracy in all its forms, and where justice is locally constructed among the poorer classes. Residents in these differentially democratized areas conceive of the very possibility of citizenship through their immediate experience.

Brazilian social relations are marked by exaggerated inequality, and this is true as well for the application of the rule of law. In 1997, a twelve-page document titled "Map of Risk of Violence—City of Rio de Janeiro" was published by the Center for the Study of Contemporary Culture.[17] Researchers found that the risk of being a victim of homicide in Rio de Janeiro is low during infancy but rises spectacularly during adolescence, reaching its peak in the twenty- to twenty-four-year age-group; after that, the risk of death by intentional homicide decreases with age.[18] Not surprisingly, the researchers also found a stark contrast between the wealthy and poor regions of the city. People living in different neighborhoods are exposed to different risks and levels of violence. For example, in 1995 in Padre Miguel, a neighborhood on the periphery of Rio de Janeiro that encompasses Felicidade Eterna, there were 50 homicides of people between the ages of fifteen and thirty-four within a total population of 21,745, making the estimated homicide rate 229.9 per 100,000. In Bangu, another neighborhood close to Felicidade Eterna, there were 92 homicides within a total population of 76,133, making the homicide rate approximately 120.8 per 100,000.

We need only to look at the *bairros nobres* (literally "noble" neighborhoods, meaning wealthy neighborhoods) of Rio de Janeiro to get a sense of the contrast. In Gávea (a "noble" neighborhood in the Zona Sul), for example, there was a single homicide in a population of 23,228, making the homicide rate 4.3 per 100,000; in Copacabana, there were nine in a population of 46,117, making the homicide rate 19.5 per

100,000.[19] These numbers indicate how startlingly high homicide rates are in peripheral neighborhoods or the brown zones.

In the case of Rio de Janeiro and in terms of absolute numbers, Alba Zaluar (1995) calculated that the number of homicides in Rio de Janeiro had indeed tripled between 1980 and 1995, rising from 2,826 murders in 1980 to 8,408 in 1994.[20] This epidemic of violence seems to differentially affect male and female youths in the same age category. Approximately twenty-two boys die for each girl in the fifteen- to twenty-four-year-old age range (Cardia 1997:27).

Using another indicator of violence, the researchers collected the numbers of intentional homicides (*homicídios dolosos*) and intentional injuries *(lesões dolosas)* in each of the thirty-eight civil police precincts *(delegacias)* within the municipality of Rio.[21] Bangu had the third-highest number of intentional homicides (276) and the second-highest number of intentional injuries (904) registered for 1995. Again, the numbers were much lower in the Zona Sul and city center, areas with much higher standards of living than the city's North and West Zones. The authors of this study point out that the risk of suffering violence in its extreme form—homicide—is up to seven times higher for residents of certain areas (the North and West Zones of the city) as compared with other areas, and that residents of the Zona Sul are—relatively, at least— spared this form of violence.

From these statistics, it is clear that violence is experienced in profoundly different intensities according to socioeconomic class. This structure of inequality extends to the police forces and to how, subsequently, the police forces mete out different punishments based on class and race.[22] It also influences how the police forces are perceived by the populations most affected. The institutionalized brutalization of the poor by the police is exercised in a number of routine forms such as torture, coerced confession, extortion, and other physical punishments, including execution (Mingardi 1992 and Kant de Lima 1986). It is clear that, historically, the policing forces in Brazil have been useful in securing the social control of the lower classes (Holloway 1993).

Because the poor are criminalized, they bear the burden of corrupt dealings with the police. The lower classes' fear and distrust of both the civil and military police are extreme, a finding easily detectable in surveys but also discernible in the ways residents of low-income neighborhoods think about, talk about, and actually deal with police officials in their everyday contexts.

Robert Shirley (1990), an anthropologist working in a squatter settlement in Porto Alegre, suggests that there is a level of community cohesion in low-income neighborhoods that is built around the common dislike and distrust of the police, a sentiment I also found in Felicidade Eterna. The majority of residents in Felicidade Eterna were honest and hardworking, but their greater sympathy toward the gangs than toward the civil and military police forces was palpable. Perhaps this is true in part because they accepted banditry as an option in the face of extreme poverty. While it may be useful for analytical reasons to reject the relationship between criminality and poverty, the trajectory into criminality by young men as a form of local knowledge (and a vehicle of advancement) still serves as a powerful explanation among the poor for why the attraction to the gangs is so high.

As Philippe Bourgois (1995:141) has argued, when it becomes clear that the labor market will accommodate young, uneducated (in this case, black) men only in poorly paid service work, as so many men in Felicidade Eterna came to realize, then a viable alternative, and one that fits in with a certain machismo desire—such as the desire to carry a gun[23]— is to join a gang. I remember being told in 1995 that Lucas, Glória's adopted-in nephew, had chosen to become a gang member *pra comer* (in order to eat). A popular song that describes an innocent who becomes a bandit just so "he can eat a fucked-up piece of bread" expresses well this popular explanation regarding the social foundations of banditry.[24] Lucas had followed his cousin Pedro Paulo into the Comando Vermelho gang in Rocinha, his explanation echoing Pedro Paulo's—so that he would not have to "work like a slave at slave's wages, like his mother."

A NOTE ON OPPOSITIONAL CULTURE

It is clear to me that in Rio everyone grows up knowing their place and their chances for success within the system. The middle-class child knows that he or she must do well enough in school and master the vestibular examination in order to advance educationally and occupy a middle-class position. In places like Felicidade Eterna, it is hard to convince the young people that there will be mobility for their generation. They have seen the generational continuity of poverty, despite the hard work of their elders. While individuals such as Glória represent one kind of honest worker in this system, she also represents the lowest rung of occupational possibilities. For many years, her hard work never provided enough for her to make ends meet. Pedro Paulo and Lucas were the two young men who seemed to get away from Glória, men who in their resistance to the system and to the idea of honest work at slavery-style wages chose the short and tense lives characteristic of the world of gangs and drug trafficking. Glória's other children all chose to work at honest, low-paying jobs.

The oppositional culture that the gangs represent is a direct response to long-term, historically conditioned economic oppression. As stated earlier, gangs provide more than economic opportunity, however. They fill in where the state is absent, and they mete out justice within an alternative system of revenge practices. They have, therefore, become an enemy—and competitor—of the state.

THE DISDAIN FOR THE POLICE

The relationships between favela residents and the police produce a structure of regular violence practically unknown to middle- and upper-class citizens. The poor thus experience the police forces as part of the everyday violence present in their neighborhoods. For them, this relationship is complex, ambivalent, and ambiguous. While the relationship of the middle and upper classes with the police forces is also complicated, it is different because it operates within a system that grants a certain amount of both immunity and impunity to those with the status and the resources to protect themselves.

The lower classes' disdain for the civil and military police forces has both a historical and a contemporary explanation. Thomas Holloway's (1993) historical reading of the institutionalization of the policing system in nineteenth-century Rio de Janeiro illustrates the possible continuities between the development of the civil and military police forces during the nineteenth century and their repressive role among the lower classes in contemporary Rio. His argument emphasizes the fact that police institutions developed during the nineteenth century were designed to address the problem of disorder in the streets experienced by the Brazilian elite when slavery was nearing its end and as more of the "free" lower classes were able to occupy public spaces. For Holloway, modern police institutions developed precisely to ensure the continuity of traditional hierarchical social relations into the impersonal public space, with political elites creating institutions that would enforce their own measures of acceptable and unacceptable behavior (5–6).[25]

It is not only violence that became normalized in policing tactics. Graft and corruption also became and continue to be part of institutionalized policing in Brazil. In an ethnographic portrait of the police forces in Rio de Janeiro, Roberto Kant de Lima (1987) recounts the attempts of one Rio deputy who refuses to accept money from *jogo do bicho* (illegal numbers game) and the ways in which he is systematically demoted in his career for refusing to play into this kind of corruption.[26] Guaracy Mingardi (1998) makes a similar point with regard to the situation in São Paulo and suggests, in line with Holloway's continuity thesis, that corruption, in addition to ordinary violence, has been thoroughly institutionalized throughout the police system.

THE CRIMINALIZATION OF THE POOR

In effect, the literature agrees that the rule of law "belongs" to the elite only, much as other material "goods" are distributed in Brazilian society. The structure of inequality extends to the police forces, where documented incidents of brutality have reached absurd proportions; such abuse is carried out to a much greater extent and with much greater impunity against the lower classes. Conversely, those who speak in defense of human rights and against the police involved in illegal activities—including death squads[27]—are viewed as supporting the "privileges of bandits" (Caldeira 1991:162). This is a modern form of Brazilian governmentality,[28] where the police forces distinguish between the kinds of rules to be applied depending on which segment of the population is being dealt with. In the elite and middle-class regions of the Zona Sul, some version of the traditional rule of law functions, whereas in favelas such as Felicidade Eterna, it does not.

This differential experience of the rule of law on a day-to-day basis and the "naturalization" of this difference by the middle classes and the elite are part of the ideological system that has resulted from the elite's criminalization of the poor and the poor's internalization of these beliefs.[29] Nancy Scheper-Hughes (1992), writing about a shantytown in Northeast Brazil, describes the ideology of the "dangerousness of the poor," in which the poor are seen as being naturally "guilty of criminal needs" while the crimes of the wealthy are understood as part of a larger, less controllable system. This ideology enables a government to turn its military against its own citizens? "What, then, is the rationale for turning a military, wartime arsenal against private citizens? What crimes have they committed (or do they threaten to commit)? What makes some citizens assume the character of 'threats' or 'dangers' to the state so as to make violence an acceptable form of social control, the legitimate 'business' of the police?" (Scheper-Hughes 1992:224). Scheper-Hughes suggests that this attitude encompasses a racial ideology, noting that the great majority of homicide victims and victims of police brutality are not only poor but also nonwhite. Other prominent Brazilian researchers of violence in Rio de Janeiro have noticed the racial imbalance in homicide rates and police brutality but have been extremely cautious about proposing race as a determining or causal factor.[30] Rather, there is much greater comfort in speaking through the idiom of socioeconomic or class differences rather than through the idiom of race. Scheper-Hughes, too, notices this reluctance to speak about the racial direction of everyday violence and mentions the acquiescence of the people who submit to the workings of a hegemonic discourse that is often contrary to their own class and race interests. She asks, "Why is there so little expressed (or even submerged and seething) outrage against police and death squad terrorism in the shantytown?" (225). Scheper-Hughes argues that in the Northeast, crimes of the poor are naturalized in racial terms. In this context, young black men are thought to steal because it is in their "nature," "blood," or "race" (224). Further, everyday violence is routinized in the numerous public rituals that bring people into contact with the state in public clinics and hospitals, in the civil registry office, in the public morgue, and in the municipal cemetery. Thus, the more extreme forms of human rights violations—such as homicide and death by police forces—are part of a larger context of "wholly expectable, indeed even anticipated behavior" (229).

> Under the political ideology of favors and privileges, extended only to those who behave well, human rights cannot logically be extended to criminals and marginals, those who have broken, or who simply live outside, the law. When this negative conception of human rights is superimposed on a very narrow definition of "crime" that does not recognize the criminal and violent acts of the powerful and the elite, it is easy to see how everyday violence against the poor is routinized and defended, even by some of the poor themselves. (228)

Caldeira (2000:187) argues that the working classes remain in a state of constant confusion and ambivalence with regard to their evaluations of police violence. This leaves them with the alternatives of either reacting privately and taking justice into their own hands or supporting the use of deadly force by the police and others against alleged criminals (187–199). It is, ironically, the lack of alternatives that leads people into the paradoxical position of supporting violent police actions that would then increase their own chances of victimization. Much of this confusion among the working classes stems from the fact that "the two main characters of the universe of crime—the criminal and the policeman—are not opposed but compared" (186). Indeed,

> If one takes into consideration the arbitrariness and violence of the police, the constant confusion (workers mistaken for criminals, policemen mistaken for criminals), the identification of criminals with policemen (both symbolic and material) and of both with poor people—in sum, the context of uncertainty, confusion, and fear of both policemen and criminals—one can only conclude that the police are far from being able to offer a feeling of security to the working and lower middle classes. The population often feels pressed against the wall without alternatives. (189)

Caldeira's argument points to the ways in which the delegitimation of the rule of law becomes a viable alternative. But while the rich can choose to ignore the law, the working classes are, according to Caldeira, made to feel that they are left without alternatives inside that order. Within this system, the wealthier classes do not have to follow the rules; they can simply avoid them.

Caldeira's argument can be extended to the poorest stratum—one that is more economically disadvantaged than the working-class Paulistas she portrays. I would argue that the working and subemployed classes in Rio's periphery have indeed found powerful alternatives to the order that has traditionally trapped them, and that these exist in the form of gangs, both local and paralocal. It is in this sense that we can view the rise of drug-trafficking gangs and the continued rejection of the police within the shared context of a delegitimized rule of law. These gangs provide an alternative justice system—a parallel state, if you will—among the poorest, who thoroughly reject a corrupt police force and, in their everyday lives, seek some organized entity that can administer "justice" in the local arena.

"PARALLEL STATES"

If we accept Thomas Holloway's (1993) continuity thesis regarding the institutionalization of graft, corruption, and repression as part of normal policing in Brazil, it follows that local poor communities would similarly have to develop some sort of force to protect themselves from the daily injustices in their own context, as well as from unprotected contact with police. Elizabeth Leeds (1996), drawing on theories of state-making and social banditry, analyzes the role of the contemporary Brazilian state as "protector" and its dynamic with the drug-trafficking gangs, which, among other things, serve as "local-level protectors." With no reliable, noncorrupt police presence, the local bandidos and the bandidos from the larger gangs in the major favelas perform internal security and crime control functions. They judge and punish thieves and other delinquents, meting out sentences that can include beatings, nonfatal shootings, and executions.

Historian Eric Hobsbawm's (1959) argument concerning social banditry in southern Europe, and in particular the Sicilian Mafia, explains that the relationship between gangs, local populations, and the state can be perceived in a productive manner:

> The word *Mafia* stands here for several distinct things. First, it represents a general attitude towards the State and the State's law which is not necessarily any more criminal than the very similar attitude of, let us say, public schoolboys towards their masters. A *mafioso* did not invoke State or law in his private quarrels, but made himself respected and safe by winning a reputation for toughness and courage, and settled his differences by fighting. He recognized no obligation except those of the code of honour or *omertá* (manliness), whose chief article forbade giving information to the public authorities. In other words *mafia* (which will be spelled with a small *m* when used in this sense) was the sort of code of behaviour which always tends to develop in societies without effective public order, or in societies in which citizens regard the authorities as wholly or partly hostile (for instance in jails or in the underworld outside them), or as unappreciative of the things which really matter (for instance in schools) or as a combination of both. (32–33)

Hobsbawm thus laid out a broad definition of the Mafia as a rural phenomenon, but one that had parallels in urban Palermo. According to Hobsbawm, the Mafia

> provided a parallel machine of law and organized power; indeed, so far as the citizen in the areas under its influence was concerned, the only effective law and power. In a society such as Sicily, in which the official government could not or would not exercise effective sway, the appearance of such a system was as inevitable as the appearance of gang-rule, or its alternative, private posses and vigilantes in certain parts of *laissez-faire* America. What distinguishes Sicily is the territorial extent and cohesion of this private and parallel system of power. (35)

In Hobsbawm's analysis, the rise of the Mafia was a major incident in the development of rural capitalism, with the heads of the local Mafia being men of wealth or of the middle class who eventually helped to transfer power in the "parallel system" from the feudal to the rural middle classes. Anthropologist Anton Blok's (1974) historical ethnography of a Sicilian village similarly examines mafiosi in their role as political middlemen. Blok views the incorporation and continuation of corruption within the modern Italian state as part of the evolution of the Mafia. In the epilogue to *The Mafia of a Sicilian Village, 1860–1960,* his message regarding the long-term corrupting effects of this form of development is rather pessimistic:

> Sicilian *mafia,* understood as *the collusions themselves* rather than as something separate from them (a common but fallacious conceptualization), presents itself as an effective force in present-day Italian politics, reflecting the stage of development of Italian society at large. Corruption, and *mafia* for that matter, are inherent parts of societies in a relatively early phase of State-formation. Can one ask Sicilians to act as citizens when most of them still are and consider themselves as subjects of powerful local and regional magnates upon whom they depend for protection and making a living? Under the present conditions, the State can only remove the most outstanding symptoms of *mafia* and corruption. It is to misunderstand these conditions and the specific stage of development of Italian society, to ask for and expect more substantial forms of short term intervention. (228–29)

Leeds (1996), applying these theories of state–social banditry relations to the Brazilian urban gang phenomenon, describes the power vacuum—the absent state in the local favela context—that is filled by the drug-trafficking gangs and their leaders. Leeds coherently describes the networks of larger gangs and their alliances with the smaller local gangs—a structure that because of obvious research limitations has not been written about sufficiently. Leeds has likened the local gangs in Rio de Janeiro and their role in meting out local justice to a "parallel state." She understands the formation of parallel states in the Rio favelas to be a process through which other power brokers become necessary to occupy the void created by an absent state authority. Leeds concurs with the arguments of both Blok and Hobsbawm—that social banditry becomes a form of self-help in the context of economic crises and social tension. Social bandits arise and are successful in the absence of a reliable state.

STATE AND BANDITS AS PERPETRATORS OF VIOLENCE

Thus far, I have suggested that in the absence of a rule of law in the poorest neighborhoods, gangs do more than merely traffic drugs. This is important because it means that even if the drug trade were to be successfully halted, or the major leaders captured, the demand for a strong gang at the local level would not necessarily diminish. The gangs, it should be emphasized, serve not only as protectors from other, outside gangs, but also as mediators in the face of a violent and corrupt police force.

Besides being institutionally corrupt, the police have more recently been accused of participating directly in drug trafficking. Mingardi (1998) documents cases in which military police have been used by drug traffickers or have become involved in the assassination of drug traffickers in order to keep the product and the profit for themselves.

Another growing trend is that police are not making arrests or carrying out their jobs while on duty but instead are doing away with opponents while off duty. The death squads that have received attention since the early 1970s are one manifestation of this, but there are other examples. A news article in the *Folha de São Paulo* supports this observation, citing a 1992 study which revealed that more than a fourth of the corporals and soldiers of the military police in São Paulo (27.08 percent) do not go to work in uniform because they feel insecure. They do not want to be identified as military police because they fear being a target of vengeance.[31]

Mingardi (1998) argues that in Brazil, organized crime has infiltrated the state. The state itself cannot be a reliable institution in terms of having the goodwill or the ability to relegitimize the rule of law, or to carry out other aspects of reform because the state itself is thoroughly compromised:

> My central hypothesis is that Organized Crime cannot exist on the large scale without having some type of accord, or collusion with sectors of the State. The research identified at least two different types of relationship between Organized Crime and the State. The first type of accord is merely financial, bringing corruption to members of the repressive apparatus, administration, and some professional politicians. The second case consists of something more than the relation between corrupted and corruptor. Organized Crime exercises its political influence through control of a series of clients. (18)

Many of Mingardi's examples focus on the corrupt nature of the military police. Although his study was based in São Paulo, he compares that city with Rio throughout the book. Mingardi summarizes two peculiarities of Rio drug trafficking, characteristics that seem to lend credence to his organized crime model: the existence of bocas de fumo that have functioned in the same locales for decades and the hegemony of large imperialist drug-trafficking organizations such as Comando Vermelho and Terceiro Comando. These two organizations represent themselves as victims of society, friends of the poor, and protectors of a particular region

(131–32), qualities that Mingardi considers indicative of an organized crime model.

Mingardi's and Blok's analyses appear to be contradictory. Mingardi implies that a corrupt state is necessary to maintain organized crime, whereas Blok argues that it is organized crime itself that replaces the weak state and insinuates itself into the very process of state-building. Both of these positions attempt to explain contemporary manifestations of corruption at various levels of government. If Mingardi is correct, however, the process of democratic consolidation will be considerably slower and muted than if, as Blok suggests, these manifestations are merely part of a longer-term evolution of a democratic state.

RETURNING TO THE MURDER: THE DEATH OF ADILSON

It was July 1998, and I had recently arrived in Rio de Janeiro for a return visit to Felicidade Eterna. I had just seen Adilson alive on the previous day. He and his four-year-old son, Diego, happened to be on the same bus coming from the Zona Sul that Glória and I were traveling on. He told us about what had happened in Vila Maria. A few days earlier, José Pedro, a young man from Felicidade Eterna, had been killed there as a payback for the deeds of his brother Leandro, who, a few months earlier, had bungled a bus assault and carelessly caused the death of a *colegial* (high school student) from Vila Maria. I remember Adilson saying something I did not understand at the time: that "somebody had to die" for the accidental murder of the student. He did not seem surprised that José Pedro, as the brother of Leandro, would have been chosen in that particular moment.

Adilson had, at one time, been a casual member of the gang in Felicidade Eterna, and later a member of a larger gang based elsewhere, but for a few years he had completely withdrawn from gang involvement. I had known Adilson since 1991. At that time, he was a young man of seventeen—the boyfriend of Filomena, one of Glória's teenage girls. They did everything together, and when Filomena was kicked out of her mother's home in 1992 at the age of fourteen, it was Adilson who took her into his own home in Vila Maria until Filomena had made peace with her mother. In 1995, Adilson and Filomena together built a small shack approximately the size of an American double bed on Glória's little *quintal* (backyard, residence) in Felicidade Eterna. They painted the name

"Diego" along the top of it, referring to their first and only child, who was born in 1994.

Filomena and Adilson separated in 1997, and Adilson took custody of Diego, moving with him back to his mother's house in Vila Maria, a large, well-organized favela a few miles from Felicidade Eterna. Filomena moved to Duque de Caxias, a city in the infamous Baixada Fluminense, back to the neighborhood she had known as a young girl.[32] Filomena allowed Adilson to take Diego because she was having trouble finding work and also because she wanted to pursue other men, a process inhibited by having a child to take care of. Less sympathetic interpretations of Filomena's behavior by friends and neighbors depicted her as an uncaring mother, one who was more interested in snagging a boyfriend than in caring for her own child. Mutual friends of Filomena and Adilson took it for granted that although the couple had separated after numerous physically violent fights, and Filomena had since become involved with other men, Adilson was still quite devoted to her. They explained his customary visits to Felicidade Eterna in this context, as well. He would visit regularly with his former brother-in-law Tiago, who by 1998 had built his own tiny shack on Glória's quintal, and Celso, whose shack was on the other side of Glória's property.

Adilson had lived in Felicidade Eterna on and off between 1992 and 1997, and during the early 1990s he had worked for a large organized gang (not one of the imperialist gangs, however) outside of the favela. He had an illustrious career as a *dissolvedor de corpos* (literally, body dissolver), the person who makes bodies disappear after people have been murdered. I remember that we were all a little afraid of him in 1995 because he typically carried around a *trinta-oitão* (big .38 pistol). When he disappeared at night, Glória's children and I would try to imagine what he might be doing and, half jokingly, would describe how difficult it must be to carry heavy, dead bodies from one place to another. We pictured the things he might have to do, such as cutting off body parts and burying them in scattered places or, alternatively, burning corpses. In the style of the nervous black humor characteristic of my companions, we were able to find comfort in our comical imaginings.

Adilson's relations with the local gang in Felicidade Eterna seemed to be stable and without problems up through 1995, despite various shifts in the local gang structure. He was involved with the gang but was not one of its central members. Everyone knew that he was more thoroughly involved with bandits elsewhere, and his interactions with local gang members in Felicidade Eterna were such that they knew they could count on him to support them, but that his obligations were mainly with his other gang.

Sometime during 1995, Adilson decided that he wanted to opt out of his dangerous and disturbing profession, but he had been told that the members of his primary gang would never allow it because "he knew too much." Some say that Adilson's desire to leave *a vida* (literally, "the life") was inspired by fatherhood, and others say that in carrying out his job as dissolvedor, he realized that it would not be too long before his own body would be getting "dissolved," given the alarming death rate among his closest colleagues. Despite the dangers, Adilson decided to try to leave his life of crime behind him, and this included his occasional affiliation with the local gang in Felicidade Eterna.

Since Glória still maintained ownership of her old shack in Duque de Caxias, it was planned that Filomena, Adilson, and Diego would move there, waiting out some time to see how Adilson's disappearance would affect his former colleagues. According to Glória, during the course of the next few months, major leaders of Adilson's gang were killed off or sent to jail, so that within a relatively short time span—less than a year—he was able to emerge from his hiding spot and return to Felicidade Eterna, more or less "a free man." The situation had changed within the local gang structure as well, and Adilson's desire to stay uninvolved was respected by those who remained. Adilson and his young family moved back into their tiny shack in Glória's yard, and he began working as an office boy in Leme, a neighborhood in the Zona Sul of Rio, until he and Filomena separated. Adilson's main concern after leaving "the life" had been to stay out of trouble. This meant staying clear of gang conflicts of any kind and earning an honest living.

However, on a warm afternoon in July 1998, he had the misfortune of being present in the streets of Vila Maria, the favela his mother lived in and where he had gone with Diego after he and Filomena separated: *"Um belo dia"* ("One fine day," as storytellers in the favelas of Rio often say at the beginning of a particularly gruesome story), José Pedro, a slow-witted *maconheiro* (pothead) from Felicidade Eterna who often visited Vila Maria to buy drugs, arrived there to buy marijuana. The police had actually caught his brother Leandro *em flagrante* (in the act) as he attempted to escape his bungled assault, and he was sent to prison, but the family of the dead student still demanded that their local gang revenge the death of their kin. So when it became known that José Pedro had naively shown up to buy his usual stash of marijuana, he was already in danger.

The gang members in Vila Maria quickly discerned that José Pedro was Leandro's brother and determined that he was a suitable target for revenge. José Pedro became the corporeal payback for the high school student. Adilson, unfortunately, happened to be hanging around that day and, like so many others, witnessed the Vila Maria gang cursorily question and then murder José Pedro.

When I ran into Adilson on the bus only a few days after José Pedro's murder, he told me how José Pedro had died and explained that he was killed as a substitute for his brother, Leandro. Adilson felt there was nothing he could have done in the situation. He could see the "logic" of the killing from the perspective of the gang and the immediate relatives of the student; somebody "had to die" for Leandro's bungled assault and for the death of an innocent. It apparently was not enough that Leandro himself was rotting in jail. Something more had to be done. Adilson kept repeating, *"Tinha que morrer, tinha que morrer mesmo."* ("He had to die. That's how it is, he had to die.") José Pedro "had to pay" for the sins of his brother, Leandro.

When the Felicidade Eterna gang found out that José Pedro had been killed in Vila Maria after innocently wandering in there to buy *maconha* (marijuana), they, too, vowed revenge: *"Um foi lá e ficou. Agora, um de lá vai ficar aqui."* ("One went there and stayed [died]. Now, one from there is going to stay [die] here.") But they were also disturbed that Adilson had been a witness but had not tried to intervene on José Pedro's behalf. They were angry about his disloyalty, even though he was no longer a true gang member. Celso, Adilson's compadre who was friendly with some of the local gang members, warned Adilson that the gang was talking about avenging the murder and that he was a possible target. Adilson, hardened by years of hanging out with more professional paid killers, considered the Felicidade Eterna gang at the time to be unprofessional, "small-time." His response to Celso's warning had been *"Quem fala não faz."* ("The one who speaks doesn't act.") Days later, after an evening of playing cards with Tiago, Adilson was murdered on the steps of Celso's shack in Felicidade Eterna.

The police and the personnel from the medical institute arrived approximately twenty-four hours after the shooting, not long after Tomás, the newly elected president of the Residents Association, called them from the newly installed orelhão. Tomás waited long enough to ensure that everything would appear normal and that the police would not have many leads by the time they arrived; he was smart enough to stay out of gang-related business.[33]

What more is there to say about this particular death? Residents living near the site of the murder—Tiago and Celso—were petrified of what Adilson's death on their property could mean to them. Adilson's family was large, and he had many brothers who were either bandits or policemen. Within hours, Glória's extended family and Celso's family temporarily moved out of the area, fearing that, given the circumstances of his death, Adilson's family would eventually seek revenge.

In this case, the series of revenge killings had been swift. But a lingering climate of fear gripped those residents who were friends of Adilson. People began to wonder if their own bodies could provide the payback in another round of revenge killings. Anything seemed possible. The families connected to the local gang members were the most fearful, sensing that in this game of revenge, the next to fall was somehow less predictable. Most other residents had a vague idea of why Adilson had been murdered, but if they were not connected to any of the individuals involved, they considered themselves relatively safe as long as they kept far away from the trouble. Overall, a sense of insecurity hung in the air long after this murder. As one resident quipped, "*Vingança é um prato que se come frio*," literally, "Revenge is a plate that one eats cold," meaning that revenge could come much later, when one is least expecting it.

WOMEN, OPPOSITIONAL CULTURE, AND RELIGIOUS CONVERSION

When Filomena was informed of Adilson's death, her first response was, "If only he had still been in the church, then perhaps they would have spared his life." Filomena had experienced the awakening of her religious feelings during the time she was hiding out in Caxias with Adilson. She had gone in and out of serious conversion, however, until Adilson's death. In the aftermath of his death in 1998, Filomena renewed her faith and joined her sister, Soneca, in becoming, once again, a member of the Assembly of God Church.

Having known Filomena and Soneca since 1991 and having understood, at some level, certain of their attitudes concerning religion, I was surprised at their conversion. Both sisters had always loved to dance—an activity strictly prohibited by the church. Throughout the years I had known them—as preadolescents and adolescents—religion was one of the many aspects of everyday life that they made fun of relentlessly. As children, they had been forced to enter and drop out of a variety of religions according to the impulses of their mother, who would join

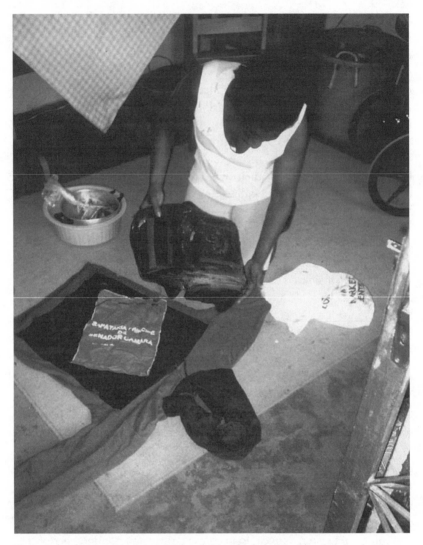

Figure 13. Glória examining Adilson's bloodied clothes after his death. Photograph by author.

churches and then, during times of disillusionment, deliberately change
allegiances and then poke fun at them.

   In retrospect, however, I suppose I should not have been so surprised,
given the known context of the Protestant religions in Rio de Janeiro. According to ISER (Instituto Superior de Estudos da Religião, 1996), the
Pentecostal temples are located in the poorest neighborhoods of the city

and attract those with the least income and formal education, characteristics of many residents of Felicidade Eterna and particularly Glória's family. At a time when it consisted of only about a hundred shacks, Felicidade Eterna supported six houses of worship. According to the ISER study, approximately 69 percent of the members of these churches are women. Thus, Soneca and Filomena were not anomalous in terms of their desire to join. Nevertheless, their choice to become crentes at this particular moment in their lives merits examination.

I would like to offer here a set of reflections on the meanings of religious conversion in the context of urban violence. I offer the possible interpretation that residents, and particularly women, of the lowest-income neighborhoods are using the strategy of religious conversion to ward off the effects of the slippage in the rules of everyday violence happening around them. It seems possible that religious conversion, especially to Protestant religions such as Assembly of God, has taken on a new meaning within the context of the high levels of violence that shantytown residents such as those in Felicidade Eterna regularly experience. It seems as if women are choosing religious conversion as a form of oppositional culture, one that resists male oppositional culture, namely, gang membership and participation in urban violence.

Individual friends from the network of people I came to know in Felicidade Eterna often espoused the opinion that "things are continually getting worse," and this discourse applied equally well to both the general economy and the levels of violence that they were forced to accommodate to. With regard to the levels of violence, Felicidade Eterna had certainly survived many unstable periods since the early 1990s. To name but a few of the deaths that residents either witnessed or were close to: Sílvio, Soneca's boyfriend, had been killed by gun crossfire only months earlier; Jairo had been killed, by either civil police or some other group, probably not for any deed he had carried out but as a revenge for the deeds of his brother, Breno; José Pedro had been killed for the mistake his brother Leandro committed in the bungled assault of a bus; and Adilson was killed for not intervening in José Pedro's murder.

Marília summed up the unpredictable nature of the more recent violence when she explained why she did not want to go shop in a neighborhood where we used to go years earlier, saying, "They [even] killed a pregnant Christian woman there."[34] Based on these collective experiences, there was an increasing sense that it was no longer possible to tell who might be killed for the deeds of whom. There was a logic to the game, that is, people were killed for reasons; there was an alternative justice system that had become institutionalized, and both gangs and police were involved. But in the always shifting personalities and sets of relationships between bandits and police, it was impossible to know for sure how justice would be defined in any one particular moment. People commented that it used to be that one did not kill one person for the misdeeds of another, but now this rule was less reliable. It used to be that women were excluded, but this seemed to be breaking down as well.

The lure of the neo-Pentecostal or evangelical religions has its own history within the field of anthropology. Sidney Mintz wrote as far back as 1960 in *Worker in the Cane* about the influence of revivalist churches in Puerto Rico of the 1940s:

> The revivalist churches have exercised a remarkable influence in recent years, particularly in underdeveloped countries and among people who are poor and subjected to rapid social and cultural change. They appear to be strongest in rural areas but also win many adherents in urban slums, whether in Johannesburg, Kingston, or Detroit. Their proselytes may be former tribesmen or former Catholics; one thing they rarely seem to be, however, is former ecumenical Protestants. The revivalist churches are the churches of the detribalized, the deculturated, and the disinherited. They fill many needs for lower-class people who, one way or another, have lost their stake in "the old ways." The revivalist churches provide an important source of recreation, and this should not be disparaged. They provide group membership, with all the psychological satisfactions such membership can give. (258)

Mintz further suggests that in the decision of Taso (the sugarcane worker who is the central character in Mintz's ethnography) to join a revivalist religion, there is room for a Weberian explanation, that is, that these churches provide a worldview that is "remarkably congenial to growing mobility aspirations in a society that is becoming Westernized" (266).

More recently, anthropologist John Burdick (1998) examined three forms of popular Christianity in Brazil: Pentecostalism, popular Catholic devotion to the slave-saint Anastácia, and the "Catholic inculturated Mass."[35] He studied these popular religious forms among Afro-Brazilian women in nearly the same context described throughout this book—among low-income women living in the Zona Norte and the Baixada Fluminense in Rio—and reported that these religious experiences move people to create new social identities. Burdick found that almost all the black female evangelicals had a much stronger stance against racial prejudice, "from the commonsense feeling that prejudice was wrong, to a much stronger moral stance bolstered by their new evangelical understanding" (144).

Burdick's book seeks a dialogue with political activists, especially black consciousness movement activists, asking them to reconsider their seemingly negative position toward the new religious convictions taken up by the poor. Burdick recognizes and addresses the common activist position that views these movements as lacking in political commitment, as passive in terms of political action, or, even worse, as breeders of various forms of false consciousness. While the criticisms made by political activists are worthy of consideration, it must also be recognized that these religious movements, albeit with agendas of their own, are out there in the trenches providing one of the few types of bodily protection available.[36]

Burdick suggests that political activists might actually look for support among previously rejected groups, particularly religious groups, and proposes that a broader perspective on these groups is required. In the process, he argues that such religious proclivities cannot simply be dismissed as breeders of false racial consciousness—a boon to anthropologists who still struggle to find meaning and logic in a more emic perspective.

Burdick argues that these churches have a positive effect on black self-esteem, as evidenced in the encouragement of light-skinned boys to marry dark-skinned girls and the telling statistic that white evangelical women were more likely than other Brazilian women to marry black men. Indeed, Burdick suggests that the fact that more black Pentecostal women marry whiter men may be the result of a strengthened sense of black pride rather than some sort of "false consciousness" propelling them toward whitening.

I agree with Burdick that it is too simplistic to reject conversion experiences as examples of false consciousness. It is, I would argue, useful to see them as a response to everyday violence, a gendered form of oppositional culture. This religious response is, in many ways, a response to young black women's own everyday context, where they see the young men in their communities going astray, getting involved in gangs and drug trafficking, and winding up dead. To some extent, their oppositional culture—a flight into a religious world that prohibits drinking, advocates moral redemption, and still believes in honest work—is as apolitical as gang activity. Quite unlike gang activity, however, successful religious conversion of men would take them out of the gangs and save their lives, even if it would not offer them stable employment. Religious conversion may actually be a form of women's oppositional culture that is a response to men's oppositional culture.

More generally, recent research on the rise of evangelical religions in Latin America has suggested that these religions are embraced by the poorest communities and that a number of gender-related issues can help explain their popularity and appeal.[37] In one particularly optimistic interpretation, Elizabeth Brusco (1995), working in Colombia, argues that the evangelical movement is a "challenge to the prevailing form of gender subordination," describing it as "an especially powerful ideological tool that radically alters sex role behavior, promotes female interests, and raises the status of women" (136). Burdick (1993) also found that women from these low-income communities have more room in these religious spaces to discuss domestic conflict than they did in other (even politicized) church movements. Similarly, Machado and Mariz (1997) argue that the attraction of Pentecostalism and charismatic Catholicism lies in their ability to deal with problems that have been considered private, such as domestic violence suffered by women.

These insights can be employed in the case discussed here. Both sisters attempted to persuade their partners to join the Assembly of God Church while they were still involved with them, although the characteristics of each of their partners, as well as the partnerships themselves, were quite different. I would argue that these women's fluctuating religious fervor was, in addition to religious conviction, at least partly influenced by a desire to distance themselves (and potentially their partners) from the real or potential conflicts in which the men were enmeshed.

For Filomena and Soneca, changing out of voguish skintight shorts and into long white skirts signaled their renewed allegiance to the church and their personal transformation, at least in terms of how they desired to present themselves to the outside world. Neither was successful over the years in persuading her partner to become a crente, nor did either of them become fully devoted members of the church themselves. In part, as both explained to me, they had become members of the church because of a saintlike *pastora* (female pastor), Sister Iara.[38]

Both sisters had become involved with men who at one time or another had been involved in criminal activities. Filomena had been with Adilson since she was a young girl of fourteen. He had been her first love, and they had, for a time, raised their child together as a couple. At the time of his death, they had been separated a little over a year. Filomena had enjoyed only minimal success in convincing Adilson to join the church while they were still together. He occasionally accompanied Filomena to church in his suit and white shirt and tie, but he never became a bona fide member. After their separation and until his death, Adilson showed no interest in the church.

Filomena attended Adilson's funeral, despite her fears that his family would cast blame on her, since they believed his continued attachment to her led him to spend time in Felicidade Eterna, the location of his murder. Adilson's mother, Lívia, was so devastated by the death that she did not attend the funeral. His siblings were silent during the services, which was later interpreted by Glória as proof of their deep suffering, as well as probable evidence of their plans for retribution. Filomena became nervous as Adilson's family's desire for vengeance and the unrest between gangs became clear. She decided against attempting to retrieve a refrigerator she had lent to Lívia some time earlier. In the days following Adilson's funeral, Filomena dug out her long white skirt and white blouse from her pile of clothes and began writing long letters to Sister Iara, expressing her renewed belief in God, her belated realization of the love she still felt for Adilson, and her desire to return to the fold.

Soneca's story differs from that of her sister. Soneca's partner, Sílvio, was a segurança for a drug boss and came from a much more comfortable socioeconomic background than Soneca. He lived on one of the asphalt streets adjoining Felicidade Eterna, and his family lived inside a walled compound with tile floors, an outdoor patio, and numerous rooms and bathrooms. He was also much lighter-skinned than Soneca, a quality about which he never ceased to remind her. Sílvio had made it known to Soneca that he was not interested in having a serious relationship with her because of her dark skin color. He told her repeatedly that he would never marry a preta like her.

Despite the unmitigated agreement among Soneca's friends in Felicidade Eterna that Sílvio was a racist, this was the young man with whom Soneca was *apaixonada* (in love with). When she became pregnant with his child in 1995, at the age of seventeen, she decided to go through with the pregnancy even though she had been told that she should not have children because of a condition related to her sickle-cell anemia. Sílvio also impregnated his mother's stepdaughter (a girl who lived in his household) at about the same time he impregnated Soneca, but at the time of his death, he was planning to marry a third woman.

According to Soneca, Sílvio died in the line of duty while trying to protect his drug boss during a shoot-out. Soneca, who was six months pregnant at the time, had to be taken to the hospital directly from the funeral, where she had threatened to jump into the grave, accompanying Sílvio in death as she had wanted to do in life. "I am not sure," she repeated, "that I can go on living without him." From then on, Soneca was in and out of the hospital until she gave birth prematurely a couple of months later. During this time, she also purportedly lost her faith (perhaps

Figure 14. Filomena and Diego just days after Adilson's death. Photograph by author.

temporarily) in God and in the church. Although she continued to feel connected to the generous and kindly Sister Iara, she felt more or less apathetic toward the organized aspects of religious life. Soneca had joined the church with a *propósito* (purpose, intention): she had hoped that her faith would bring Sílvio to her side and keep him alive in his dangerous line of work. When Sílvio was killed and his alliances with other women had been confirmed, she experienced a crisis in her faith and wondered why circumstances had turned out the way they had.

I would here offer another defining aspect of these revivalist religions, one that builds on the work of the previously cited scholars but also takes into account the lived experiences of everyday violence that women such as Soneca and Filomena attempt to survive. An additional attraction of these religious groups is that they offer a place to turn to and a definitive break from the experiences connected with violence. Religious belonging offers to women the bodily discipline—the clothing and bearing—that suggests they are "out of the game." One message, among others, that religious belonging and the public display of that belonging transmit is that the person is an honest citizen. It is one concrete way—one of the very few—in which one can still be poor (and dark-skinned) and be saying and fortifying through clothing a definitive message: this person is far from the world of drugs, crime, violence, and trouble—in the church's language, closer to God. The effect of this protective camouflage is to shield the wearers from the forms of violence that affect them, sometimes as a result of being the mothers, sisters, and lovers of men in trouble. It is a way for the poor to decriminalize themselves in a society that criminalizes them.

It is perhaps not mere coincidence that these stricter religious orders are having their greatest success precisely in the brown zones. Such religious groups are in the position to actively address and specify regimes of the body; crentes are required to dress in a particular way, to refrain from dancing, and to remain abstinent from alcohol. For those residents who suffer the injustices that are usually considered "private" problems—physical or sexual abuse against women and children, for example—their only recourse, other than such religious control of the body, is the gangs who control the body through acts of vengeance, or the police whose operative vision is one that views all residents of favelas as criminals. In the sense that these religious movements see all people as equal in the eyes of God and simply prohibit particular behaviors, their subjects are able to live outside of the absent or corrupted state, and without the gangs. I would argue that the religious groups provide an alternative to living within what Leeds (1996) has called the "parallel state."

It is interesting to remember that both Filomena and Soneca joined the Assembly of God Church while being involved with men who were heavily engaged in dangerous criminal activities. On the one hand, their joining could be seen as an attempt to save their partners. But there is another interpretation. They were also trying to publicly and symbolically distance themselves from the men they loved. Given the sense that women and children are no longer safe from gang violence, women who do become entangled with men who are involved in dangerous activities are definitely at risk. Those who would never before have been considered legitimate targets—young women, for example—now need to reaffirm an identity separate from the men in their lives in order to distance themselves from the periodic cycles of revenge that plague the parallel state. Symbolic clothing, in the service of religious belonging, reaffirms the once taken-for-granted status as a nontarget. Religious belonging has become not only an indicator of faith but also a protective symbol of neutrality and nonparticipation in the escalating violence occurring among police, bandits, and police-bandits.

By 1998, Glória's two youngest daughters were barely twenty years old, and both were already widows with children. Neither of their young male counterparts had survived past their twenty-fifth birthday. Both young women had expressed and then retired their faith in God an inordinate number of times.[39]

This chapter has documented the ways in which the rule of law is distributed unequally in Brazil, a quality that Brazil shares with other states still in the process of democratic consolidation. I have argued, along with others,[40] that the poor residents in the brown zones of Rio de Janeiro are criminalized by the middle classes and elites. Survey-style polls that have been administered to the poorest segments of the working classes have found that they are in the position of supporting measures that increase violent police action, a position that other authors find "paradoxical" (Holston and Caldeira 1998). But if we look closely at what is happening over time in the brown zones that have been removed further and further from the benefits of economic well-being and the institutions and organizations that make up that place called "civil society," we find a different set of actors gaining local powers of their own. One such group is the local gang that crops up in such areas and winds up protecting local populations and mediating between their communities and larger, more imperialist gangs and police. The absence of the state in such areas means that these local gangs provide a parallel or alternative rule of law that deals with "private matters" which the state is unable and unwilling to address within these brown zones.

CHAPTER 6

Partial Truths, or the Carnivalization of Desire

The shift, from seeing sexual intercourse as a right of
husbands and highborn men toward wives and low-status
women, to seeing it as an expression and proof of deep
personal regard in all social classes is recent, imperfect, and
incomplete. Sex-as-love competes ineffectively with sex-
as-debauchery, sex-as-obligation, sex-as-right, sex-as-
degradation.

> L. A. Rebhun, *The Heart Is Unknown Country: Love in the
> Changing Economy of Northeast Brazil*, 212

Marieta, Glória's godchild and the daughter of Joana—owner of one of
Felicidade Eterna's home-front bars—was born in late 1991 and was
eight months old when I left the shantytown in 1992. She was a pudgy
infant with an expressive face and was often seen perched precariously
on the hip of her ten-year-old brother, Camargo, who would show her
off at Glória's shack on the barreira, where she would be passed around
among the cooing children, adolescents, and adults. When I arrived back
in Felicidade Eterna for a visit in May 1995, Marieta was a chubby toddler, bright but not very talkative for her age, with a pacifier permanently
affixed in her mouth. The pacifier had become her trademark; she rarely
took it out of her mouth, and then only to answer questions posed to her
with a curt and definitive "yes" or "no." This laconic aspect of her toddler character was well appreciated by her friends and neighbors.

At birth, it was noted that Marieta had a rather small but odd-looking
growth on her *bundinha* (little buttocks). Her mother had been told to
wait a couple of years before having it reexamined by a doctor, and so
when Marieta reached the age of four, Joana brought her to a local clinic
to have it looked at by a female physician on staff. When the doctor asked

Marieta to turn over with her pants down so that she could examine the growth, Marieta yanked the pacifier from her usually silent mouth and uttered her soon-to-be infamous phrase, "In my aaaass, noooo, idiot!"

These words would, in the days and months to come, become the punch line of a joke that Glória and Marieta repeated to friends and neighbors. They had the routine worked out like veteran performers. Glória would look at Marieta and ask her, "What did you say to the doctor?" and Marieta would respond the same way each time, angrily pulling the pacifier out of her mouth and defiantly shouting, "In my aaaass, noooo, idiot!" at which point everyone, including Glória and little Marieta, would break into convulsive laughter.

SEXUALITY IN THE CONTEXT OF LOCAL CULTURE

I embark on the intellectual project of this chapter in a rather hesitant and tentative fashion—more so than in other places in this book—because I recognize the alertness that must be maintained when attempting to carry out and report on any research that engages poverty and sexuality, thematic areas of knowledge production that can all too easily be used to control and revictimize marginalized populations. This project is generally challenging because of the ease by which the information here could be distorted.

I must ask the reader to attempt to avoid his or her own ethnocentrism and versions of either Western feminism or classism here, for what I am arguing is not necessarily unique to the Brazilian lower classes, nor even to Brazil. I offer this chapter as one that provokes, that makes it possible to think about the reasons that some things are said and some are left unsaid with regard to sexuality in the flow of everyday interactions. This chapter confronts the peculiar form of machismo that is present in places like Felicidade Eterna, one that is naturalized and normalized within the flow of everyday life and in which men and women both participate. It is about the lack of alternative public discourses that make their way into the lives of people living in Felicidade Eterna.

I argue that there are a number of disturbing elements that structure everyday sexuality in places like Felicidade Eterna, but that there is no easy way to confront these elements because the discourses that would be necessary to battle these problems are either not well developed, not disseminated beyond the reaches of the middle and upper classes, or simply taboo. In part, it seems, any critique of sexuality is difficult for women to carry out because of the reigning Carioca identity that loudly speaks of a sensual, tropical sexuality, one that has triumphed in a kind of Brazilian carnivalization of desire. My point is simple: this carnivalization of desire is largely, although not entirely, a masculinist vision of desire and transgression. As a result, counterdiscourses to this particular vision are difficult to develop.

DISCOURSES OF SEX-POSITIVENESS

He was an older man, perhaps over sixty-five and certainly retired. He wanted to know where I had been the last two years. I told him that I had been carrying out research in Brazil. "Brazil!" he exclaimed. "I was there, oh, it must have been more than thirty years ago, consulting on an engineering project in Rio de Janeiro, but I will never forget it. Such beautiful women and running around practically naked on the beach. It's a paradise. Just paradise." Then he paused for a minute and thought dreamily to himself. Meanwhile, I was amazed at his vivid and excited sentiments about Brazil and wondered what experiences he had there and what it must have been like thirty years ago. Then, he added, "For men, of course, it's a paradise for men."

Author's fieldnotes, New York, September 1992

I am not the first visitor to Rio de Janeiro to remark on the importance of sexuality to Carioca identity.[1] According to some contemporary anthropological interpretations of brasilidade, or Brazilianness, sexuality is central: "While sexual life in North America or Europe has been treated as an essentially individual phenomenon, in Brazil it has also emerged as a central issue at a social or cultural level, and has been taken, for better or worse, as a kind of key to the peculiar nature of Brazilian reality" (Parker 1991:28). While I would perhaps be more hesitant than anthropologist Richard Parker (1991) about interpreting sexuality as central to *all* of Brazil, I do take it for granted that sexuality is a key metaphor used by Cariocas in their everyday language and description of almost all aspects of social life. Sexual joking and teasing, likewise, seem to be a friendly aspect of even the most benign social relations, acting as a kind of verbal confirmation of the centrality of sexuality to social life.

The documentary film *O Amor Natural* (1996), by Heddy Honigmann, captures well the permissive and celebratory sexuality of Rio, as
well as the inherent comfort level around expressions of eroticism and
sexuality that range across class-, color-, age-, and gender-distinct Carioca subcultures.[2] Heddy Honigmann selects a series of interviewees and
explains to them that she is interested in their interpretation of some previously unpublished erotic writings by the Brazilian poet Carlos Drummond de Andrade.[3] The premise of the film is to explore how different
individuals interpret this previously unknown poetry. The film explores
elements of Rio's diverse population, transmitting to the viewer an implicit message about the special attitude that Brazilians have toward their
own bodies and toward eroticism in general. Among those interviewed
on film by Honigmann are an aging female Olympic swimmer; two
middle-class women lying on a beach in the wealthy Zona Sul who are,
on camera, inspired by the poetics to discuss the hottest sexual moments
of their pasts; an elderly widower from a lower-class background who,
surrounded by his children, is encouraged by his daughter to brag about
his sexual excesses—certainly a humorous display of his ongoing expression of a particular kind of masculinity. The film celebrates Drummond without pretense and serves as a monument to brasilidade—of a
"sex-positiveness" that is both real and palpable. This film supports the
notion that sexuality is central to Brazilian identity and that Brazilians
are proudly interested in and devoted to their own particular form of
normative heterosexuality. Brazilian sexuality is, of course, more concerned with buttocks than with breasts,[4] a lesson properly transmitted to
a foreign audience, but where the film truly entertains outsiders is in presenting the ways in which elderly Brazilians—both men and women—
engage in sexual talk and banter. What the film manages to convey—
especially to a non-Brazilian audience—is the fact that Cariocas possess
an open, permissive approach to sexuality. The participants in the film
are shown reading explicitly erotic poetry without embarrassment and
with a great deal of good-natured humor.

The presentation of elders as capable of expressing interest in sex and
the presentation of a daughter encouraging her father to speak of his in-
fidelities appear in an equally amusing light. The film entertains and captures an important partial truth. Cariocas do possess a "sex-positive" attitude toward life. At the same time, however, nobody attempts to ruin
the fun or to disrupt the narrative of sexual permissiveness. Nobody
asked these same participants about more contested aspects of sexuality,
such as their feelings about male and female homoerotic behavior, or

even the more well-known gendered double standard on fidelity. Importantly, no women in the film were found to be bragging of their extramarital sexual excesses.

Sexual teasing and banter are common in Felicidade Eterna. These everyday practices of sexual joking and teasing are particularly interesting because of what they potentially reveal about the local sexual culture. They permeate everyday relations and allow for commentaries that might be more difficult to speak about directly. Instead, messages are transmitted through the subtlety of humor.[5] Being clever with words and stories has value, as does the ability to respond appropriately to a joke. Bawdy sexual humor is heard endlessly, and it is practiced by young and old alike. This is why, at some gut level, I can readily appreciate what Honigmann captured in her film. She captured a partial truth, one among many others. Honigmann's recognition of the seemingly ageless interest in sex talk was something I myself had experienced through Glória.

One of Glória's favorite stories was about her own mother, Valdirene, who, over the last thirty years or so, had become a prudish, strict woman, a crente, a devout member of the Assembly of God Church. I learned about different aspects of Valdirene's character while on a three-hour bus ride to the outer edges of the metropolitan area of Rio, accompanying Glória on a surprise visit to her mother's community. When we finally stepped off the bus, Glória and I had to hike many kilometers along dusty roads to track down Valdirene because, having visited infrequently over the years, Glória had forgotten how to get to her mother's house. Every kilometer or so we would call out to a person along the road, asking if he or she knew where Valdirene, "the crente," lived. We finally found Valdirene's house, a small cement dwelling at the side of the church, and seconds into this mother and daughter reunion, Valdirene launched into a story about a recent dream. I thought my Portuguese had suddenly gone bad, because after hearing about Valdirene's religious conversion, I did not expect to hear what I heard. Valdirene was describing in great detail a dream about the erect penis of her long-deceased husband, Glória's father. Valdirene told Glória that when she woke up, "It [the erect penis] had disappeared." *"Estou joinha minha filha, estou joinha"* ("I am joyful, my daughter, I am joyful"), she exclaimed, and repeated these words over and over again to Glória, as if thankful for the mere opportunity to still dream of sex. Glória, amused by this story, occasionally looked over at me and winked, reassuring me that I was understanding it all correctly. In the months following this visit with her mother, Glória would use the story of Valdirene's dream to entertain her children, friends, and neighbors about her estranged and highly religious mother. Glória would imitate her mother's toothless grin and frail body and exclaim, "I am *joyful*, my daughter, I am *joyful*," a phrase uttered by the faithful during mass but also by Valdirene in celebration of her erotic dream.

Nelsinho, the adopted son of Elis, Glória's *travesti* (transgendered person, in this case male to female) neighbor, was often teased as a young child.[6] When he was fifteen months old, Soneca, who was Nelsinho's official godmother, would grab his penis affectionately and, holding it upright in her hand while waving it back and forth, would tease, *"Você é como galinha, sua mãe cria pra depois comer"* ("You are like a chicken, your mother raises you to later eat you"). While it would have been in poor taste to directly challenge what appeared to many women in Felicidade Eterna as Elis's imperfect bid to portray herself as a woman, she (through her son Nelsinho) had become the object of ridicule, although she was also adored and admired as a good person and a solid friend by many. In public, residents of Felicidade Eterna treated Elis as if she were a woman; they referred to Elis as "she" and listened attentively to her tales about working in the kitchen of an upscale motel. Women exchanged gossip with her and complained about men with her. Privately, however, the fact that she did indeed have a penis was a theme that provoked remarks, both derogatory and humorous, including those made about her son. Over time, Nelsinho had learned to respond to the constant teasing. Once when Glória asked Nelsinho whether or not Eber, his father and Elis's partner, was home, he turned to Glória and replied sarcastically, "Why? So you can grab his dick?" Glória recognized the humor in this child's response but also wondered privately if Nelsinho would not turn out to be a little *fresco*, literally fresh, in the sense of being naughty, but here also referring to the possibility of Nelsinho turning out to be an effeminate man, or "sissy," later on.

THE CARNIVALIZATION OF DESIRE

An in-depth exploration of humor in the form of sexual teasing or sexual joking leads us to an analysis of Brazilian sexuality that goes in a different direction than the standard story of sexual permissiveness and sex-positiveness that has been presented in academic literature and popular culture. These representations, while capturing a partial truth, also demand critical reflection.

Sexual permissiveness and even sex-positiveness are social facts that describe social relations in Rio de Janeiro and capture important aspects of this local culture. Brazil's self-promoted image as an eroticized "tropical paradise" is an accurate one. There is a sense of bodily liberation, expressed in body language, dress, flirtation, and exuberant dance that grounds Carioca bodies differently from North American or Western European bodies. I was regaled with stories about other anthropological fieldworkers who had preceded me and who were "eaten" by Brazilian culture, foreigners who were slowly seduced by the reigning sexual culture and who rediscovered their bodies in the Brazilian context.[7] I, too, have witnessed this transforming experience, and I do not doubt its veracity. Carioca culture, for example, is immediately recognizable in its penchant for clothing styles that hug and accentuate the body, particularly the buttocks. During my own fieldwork, I moved slowly in this direction, away from wearing baggy and somewhat unflattering North American clothes and toward wearing more tight-fitting and revealing Brazilian clothes. This was partly an attempt not to stand out, and it worked.

In Rio de Janeiro, public flirtation is an elaborate and beloved game, not scrutinized as an objectification of women's bodies but rather appreciated as pleasurable and complimentary of women's bodies. Brazilian women friends of mine from the middle and upper classes, most of whom have a very ambivalent attitude toward North American feminism and some of whom are approaching middle age, told me that they honestly enjoyed the attention of flirtatious exchanges, and that being publicly recognized as sexually desirable is important for them. Being ignored is considered true punishment—a fate worse than death. I was told over and over again that Brazilian women of all classes enjoy being looked at, complimented, and considered sexually desirable. One of my Carioca friends—a professional woman in her early thirties—who spent years studying in the United States remarked that she always looked forward to getting back to Rio because in the United States she felt ignored, especially by men.

Implicitly, much of the important anthropological work on sexuality in Brazil has emerged out of a lineage of male scholars interested in male homoeroticism. Much of this work was groundbreaking within the context of scholarly research at the time it was written. For example, Peter Fry (1982a) posited that male homosexuality in Brazil consisted of two distinct types, an upper-class model and a lower-class model. Fry believed that the upper-class model was a kind of "import" from Western

Europe and North America that adheres to a conceptualization of homosexuality that connects one's sexual and social identity with one's sexual object choice. The lower-class version recognized the categories of *homens* (men) and *bichas* (meaning worm, a term used derogatorily to refer to effeminate men and translating as something similar to "faggot" in English) and was a dualistic model of active and passive partners who divided along both sexual and social gender roles. Within this model, homens were understood to be the active, penetrating men who maintain their masculine identity regardless of whether their sexual object choice is male or female, and bichas were understood to be the passive, receiving partners who represent effeminate men and whose masculine identity ultimately is compromised by their social and sexual role.

Over time, a number of anthropologists, building on Fry, have charted important elements of Brazilian sexuality. They wrote about topics such as masculine prostitution in São Paulo (Nestor Perlongher 1987) and homosexual identity formation and political organization in São Paulo (Edward MacRae 1992), extending this literature in important and creative ways.

Richard Parker (1991), building on Fry's understanding of the homem-bicha binary construct, illustrated how the structures of activity and passivity are used to genderize, eroticize, and categorize the Brazilian sexual universe.[8] Parker suggests in this early work that sexuality in Brazil has a liberatory quality, one that encourages various forms of transgressive play. But transgression, finally, seems to be patterned by traditional gender relations, with men being expected to act as transgressors and women playing the role of "boundary-setters" (Goldstein 1994a).

Historian James Green (1999) has recently suggested that much of the anthropological work in the last two decades may have overestimated the extent to which Fry's (1982a) binary applied to the various sexual subcultures that existed in Brazil since the early twentieth century. Contrary to Fry and those who built on Fry's ideas, Green suggests that subcultures of effeminate and noneffeminate men with homoerotic desires existed prior to the introduction of Western European medicolegal ideas.

Feminists have also produced a significant body of work about sexuality in Brazil, but they are cited much less often in the anthropological literature on sexuality. One possible reason, based on my understanding of the place of feminism in Brazilian intellectual life, may be that the feminist literature produced in Brazil was viewed as too essentialist. Another, possibly even more powerful, reason is that feminist literature on sexuality was perceived to be too "sex-negative." One could argue that Brazilian feminists have attempted to avoid what is perceived as radical North American feminism, a feminism that criticizes normative gender relations and heterosexuality but also may appear to be sex-negative. Brazilian feminism has had difficulty directly confronting issues that touch upon the body and upon sexuality in the context of heterosexual relations. In the avoidance of these difficult areas of inquiry, it becomes difficult to unearth other stories, those partial truths that hint at the less certain aspects of sex-positivism.

The following anecdote related to sociologist Rose Marie Muraro, the author of *Sexualidade da Mulher Brasileira: Corpo e Classe Social no Brasil* (*Sexuality of the Brazilian Woman: Body and Social Class in Brazil;* 1983), may prove instructive in terms of understanding which public discourses—in the form of academic knowledge production—become acceptable over time, and which do not. Muraro's case provides an interesting window into the process of intellectual marginalization of certain feminist writings about sexuality.

According to political scientist Sonia Alvarez (1990:89–91), in 1971, Rose Marie Muraro, at the time, managing editor of *Vozes* editorial house, the same company that translated North American feminist author Betty Friedan's book *The Feminine Mystique* (1963) into the Portuguese language, invited Friedan to Brazil to speak. Alvarez notes that at the time, two distinct middle-class women's networks provided the organizational bases for nascent feminism in Brazil: a university- and militant opposition–based network of younger women, and an academic- and professional-based network of older women. Alvarez notes that two distinct feminisms emerged during this period of military dictatorship: one that would ultimately be invited to join the left in its attempt to reorganize the country and another that became perceived as the struggle of bourgeois lesbians against men and was considered unacceptable and alien.

Alvarez argues that the women's movement in Brazil positioned itself self-consciously in relation to the politics of public and private spheres. The organized left was cautious about backing any of the more radical gender-based demands of the women's movement, such as those that touched on the private sphere, or the body, as in the case of legalized abortion. It follows, as well, that legislation around issues that relate to sexuality would also be cautiously approached. Muraro's ambitious book, based on interviews with middle-class people in Rio de Janeiro, farmworkers in Northeast Brazil, and factory workers in São Paulo, took on a series of complicated issues related to sexuality and social class. Despite the fact that Muraro herself had earlier denounced Friedan's brand of feminism, her work seems to have been neglected by those contributing to the anthropological literature on sexuality.

Here I would like to speculate about why—apart from personal differences between authors that I may not be aware of—the anthropological literature on male homoeroticism seems to have completely marginalized works such as Muraro's. Two complementary processes seem to have been at work. First, the divisions within Brazilian feminism served to taint any feminism that addressed issues of sexuality in ways that echoed North American versions at that time. Second, scholarly anthropological works produced during the same period, which were notably not necessarily considered controversial at the time, were devoted to exploring the more permissive and carnivalesque aspects of Brazilian sexuality and not as interested in the more normative aspects of traditional gender relations. On the one hand, this early interest in male homoeroticism in Brazilian sexual culture represents a courageous and exceptional case of scholarship that in some respects preceded the emergence of "queer theory" in the European and North American context. On the other hand, it has led to a form of unintentional neglect with regard to research on other forms of sexuality. Perhaps this is an opportune time for feminist anthropologists to rethink and reconceptualize sexuality studies in Brazil.

I began this chapter with the description of a joking routine performed by a little girl, Marieta, and her godmother, Glória. The context of this popular humor—at once sexualized and communicative—is an expression of discontent that is rarely given much importance as a counterdiscourse among the more standard sex-positive discourses that are heard every day. Without understanding the humor here, one would be left with just the face value of talk and thus an emaciated view of the range of events that occur and are commented upon.

My efforts here are not meant as a complete replacement for or negation of sex-positiveness. I suggest, rather, that there is a neglected aspect to the overtly sex-positive narrative that has been emphasized by a lineage of scholars focusing on male homoeroticism and the more playful aspects of transgression. In the absence of a feminist critique of gendered power relations and normative heterosexual relations, some partial truths have remained hidden. The inability to speak critically about sexuality leaves poorer, darker-skinned Afro-Brazilian women in the position of second-class sexual citizens, unable to fully critique some of their own local subculture's particular approach to sexuality. Their discourse, however submerged, does occasionally find voice through their humor, and this humor provides a critique of everyday sexuality, a counterdiscourse that registers a definitive "crack" in this standard vision of sex-positiveness and begins to build a broader, deeper—and perhaps more troubling—picture of sexuality in contemporary working-class Rio de Janeiro.

ETHNOGRAPHY: LOCAL SEXUAL CULTURE IN FELICIDADE ETERNA

Sexual/Eating Metaphors, Subversion, and Creative Resistance

Among the people I came to know in Felicidade Eterna, as well as in signs available in the broader popular culture, metaphors about food and eating were often used to express ideas about sexuality. The word *comer*, which means both "to eat" and to actively consume another person sexually, is connected to male sexual activity. Women and others perceived as being in the sexually passive position are generally the metaphorical receivers, and they *dar*, or "give." It is thus possible to retranslate a number of Brazilian sexual identities into consumption metaphors—put most simply, you are defined by whether you are a person who eats or one who is eaten, that is, whether you are active or passive in the consumption process, and not by *what you consume*. The standard understanding of maleness and male identity in the Brazilian construction of sexuality[9]—more common among the popular classes—is that a man who eats other men and assumes the public status as the active sexual partner can maintain a firm male identity as an homem, while the passive partner, the bicha or viado, considered the recipient in anal sex, loses status. In this same context, a man who is cuckolded becomes a *corno* (horn, a man with horns), feminized by his partner's infidelity.[10] Within this particular sexual hierarchy, females are to be consumed, and they are viewed negatively when they assume the role of "active" consumers. This explains, in part, why calling someone a whore or a prostitute *(mulher da rua)* in this context has such negative connotations: such women are "dangerous" because they are outside of the home and because they do not act like other women. By being perceived as *active* sexually, they are causing a category disturbance. Similarly, women who consume too many sexual partners are referred to as *galinhas* (chickens) and *piranhas* (piranas or meat-eating fish), and both of these animal metaphors have negative connotations.[11]

The women living in Felicidade Eterna are able to subvert the social and moral order that idealizes men as eaters and women as those being eaten, resisting the social control embedded in these discourses through joking and storytelling. They, in turn, are empowered by this subversion, thus to some extent setting their own standards for acceptable sexual behavior. Women are involved in a type of creative metaphorizing that aims to subvert idealized notions about "who is eating whom," and in the process they make claims about their own personhood. They can *corn-ear* (put horns on, cuckold) their male partners by going out to "eat" other men. As a result of a woman's real or implied infidelity, her partner is perceived as turning into an animal himself, becoming a corno, or cuckold, and "growing horns."

"Eating" metaphors point not only to the nature of gendered sexual power relations where men are eaters and women are to be eaten but also to the intimate ways in which economic and sexual aspects of normative gender relations are intertwined. Women expect men to be providers, and this is a key element in a woman's recognition of a partner's good qualities. These economic expectations are woven into the fabric of daily life, and people use the metaphors of sexuality and eating to express their dissatisfaction with the status quo. The metaphors of eating and sexuality are turned upside down through humor, which functions as a window expressing their resistance to the traditional metaphorical and real constraints on their (sexual) selves.

Women do make men grow horns; they also actively seek out boyfriends with resources and demand food from them; they even break off relationships with men who literally consume too much and produce too little. And they tell these stories to one another, exercising and reaffirming among themselves a kind of subversive power, perhaps partly commodifying men and men's resources in response to their own commodification as sexualized, racialized, and exoticized Others.

Susan Bordo (1993) notes two waves of Foucauldian-influenced feminism—the first wave emphasizing his work on "discipline," "docility," "normalisation," and "bio-power," and a second, more "postmodern," wave emphasizing "intervention," "contestation," and "subversion." This call for the analysis of subversion, however, must be linked to an analytics of gendered power relations, enabling the examination of consistent forms of gendered social control. Glória, for example, retained her own pragmatic view that enabled her to call upon her male partners to be cooperative providers for her family. If they did not cooperate, one option she occasionally exercised was to deprive them of sex. She would, somewhat jokingly, talk about times of necessity in the past when she had to be extremely hard-edged about her well-developed pragmatics of exchange:

> I always ran behind, look, the day that I don't have money working, since I work by the month, I go out looking for that temporary work to give my children something to eat. I would go out on the street, I am not ashamed to say it, that's what I did. I would go out and arrange for a lover, go out with him and he would have to pay to go out with me. If not, I wouldn't go. I would say to him, "at least give me the soap to wash the bottom of my panties, since I am not going to go out and dirty my panties and then after have to spend money on soap." I would say that, I am not lying, it's the truth, God is watching. (Glória, taped interview, 1992)

Glória and her network of female friends and family in Felicidade Eterna have two major complaints about male privilege and the more generalized shortcomings of their male partners. First, they complain that men are inadequate economic providers, either not earning sufficiently or not sharing their wages appropriately to adequately care for their families. Second, men are not to be trusted in terms of fidelity. Men, according to women, are likely to fool around no matter who their stable partner is; this is simply a taken-for-granted fact of life. Women, too, can be adulterers, but the perception is that they are less often and then only as a means of revenge or payback rather than an act in and of itself. Because of the naturalized ways in which male sexuality is perceived—animal-like, uncontrollable, thoughtless—male infidelity is disliked but perceived as part of the normal repertoire of male behavior. This is not necessarily so in the opposite situation. Women are expected to be loyal to their partners simply because they are women, and their disloyalty shames and dishonors their partners, transforming them into the despicable and pitiable corno. Women work hard, however, to subvert these naturalized forms of male privilege and prevailing double standards.

Whenever Glória would talk about her on-again, off-again relationship with Zezinho (little Zé), her boyfriend in the early 1990s, she would recite a litany of complaints about him and then, finally, would sigh and say, *"Eu gosto dele"* ("I like him"), meaning she liked him sexually. When Zezinho and Glória first met, Zezinho was married and living with Lucina in Felicidade Eterna. The women of Felicidade Eterna, who kept abreast of all the twists and turns of favela gossip, thought that Lucina eventually grew tired of being beaten by Zé on a daily basis, and one day fled Felicidade Eterna with "Sandrão A Policião" for a home in a neat lower-class neighborhood, leaving Zé alone in their small shack with all six of their small children to care for. Three children were rescued by Lucina's mother, Dona Madalena, who still lived in Felicidade Eterna, and the remaining youngest three were adopted in by Glória, Zezinho's mistress at the time. Zezinho had impregnated both his wife and Glória at about the same time eight years earlier, so when Glória inherited Zezinho's children, Félix (Glória's son with Zé) also gained his half brother, Aguinaldo (Lucina's son with Zé), as a housemate.

Glória sustained this suddenly enlarged household on her meager income as a domestic worker. Zé worked occasionally as a fix-it man, accompanying Glória to the Zona Sul to find work, but ultimately, discouraged with this grueling form of day labor, he drank most of what he earned and did not contribute much to the household. Thus, Glória found, over time, that Zezinho fell far short of her expectations in numerous, fundamental ways. Glória's children often told me with biting humor how, in Zezinho's house, the number of rats outnumbered the number of humans and that the level of dirtiness and disorderliness that the house reached soon after Lucina's departure was proof that he could not really manage things without a woman. In her explanation of why she finally ended her long liaison with Zezinho, Glória proclaimed that he was taking more than he was contributing, specifically eating more than his fair share of meat and other food in her household. Zezinho, she criticized, would always take half or more of any meat he brought home, in spite of the fact that he had brought three children into her home and that Glória already had another nine to feed from the same portion.

Glória's final breakup story with Zezinho, in 1994, ends with a sort of poetic justice—a physical response to a metaphorical claim. Shortly after having fought and separated, Glória and Zezinho found themselves drinking next to one another at Joana's bar, and a fellow drinker—not from Felicidade Eterna—asked, out of curiosity, what their relationship to one another was. Before Glória was able to describe him as her ex-partner, Zezinho himself proudly answered, "I am eating her."

Glória, incensed by Zezinho's claim and choice of metaphors, seized the opportunity and smacked him hard in the face, bloodying his nose. The use of this eating metaphor was insulting, especially since she considered Zezinho by that time to be a leech—all along "eating" her hard-earned wages without contributing much of his own earnings to their combined household. In this context, his power-invoking claim to be "eating" her was a humiliation and a sign of disrespect beyond what Glória could bear, and it led to her own use of physical violence.

I was often present during Glória's retelling of the story of how she "beat up Zezinho and made him bleed." In her renditions to several groups of kin and friends, she never failed to emphasize the appropriateness of her response to his insolent remark and seemed to derive a great deal of pleasure from having put an end to Zezinho's "carnivorous" claims by shedding his blood. Glória was not about to be dominated permanently by any man—either physically or metaphorically.

Soneca, Glória's daughter, also uses "eating" metaphors to explain how she conquered a man and transformed him from a consumer of her body into a provider for herself and her pregnant (and hungry) sister, Anita. Again, here, as in the case of Glória, it is in the inversion of the taken-for-granted metaphor where humor is found and meanings are made. In describing an affair she carried on for a number of months as a young teenager with a married neighbor, Soneca emphasized how she induced him to use his money to buy food *for her* rather than for his own family, a feat she described with a good deal of pride. According to Soneca, everyone assumed that "he was eating her," but in reality, he was not eating her at all. To be able to motivate the man who was "eating her" to provide luxury food items for her and her sister was a way of making herself powerful. At the age of seventeen, Soneca reflected on the affair she had three years earlier:

> In the beginning, we didn't do anything. He lived next door. . . . I was friends with his wife. She never discovered what was going on. . . . I liked this *aventura* [affair]. I got fat. I came home with money. I came home with *bombons* [candy] for Anita. When I left him I was fifty-three kilos. Now I am *sequinha* [a little dried out, wasted]. I got fat on his account. I went to many hotels. I went to the vacation house. I visited places I didn't know before. I went out with many others, but nobody ever said anything to him. He was a corno but a corno who gave me things. (Soneca, taped interview)

Soneca was obviously proud of her ability to use her seductive capabilities to gain something in exchange. They were part of the tool kit she employed to help survive during difficult economic times. Soneca had registered her mother's perspective on a woman's right to claim payment from partners and, dutifully recalling her words, lived out Glória's maxim with regard to herself and her sister: "I never let my children experience hunger. Whenever I had problems, I would get a boyfriend."

Of course, not all women were as brazen as Soneca, who actually took pride in being able to use her youth and beauty to survive and even "get fat" within the context of a mistress relationship. More mature women, such as Darlene and Eliana, likewise, spoke of the "payoff" they expected from men; in the cases presented here, both of them describe situations in which they figured as the "other woman." Eliana had her last child, Wanderlino, with "O Sargento" ("The Sergeant"), to whom she has been a mistress since 1985, the year after her husband died.

> When I met the father of my smallest here [she said pointing to her youngest child, Wanderlino]—he's a marine, a sergeant in the marines. When I met him, I met him while on a bus. I was working downtown near the Central. . . . He used to come two or three times a week . . . around midnight or one in the morning. Nowadays, he is getting home late and he is tired. He only comes once a week. But every week he is here. He lives with the other [woman]. . . . He helps a lot with things around the house. At times I am stupid, I don't request or demand. My deal with him is that if I am needing something I go to the telephone and the same day he brings it. . . . I am a widow, and widows have a pension. I am a pensionist, so my pension is a minimum salary. So with my salary and with the pension, it wasn't enough to buy a television. If I have a television, it is because he gave it to me. This refrigerator, he gave to me. If I have a roof, it was he who helped me. (Eliana, taped interview, 1995)

Similarly, Darlene, Glória's friend who was a sex worker in downtown Rio, spoke candidly about her "interests" in a boyfriend she was seeing in 1998, a man named Brunó, twenty years her senior, who earned between four and five salaries per month as a painter and a fix-it man. Darlene commented in an interview, "I don't intend to stay with this guy. If a better opportunity comes along, I am out of here. *Minha estrela não há brilhado ainda não.* [My star hasn't shown yet.] Bandit I don't want. . . . I have been with them, but not seriously. Police neither. I am scared of being a prisoner."

Sarlete, a young teenage neighbor of Glória's in Felicidade Eterna, was referred to by the dubious nickname "Buceta Assassina," or "Killer Pussy," by her friends. Dilmar, the leader of the local gang of Felicidade Eterna in the early 1990s, and Sarlete were lovers, and his liaison with her proved fatal for him. In 1994, when Sarlete was only fourteen, she told her age-mates, the boys in Dilmar's gang, that Dilmar was planning to betray them. Dilmar had, by that time, already come under suspicion because he had poorly calculated a butcher shop robbery; he had sent some of the local boys to carry out the job, but when the boys arrived at the shop, the owner seemed to have been warned in advance and was ready for them with a team of heavily armed guards. Two of the three boys managed to flee the scene, but one was captured and shot, and then left to die in an alleyway. After the robbery the boys continually wondered among themselves if Dilmar, for some reason, had set them up. In any case, Sarlete's information fed their fears, and rather than risking their own futures, they decided to carry out a preemptive strike. Sarlete aided them in their plot. One evening, while Sarlete was awaiting a tryst with Dilmar in her shack, the boys caught him off guard, walked him out to the field next to the favela, and killed him with his own gun, despite his repeated declarations that he had not betrayed them.

Sarlete proudly narrated these events for me in 1995, speaking in whispers, making me promise, in serious tones, not to tape-record the interview. Approximately a year after Dilmar's murder, the residents still felt a bit nervous and vulnerable in a place with no organized local gang structure of its own. Sarlete was also nervous because she was in a new relationship with a policeman who visited her out of uniform and never told anyone about his profession. Sarlete earned her nickname, "Killer Pussy," because so many of her boyfriends over the years seemed to be either police or bandits. Further, she explained, "They died after having eaten [had sex with] me,"[12] a joke that made clear the power she felt through her sexuality, one that could cause death for those who ate her.

Although eating is understood to be more powerful than being eaten—and being male entitles one to do the eating—here was a reversal of that normal scenario. Women often took the opportunity to subvert the given metaphorical structure: Glória whacking Zezinho, Soneca manipulating a man to provide her with food she would not normally be able to afford, Eliana and Darlene gaining economically from long-term liaisons with married men, and finally Sarlete "killing" the men who ate her. All of these are examples of women overturning the gender hierarchy embedded in the eating metaphors that make men symbolically dominant in the language of sexuality.

In their jokes about men and about "who's eating whom," as well as in their actions, women reveal their ability to turn metaphors and reality on their heads. The story about Soneca as the "other woman" reveals how, in a case where she perceived that others might see her as "just another woman willing to be the other woman" and therefore being taken advantage of, she was able to subvert that meaning and supply her own narrative, describing how she was able to acquire economic goods she herself could not afford. Sarlete's embrace of her nickname and defense of her identity as a "woman who eats" is another example of creative resistance to simple passivity. But in spite of women's creative resistance to the dominant metaphors of consumption and sexuality, they nevertheless would strictly adhere to some standard cultural scripts that inevitably reproduced aspects of the sexual hierarchy they worked so hard at times to subvert.

FROM BOYS TO MEN: NORMATIVE MASCULINIZATION AND HETEROSEXUALITY

Class-specific regimes of sexuality do exist. A good portion of the pride among this segment of the working-class Carioca population, I would argue, lies in their belief that even if they are not blessed with great material wealth, at least they have "good sex" and lots of it. It is the one abundant good that is perceived as inexhaustible and available—and it is free. One of the women I interviewed in a factory in São Paulo used a series of foods and their meanings to differentiate herself and people like her from os ricos (the rich), whose sex lives, she maintained, are as weak and bland as their diets:

> The poor man eats well, a feijão [bean soup] with meat inside, a mocotó [soup made from the hoof of a cow], carne seca [beef dried in the sun] inside the feijão. . . . [13] What I ask is the following, "Is the rich person going to eat all of this?" He eats only jelly and cheese. Bread and butter. What strength does that have? For this reason, they lose their potency early. At times, the poor man is feeling weak and he sends me to make a mocotó. . . . It makes you strong. I know because I am from Bahia. I make it. The rich person doesn't eat feijão. The iron is there. The bed [sex] of the poor person is better. Because of the food. (taped interview with female factory worker in São Paulo, thirty-eight, migrant from Itabuna, Bahia, 1992)

Among working-class Cariocas, it is considered unhealthy for men to go too long without sex: it can provoke insanity. Here, as well, a class thread runs through the gender role sexual expectations: there is the desire to provide boys with sexual experiences so that they can be knowledgeable about and fulfill their sexually active role. As part of the expected ritual of turning a boy into a man, boys are encouraged and expected to become active seducers.

It was a hot, lazy afternoon in 1992 in Felicidade Eterna, and Glória had planned to take a day off from working. I knew she was serious about her intentions because the night before she drank numerous beers and several glasses of her traditional café, allowing herself to relax completely and give herself over to a day of rest and recovery. Many of the children and her cherished childhood friend Eliana were hanging out that day in the tiny shack, seeking refuge from the sun and having an easygoing conversation. Glória became serious at one point and declared that

she needed to get after Roberto (the oldest boy in the large family) to take
Lucas, who was soon to turn eighteen, to visit a prostitute. The following is a section from the taped interview of that day:

> *Glória*: Who is in bad shape is Lucas. Lucas, the one with the *chouriço*
> [sausage, referring to his lips], is going to be eighteen in May, and
> he never *deu uma bimbada* [screwed around] that I know about.
> (Glória and Eliana laugh.) The other day I was telling Roberto that
> he has to take Lucas to the *zona*. And not the Zona Sul but the
> *zona da puta* [prostitution zone] of women.
>
> *Danni*: Why?
>
> *Glória*: *Dar uma bimbada.* [To have a little screw.]
>
> *Eliana*: After he learns, then you are going to see what happens.
>
> *Glória*: In the zona, you pay cheaply and you don't have any responsibility.
> There he puts her *calcinha no chão, dinheirinho na mão* [little
> pantie on the floor, little money in the hand] and that's done, it's
> over. *Vapt-vupt* [It is fast].

Glória was concerned that this eighteen-year-old boy have a sexual experience, and she was determined that he have it without the possibility
or responsibility of impregnating a young girl. There is a consistency to
Glória's desire to plan for Lucas's first sexual experience. First, Glória believes that men "naturally" must have access to sex. Men are like animals, and it is natural for them to fulfill what she considers a basic need.
On the other hand, she would like her daughters to remain virgins for as
long as possible, if only because their enforced virginity guarantees that
they do not become pregnant and bring another mouth to feed into her
house. Their own desires to become adult women, however, and to
achieve their own standards of adult femininity have over time led all her
young daughters—Anita, Filomena, and Soneca—to become young
mothers, much to Glória's dismay.

Glória explains to her guests that sending Lucas to the prostitution
zone is the only way for him to get a girl, since he lacks certain male qualities necessary for being a successful seducer. According to Glória, Lucas
"não tem papo" (cannot talk well, does not know the art of seduction).
Lucas, nicknamed Borbulho (Bubble), was of particular "worry" to
Glória because he was quite shy and rarely spoke. When he spoke, Glória
teasingly observed, his sausage lips made him sound as if he were producing bubbles rather than talk. This characteristic, she thought, was
simply not going to get him anywhere with a woman. She felt, therefore,
that he might need some prodding, and sending him to the zona seemed
to be an appropriate solution. Glória made us all laugh uproariously

with her imitations of Lucas attempting to "sweet-talk" a woman into having sex with him—and of course, in her mind, not succeeding. It was not a case where he was exhibiting any obvious nonmasculine behavior; rather, he just seemed completely disinterested in sex, and this was the cause of her motherly concern.

Glória's double standard regarding the first sexual experiences of her male and female children is not unique to her as an individual.[14] For Glória, this double standard is consistent with a broader set of ideas about how male and female sexuality naturally operates. She wants Lucas and her other sons to gain sexual experience and become knowledgeable about sex so that they can be sexual initiators, and she wants her daughters to remain virgins until they are ready to commit to a steady partner who can support them.[15] Glória and the other women in her age cohort know that teenage sexual experience frequently leads to pregnancy, but the high cultural value placed on children and motherhood, as well as the possibility of starting their own lives, also attracts young girls to early childbearing. Young men gain knowledge and their first sexual experiences with those who are not necessarily potential partners— and this can mean with female sex workers or even through homoerotic encounters in the context of boy-boy relations in what has been described as *fazendo meia* (doing half) or *troca-troca* (exchange-exchange).[16] Women, in order to remain "good women," are expected to attain their early sexual experiences directly from their male partners and ideally as inexperienced virgins.

Young women in Felicidade Eterna, however, were nothing like the older women whose stories I heard in the context of São Paulo–based women-only focus groups thematically organized around sexuality and AIDS prevention. Many of the women in these groups shared their traumatic stories of losing their virginity, framed as a loss of childhood innocence as well as a violent female rite of passage into normative heterosexual relations. Younger women in these same groups, much like the younger women in Felicidade Eterna, were in different positions in that the ideal of virginity was waning and yet they feared being labeled a variant of "bad women," possibly risking being barred from steady relationships with responsible men. In Rio, the ideal of virginity before partnership seemed to be far more distant from the reach of young women, and my young female friends in Felicidade Eterna were perfect examples of this generational distancing from the norms of virginity that held during their mothers' generation. Instead, these young women straddled an awkward position. From the amount of sexual discourse and teasing they were privy to from an early age, it would be impossible to grow up in Felicidade Eterna and have no sexual knowledge at all. It would be perfectly easy, however, for these same women to be completely unaware of available birth control methods or to be unable to afford them. Interestingly, the abundant sexual discourses have not necessarily produced any substantive knowledge about reproductive health, pregnancy prevention, or HIV transmission. Recent statistics show that between 1993 and 1998 the birthrate in Brazil increased by 31 percent among girls aged ten to fourteen and 19 percent for girls aged fifteen to nineteen.[17]

Glória's son Tiago was, like Lucas, considered shy and sexually inexperienced at fifteen. He also was extremely helpful around the house, assisting Glória and Soneca to keep the family together. He most often was sent on errands to buy things, but he also knew how to cook, and he was kind and patient with the younger children. He even occasionally took care of Juliana, the paraplegic daughter of Marília next door. For these reasons, he was often teased and called a bicha, taunted to get tougher, and goaded to become sexually active. His sister Soneca continually teased him by reminding him about his lack of sexual experience, telling him about the belief that when a man goes for a long time without sex, sperm *"sobe à cabeça e fica doido"* (rises to the head and makes you crazy). She would say, "You are like *queijo minas.*" *Queijo minas* is a kind of hard, white, salty cheese common in Brazil; according to Soneca, it also refers to somebody who has gone for years without having a sexual relation. Similarly, Soneca explained that *polenguinho* (a soft processed cheese available in triangular packages) is a person who has gone for months without a sexual relation, and *requeijão* (a cheese with a consistency similar to yogurt) is someone who has gone weeks without having had a sexual relation. Soneca's taunts would erupt during fights or even just during daily teasing sessions.

SACANAGEM, TRANSGRESSION, AND FEMALE BOUNDARY-SETTING

Sacanagem is an important organizing concept in the realm of Brazilian sexuality. Parker (1991:102) accurately describes sacanagem as linking "notions of aggression and hostility, play and amusement, sexual excitement and erotic practice in a single symbolic complex." Sacanagem can be good or bad—it can describe an act that gives pleasure as well as one that hurts or humiliates another. Sacanagem is often applied in the context of sexuality that borders on the transgressive; in the context of focus-group interviews with women, it came up in discussions about their feelings about anal sex. For some, it was fun and pleasurable. For others, it became a point of contention because men seemed to request it, whereas women usually expressed more ambivalence about it (Goldstein 1994a). As Parker (1991) points out, boys are sometimes initiated into anal eroticism with other boys through such same-sex games as fazendo meia or troca-troca. But these homoerotic games are usually initiated by older and stronger males who exert their power over younger and weaker boys, claiming masculine sexual identities for themselves in the process of violating and symbolically feminizing others. This aspect of sacanagem points to the more ambivalent and negative aspects of transgression in the context of sexuality. Women are often cast in the role of sexual boundary setters in this transgressive complex. And ideal men are, to some extent, expected to transgress. In the context of protecting young girls' bodies, this can be problematic. In Brazil, the age of consent is fourteen, although in April 1996, the Brazilian Supreme Court sent down a decision that threatened to lower the age of consent to twelve.[18] In Felicidade Eterna, local rules regarding teenage sexual behavior are contentious and influenced by broader economic, racial, historical, and institutional factors—ones that I have touched upon throughout this book.

In this context, there was a great deal of taken-for-granted local cultural knowledge regarding sexuality that took a long time for me to begin to comprehend. In part, at least, I think I was influenced by my own initial perceptions of sex-positive Rio, so I was not prepared for the kinds of precautions that women took in dealing with men outside of their own families. On Glória's street on the barreira and beyond, stories of child and adolescent sexual abuse were pandemic and were not treated as extraordinary at all.

A JOKE THAT EVEN GLÓRIA DID NOT FIND FUNNY

A few months after breaking up with Zezinho, Glória hooked up with Mauro, a retired marine who worked as the pai-de-santo (literally, father-of-saint, religious leader) of a congregation of practitioners of Umbanda (an Afro-Brazilian religion).[19] Mauro lived in a small, two-room cement house behind the terreiro (temple where Afro-Brazilian religion is practiced). Glória decided to give her relationship with Mauro a chance, and so she began by moving out of her own shack during most of the week and spending her off-work time with Mauro in his home in a neighborhood a few kilometers from Felicidade Eterna. During that time, she sent home enough food and money to her children on a daily basis so that they would be taken care of. She left Soneca in charge of the younger children and saw her regularly. This happened to be during a period when Soneca and Glória were employed together as domestic workers, and their daily schedule together was a hectic one that had them traveling by bus late at night from the Zona Sul to the Zona Norte.

During one of these late returns to the Zona Norte, they both decided to spend the night at Mauro's house so that neither of them would have to walk alone at night. Soneca, however, had a deep fear of the statues of *exús* (ambiguous spirits that are thought of as tricksters and, in some ways, devil-like in Afro-Brazilian religions) that Mauro had standing in the corner of his living room. Soneca was expected to sleep alone there, but, overwhelmed by her fears, she begged her mother to let her sleep in the adjoining room where Glória and Mauro usually slept side by side on a large piece of foam on the floor. Sympathizing with her daughter's fears, Glória permitted Soneca to curl up and sleep next to her after their hard day of work.

Mauro, arriving home later that evening and realizing that he would be sleeping with both mother and daughter that night, jokingly declared in mock protest, "I am going to eat both mother and daughter tonight if she [Soneca] sleeps in the bed here with us!" Mauro was, it seems, annoyed that his newly gained privacy with Glória was being violated because of a grown child's silly fears. Glória, however, did not find his remark funny; she immediately packed all her belongings into a few plastic sacks and, with Soneca half asleep beside her, walked back the three kilometers to their shack in Felicidade Eterna. She remained angry and distant from Mauro for the next two weeks before finally forgiving him and accepting his explanation that he was "only joking."

Mauro's remarks were not taken lightly, even among a group of people who, as I have illustrated, have a distinctly bawdy and transgressive sense of humor and who never miss an opportunity to tease about sexuality in explicit ways. But Mauro had implied an all-too-real sexual threat associated with stepfathers that ultimately undermined the humor in his complaint.

Marília, Glória's next-door neighbor, after hearing Soneca's version of what had happened, summed up her feelings about stepfathers and men outside the family with the comment, "The one who raises you does not eat you." Marília's logic was simple and taken for granted. Once I became aware of this maxim, I started to recognize it often. Women had an entire set of discourses specifically about the danger of stepfathers, and yet they were comparatively quiet on the question of biological fathers.[20]

Figure 15. The exús that Soneca feared in Mauro's house. Photograph by author.

Within this local construction, women speak of dangerous men as *padastros* (stepfathers). The category itself almost provides the explanation of behavior that is part of an expected repertoire of transgressive male sexuality. Stepfathers, or merely men who are considered outsiders to the family unit, are perceived as dangerous, and women, accepting this danger as part of the natural order of things, practice all kinds of precautions to protect their children from these men's transgressions.

Filomena, Glória's rebellious fifteen-year-old daughter, was banished from Glória's household in 1992 after a heated confrontation with Glória. She ran away to the home of her boyfriend at the time, Adilson, where a visiting male family member attempted to sexually take advantage of her:

> It was the husband of the sister of Adilson's sister-in-law. There, he tried to abuse me. I was lying down on the sofa, and he began to pass his hands over me, and I was dying of fear there. I was thinking in my head, "If I tell the others I will have to go from here and I am going to sleep on the street. I am going to pass through everything that I passed, stay sleeping on the street under the rain. I am not going to tell anyone." I stayed there and remained quiet with him passing his hands over me. Then everything came crashing down and I started to cry. Then I went to where Adilson was and I started to cry. Adilson said, "What happened? What happened?" and I started to cry telling him. Then he wanted to fight with him, but I said to just leave it and to not do anything. (Filomena, taped interview, 1992)

Filomena was not necessarily surprised by what happened. She had given the impression that she was a teenager without a home, arriving as she did late in the evening at Adilson's door. At the time, Filomena lacked alternatives. Having fought with Glória, she had no home to return to except "the street." Later, Filomena explained how it was that she appeared to others, providing the explanation that her vulnerability—her status of being thrown out of her own household—as the reason for the man's actions: "Later, when Adilson's father found out what happened and he invited me to live there again, he said, 'Ahh Filomena, I thought that you were that way—a girl without responsibility, that you were that way, *avoada* [flighty, loose, tricky].' And I said, 'No, Seu Jesus, but it's o.k.'" As Filomena understood the situation, her appearance as a child off the street made her vulnerable to the sexual advances of men.[21] When women cross out of the boundaries of the house and onto the street, they are categorized as women of the street, loose women, those not bound by the rules of the house that normally protect them.[22] Male sexuality spans both the private world of the casa and the public world of the rua, but acceptable female sexuality is symbolically bound within the walls of the house—in the most private sphere. In classic symbolic anthropological language, when women cross out of the house, they become "like matter out of place" (Douglas 1966) or a mulher da rua, and therefore open to the advances of men.

Filomena had already internalized a sense of herself and her sexuality as fundamentally unprotectable outside of her own home. The simple act of leaving home and being unprotected outside the womb of her own family, and especially of her male kin, turned her into what naturally appeared to others as a "flighty" girl, one who might not mind and might even welcome the sexual advances of men. It is assumed, likewise, that men would sense her unprotected state and prey upon her vulnerability. To men, women in this situation are perceived as already sexually experienced and most likely "ruined" for the purposes of any decent relationship with a man.[23]

This juncture brings me to one of the more heatedly debated points between theorists weighing the possibilities of a Foucauldian versus a feminist approach to sexual abuse. Kate Soper (1993:35) argues that Foucault does not offer any clear picture of the "interrelationships between bio-political and socio-economic dimensions of female subordination" and that he retains a universalizing and gender-blind approach not very different from the liberal-humanist and Marxist accounts of power that he worked so hard to separate from. For Soper, Foucault's genealogy of ethics is centered on the desire and comportment of elite male citizens. She takes issue with Foucault's analysis of the Lapcourt incident, a passage in *History of Sexuality Volume I* (1980[1978]) in which Foucault notes the interventions that were brought to bear on a simple-minded farmhand who, in 1867, obtained what Foucault referred to as "a few caresses" (31) from a little girl. Foucault uses this example to show how an entire machinery of discursive power is brought to bear on what he considers a small, insignificant incident:

> The pettiness of it all; the fact that this everyday occurrence in the life of village sexuality, these inconsequential bucolic pleasures, could become from a certain time, the object not only of a collective intolerance but of a judicial action, a medical intervention, a careful clinical examination and an entire theoretical elaboration. . . . So it was that our society—and it was doubtless the first in history to take such measures—assembled around these timeless gestures, these barely furtive pleasures between simple-minded adults and alert children, a whole machinery for speechifying, analyzing, and investigating. (31)

Soper points out the limits—at a fundamental level—to Foucault's discourse theory in addressing sexual abuse. Soper's (1993) remarks read as a set of suspicious, although quite humorous, rebuttals to Foucault's particular blindness with regard to this incident:

> Could it not be that what is significant about *his* discourse upon it is the extent to which it may be exonerating, displacing and repressing the "event" that it is really about: this "alert" (terrified?) little girl, who runs to her par-

ents to report her "inconsequential bucolic pleasures" (her distress at being
slavered over in a ditch by a full-grown, mentally disturbed male?), thus
summoning forth a "collective intolerance" (alarm and sympathy?) over an
episode remarkable only for its "pettiness" (for the fact that something of
this kind was for once accorded the attention it deserved?)? (42–43)

According to Caroline Ramazanoglu (1993), Foucault presents a special
challenge to feminism because of his conceptualization of domination
and subordination as the "effects" of power rather than as proceeding
from a specific source of power. Accordingly, she argues that Foucault's
version of social constructionism ultimately helped to liberate feminists
from the "stink of biological essentialism" but did not really add much
to how feminists understand the body from the vantage point of subordinated women's lived experiences. Maureen Cain (1993), following this
line of reasoning, points out that "not all relationships in which people
live are expressible in discourse" (74), and she suggests that feminists go
beyond Foucault in theorizing feelings that have no discourses. She urges
an exploration of the unspeakable.

In 1992, I came to know Alzira, a woman who lived just a few shacks
downhill on the barreira from Glória's home. She was a single mother at
the time, and a recovering cocaine addict, working as a piece-rate seam-
stress and living with her two teenage daughters, Adriana and Sarlete.
When she was a teenager, she had her first child, a son, whom she gave
to her mother to raise. Later, she married and lived for fifteen years with
Reinaldo, giving birth to her two daughters. After leaving Reinaldo in
the early 1990s, she had an affair with a *macumbeiro* (one who practices
macumba, an Afro-Brazilian religion) by whom she became pregnant
and who threatened her with death (via macumba) if she did not have
the child.

After giving birth, Alzira gave her newborn baby girl to her teenage
daughter Adriana to raise. Alzira had finally worked up the courage to
end her affair with the macumbeiro and soon after became involved with
another man. Adriana, only fourteen years old at the time, would tote
her baby sister around Felicidade Eterna as if she were a doll. I knew
Alzira cared about her daughters and that she worked hard as a seam-
stress to keep her small family well fed and clothed. Alzira made it clear
that she preferred to leave her three daughters alone in her shack rather
than subject them to the possible sacanagem of a man who was not their
father. Reflecting on her choices of partners, Alzira lamented the fact that
she spent fifteen years defending herself from her husband's beatings. Ap-

parently, he had few commendable qualities. She described him as a poor provider and a drug addict prone to extremes of violence. Nevertheless, years later she still considered the possibility of reuniting with him because "at least he respected his daughters."

Marília, Glória's young neighbor, who was twenty-three at the time I interviewed her in 1995, began a difficult period in her life at age eleven, when her own mother suddenly collapsed and died. After being shuffled around among her network of godparents and encountering hardships in each of their homes, she sought out the godmother of her youngest brother, a woman whom she remembered from her childhood as somebody she liked a great deal. Marília managed to track down this woman and was invited to live in her household, together with the godmother's three young daughters aged approximately ten, eleven, and twelve. Marília remained there almost a year. This godmother happened to be much more financially secure than Marília's family, and she welcomed Marília into her household, vowing to pay her school expenses. She treated Marília as if she were a daughter, and initially Marília was content to be there. One day, however, the godmother confided in Marília that some years earlier she had had to send her oldest daughter off to live in another household because of an accusation of sexual abuse by her daughter against her current husband, the father of her three younger daughters. Concerned that another girl not of his own blood was living so closely with them, the godmother decided to warn Marília about this past history and requested that Marília tell her of any sexual offenses.

The godmother believed that her oldest daughter had been truthful about the abusive behavior of her stepfather, and she sent her away to protect her; at the same time, however, she believed her three other daughters would be safe, since, after all, they were his own children. Here again, the discourse of sexual abuse was bound within a discourse about stepfathers. This abuse, while not exactly acceptable, was understood within a certain logic about male sexuality and its limits. The only act that was perceived as heinous within this particular logic was the case of incest between a biological father and daughter or son or by a father who had participated in the raising of a child from a very early age. For all these reasons, the godmother was alerted by Marília's presence in the household, recognizing that a fictive kinship relationship would not be able to protect Marília in this case. As it turned out, her husband did make sexual advances toward Marília, and the outcome was that Marília wound up leaving the house, much like the godmother's oldest daughter. When it became clear to Marília that I was not understanding the logic behind the decisions that were made, she finally, in one conversation, offered me the following explanation to my query about why this woman would choose to stay with a husband who abused the other women in her own household:

> *Danni*: I don't understand. She suspected her own husband?
>
> *Marília*: Yeah, because he had already attempted to abuse her elder daughter because she wasn't his child. She was the child of another man, outside of the three she had with him.
>
> *Danni*: She was at what age?
>
> *Marília*: She was nine years old.
>
> *Danni*: And this man attempted to abuse her?
>
> *Marília*: Attempted to abuse her.
>
> *Danni*: How is it possible?
>
> *Marília*: Yeah, she left for work and the girl was sleeping. He was fooling around with her clothes, attempting to abuse the girl.
>
> *Danni*: Really?
>
> *Marília*: Then she ran to the neighbor's house and stayed there until her mother arrived and when her mother arrived she told her everything. Her mother sent her to her grandmother's house, but she also didn't want to leave him. She liked him. . . .
>
> *Danni*: Didn't want to leave him? [in disbelief]
>
> *Marília*: The girls studied all morning, and I studied in the afternoon. He came home earlier one day and said, "Marília, make a coffee for me." Then I finished making the coffee, and he took off his clothes and passed only in his underwear to the bathroom. When he returned, he grabbed me. He grabbed me and began to rip my shirt. Then, to defend myself, I grabbed the pot of hot coffee and threw it on top of him. (Marília, taped interview, 1995)

In the aftermath of these events, Marília's godmother informed Marília that she would no longer be able to stay in her home. Marília protested that she wanted to stay (another aspect that I did not quite understand), but her godmother insisted that she leave. As Marília explained it finally: "Because she wasn't going to leave him because he was the father of her children. She liked him, and if she didn't leave on account of her daughter, would she leave on my account?" Isadora had experienced a similar friction with her mother, Dona Darcilene, now an elderly resident of Felicidade Eterna. Although Dona Darcilene lived just an alleyway away, Isadora's relationship with her mother was not as warm as it might have been. Isadora eventually explained that there were many issues between herself and her mother, stemming from the distant past, the time of

Isadora's adolescence. Isadora's biological father had died when she was only nine, and her mother soon after met and paired up with Isadora's first stepfather, a man named Oduvaldo. Oduvaldo was practically a "gypsy" by nature—he was always moving, and they never stayed in one place very long. Isadora explained her relationship with her mother in an interview in 1992:

> *Isadora*: I worked with him, pushing wood and manioc to the factory at this fazenda. And he didn't want me to have a boyfriend at this age, but I had one. But I dared and dated this guy. He was much older than I was—the father of Afonso and Edeli. So I started to date him, and he [Oduvaldo] didn't like it. I don't know. . . .
>
> *Danni*: Jealousy?
>
> *Isadora*: Jealous of me. . . . I think he wanted me, as well.
>
> *Danni*: That he had eyes for both of you? [You and your mother]
>
> *Isadora*: [Gesturing with her head to mean "Of course"] But I defended myself very well. I defended myself very well because I knew that he wasn't my father, so he had second intentions. Because many times he demonstrated this. Touching determined parts of my body, you know? So this left me with my eyes always open.

As Isadora explained to me, she believed that her stepfather, Oduvaldo, was "waiting for me to grow up, thinking that I was for him," and for this reason she felt she needed to get out of the house as quickly as possible. Thus, by the age of twelve, she had already decided to run away from home with a man ten years her senior, in part because she feared Oduvaldo's advances. Dona Darcilene, whom I interviewed separately about these same events, was also able to recall Isadora's problems with her stepfather: "She didn't like him at all. When he came into the house, she left. She only came into the house when he was sleeping. She was afraid of him. Danni, I suffered a lot in this world. I always ask God that nobody suffers the same thing I suffered—what my daughter suffered." After Isadora's departure, Darcilene gave birth to two of Oduvaldo's children and continued to live with him for several years. According to Darcilene, they "lived fighting," and he was a poor provider. She finally achieved some peace when he disappeared from her life. When I asked Isadora how she felt about her mother choosing to stay with a man whom she had felt was abusive toward her, she said that she and her mother now can both agree that he was a bad thing in their lives and that they have since resolved to forget about that time and not mention him anymore.

In 1991, Elis and Eber adopted Nelsinho together, and Soneca was declared "a godparent." Elis's mother aided Elis in the process by helping to locate a young girl who wanted to give up her child for adoption and then by signing the necessary legal documents to register the child legally under her own name. Although Elis turned out to be an excellent mother, because she was a travesti, "the authorities" would not have approved her documentation had she attempted the adoption on her own. Elis described her youth as troubled, largely because she was perceived to be an extremely effeminate boy. But aside from early tauntings by other children and adults who felt she was not on her way to becoming a properly gender-socialized boy, Elis bitterly recalls having had to deal with a stepfather who sexually abused her throughout her youth.

According to Elis, she was a homebody, mostly because her mother kept her prisoner in the house. Elis was close to her sister and her sister's friends, playing with dolls, playing house, and making food. But it was also in her own house, she says, where, *"eu me perdi"* ("I lost myself," meaning her virginity). And, as she explained in an interview, she is still *revoltada* (disgusted) with the fact that it happened with her own stepfather, a man who abused her and then blackmailed her with threats of violence if she told anyone:

>   *Danni*: What age were you?
>   *Elis*: At the time, I was eight years old, more or less.
>   *Danni*: Eight years old? And he abused you?
>   *Elis*: I was eight years old—and there it began, you know? That was the first time. I think the tendency was going to appear because I was always a different person, I think, you know? I was always different. I don't know. My mother lived with him for fourteen years.
>   *Danni*: Fourteen years, and she never knew?
>   *Elis*: She knew. Later she knew everything, but—
>   *Danni*: And she was disgusted, shocked?
>   *Elis*: With *me,* not with him.
>   *Danni*: With you? But you were a child?
>   *Elis*: Because she thought, she thought that I was—that I was being the seducer—that was what I wanted—that it was shamelessness on my part. Not on his. I always told her that it wasn't that way.
>   *Danni*: How is it possible? A child of eight isn't guilty of anything.
>   *Elis*: I always told her that *he* was wrong, you know. That it wasn't me. She always said he was right. I didn't get upset. He would threaten, "Don't say a thing. If you tell you are going to see." I don't know what, he was always blackmailing and he would always come [to abuse me]. I was always afraid that he would come looking for me

and everything. I don't know, it was a part, you know, that made a mark on me and everything, a giant disgust with everything. From then on—the rest—what I did was for myself, was my own spontaneous and free will, you know?

The literature on Brazilian travestis, much of which is focused on those who are sex workers, reveals many of the abuses they suffer in different phases of their lives.[24] Elis's history of abuse by a stepfather is not unique to the life stories of travestis; it is also not unique in the context of young women's coming-of-age stories.

PARTIAL TRUTHS

There was a great deal of consistency across many of the stories I heard. All of them ended with women making choices to remain with either an abuser or a "potential" abuser (such as Alzira's case)—with "potential" in this context meaning any man not fully related or committed to the protection of the child. Without the institutional and juridical mechanisms available to the middle and upper classes, poor women are left as the guardians against a socially constructed transgressive male sexuality. The other consistent theme to these stories is the underlying belief that teenagers, and even very young children, are sexual and have sexual desires; they are seen as having agency, even in relations with older, more powerful adult males. This realization is nevertheless perfectly consistent with what I have argued about childhood among the poorest classes more generally. These particular aspects of local sexual culture, on the one hand, create what appears to be an epidemic of child sexual abuse; on the other hand, they point to a strange expectation—and subversion—of sexually transgressive male behavior. The ambiguous years—when children are preteens and teenagers—are especially problematic in this setting because there are few well-developed psychological and medical discourses that are readily employed by those in the poorest classes. Such discourses, we know, tend to desexualize children in particular ways, an outcome that I would argue has taken hold among the middle and upper classes. But in the poorest classes, there seem to be specific class aspects that may leave young girls and boys vulnerable. According to Foucault (1980[1978]), "We must return, therefore, to formulations that have long been disparaged; we must say that there is a bourgeois sexuality, and that there are class sexualities. Or rather, that sexuality is originally, historically bourgeois, and that, in its successive shifts and transpositions, it induces specific class effects" (127).

The understanding of this behavior evolves as much out of the local culture's training of young boys for manhood, a training that constructs masculinity and masculine sexuality as aggressive and even predatory and that punishes gentle men, such as Tiago, who are sexually inexperienced. It is embedded in Glória's concern that Lucas travel to the prostitution zone to "have a little screw," because he does not have the seductive skills, the good *papo* (talk), to convince a woman to have sex with him. It is embedded in the almost clichéd adage that functions as a warning for all that "the one who raises you doesn't eat you," but be careful of the other ones who have not raised you! It comes from the sense that a girl like Filomena, who was temporarily "on the street," may be constructed as "loose," thereby viewing as normal the behavior of a man who preyed upon her.

If we consider the originating metaphors used to express the highly gendered and hierarchized ideal where men are "the eaters" and women are "the eaten," we see that women sometimes manage to subvert the ideal and to speak in a language of resistance—such as the case with Glória and Zezinho, Soneca and her affair, and Sarlete, the Killer Pussy. But we also see that women are constrained by a number of factors, not least of which is the local sex-positive language and attitudes that make it hard for women to protest male infidelity or to govern transgressive male sexuality, even when it negatively affects their children because these characteristics are sanctioned and built in to what is considered normal sexuality and because, as many women complained, "this is how men are."

I return now to the story that opened this chapter to help the reader understand why Glória found Marieta's exclamations to the doctor who wanted to examine her bundinha so amusing. I have tried to provide a context of everyday stories and everyday expectations around aspects of local sexual culture in Felicidade Eterna so that it would be possible to comprehend Glória's laughter over Marieta's exchange with her doctor. Glória found it comical that Marieta heeded—almost in excess—her mother's warnings concerning outsiders (including Marieta's older brother and stepfather) that nobody should be allowed to touch her vaginal or buttocks areas and applied it to the case of a female doctor who simply wanted to examine a growth there. What everyone in Felicidade Eterna understood implicitly about this story was the fact that Marieta had a stepfather and that, like other young girls in Felicidade Eterna, she was probably warned by her mother to defend herself against anyone who might prey on her body.

CHAPTER 7

What's So Funny about Rape?

There's only a mad logic here, no resolving. Your brother said
something, he said, "You've got to have a sense of humor
about all this—otherwise it makes no sense." You must be in
hell if you can seriously say things like that. We've become
Medieval.

Michael Ondaatje, Anil's Ghost

One fine day in 1995, Marília, Glória's twenty-three-year-old neighbor,
announced the following to her husband Celso, who worked nights as a
"roadie" for the samba bands that played on the weekends in the large
favelas in the Zona Sul and was just returning early in the morning after
a full night of work:

> "*Puxa* you are hard to kill, ehh?"
> "Why?" he asked.
> "Because I put rat poison in your drink this morning, and you didn't
> die." (Marília, taped interview, 1995)

Marília and Celso lived together in the makeshift shack immediately
adjacent to Glória's. Approximately the same size as Glória's small quarters, it was set up in a slightly different manner to accommodate the
young couple and their three children, who all slept together in the
queen-size bed that took up most of the fifteen-by-ten-foot room. Their
shack sported a refrigerator, a fan, a "new" television and stereo system,
and a small toilet area that was separated from the tiny kitchen area by
a cloth curtain. Juliana, Marília's five-year-old paraplegic daughter—
severely brain-damaged and unable to walk or talk—was a permanent
resident of the large bed. Unable to afford a wheelchair or any form of
professional physical therapy, Marília could only ease her daughter's
frustrations by gently changing her position in the bed during the day so
that she would be more comfortable.

Soon after Marília's confession to Celso, he took off for his day job as an unarmed security guard at a large food store in the center of Rio. He was hoping to accumulate enough money in the next few months to take the training course that would enable him to purchase and carry a gun; this, he hoped, would provide him a raise in his salary. After he had left Felicidade Eterna and made his way to the bus stop, word soon spread that Marília had attempted to kill Celso but that he had not died. Soneca, Tiago, Filomena, and I heard the news and made our way the few steps over to Marília's shack to find out what was going on. Tiago, as usual, began gently cooing and playing with Juliana on the bed, trying to keep her happy and entertained, since she was a bit stirred up with all the noise and excitement taking place around her. Neighbors periodically popped in and out of the shack, using the common ritual of borrowing—cigarettes, salt, or sugar—as their pretense for catching fresh pieces of Marília's gossip.

In short, the day before, Marília had tried to poison Celso by putting a few spoonfuls of rat poison in his morning juice. Marília told everyone what she had done without a trace of guilt, with even a playful smile on her face. She and everyone else present thought it was hilariously funny that after all her determined effort, Celso did not die. She had been sure that she would return later to her shack and find him dead, with Juliana, as usual, drooling all over herself and Guilherme, who loves his father, banging his head against the wall in grief. Since Celso was a drug user, she believed that his death would be mistaken as a drug overdose. "I would say that he died of sniffing. Since he takes so many drugs anyway, everyone will think it was a drug overdose." I decided to ask Marília a straightforward and simple question: "Why did you want to kill your husband?" What followed was a four-hour response. Marília urged me to turn on my tape recorder because without knowing how much she had suffered in her life in general, and specifically in her marriage to Celso, I could not possibly understand her full motivations.

That day, I recorded Marília's detailed life history. Her narrative traced her birth in a Rio favela, the involvement of two of her siblings in crime and drug traffic, and her mother's sudden death. It chronicled Marília's eleven-year circulation through her entire network of godparents, people she had hoped would provide her with a safe place to live in the aftermath of her mother's death, but who in each case disappointed her with bad treatment and varying levels of abuse.

Celso and Marília dated briefly shortly after Marília had returned to the home of her father, having given up the pursuit of her godparents. She dated Celso and quickly lost her virginity. Fearing what her father would do to her if he found out, Marília fled to her mother-in-law's house, despite the fact that her relationship with Celso was souring; soon after, she gave birth to her first son, Guilherme. Based on a rumor propagated by a vengeful neighbor, Celso came to believe that Marília was secretly seeing other men. His response was to court other women and to neglect his young family. He would tell Marília, "Since you are seeing other guys anyway, you are going to go hungry." Marília, desperate to feed her children, went out and found work as a faxineira to support herself and her child, while Celso continued his philandering. Eventually, during a reconciliatory moment, Marília became pregnant with their second child, Juliana, whose early childhood was spent in and out of hospitals in a quest to find out what exactly was wrong with her. Marília accompanied her daughter through these internments, soliciting help from a coroa during difficult financial times, when Celso failed her completely.

Marília eventually moved back in with her bad-tempered father, who had told her when she was a child still mourning the death of her mother that his house was too full and that he had no room for her. His inability and unwillingness to care for all his children after his wife's death was what originally sent Marília on her first series of misadventures in the homes of godparents.

Marília insisted that I listen carefully to the litany of offenses she suffered throughout her brief twenty-three years of life before proceeding to explain why she had attempted to kill her husband. Indeed, her life history reads like an exaggerated embodiment of the idea that "everything that can go wrong will go wrong," but I knew that her story was not at all atypical. At each turn, Marília met her tortuous fate with a great deal of courage and fortitude, always finding a way to survive, often managing to trade in one form of victimization for another that, initially at least, had appeared better. But these turned out to be as bad as or even worse than the original problem she was fleeing.

What made Marília's final story about her attempt to kill Celso so amusing to her audience is that by the time we had heard about the tragedies she had survived, we were all, in a sense, rooting for her to experience success at something. It seemed fitting that Marília finally reached the end of her rope with her abusive, unfaithful husband, and that even in this case, things did not turn out as she had planned. In the end, "He was difficult to kill," just like the rest of her problems.

The day before, Marília had been preparing Celso's morning coffee and, realizing that they had run out, offered him an orange-flavored powdered drink known as Ki-Suco. The night before, Soneca and Sarlete, her young, single neighbors, had been primping to go out to dance at the local pagode, and they urged Marília to go along with them. She knew that Celso was working a gig that night and calculated that she could go out and enjoy herself with her friends and return home in time to receive him in the early hours of the morning—his usual hour of return. But Celso returned early that evening and found out that Marília had gone to dance with her friends, an act he had categorically prohibited. Celso's position was that Marília should never go out in the evening and leave their children unattended. He also was concerned that she not participate in a public dance without him, for he feared being cuckolded. While at the pagode, Marília caught a glimpse of Celso and immediately fled for home, fearful that if he had seen her, he would beat her up first and ask questions later, his usual approach. But she must have slipped away in time, because Celso actually arrived at home that night without making a fuss. Although he went to bed peacefully, Marília's fears grew throughout her sleepless night. She imagined that perhaps he was merely waiting for morning to confront her and was certain that, despite her explanations, he was going to hit her. "Whatever happened he was going to hit me. And I was saying to myself, 'You are going to hit me [only] if it were another day.'" She had decided, once and for all, that she was not going to put up with his abuse anymore. That night, she decided to put rat poison into his morning drink. "I don't like him anymore, and I wanted him to stop screaming in my ear," she explained.

Given the drama of her life and the litany of victimizations she had survived, the fact that Celso did not die—even from a fistful of rat poison—came across as a final moment of absurdity. Marília recognized that even in the strongest, most active moment of her resistance, things can still go wrong. Yes, Celso, like so many of Marília's problems in life, proved "difficult to kill."

AN EVENING OF TERROR IN DUQUE DE CAXIAS

Of all the subjects addressed here, the laughter in the following story may be the most difficult to grasp because it deals with the painful and devastating experience of a rape. It is a context in which the laughter seems to be truly inappropriate, offensive, "out of place." But it is important to interrogate the absurd humor here, to understand on which pivotal details the humor is built and on which details suffering is felt.

Shortly before and catalyzing their decision to move to Felicidade

Eterna, Glória and her family had been assaulted in their home in Duque de Caxias, a poor but working-class neighborhood with asphalt streets and sturdier shacks (see maps 3 and 4). Lucas had been ordered to secure the windows and doors of their home that night, a ritual done with great care before bedtime. Somehow, he had failed to lock one of the wooden windows correctly. Soon after the family settled down to sleep, two men claiming to have guns stood close to the poorly shut window and demanded that they be let in to search for a certain "Cesar," whom they claimed was a member of a rival gang.

At the time Glória was living with Ignácio, also known as "Gordo," or "Fatty," because of his large frame and belly, who was a drummer in a neighborhood pagode band. He often stayed out most of the night playing at gigs, returning home only in the early hours of the morning. Glória's children at the time were all quite young, and she had, because of them, purposefully moved far away from her gang-member son, Pedro Paulo—who had stayed in Rocinha—so that her family would not be subjected to the rivalries wrought on innocent family members by opposing gangs. When the two assailants knocked on the window, Roberto, closest to the window, was the first to hear their threats. Roberto screamed out for his aunt Glória in the next room and told her that there were some men outside who wanted to get in. Thinking that it was simply a case of a mistaken identity—she did not know of any "Cesar"—Glória decided to open the door and let the men in. She knew that once inside they would see that there was nothing worth stealing. Nevertheless, before opening the door, she pushed her two youngest daughters, Soneca and Filomena, under her cot to hide them. Upon entering, the men told all the children to get on the floor in the bedroom with their heads covered, and they singled out Anita, Glória's oldest daughter living at home, and Cláudia, Glória's niece, and kept them in the front room together with them. When the two assailants were convinced that "Cesar" was not actually there, they decided to rape Anita and Cláudia, who at the time were only fourteen and fifteen years old. Glória and her other children, trapped in their tiny bedroom, could hear Anita and Cláudia screaming through the door, just a few feet away. Desperate to stop the rape of her daughters, Glória tried to get the men to open the door by telling them that she badly needed to use the bathroom. Unconvinced that the assailants were actually armed, and priding herself on her physical strength, Glória planned to overpower them once they opened the door. At that moment, however, Ignácio returned from his evening of drumming and interrupted the assailants, who met him at the doorway. They instructed him to place his hands high in the air, and Ignácio, renowned for his smooth talking, began trying to reason with them. They quickly lost patience with him, accusing him of "talking too much," a crime that resulted in the robbery of his wristwatch, one of his most beloved possessions. The rapists then began asking about the few household goods that were visible, demanding to know whether the television set was color or merely black and white. Despite the seeming worthlessness of the goods, they gathered together the stereo, the fan, and the television at the doorway, picked up the television and the fan, and told everyone to remain still and quiet, warning that they would return shortly to retrieve the stereo. Fifteen minutes after the men left, Glória realized that they would not be back. She grabbed a large kitchen knife and urged Roberto and Ignácio to join her in going after them. They did, but they were unsuccessful in tracking them down.

These events took place in 1988, and over the course of my fieldwork, I heard the details of that night in various renderings, both from Glória and from her daughters. Glória used the story to explain why she and her family abandoned a home in a "real neighborhood" to move back into a favela, and also to explain why Glória left Ignácio, the fat drummer who had been at least a somewhat decent provider, for a former lover, Zezinho, a skinny alcoholic and a poor earner. It was in these later renditions of the events of that evening that I initially recognized my own sense of Otherness and distance from my friends. When I first arrived in Felicidade Eterna, I could not imagine what anybody could find funny about the terror of that evening in Duque de Caxias.

Over time, however, I was able to grasp the humor of these stories and recognize that what appeared to me to be "laughter out of place" was actually laughter quite accurately "in place." It was not that rape was something acceptable or easily dismissable to Glória and her daughters, either. Rather, rape is an extremely serious offense, one that provokes all kinds of retaliatory violence. The rape of a child in a shantytown, for example, can provoke a gang to murder. Husbands, fathers, and brothers try to protect the bodies of their wives, daughters, and sisters, to which their own honor and reputations are tied. But while all this is true, it is also true that women are sometimes left without the protection of their male relatives or anyone at all; sometimes women find that the protection afforded by male relatives comes at its own high cost.

The telling of the robbery and rape story provided a way for sexuality, violence, and female victimization to be dealt with through humor. Over time, I also found that the story became a pivotal event around which discussions revolved about the expectations women had for the men in their lives. For example, throughout the years, Glória and her daughters often came into conflict over their differing opinions about stepfathers and boyfriends. In a general sense, Glória's children did not really appreciate Glória's boyfriends, especially in their role as stepfathers. Glória, on her part, did not approve of the boyfriends her daughters chose, boys who would impregnate her daughters and then either eschew their responsibilities as fathers and providers or fulfill them only partially. I realized in the end, however, that these stories, aside from their humorous twists and turns, also revealed a great deal of suffering that otherwise would have remained silenced.

SONECA'S VERSION OF THE STORY

Anita had already lost her virginity, so it hardly hurt at all. But Cláudia was still a virgin (laughter), so it hurt a lot. She was a virgin [cabaçinho de mamãe]. When the rapist went to Anita, she screamed, "Don't come to me, go to her!" She screamed as loudly as Cláudia. . . . Cláudia went crazy right after that night. . . . Anita didn't pay any attention [não ligava] because she wasn't a virgin anymore. It was only Cláudia crying, only crying, crying. And who took away the most damage that night was Cláudia, right? Anita was faking [damage], saying that the pregnancy was from the rapist, but it wasn't. It was from Gabriel, her boyfriend. . . . After that whole scene, Cláudia was completely crazy and my mother told her to take a bath. Cláudia was crying all the time. Cláudia is the one who suffered the most damage, right?

Soneca, taped interview, 1992

In 1992, approximately four years after the robbery and rape, I was sitting with Anita, Soneca, and Glória's other children in their shack in Felicidade Eterna and was asked, almost formulaically, whether I had ever heard about that night. Of course, I already had, but it was a story that they obviously wanted to tell again. Soneca began with the punch line, which was the fact that Anita screamed as loudly as Cláudia on the night of the rape because, having recently lost her virginity, she was afraid of what Glória might do to her if she found out that she was no longer a *moça* (girl), but instead a woman. Soneca teased Anita by pointing out to me and the rest of her audience how cowardly Anita had been that evening. But she also relayed her own displeasure about Glória's attempt to control her daughters' sexuality, reminding everyone of Glória's standing threat to banish them from the house or to place hot pepper in their vaginal areas if they dared to lose their virginity.

Soneca downplayed Anita's trauma because Anita had already lost her virginity and therefore "it didn't hurt hardly at all." But Soneca became much more serious when she described what had happened to Cláudia, emphasizing the fact that "Cláudia lost the most that evening." This latter piece of information was essential to her comprehension of the different degrees of hurt experienced out of this violent scene, and it provided her with the context to tell us the broader story—the part she and the others actually found amusing: both Cláudia and Anita had, at the time, presented themselves to Glória as if they were both still virgins. Soneca did not lose the opportunity to tease Anita by reminding her of her cowardice that evening in pleading with the two men to get off her and go to Cláudia, despite her own, "less vulnerable" status. According to Soneca, Anita orchestrated her screams of anguish to be as loud as Cláudia's so that nobody—but especially Glória—would suspect that she was no longer a virgin. Soneca exaggerated Anita's cowardice, in regard to both the rapists and Glória, and revealed her "false cries" as funny. This twist manages to turn an evening of terror and violence into a story of Anita's cleverness and resourcefulness in the face of Glória's protective stance around her daughters' sexuality. While I came to understand what elements made the story so funny to Glória's children years after the event—I eventually "got" the joke—I still found it difficult to join in the laughter when listening to these particularly dark stories.

Soneca then extended her critique to Ignácio. She reminded everyone that, upon his arrival at the door of the shack, the robbers instructed him to place his hands high in the air and then swiped his wristwatch. Soneca, quite slight and bony, managed to stand tall at this moment, pushing out her belly, indicating the fact that Ignácio was overweight, a big man. She even managed to deliver some convincing but obviously false sneezes, a characteristic of Ignácio's when he was nervous. As Soneca told this part of the story, she and the other children were crying with laughter. "The robbers," Soneca continued, "were still doing their business" with the girls when they were interrupted—by his arrival and his sneezes—and so they had to deal with him. They demanded Ignácio's wristwatch as payment for his offense of "talking too much," and his material loss became the main focus of his lament about that evening.

Soneca continually reminded everyone of Ignácio's selfish focus on "his own losses" rather than on the losses experienced by the girls, a detail that condemned him in the eyes of Glória's children and eventually Glória herself. Cláudia suffered enormously from the trauma of that night, as did all of Glória's children. They could not "forget the faces" of the two men, and during the next few months, no one in the little shack slept soundly. With time, Glória too, finally gave credence to her children's complaints about Ignácio, and one day, acknowledging his narrow self-interest, abruptly packed up all their belongings from the Caxias household, informed Ignácio that she was leaving him, and traveled to the small shack she had purchased in Felicidade Eterna, where she took up once again with her former lover Zezinho.

BATTLING MOTHERS AND DAUGHTERS

This night of terror also served Anita as a vehicle for commentary about her coming of age within Glória's often harsh disciplinary regime. On a lazy Sunday afternoon in 1992, Glória, Anita, Soneca, and a few of Glória's friends and neighbors were enjoying each other's company. Soon, though, the scene became a stage for competition between Glória and Anita, both of whom used the night of the rape as a vehicle for airing their conflicts. They had come to disagree about the appropriate time for a young girl to engage in a sexual relationship, and they used their distinct perspectives about the night of robbery and rape as critical commentary. Each of them wielded humor as a kind of weapon—to either highlight or mask particular details of the event.

As it happened, Anita discovered she was pregnant shortly after the rape, and Glória used all her hard-earned Christmas money on remedies to help Anita abort, assuming that the pregnancy was the outcome of the rape. Anita was, in fact, already pregnant by her boyfriend, Gabriel, with whom she had been sexually active for some months. In Anita's version of the story, she tells of how she felt deathly afraid of her own mother— more afraid of her than of the rapists. Anita used the story to explain the extent of her suffering under Glória's strict command. According to Anita, the terror of the rape paled against Glória's threats: "My mother told everyone that as soon as the girls lost their virginity, they could all get out of her house and live on the street as far as she was concerned. She wanted us all to get married and not have all of us pregnant around her. She was already telling me that I lost it [referring to her virginity] when I really hadn't. I was being judged as if I had lost it anyway, so I would go out the window and do it. That's how I lost it, because of my mother, talking too much." For Anita, one excess, her mother's "talking too much" and accusing her of not being a virgin, led to another excess, her own loss of virginity. Having long before tired of the selfish abuses of Ignácio within their household, Anita saw her budding relationship with Gabriel as a respite from her troubles at home. Because Ignácio lacked the legitimacy of a "real" father, his nasty routines of hitting the children for what he considered bad behavior or, alternatively, requiring them to beat one another were even more resisted than they might have been.[1] Glória's children thoroughly disliked him and constantly urged her to leave him, but she had been unwilling to do so until after the rape. As Anita clearly pointed out, Ignácio's single-minded concern over the loss of his wristwatch the night of the rape epitomized his long-held indifference to the concerns and sufferings of Glória's children.

Just as Anita was beginning to gain the sympathy of her audience with her indictment of Ignácio, Glória became restless and jumped up to offer her own account of the event: "In the time of the rapists, I ran from hospital to hospital with Anita, but it was me who bought all the medicines. Meat, food, it was all me. Then I paid Manuel to do a macumba, since my saint was far away. All of my money was paying for macumba for Anita. All of the money I had earned for Christmas went for this, I barely got a gulp of sugarcane brandy for all of my work. Go take it in the ass [referring to Anita]." Glória reminds everyone that Anita never gave any indication at the time that the pregnancy was a product of her budding romance with Gabriel, nor that she might have wanted to have a child. Glória, assuming that the pregnancy resulted from the rape, insisted on helping Anita to abort. She dragged Anita to a macumbeiro for counsel and bought her anal suppositories and stomach ulcer pills, over-the-counter remedies that were commonly used to induce abortion. When Glória eventually learned the truth, months after the rape, she was furious at Anita for having duped her. It only added fuel to her argument that, ultimately, both her children and her own lovers were taking advantage of her generous, hardworking nature. Even years later, I sensed through Glória's biting humor that she was still peeved. For Glória, Anita's pregnancy was irresponsible, because neither Anita nor Anita's boyfriend, Gabriel, was working at the time. From her perspective, Anita should not have been screwing around, since she was not able to deal realistically with the consequences of a pregnancy. Glória laughed about her own past threats to her daughters, never carried out—hot peppers on their genitals—and justified herself by elaborating on Anita's case. She explained that, ultimately, she hoped her verbal threats would deter her daughters from entering into premature sexual relationships and risking pregnancy.

By 1992, the time of these conversations, Anita had settled down and made a home with Gabriel. That year, she gave birth to her first daughter, Gabriela. With Glória's assistance, Anita had successfully aborted her first pregnancy, but later her relationship with Gabriel deepened, and she began living with him in a common-law marriage. According to Anita, he was doing his job of properly supporting her and their baby. During this conversation, Glória disagreed with Anita's assessment of her financial support from Gabriel and seized the opportunity to chastise her daughter for not demanding more from her partner: "Who is banking whom? When a man supports, he has to give you from the top to the bottom. What is he doing? [referring to Gabriel] He only gives you enough so that you don't starve. The maternity clothes, I gave. Every single time, he should have bought all the clothes. He doesn't support you properly."

Glória's retelling of the rape and robbery story in front of her friends and family provided the opportunity to criticize teenage pregnancy and express her own expectations and frustrations regarding a man's obligation to provide financial support to his family. Clearly tired of supporting her children and their offspring, Glória was also fed up with supporting her own irresponsible boyfriends. Ideally, Glória wanted her daughters to demand more economic support from their male partners. But demanding this form of financial participation from male partners is not always easy. Men resist contributing too much, especially to women who already have children with other fathers. Male economic participation is often the main issue for women in a romantic relationship, and it is hotly contested territory.[2] Glória's own economic reliance on the help of men, including her relationship with the bullying Ignácio, probably inspired Anita to seek escape from home through her relationship with Gabriel. Women often find themselves escaping one form of victimization in their lives by entering another, often equally troublesome, situation.

All these women were talented storytellers. They highlighted their own suffering in their own narrations. Each of them managed to turn the evening of the robbery and rape into an amusing story that also served as a thinly disguised tale of the troubled nature of male-female relations and of everyday life. The retelling of the rape story through attention to various humorous details allowed for the venting of anger about a series of issues that would normally be difficult to discuss in a straightforward manner: the abuse of women by warring gangs, the misplaced priorities of stepfathers, and the desire of women for men to provide economic stability.

A NOTE ON THE LEGAL UNIVERSE AND RAPE

Why is it that such egregious forms of violence as rape are met by women with a kind of absurd humor, a show of laughter through tears, rather than by some other more organized response, such as that connected to an operating legal system? Because of their distrust and fear of the police, it is highly unlikely that my friends would ever report heinous crimes—even rape—to the authorities. But to take this argument further, I want to suggest that the legal system itself—assuming that a case of rape of a lower-class woman finds its way there—is still, even today, hindered from hearing the perspectives of impoverished women due to a combination of anachronistic legal codes regarding class (and therefore race), gender, and sexuality.

Evidence from social historians suggests that differences have existed between popular and elite culture on a number of scales—but especially sexuality—since early in the twentieth century. Esteves (1989),[3] writing about Rio in the early 1900s, argues that lower-class women were actively creating their own subculture, one that did not place as much importance on virginity as did the elite culture of the time. Esteves examined the perspectives of sexuality embedded in court cases of rape, moral offense, and kidnapping during that period. She found that lower-class women making accusations of rape in court were forced to adopt a more elite view of sexuality in order to approximate judiciary views of sexuality that were dominant in elite culture at the time. Because the local cultures of women differ according to class position, women from the lower classes, who might not place much importance on their loss of virginity, would be forced to feign an interest in their own virginity to prove their credentials as "honest" women. These young women from the lower classes had to hide their true values and beliefs about sexuality from their middle-class neighbors and bosses who would not approve of their attitudes and/or behavior.

While perhaps the distance between elite and popular culture sexuality no longer exists in this extreme form, some of the cultural norms of the dominant classes have become embedded in the legal system, making the criminal act of rape—by either an unknown or a known person, as well as other crimes against women inside of family life—difficult to adjudicate in court. In an analysis of court cases carried out in six Brazilian state capitals between 1981 and 1986, Ardaillon and Debert (1987) argue that rape has been difficult to adjudicate in the Brazilian court system because it relies on stereotyped gender views of both the perpetrator and the victim. They found, for example, that it was difficult for younger women who were not virgins or, in the case of older women, those who were not in one stable partnership with a man, to meet the court standard of an "honest" women and thus to win a rape case. As late as the 1980s, anachronistic definitions of female honor were still codified within the legal system.

Although the Supreme Court in 1991 struck down the "defense of honor" as a justification for wife killing, the courts have been reluctant to prosecute and convict men who attack their wives, especially if there is evidence of infidelity. In a very general sense, the courts are caught in anachronistic understandings of class, gender, and sexuality, thus leaving women—but especially impoverished women—with little or no legal recourse in their everyday negotiations with men, gangs, and criminals. The best they can do in this situation is to seek the protection of another (possibly abusive) male or, as in Marília's case, carry out either real or halfhearted attempts to protect themselves. Women do, in fact, become violent in these situations, but they also laugh—darkly—about the impossible situation they find themselves in.

BLACK HUMOR AS THE ONLY RESPONSE

I have implied throughout this book that "taste," when applied to the aesthetics of humor, is not a neutral concept. Humor can only be understood in its place, and place is always circumscribed by relations of class, gender, race, and sexuality. The sustained absurdist discourse that produces laughter over the failed death of an abusive husband or that takes a rape as its point of departure, suggests that certain forms of black humor may originate within the dominated or the "popular" classes because it is their only recourse in a universe of limited options.

Beyond the range of any social system's options, there is only laughter. The content of the humor—its "bad taste"—substantiates the possibility that these dominated classes, caught in a set of limiting circumstances, have few options beyond absurdist laughter. What at first may have appeared to readers as merely humor in "bad taste," I hope, has by now become a comprehensible response to a moral and legal system that is currently incapable of addressing the grievances of women in the dominated classes.

CONCLUSIONS

Throughout this book, I have argued that understanding humor, especially laughter "out of place," provides a unique window into how impoverished working women in the shantytowns of Rio de Janeiro understand and experience their lives. Each of the preceding chapters has provided stories that became understandable as "funny" only when the full context of the story was described. When I speak of ethnographic context, I refer not only to the ideational systems within which actors become agents but also to the power relations within which actors are restricted. Glória's laughter about Dona Beth's distress at her daughter's attempt at "independence" can be understood only within the context of Glória's desire to see her own daughters become adult women and leave home, despite a barely subsistence-wage economy that encourages them to seek partners for economic support and to commodify their own bodies. Glória's teasing of her nephew Roberto about his dark skin color is comprehensible only when we understand the individual and social reasons behind the current complicated forms of race relations in Brazil. When Glória meets up with her ex-partner and tells him of their son's recent death in a gang shootout with police, she is moved to laughter by this man's tears because he had never shown any interest in his own offspring until that moment. As she explains, she had already been worn out by her struggles with Pedro Paulo and the tragedy and violence he courted; she had long ago "run out of tears" for him. Celso, Marília's husband, jokes with me about the fact that the blood on the street where his compadre Adilson was murdered is now "clean" and therefore no longer represents something to be frightened about. This, indeed, is nervous laughter, laughter inspired by fear and bewilderment regarding who might be the next target. Marieta, Glória's young godchild, is prompted to scream at the female doctor examining a growth on her buttocks because she has been taught to protect herself from strangers who might want to violate her body. Women in these settings are continually striving to mediate their perspectives on sexuality in a society that is incredibly sex-positive but that does very little to protect the bodies of women—even young women—from transgressive male behavior.

Using humor as a starting point, I have tried to describe the deepening layers of the context—the daily structuring of class, race, gender, sexuality, and violence in Felicidade Eterna—in which these jokes and stories are embedded and entangled. Such context allows us to "get" the joke, even as the humor both masks and reveals (often in very complicated ways) the very structures and hierarchies on which the humor depends.

I hope that this book, as a whole, makes clear that these women are not merely passive victims of the structures and discourses of domination that constrict their lives. While they do enact and reproduce these structures—they "live" them—these women also, in fact, often strenuously and creatively resist them. Sometimes, indeed, most often after having put up a good fight and after having done all that they can do, the only thing left for them is laughter and, perhaps occasionally, a little taste of justice.

The ethnographic data presented throughout this book lead us to ask the obvious question, namely, *What is to be done?* This is a question that I hesitate to answer in anything more than the most general terms, but I know I must somehow address it because of the potential call for action that the stories told here bring forth. One of the most pressing questions in the coming years will be how to extend a democratic rule of law to the lower classes—into so-called brown zones. I have shown how large segments of the working classes have known only police brutality and in desperation have come to rely on the gangs as an alternative to the state's rule of law in their neighborhoods. The middle and upper classes will need to address this differential application of the rule of law, or they will witness an even greater threat to their desire for democratic consolidation. They will need to work in favor of human rights, even for those whom they have mistakenly condemned as criminals.

Twelve of Glória's fourteen children are currently working at "honest" jobs, earning little, but surviving. Only two of her children "went bad," as she would say. Middle- and upper-class activists will need to support mothers like Glória, whose own life story—slavelike labor and little social or economic advancement—has provided the ammunition for some of her sons (Pedro Paulo and Lucas) to become bandidos. Democratic consolidation cannot occur without reform of the police forces and an end to the human rights abuses and corruption within that institution. It cannot occur without a credible rule of law that is applied to citizens without distinctions of class, race, or gender. In a country where white-collar crime is rampant, yet practically never punished, a true overhaul of the police and justice system would have to bring to an end the privilege of the dominating classes to sidestep and ignore the parts of the law they find inconvenient.

Beyond the immediate economic benefits that the drug trade is purported to bring to some segments of society, the gangs of varying sizes and levels of organization involved in trafficking also provide an alternative rule of law in impoverished neighborhoods. Before their utility becomes archaic, however, an entire system of "good faith" social services would need to be put in place to treat the everyday private injustices that are currently being handled by such organizations. The courts would need to be reformed into a believable set of institutions that could deal with the many different levels of crime and abuse.

Although Brazil is currently experiencing a moment where democratic institutions are estimated to be consolidating and the possibilities for new levels of participation are hoped for with great optimism, the process is uneven and proceeds slowly through the class structure, leaving those at the very bottom isolated from many of the benefits of a true civil, social, and political democracy. Unfortunately, as Leeds (1996:47) notes, "although procedural democratic practices may have returned for the middle classes, nothing inherent in the transition to democracy guarantees either procedural or substantive democracy for the lower classes."[4] In the last hours of preparing the manuscript for this book, I have a sense of optimism. It is December 2002, and Lula, the Workers Party candidate, is poised to take office as president of Brazil. This fact may help constitute a new era in Brazil's quest to consolidate its democracy and to support a more equitable rule of law across its many regions. Perhaps, when all these reforms are accomplished, we will witness a momentous change in the laughter of these people.

In the many discussions I shared with Glória, I was reminded of how upsetting the crime at her home had been to her. Glória moved her family away from the house in Caxias soon after the crime because everyone was traumatized by the event and feared that the two men would return. She never reported the robbery or rape to the police. Instead, Glória and her family demanded revenge against the intruders through an appeal to her local gang. In short, she made it known that she would be delighted to see the rapists dead. Indeed, Glória vowed that night that she would not rest until "the two who had done sacanagem to her daughters were in their graves."[5] When the news came that one of the rapists had died violently in a nearby gang war, Glória, Anita, Cláudia, Soneca, and the rest of the family were absolutely delighted.

Notes

INTRODUCTION

1. Later, during a research project I carried out briefly in 1994 in Hungary with Jewish Holocaust survivors (Goldstein 1995a, 1997), I again recognized among some of my informants that strange ability to find comedy in the midst of tragedy. In the case of Jewish humor, aesthetics comes into play as well. The controversies that surrounded the film *Life Is Beautiful* (1997) come to mind. Some audiences found the film to be "in poor taste," with its comedic spin on the Nazi era, the Holocaust, and concentrations camps.

2. Throughout years of living in Spanish- and Portuguese-speaking Latin America, I have observed that what takes the longest for outsiders to learn is what it is exactly that people find funny—what it is that people laugh about together. In fact, it is perhaps too trite to say it so directly, but laughter can open up a world of meanings about a particular subculture that would otherwise remain hidden and unknown. One would think, given this inherent power, that anthropologists would have spent a great deal of time exploring humor, but this has not been the case. Much of the work on humor is to be found in the literature devoted to folklore. While the general literature on humor and laughter is vast and beyond the scope of the present work, I would like to provide an abridged list of major guideposts for where to start. Freud (1963[1905]) and Bergson (1956[1911]) are de rigueur starting points. Morreall (1987) provides a useful guide to philosophy's interest in the field, and Mulkay (1988) provides an excellent review of sociology's interest in the field. Apte (1985) is an important contribution that summarizes much of anthropology's interest in the field. See also Parkin's (1993) review article of anthropological approaches to joking; McGhee and Goldstein (1983); and Gay (1993), "The Bite of Wit," which includes a useful bibliography, as does Morris (1991).

3. There is also a wide and varied literature that analyzes the role of women and humor, a literature that attempts to address and often debunk a late-eighteenth-century idea that women had no wit. There are many good starting places. See, for example, Sheppard (1986). Some feminist folklorists suggest that joking may be one of the strategies of coding that women use to refuse, subvert, or transform male dominance. See Radner (1993), Lakoff (1975), and Tannen (1990).

4. There has been a similar problem for the new historians in other contexts who seek to write the history of popular culture but are faced with a dearth of original documents written by the people themselves. Ginzburg (1976) addresses this problem in *The Cheese and the Worms*. There are many notable exceptions among Brazilian historians, such as Esteves (1989) and Fausto (1984), who, for similar reasons, have turned to court proceedings in order to read into women's popular culture. See also Caulfield (2000).

5. See Escobar's (1995:153) discussion of ethnographic writing.

6. The one million number is seriously debated, and I have cautiously adopted this number at the low end. Much of the census data is now available through the Web, and for the most part, those numbers are often drawn from and reconfirm those of the Instituto Brasileiro de Geografia e Estatística (IBGE; Brazilian Institute of Geography and Statistics). It is estimated that the municipality of Rio de Janeiro—the city proper—has a population of 5,551,538. The vast metropolitan region, however, was estimated to have a population just above 10 million and the state, approximately 13 million. See the on-line IBGE Web site: www.ibge.gov.br/cidadesat/default.php. See also IBGE (1996, 1997a). Julio César Pino (1997a) estimates that in 1991 the city of Rio de Janeiro contained 661 favelas housing 962,793 persons in 239,678 shacks. See also Pino (1997b).

7. *Quarto de Despejo* (1960) was published in English as *Child of the Dark: The Diary of Carolina Maria de Jesus* (1962).

8. Levine (1994) argues that this first book and her subsequent publications unmasked the myth of Brazil as a racial democracy, but since the unmasking was coming directly from an "uppity" black woman from the slums, elites from both sides of the political spectrum had trouble with her personality and with her perspective and therefore ignored her later works. See also Levine and Meihy (1995).

9. Bakhtin's (1984[1965]) analysis of the unofficial folk culture of the Middle Ages in *Rabelais and His World* offers an interesting starting point for thinking about the place of laughter in social life.

10. I also had the opportunity, during my graduate school years at the University of California–Berkeley, to sit in on some courses of the great folklorist Alan Dundes, whose bountiful work includes solo-authored books and articles, compilations of articles, and edited volumes, many of which deal either directly or indirectly with Jewish humor. I appreciate his insights into humor and offer the interested reader just two guideposts here to his extensive contributions to the literature on Jewish humor. See, for example, Dundes and Hauschild (1983) and Dundes (1985).

11. Some writers have claimed that as Jews become absorbed into the main-

stream North American culture, what made them distinct—Jewish humor, Jewish sensibility, and the Jewish perspective—may actually be disappearing. See Horowitz (1997).

12. Freud's (1963[1905]) analytical position on jokes is perhaps the original source of this perspective. Freudian joke theorists disagree about whether or not jokes must be aggressive. Oring (1992), for example, argues against seeing jokes purely as aggressive, a view that has been favored by Dundes. See, for example, Dundes (1987) and Koestler (1989[1964]).

13. See, for example, Oring (1994). Oring sees humor as a sort of "escape valve" for the suppression of sentiment, a phenomenon that has accompanied modernity.

14. A book edited by Powell and Paton (1988), which carves out a subfield devoted to the sociology of humor, takes as its central concern the question of whether humor can be analyzed within a resistance model or rather more as a form of social control used by the dominant groups to maintain their power over subordinated groups.

15. See Thompson (1974, 1978).

16. This is a playful reference to Foucault's position on the relationship between truth and power and the role of intellectuals in constituting a new politics of truth. See Foucault (1980:109–33).

17. The text of this talk was later published by Prickly Pear Pamphlets (North America), Charlottesville, Virginia. The first edition was published in 1993 and this later edition, in 1999. Founded in 1993 in Cambridge, England, by anthropologists Keith Hart and Anna Grimshaw, Prickly Pear describes itself as finding its inspiration for the first series in the "eighteenth-century figure of the pamphleteer, who circulated new and radical ideas to as wide an audience as possible." The Web address of the press is www.people.virginia.edu/~mee7x/pricklypear.html.

18. Attributed to Freud in Bartlett (1980:679).

19. In her epilogue to *Encounters with Aging,* Lock is here commenting on the distinction between hegemony and ideology as set out by Comaroff and Comaroff (1992:28).

20. An example of how humor was used in a specific instance of upsetting group boundaries can be seen in the surrealist political and artistic movement, which used humor to assault the aesthetic tastes and values of the middle and upper classes. Surrealism is dated from the period between the world wars (1924–40). André Breton is recognized as its founding figure, a writer whose book *Anthologie de l'humor noir* (1966), originally published in 1930, set out to detail the relationship between comedy and darkness. Black humor was envisioned as one of a number of powerful poetic weapons. For Breton: "Black humor is bounded by too many things, such as stupidity, skeptical irony, joking without seriousness . . . (the enumeration would be long), but it is preeminently the mortal enemy of sentimentality" (Breton in Pratt 1993:17). Breton and the surrealists understood sentimentality to be a characteristic of bourgeois culture; it therefore became the object of derision for the surrealists, which helps explain why their art is based on shock, absurdity, demented humor, and the incongruous juxtaposition of subconscious and fantastic imagery—a decidedly unsenti-

mental assault on bourgeois taste. It was intended to be aesthetically displeasing and ungratifying—the whole point was to disturb. For Breton, black humor became a discursive weapon that could be used to symbolically contest the dominant discourse of society; accordingly, it was potentially antididactic in that its purpose was to revolt against the prevailing dominant ideology. Breton's book, published at the end of the surrealist period, makes the definitive link between forms of human communication, whether jokes, poetry, literary experiments, or humorous stories and politics. The surrealist painting style, literature, and poetry were inspired greatly by Freud; they sought to reunite exterior and interior realities, conscious and unconscious realms of experience. In painting, perhaps the most famous image associated with the period is that of Dali's melting clocks in *The Persistence of Memory* (1931), an indictment of the bourgeois notion of "modern" time and a critical commentary on the controlling and dominating effects of industrialization and capitalism. The cinematic productions produced in this period, such as *Un chien andalou,* directed by Dali and Buñuel (1928), and *L'age d'or,* directed by Luis Buñuel (1930), inspired later trends and movements within literature, cinema, and the visual arts more generally.

Breton's leadership in the movement, intimated in his writings (1978[1936]), clearly illustrate the movement's interest in supporting the working classes through artistic subversion. His essay "What Is Surrealism" (1978[1936]) served as an affirmation of the connectedness between the surrealists and the working classes: "Let it be clearly understood that for us, as surrealists, the interests of thought cannot cease to go hand in hand with the interests of the working class, and that all attacks on freedom, all interference with the emancipation of the working class and all armed attacks on it cannot fail to be considered by us as attacks on thought as well" (140–41). Eventually, however, the movement was unhinged by internal bickering about the relationship between artistic production and political engagement. A point to be noted about the surrealists is that they were intellectuals—for the most part from the petite bourgeoisie—critical of fascism and sympathetic to the Bolshevik revolution. They were, in short, critical as well of the destructive aspects of rationalism and of the human exploitation brought about by capitalism. Much of the internal bickering within the surrealist movement spun around tensions concerning where exactly different members stood on the relationship between their art and their politics. Importantly, the surrealists wanted to make fun of bourgeois pretensions, despite their own bourgeois roots. The philosopher Walter Benjamin (1978b), writing between 1927 and 1933, characterized the surrealists as an example of a case where the French literati—the intelligentsia—experienced great difficulty in making contact with the proletarian masses whom they wanted to support politically, pointing to the more generalized difficulty of being a "class warrior" when you are not of that same class.

As a contemporary term, surrealism conjures up a diverse body of material ranging from the theater of the absurd to magical realism, to the films of the Spanish director Pedro Almodovar. What holds these diverse forms of communication under the heading of black humor is their desire to spawn laughter from the absurdity and tragedy of the human condition.

21. By using the term "black" here, I am referring to the humor form set out by Breton in his *Anthologie de l'humor noir* (1966). I am also attempting to provide some of the context for the use of the word "black," because of the negative, racialized meanings invoked through the naming of this humor form. To get around this dilemma, I have tried when possible to substitute other words throughout the text.

22. See, for example, Mukerji and Schudson (1991).

23. There seems to be a bit of comic subversion on Tuttle's part here. Bartlett (1980:756, footnote 6) explains that Tuttle wrote a letter to the *New Yorker* dated December 8, 1934, in which he describes the architecture, from which he is recoiling, as collegiate Gothic, one "that had been designed expressly . . . to enable yeomen to pour molten lead through slots on their enemies below. As a propitiatory gift to my gods . . . and to make them forget by appealing to their senses of humor, I carved the inscription over the door."

24. Rafael Sabatini (1875–1950) was a French writer whose book *Scaramouche: A Romance of the French Revolution* (1999[1921]) describes the adventures of Andre-Louis Moreau, a man who vows to get even with the Marquis de La Tour d'Azyr for the death of his friend. The book begins with the same quotation Tuttle used, and Sabatini had the epitaph placed on his gravestone. The *scaramuccia* is also a stock trickster character of the Italian theatrical form known as commedia dell'arte, a figure depicted as an unscrupulous and unreliable servant. In the French theater of Molière (1622–73), the character Scaramouche was closely associated with the Italian actor Tiberio Fiorello, who was able to present it as a comic servant, one who would weep instead of laugh and laugh instead of weep. See www.britannica.com/seo/s/scaramouche/.

25. The quotation ends with "and that was his only patrimony." Rafael Sabatini, *Scaramouche* (1999[1921]), quoted in Bartlett (1980:756).

26. See Alvarez and Escobar (1992) and Alvarez, Dagnino, and Escobar (1998).

27. A perfect example of this was the military presence and curfew set during the United Nations Conference on Environment and Development—also known as the "Earth Summit" of 1992—held in Rio de Janeiro. Because of the international presence, the crackdown on shantytowns and on poor neighborhoods more generally was intensified.

28. See, for example, Lavinas et al. (2001).

29. See Holy Bible (authorized or King James version) (1955[1951]).

30. This quotation by Jerry Lewis is found in *The Rolling Stone Book of Comedy*, Schiffman and Zehme (1991:82).

31. The *Veja* article that described the event claimed that the *galera* (funk dance gangs) rivalries were being carried out on the public beach. Yet the entire event had a political dimension as well. Benedita da Silva, a black woman running for mayor of the city at the time, was targeted as being connected to these youths, and some attribute her political defeat to the fear among members of the middle class that if she were elected, they could expect more of the same. See "Arruaça na areia," *Veja*, October 28, 1992, 18–22. See also Benjamin and Mendonça (1997) for more on the life of Benedita da Silva.

CHAPTER 1. LAUGHTER "OUT OF PLACE"

1. The Oswaldo Cruz Foundation is a research institution linked to the Ministry of Health, devoted to work in the area of science, technology, and public health. Information is available from www.fiocruz.br/.

2. Form of friendship defined by one's godparenthood to a friend's child.

3. Glória's two oldest children, Pedro Paulo and Fernanda, known as Falecida No. 1 (the First Deceased), were no longer living with her at the time. Their particular histories will be discussed in greater detail in chapter 4.

4. According to an on-line dictionary, Aesopian can refer to one of the following:

  1. Relating to or characteristic of the animal fables of Aesop.
  2. Using or having ambiguous or allegorical meanings, especially to elude political censorship: "They could express their views only in a diluted form, resorting to Aesopian hints and allusions." (Isaac Deutscher)

On-line dictionary available at www.dictionary.com/cgi-bin/dict.pl?term = Aesopian.

5. *Terreiro* is used to denote the religious center or space where Afro-Brazilian religious congregations meet to carry out devotional practices.

6. *Communitas,* the Latin word for "community," is associated with the work of anthropologist Victor Turner (1920–83), who in *The Ritual Process* (1995[1969]) wrote about the communion of individuals within a certain phase of a ritual.

7. According to Green (1999:295, footnote 6), the term *cidade maravilhosa* (marvelous city) was coined by Coelho Neto (1908:3).

8. This quotation is attributed to the director and film critic Arnaldo Jabor, but Ventura (1994:epigraph) found it in Paulo Francis (1980).

9. My interviews focused on such micro-level issues as household economics, farming systems, and marketing plans, as well as more macro-level political economy issues that concerned the structure and history of land tenure and agrarian reform in the region. Ultimately, our team was interested in analyzing and reporting (in digestible form) to policy makers in the Ministry of Agriculture the combination of historical and political processes—including an analysis of the minimalist land reform carried out in specific regions and the evolving forms of peasant production, such as sharecropping arrangements that, despite fertile soils, have led to the precarious situation of small-scale peasant farmers.

10. Spanish for Southern Cone.

11. They represented a broad range of leftists who intellectually adhered to some version of dependency theory to understand North-South relations and the contradictions of development in the South. They were enamored of the writings of the activist and exiled political scientist Fernando Henrique Cardoso, who at the time was a hero of the left, but at the completion of this book is considered by many as a free-trade neoliberal who abandoned his earlier leftist intellectual writings about the structure of poverty and inequality in his country. Cardoso became president of Brazil in 1994.

12. After the military coup in Brazil in 1964, the Tropicalist movement, as-

sociated with a number of musicians, became identified with a "countercultural" artistic, behavioral, and political style. See Dunn (2001) for more on this movement.

13. In 1988 Brazil passed one of the most progressive constitutions in the history of the West.

14. In Rio de Janeiro, Silvia Ramos from the nationally prominent Brazilian AIDS Association (Associação Brasileira Interdisciplinar de AIDS [ABIA]) collaborated with me on the focus group interviews; in São Paulo, Regina Rodrigues de Morais and Rosa Dalva F. Bonciani (both of the Coletivo Feminista Sexualidade e Saúde, or Feminist Collective on Sexuality and Health) collaborated with me on the focus group interviews. The project, titled "The Cultural, Class, and Gender Politics of Modern Disease: Women and AIDS in Brazil," was funded by the International Center for Research on Women (ICRW); the results of this research are available in Goldstein (1994a, 1995a).

15. We conducted a total of eighteen focus group discussions (three discussions in each community). These sessions were held in favelas in Rio (three communities) and poor neighborhoods in São Paulo (three communities). The communities in these two cities were not really comparable: those in São Paulo were "working-class," whereas the Rio favelas could more accurately be described as the working poor or sub- or underemployed. The discussion groups, each of which included five to twenty women, focused on issues related to AIDS and sexuality. The discussions lasted from two to four hours and were tape-recorded. See Goldstein (1995a) for an accounting of who was interviewed, from where, and when, and for a complete account of this research.

16. In considering the place of public intellectuals in specific national contexts, I would argue that the United States is the exceptional case in comparison to many other countries, including Brazil. Perhaps it is because North Americans admire capital more than intellect, or perhaps it is because our higher education system is expansive, creating a separate sphere of influence between academic knowledge and public life. Or perhaps, more simply, academic institutions discourage the formation of public intellectuals.

17. I am calling this a nuisance in that the middle and upper classes do recognize—and often complain about—the burdens of being a responsible patron. As I point out in chapter 2, patron-client relations in this setting are complicated.

18. The term *favelados* can be used derogatorily, but in this context it is not.

19. Da Matta has written extensively about Carnival in both Portuguese- and English-language publications. See, for example, Da Matta (1973, 1978, 1991b).

20. Recently, scholars such as Scheper-Hughes have extended and relativized Da Matta's original and frequently cited interpretation by looking for particularized meanings within specific historically contextualized communities. For example, historian Sandra Lauderdale Graham (1995[1998]) provides a wonderful description of Brazilian *carnaval* in the early 1800s, highlighting its classed character and the fact that it was largely a safe time—one without lasting danger (or persistent change), but one that acknowledged popular sentiment toward hierarchy:

> Wealthier persons "more secluded"—the phrase indicated privilege—retained their suspicions about the polluting street. They watched processions from upstairs win-

dows or vestibules, protected from jarring or unruly crowds. Not only did they not join street festivities, the rich conducted their own celebrations, but indoors. . . . By their playful turnings of customary order, they potentially disrupted order. By their gleeful breaches of the gestures of deference and obedience, common people revealed that their usual behavior was not, could not have been simply authentic. Carnaval presented—and those who ordinarily exercised authority accurately understood— that popular awareness. In fantasy, allegory, pranks, music, and exaggeration the poor played out the tensions between the house and the street. . . . The time dedicated to revelry had a fixed end beyond which carnaval's excesses could not continue. So contained, any real threat to order appeared extinguished. Carnaval provided a safe time, without lasting danger for the rich and without true accountability for the poor. (69–71)

Graham suggests that in the celebration of Carnival during the 1800s, a large segment of the working poor already lived much of their life on the streets, so that Carnival did not "invert" but rather celebrated and exaggerated the ordinary (68). Similarly, historian James Green (1999:203) recently argued that for Brazilian homosexuals who transgress gender roles and acceptable sexual boundaries throughout the entire year, Carnival "provides the opportunity for an *intensification* of their own experiences" rather than an inversion.

21. Known as the Sambadrome in English, it is the stadium where the main Carnival parade takes place.

22. I had told them about this possible book title shortly after I saw the new release of the Orson Welles film of the same title in the early 1990s, a film that had been shot in the early 1940s and then placed in a sealed vault for a number of years. The film, which focused on the political struggles of Brazilian *jangadeiros* (fisherman) during the Vargas years, was considered controversial at the time, which explains why it was not released. The official U.S. version came out in 1994.

23. The researchers and activists working on this project also discovered that women from the middle and upper classes also regularly took risks with their partners and that gender relations across the class divide were problematic in ways that hadn't been recognized before.

24. See Geertz (1973).

25. For a good example of this, see John Seabrook's (2000:32) discussion of taste in *Nobrow: The Culture of Marketing, the Marketing of Culture.*

26. See Scheper-Hughes (1992:209–10) for her discussion of "bad faith."

27. See Bakhtin (1984[1965]).

28. An anthropological text that deals with humor and laughter in a fieldwork setting would be incomplete without reference and hearty gratitude to Elenore Smith Bowen's (aka Laura Bohannon's) riveting and humorous tale of fieldwork (which often went awry) among the Tiv of West Africa, immortalized in her book *Return to Laughter* (1954).

29. Corcovado is the name of the mountain where the *Cristo Redentor,* or the Christ the Redeemer statue, sits.

30. The relationships of anthropologists and other social scientists to their informants in the field is a complicated one and too broad to address here. See, for example, Wolf (1996) for a series of articles on feminist dilemmas in the field and Kulick and Willson (1995) for articles on erotic subjectivity.

31. See, for example, Lewis (1959, 1963, 1965, 1966).

32. For an introduction to the major texts in anthropology that provoked this "crisis," see Marcus and Fischer (1986) and Clifford and Marcus (1986).

33. What Lewis—perhaps the foremost author associated with the culture of poverty school—did successfully was write well. (For examples of his work, see Lewis 1959, 1963, 1965, 1966.) His book *La Vida* won the National Book Award in 1967. His work is characterized as being qualitative and literary; his approach employed intensive case studies of families. He also received a great deal of media attention, especially because his concept was employed in the famed Moynihan Report, a document submitted to President Lyndon Johnson as a call for federal action against black poverty. This poverty thesis was named as the academic work that framed the Moynihan Report's model of poverty, one that was later accused of forwarding an image that seemed to "blame the victim." A fascinating article by Harvey and Reed (1996) attempts to deconstruct the political and academic context of the debate and argues that Lewis was a "man of the left" who was self-consciously a humanist scholar and practitioner of "ethnographic realism." They claim that much of the work that has criticized Lewis has been both unfair and erroneous, the product of leftist infighting and a form of New Age liberalism that denies the existence of class. And, rather than considering the conservative implications of Lewis's work, they argue that his work would be more productively understood as "an ethnographic starting point for developing a critical conception of poverty's superstructural foundations" (Harvey and Reed 1996:485). As such, in their opinion, Lewis's work is a celebration of the resilience and resourcefulness of the poor and not a denigration. From my perspective, it seems that Lewis did have an understanding of political and economic structures and the ways in which they construct and limit the choices of the poor, but because of his desire to get up close and to understand specific cultural logics, the broader social structure and the framing of political and economic structures are not explicitly elaborated upon in his actual ethnographic work.

The literature that points to the flaws of Lewis and his school of followers was, nevertheless, abundant. See, for example, Charles Valentine's *Culture of Poverty: Critique and Counter-Proposals* (1968). Within the discipline of anthropology, Eleanor Leacock's (1971) edited volume, a watershed critique titled *The Culture of Poverty: A Critique,* was devoted to an indictment of Lewis. The critiques ranged from methodological (problems of sampling, inadequate attention to alternative hypotheses) to substantive (whether there was such a thing as a "culture" of poverty) to ethical issues (a reference to the employment of this concept by others, such as how it was interpreted through and beyond the Moynihan Report). Also, Lewis's approach was accused of being overly psychological and lacking an understanding of social structure, thus aligning him with some of the early American "culturalists" of the "culture and personality" school.

Whether or not one agrees with the criticisms launched against Lewis and his body of work, anyone who has read his work would admit that one of Lewis's great strengths is his ability to transmit a sense of intimacy with and understanding of the consciousness of the people he writes about. His work embodies all the contradictions—both positive and negative—that we now associate with thick description.

34. Lassalle and O'Dougherty (1997:244–45) make this criticism of Scheper-Hughes (1992) as well as of Philippe Bourgois (1995).

35. These references are found in Gay (1993:372).

36. See, for example, Marx (1906–09).

37. This implication is entirely unintentional, although very difficult to entirely avoid.

38. See Taussig (1989) for a critique of these two books.

39. See W. W. Rostow (1960), the emblematic anticommunist text of its time, for a good example of the modernization paradigm that sought to explain how developing countries would eventually pass through the stages of capitalist development and reach the glory of high mass consumption.

40. For example, they point out that since about 1870, exporters of raw materials received less for commodities than the cost of finished goods imported from industrialized nations.

41. Much of the version of Brazil's history that I provide in this section is deeply indebted to the work of historians Thomas E. Skidmore (1999) and E. Bradford Burns (1993).

42. See Skidmore (1999:44) for a fuller explanation of the *exaltados*.

43. Owensby (1999:27) estimates that the number of industrial establishments in Rio grew tenfold during the time, from 1,500 to over 15,000 men and women.

44. Skidmore (1999:116) describes the corporatism during Vargas's first reign in the following passage: "The intent of corporatism was to facilitate the adoption of modern capitalism while avoiding the extremes of laissez-faire permissiveness on the one hand and total state direction on the other."

45. Populism here means an appeal to voters through the promise of public works and social welfare benefits. For a thorough discussion of pre-1964 populism in Brazil, see Debert (1979).

46. The União Democrática Nacional (UDN), initially starting out as liberal consitutionalist, early on had earned the support of the middle and upper civilian classes and army officers and even some leaders from the Communist Party. The party eventually shifted to the right politically and became known for its support of free trade and antigovernment intervention in the economy.

47. In Brazil, the vice president can be from a different party than the president.

48. Although Argentina experienced its own military coup in 1966, not long after the Brazilian one, there were many differences from the Brazilian case. To name but a few, the support of the Brazilian guerrilla movement was limited in numbers and did not have widespread support among the population at large. The military itself was divided, and civilians—in the form of political allies—were still in charge of many parts of the government.

49. See Skidmore (1999:175). See also Pinheiro (1991), who suggests a different causality.

50. See Holloway (1993) for a history of policing in Rio de Janeiro.

51. See Baer (1983).

52. See Skidmore (1999:193).

53. As I complete the editing for this book, in late 2002, Lula has won the election for president and is poised to take office.

54. As an intellectual, Cardoso was a prolific writer, authoring hundreds of articles and books. A book he coauthored with Enzo Faletto, *Dependency and Development in Latin America* (1979), is a good example of his Marxist academic writings.

55. As governor of the Federal District, Buarque instituted a program known as Programa Bolsa-Escola (School Bursary Program) that rewarded low-income parents with additional income if their children were enrolled in and attending public school. See the following Web sites: www.uol.com.br/aprendiz/n_colunas/c_buarque and www.idrc.ca/lacro/foro/seminar/caccia_pb.html.

CHAPTER 2. THE AESTHETICS OF DOMINATION

1. Glória called her Dona Beth, using the polite form of address. This form was usually reserved for employers or elders. (For example, Glória also spoke about Zezinho's ex-mother-in-law, a woman in her midsixties living in Felicidade Eterna and addressed as Dona Madalena.)

2. *Patroa* means boss in this context but also refers to the wife, or madam, of the house.

3. Lovell's (2000) recent empirical study of racial and gender exclusionary practices concludes that the majority of Afro-Brazilian women remain confined to laboring in the area of domestic services and that "gender and race intersect to differentiate women's work lives and opportunities in Brazil" (99).

4. In Brazil, wages are defined by the notion of a *salário mínimo* (minimum salary), and income level is defined by how many minimum salaries a person earns per month. One minimum wage typically hovers between $80 and $100 U.S. This amount is defined according to the *cesta básica* (basket of basic goods), which includes foods such as rice, beans, and farina, that are meant to sustain a family of four over a one-month period (Wood and Carvalho 1988:122). The minimum salary is therefore supposed to be able to sustain a family of four for a month, and it is adjusted periodically to keep pace with inflation and with a series of other consumer price indexes. Domestic workers typically earn one or two minimum wages per month. By all accounts, Beth's wages of five minimum salaries per month were exceptionally good. A very large proportion of the Brazilian population is in this earning sector, and in some regions of Brazil, this designated minimum is even lower than in the cities. Wood and Carvalho (1988) citing Lluch (1979) examine the area of demand for labor services and the rate of growth of the poor population. Wood and Carvalho (1988) predicted that "the relatively low rate of job creation in the formal sector means that the number of workers making less than the 1970 minimum wage may increase, from 16 to 22 million by the year 2000, despite high growth in output" (245). It seems as if their predictions have come true in that there are many more poor people and fewer jobs for them in the formal sector employment area. Thus a large proportion of the population remains stuck in the lowest wage-earning sectors. Another way of understanding this is to notice that even with high rates

of economic growth, the proportion of poorly paid workers increases. This occurs because of the relatively low rate of job creation in the formal sector and the high rate of increase in labor supply (Wood and Carvalho 1988:258).

5. Glória had taken in Celina's children after her death and had also adopted in Zezinho's children when she reunited with him.

6. The work card is a legal document in which the employer registers the employee's date of hiring, salary, and function. This document guarantees the worker's constitutional rights to the minimum wage, weekly paid days off, an extra monthly salary per year (called the thirteenth salary), paid holidays, pension, one month of paid vacation, and so forth. Registered women workers are granted maternity leave of 120 days, day care for their children, breaks to breast-feed, and other rights guaranteed by the 1988 constitution (Lovell 2000:100). Glória had not been a registered member of the system until she worked for Dona Beth, and thus she had been excluded from all these rights until the mid-1990s. When an employer signs a carteira, he or she contributes approximately 8 percent of the total wage, and the employee is expected to contribute the other 8 percent. Social security in Brazil dates back to the 1930s, and early on it became the dominant system for providing health care services. Social security institutions, then called Institutos de Aposentadorias e Pensões (IAPs; Retirement and Pension Institutes), were organized according to a classic insurance model: in other words, benefits and assistance depended on the ability of the category of employee in question to contribute. In 1966, the organization based on the IAPs was unified into a single institution, the Instituto Nacional de Previdência Social (INPS; National Institute of Social Security). The reform of the social welfare and health systems was legally concretized in the 1988 constitution, and a series of changes took place throughout the 1990s but cannot be fully outlined here (see Lobato and Burlandy 2000). The reorganization seems to have brought many domestic workers such as Glória into the system. Signing a work card is a major commitment on the part of an employer because it entails paying a percentage of the employees wage into the federal social security system. Social security for non-live-in domestic workers is still not universal practice, however, despite the 1988 constitution's intention to enhance the rights of domestic workers.

7. The following is a quick review of the currency changes in Brazil since the abertura. The Plano Cruzado was initiated in 1986, and the *cruzado* was introduced. Under this plan, three zeros were eliminated from the *cruzeiro*. In 1989 the Plano Verão was implemented, and another currency, the *cruzado novo*, equivalent to 1,000 *cruzados*, was introduced. In March 1990, the Plano Collor was launched, and the currency was the *cruzeiro real*, which was often referred to simply as the *cruzeiro*. In 1994, the Plano Real was launched. See Fonseca (1998) for a review of these economic programs and currency changes. The *cruzeiro* was the currency in Brazil just before the *real* replaced it in 1994. I say "at one point" because inflation was significant at this time.

8. I calculated in dollars because, at the time, inflation was extreme, and the Brazilian currency was (and still is) linked to calculations through a kind of mental dollarization. Good employers, for example, who were aware of the sky-rocketing prices of foods, would attempt to adjust wages to keep up with inflation through this kind of dollar calculating.

9. The dictionary spelling is *veado,* but in popular slang the word is written *viado.*

10. Glória lovingly and teasingly used these words to refer to her former employers, but her use of them was also part of a broader, less politically correct popular vernacular; thus different meanings would be understood depending on her audience. Because Glória knew that I was a sympathetic audience, she felt free to speak in this fashion.

11. See, for example, Pereira de Melo's (1989) statistics based on the 1980 census. They show that only 17.6 percent of women domestic workers earned above one minimum wage per month, with the vast majority earning well below one. Lovell (2000:95) more recently found that Afro-Brazilian women suffer doubly from both gender and racial inequality in wages.

12. Of course, some interpretation is involved here regarding where the middle classes end and the upper classes begin. For the purposes of this study, I am following the work of Wood and Carvalho (1988), who estimate about 20 percent of the population as constituting the middle class, and earning somewhere between five and twenty minimum salaries, with the upper classes earning above twenty minimum salaries. I am also, notably, following Owensby's (1999) notion of middle-classness as a state of mind, with the greatest division being that between manual and nonmanual labor.

13. It was not until 1998 that Felicidade Eterna had its own *orelhão* (public pay telephone) placed at the entrance. Before that time, one had to walk more than a mile to the bakery to find a public telephone.

14. I was told that Soneca had a difficult birth due to a condition related to sickle-cell anemia.

15. Cultural capital, an idea that is often associated with the work of Pierre Bourdieu (1984), is that entity possessed by a person which derives from the symbolic knowledge, aptitude, dispositions, goods, and credentials, including years of schooling, that is connected to a person's economic class. But the idea goes beyond economic and social definitions of capital; it also includes aesthetics and a range of signs that become distinguishing indicators of class.

16. It is, as Anna Rubbo and Michael Taussig (1977:48) once noted, the primary division in Colombian households: you either supply servants or you employ them.

17. See, for example, Pereira de Melo (1989); Kofes (1990); Brites (2000).

18. Because of the limits of the available census data, it is hard to get a precise reading of the numbers of domestic workers who are not registered in any formal way. Given that so many domestic workers are currently in live-out situations, the actual number of workers and their exact employment conditions are difficult to calculate. Many live-out domestic workers, for example, are known to be denied some of the benefits granted to live-in domestic workers by the social security system, such as a signed carteira (Pereira de Melo 1989:252).

19. According to a United Nations summary report (Tolosa 1996:4), the increase in service activity signifies a decline in the proportion of the population with a formal contract. Tolosa examined the National Household Survey for 1990, paying attention to the sectors in which most workers were employed. He found that the service sector in Rio was dominant, and its dominance had in-

creased precisely during the years of economic decline. Inequality worsened during the 1980s in Brazil's three largest metropolitan areas (São Paulo, Rio de Janeiro, and Belo Horizonte); of those three, Rio's inequality grew to be the worst.

20. In 1981, the Gini coefficient—the calculation that measures the level of income disparity in a country or a region—in Rio de Janeiro was measured at 0.58. In 1989 it had increased to 0.67, meaning that the level of inequality had risen significantly. The Gini coefficient measures the difference in wealth between the poorest sectors and the richest sectors in a particular country. The closer the number is to 1, the closer the situation approximates complete inequality.

21. São Paulo has a larger working class and middle class because of its leadership in industry.

22. According to the IBGE (1996), approximately 40 percent of permanent workers in the Rio metropolitan area were women. Despite the legal restrictions on employing children under the age of fourteen, they account for approximately 4.6 per cent of the workforce (overall, in Brazil). This material comes from the U.S. Department of State "Brazil Country on Human Rights Practices for 1997." See www.state.gov/www/global/human_rights/1998_hrp_report/brazil.html.

23. The exact calculation of the number of domestic workers in a population would be difficult to make, since so many of them would not appear in census material. But here are some approximations of how disadvantaged these workers are. Lovell (2000) estimates that "preta [black] women in São Paulo remained overwhelmingly concentrated as domestic workers. Forty-six percent of all employed preta women in 1991 were domestic workers as compared with 38 percent of parda [mulata] women and only 18 percent of white women" (93). Lovell suggests not only that domestic work is racialized but also that the gender gap in wages is even greater than the existent racial inequality. She finds that "Afro-Brazilian women were paid less than Afro-Brazilian men in all educational categories" (95).

24. See De Souza (1980); Jelin (1980); Saffioti (1978).

25. Rocinha, one of the most famous favelas in Latin America, is a complicated community purported to have a population of over 150,000. By now, it is one of the more established and organized communities in Rio de Janeiro. The Web site for Rocinha (www.rocinha.com.br/) describes many projects that are currently in the planning stages, including plans for a university. Rocinha became notorious throughout the late 1980s and 1990s for drug trafficking and violence. Glória, however, remembers Rocinha as a peaceful community, one without the violence that came to characterize it in later years. See also UNICEF (1985).

26. Freyre (1986[1933]:418) mentions that these became terms of endearment between whites as well.

27. See, for example, Harris (1964a:66).

28. See, Harris (1964), chap. 6, "The Myth of the Friendly Master," in which he rejects Tannenbaum's (1947) notion that slavery was "soft" in Brazil.

29. See Caulfield (2000:50–69) for a full description and analysis of the visit of King Albert and Queen Elisabeth of Belgium to Rio de Janeiro in 1920.

30. In the introduction to *Para Inglês Ver,* British anthropologist Peter Fry (1982c:17) positions his own writings about Brazil and offers some possible ex-

planations of the book's titling phrase (and for my own titling of this section). One possible myth of origin for the phrase is related to the period of English prohibition of slave trafficking (1830–88) and the camouflaged transgression of this order by Brazilian ships. Fry uses the phrasing and the myths surrounding it to talk about English and Brazilian identity, to describe how, over time, both historically and in the contemporary versions of North-South relations, each has had to deal with the possible reading of its civilization by the other. Fry lays out a series of generic binaries that have defined Brazilian identity in contradistinction to that of the British (which could also be read as broadly European). Where the British are orderly, timely, and respectful of the law, Brazilians are disorderly, not punctual, and disrespectful of the law. When it came to the English prohibition of slave trading, Brazilian navigators figured out a way to hide their illegal activities, creating elaborate schemes to appear lawful, "for the English to see."

31. The modernists were a group of artists who wanted to set out a new national identity for Brazil in relation to foreign powers; they were especially keen on breaking the colonial trend of imitation.

32. The Modernist movement in Brazil is generally understood as the movement that began to question uncritical acceptance of European aesthetic forms and sought to develop a uniquely Brazilian style of aesthetic expression in the arts and literature. It began during the Modern Art Week festival that took place in the São Paulo Municipal Theatre in February 1922.

33. Freyre's discussion of the sexual relationship between the masters and the slaves—one he recognized as dependent not only on the lascivious nature of white men but also on the compliant nature of black and mulata women—is a great deal more problematic (and is discussed in chapter 3) but perhaps is better understood within its historical context. Freyre ignored and greatly downplayed the history of coercion or rape. The outcome has been that race and sex have long been separated as topics.

34. Because most of the streets in the favelas were not paved, asphalt was associated with neighborhoods with residents of a higher economic class.

35. This refers to a person from Northeast Brazil. It can be meant in a derogatory manner.

36. This is one of many variations of language found in Northeast popular culture. In this case, *Oxente* is the agglutination of *Oh* with *gente,* which means "You all" or "You folks."

37. Motels in Rio are often short-term residences used for sexual encounters. Some motels rent by the hour and serve a working-class clientele; others serve a wealthier clientele for extended weekend retreats. They were referring to the latter in this case.

38. See, for example, Caldeira (2000).

39. While there seems to have been significant improvement in education in the 1990s, the educational level of the overall population is quite low. Overall, illiteracy for those over ten years of age is 14.8 percent, with Northeast Brazil registering a rate as high as 29.4 percent (IBGE 1997a). This picture divides radically along racial lines as well: the proportion of whites who have completed the "compulsory" eight years of elementary schooling, 29.5 percent, is more than double the 13.6 percent figure for nonwhites. Whites are almost four and a half

times more likely than nonwhites to complete a college education (Hasenbalg and Silva 1999:155). Given this disparity, it is no surprise that nonwhites hold a disproportionately higher share of the lowest-paying jobs in the informal sector. In 1987, the monthly income of nonwhites was a little less than half that of whites (Hasenbalg and Silva 1999:157). Poor families (those earning less than twice the minimum wage per month) are underrepresented in preschool and high school age groups (40 percent as compared with 80 percent for the others), and even in grade school. See the following Web site for related information: www.un.org/esa/agenda21/.

40. Recently, there has been much public discussion of the racial dimensions of educational inequality. Generally speaking, black and mixed-race people are far less represented in higher education and in high-prestige careers than their proportion in the total population. Many believe that the fate of black people in Brazil is sealed in the educational system—early—before individuals even reach the labor market. See "Baixa escolaridade realimenta a discriminação," Folha Cotidiano, C1, Folha de São Paulo, Domingo, January 14, 2001. The article refers to the research of Sergei Dillon Soares at the Instituto de Pesquisa Econômica Aplicada (IPEA; Institute of Research in Applied Economics).

This more recent finding regarding race seems to complement Pastore's earlier observation in that families would have to make it first into the working classes in order to be able to take advantage of the opportunities available through education. For example, whereas blacks represent 5.7 percent of the population, only 2.2 percent graduated from a series of higher education majors evaluated by the study. See Gois (2001).

Anthropologist Yvonne Maggie, who is quoted in the same article and has been studying racial inequality and discrimination in Brazil for many years, has now turned to examining racial inequalities in the educational system. She noted that the inequality in higher education was not really related to the difference between universities as much as to the difference in majors, with those majors of greater societal prestige having a higher proportion of white people enrolled. See also Maggie (1988).

41. I am greatly indebted to the research done on household workers over the years by Elsa M. Chaney and Mary Garcia Castro, who together published the edited volume Muchachas No More: Household Workers in Latin America and the Caribbean (1989).

42. Cultural reproduction theory, sometimes referred to as cultural capital theory, refers to the Marxist analyses of the French sociologist Pierre Bourdieu (1984, 1991, 1993) regarding the reproduction of social inequality, especially through schooling. See also Bourdieu and Passeron (1977).

43. Social movements, perhaps, are somewhere in between armed resistance and oppositional culture. While in a broad sense, one would have to admit that the success of the Movimento Negro (Black Consciousness Movement) in Brazil has not been great, one would also have to consider that in the city of Salvador, Bahia, for example, the Afro-Brazilian carnival groups have had some success in terms of creating a space for the development of black identity.

44. An interesting film version of social mobility through soccer is depicted in Solo: The Law of the Favela (1994). This is similar to the United States, where

black boys from poor neighborhoods often want to become basketball players. See Telander (1995[1988]).

45. This was in 1998, when a *real* was approximately equivalent to one dollar. One salary at that time was about 100 *reais,* which meant that Darlene had to take in twenty customers in one month in order to clear one minimum salary.

46. It may be that women's oppositional culture takes place in the form of seeking social mobility through marrying up (the commodification of love), seeking whiter or more financially secure men (whitening), seeking older men (the coroa), seeking the commodification of their own bodies through sex work, or even seeking religious conversion. All these will be discussed in the following chapters.

47. Research and literature are now emerging about Brazilian telenovelas. See, for example, Leal (1990[1985]); Araújo (2000); Fernandes (1997[1982]); Hamburger (1999).

CHAPTER 3. COLOR-BLIND EROTIC DEMOCRACIES

This chapter was published in a different form as "'Interracial' Sex and Racial Democracy in Brazil: Twin Concepts?" *American Anthropologist* 101 (1999): 563–78.

1. One of the most common ways that women were inducing abortion in this time period was through the over-the-counter stomach ulcer drug Cytotec. See Leal (1995:33).

2. See Fussell (1983) for a good explanation of how North Americans deal with class.

3. Barbara Ehrenreich (1987, 2001) has written and spoken publicly about the stereotypes perpetuated about women on welfare and has helped debunk the myth that the majority of women on welfare are African American, when in fact most are white. According to McLaughlin (1997), although the myth that most welfare recipients are African American women persists, in fact, children constitute the largest group of people receiving public assistance.

4. See Fry (1995, 1995/1996) and Winant (1994) for works that take on comparative race relations.

5. Robert Stam (1997:1) has argued that Brazil and the United States, although not identical, are indeed eminently comparable in that they share qualities in terms of both historical formation and ethnic diversity. Historian George Reid Andrews (1992, cited in Hasenbalg and Silva 1999:160) also sees comparisons of Brazil and the United States as useful. Andrews suggests that while the indexes of inequality in the United States declined after 1950, in Brazil, the same indexes remained stable or worsened.

6. There are a number of classic articles in this field of racial categories. For the anthropological articles that helped frame this field, see Harris (1964b), Kottak (1963), and Sanjek (1971).

7. The 2000 census in the United States has made changes to the race and ethnicity questions. According to the Web site provided by the U.S. Census Bureau (www.census.gov/Press-Release/www/2001/raceqandas.html), the minimum categories for race are now American Indian or Alaska Native; Asian; Black or

African American; Native Hawaiian or Other Pacific Islander; and White. There no longer was a multiracial category, but respondents were allowed to select one or more races in their self-identification. A sixth category of Some Other Race was also included. There were also two minimum categories for ethnicity: Hispanic or Latino and Not Hispanic or Latino.

8. The 1980 Brazilian census, for example, used only four categories: black (*preto*), white (*branco*), yellow (*amarelo*), and mixed race (*pardo*) (Harris et al. 1993), which avoid much of the multiplicity and richness found in everyday discourse. Everyday discourse (in Felicidade Eterna and in Brazil more generally) is often about "color," which suggests a continuum of features, encompassing skin color, hair type, and facial morphology, without positing separate racial types. The women in Felicidade Eterna, for example, usually described themselves as *morena* (brown, or mixed-race), but on certain occasions they described themselves or others as *preta* (black) and less often as *negra* (black). *Preta* and *negra* both mean black and are used interchangeably as race or color terms. Both words can be softened in Brazilian Portuguese by adding the diminutive *inha;* this lessens the impact of calling someone black, which can easily be interpreted as insulting. Maggie (1988), cited in Hanchard (1994b), notes that *negro* and *preto* are rarely used to describe friends or those with whom one has direct contact, for fear of insulting as well. I found this to be true in Felicidade Eterna, although context made all the difference.

9. See Sheriff (2001) for a recent critique of these conventional understandings of racial classification in Brazil.

10. See "A Cinderela Negra," *Veja,* July 7, 1993, 66–73.

11. The election of a black man to a high government position is a rare occurrence in Brazil. See Podesta (1993), cited in Twine (1998), who notes the extremely low numbers of elected black officials at the federal level. There is a similar dearth of black elected officials at the state and local levels.

12. Fry (1995/96) comments on what he and other writers on Brazilian race relations have noted to be a plethora of terms used in everyday conversation by low-income Brazilians. This multiple mode or reference includes words that refer to mixed race and/or mixed color such as *moreno(a)*, *moreno(a) claro(a)*, *mulato(a)*, *mulato(a) fechado(a)*, *pardo(a)*, *crioulo(a)*, *neguinho(a)*, and *pretinho(a)*.

13. To illustrate the complexity of popular Brazilian racial discourse, Fry uses the photograph of Ana Flávia and her father printed in *Veja* as a loosely constructed projective test to elicit descriptions from low-income Brazilians living in Rio de Janeiro. First, he presents the photograph so that only the faces appear. Two "negro" *garagistas* (men who care for the cars of middle- and upper-class individuals and who describe themselves as negro) questioned by Fry describe the governor and his daughter as either *mulato* and *morena* or *mulata* and *moreno*, words that are considered "polite" terms signifying mixed race. They seem to have been used interchangeably by Fry and his informants. When Fry presents the entire photograph, revealing both the upper-class context of the two protagonists and the title of the article ("A Cinderela Negra"), the two garagistas laugh. Fry suggests that the wealthy surroundings, including the palatial room and the clothing of the father and daughter, disqualified them from the category of negros in the eyes of the garagistas, causing them to burst out in laughter, as if Fry

(and *Veja*) had played a visual joke on them. The implication was that they laughed as if they were wondering, *How could Veja describe her as negra when she came from that opulent background?* Only the middle and upper classes, Fry contends, are succumbing to Americanized notions of race, whereas the popular classes continue to use multiple categories that rely heavily on signs of class.

While Fry recognizes the hierarchy within popular culture of African and European traits of inheritance, illustrated by descriptions of people as having *cabelo ruim* (bad hair) or a *nariz chato* (flat nose), he suggests that such distinctions become racist only when African features are viewed as inherently inferior. *Chato* means "lousy" in Portuguese, but together with "nose" is understood to mean flat or wide, features culturally defined as ugly and associated with African descent. Fry further suggests that there is some ambivalence in the negative evaluation of blackness, as evidenced by the large number of people who (when surveyed) choose their marriage partners across racial lines.

Fry reproduces a table from the *Veja* survey (published in the same "Cinderela Negra" article) to illustrate his point that Brazilians cross racial lines both in their evaluation of beauty and in their choice of "ideal [marriage] partners." In this survey, informants were divided into black and white racial categories (Fry mentions that the article does not state whether these are self-descriptions or descriptors used by the researchers) and then asked to choose their "ideal partner," with the choices consisting of white (branco), mixed-race (mulato), or black (negro). Fry notes what he considers the high percentage of positive responses concerning the mulato category (27 percent of whites and 31 percent of blacks said their "ideal partner" would be mulato) and suggests that Brazilians' attitudes toward one another in the realm of sexual unions give some credence to the notion that the "myth" of racial democracy may not be simply a myth.

Fry himself suggests that the survey presented in the *Veja* article is somewhat problematic because it does not reveal how the racial categories of the informants were determined. However, he uses the survey to make the point about "ideal" partners. At the same time, I would note that of the whites surveyed, 53 percent preferred a white marriage partner, and of the blacks surveyed, 14 percent preferred a white partner and 37 percent a black partner. Significantly, the *Veja* survey was not broken down by gender. Leaving gender unmarked significantly skews this survey because, as I argue, mulata and mulato (female and male mixed-race persons) are in no sense equivalent in meaning or connotation (see also Corrêa 1996).

14. It is also present in scholarly venues. A white North American colleague of mine told me of an exchange she had with a Brazilian colleague when she revealed to him that she intended to study racism in Brazil. He asked her whether she had ever slept with a black man and suggested that because Brazilians form sexual unions across color lines (and the implication is that North Americans do not), racism does not exist there.

15. Silva (1985), for example, looking at economic data on social mobility, argues that lighter-skinned (mixed-race) people do not fare better (in terms of socioeconomic mobility and social equality) than darker-skinned people, thereby challenging the idea, common among low-income people such as Glória and her relations, that lighter skin has significant advantages (see also

Shapiro 1996). Silva's findings are compelling in terms of understanding the broader implications of racism, but it is hard for me to erase the ongoing and everyday discourses of people in Felicidade Eterna that illustrate their belief that small differences in skin shade can make an enormous difference in one's life.

16. The phrase was *"subir na vida."*

17. *Coroa* as used in this chapter and this context refers to an older, richer, whiter man. The word actually means "crown" and refers to regal authority. The *Novo Dicionário Aurélio* notes its usage in slang as "one passing from maturity to old age." It also means tonsure or a bald spot on the head. The word seems to have different meanings in different contexts. Rebhun (personal communication) finds that in Northeast Brazil, the common meaning of coroa is that of an older unmarried woman, while Fonseca (1992), whose research site was in Porto Alegre, found that the word referred to a married man who sustained a single mother and her children.

18. *Golpe do baú* appears in the *Novo Michaelis* dictionary as "marriage for economic interest." The treasure chest coup refers to the fact that the woman is marrying or seducing for money. The English term "gold digger" refers to an equivalent scenario.

19. Twine (1996) encountered similar attitudes among rural Afro-Brazilian women in the northwest interior of the state of Rio de Janeiro.

20. The implicit references to the correlation between one's age and one's sexual potency reveal ageist stereotypes. Anthropologist L. A. Rebhun shared a joke from Northeast Brazil with me that illustrates a similar point and translates something like this:

> A young woman went to bed with an old man [*velho*]. She thought that since he was too old, he wouldn't manage a screw and that he would die before the first one. She says, "I am going to marry an old man, kill him, and keep his money." Arriving in the room, the old man goes to change while she is smiling and thinking, "I am going to kill this coroa." A little bit later, the old man arrived with a hard dick with a condom on and some cotton in his ears and a clothes pin on his nose. The woman got scared and asked what it all was. He responded that there are two things which make him really mad: the groans of a woman and the smell of burnt rubber!

21. See, for example, Brown (1998); Hyam (1986); Stoler (1989, 1995); Young (1995).

22. According to Collins (1990), the fusion of the Jezebel image with that of the prostitute allowed for the forced prostitution of enslaved African women in the antebellum American South. See also Gilman (1985).

23. I place "imaginary" in quotation marks as a reference to Anderson's (1983) notion of imagined community, in this case, of white Brazilians imagining and appropriating an Afro-Brazilian past.

24. A good example of this is registered in the famous one-liner delivered by the former president, Fernando Henrique Cardoso, during his first election campaign. Cardoso declared that he was born with "one foot in the kitchen," signaling his purported mixed-race heritage as well as a union involving a poor, dark-skinned woman working in the kitchen of the colonial *casa grande* (big house). See Freyre (1986[1933]).

25. See Corrêa (1996), Gilliam (1998), and Gilliam and Gilliam (1999) for excellent exceptions.

26. Historian Maria Odila Leita da Silva Dias (1995[1984]) notes that Freyre's writings rely on the "myth of the absent lady" (52). Portuguese colonizers, it was often noted, left their women at home in Portugal. Explanations of colonial behavior, especially the relations between white men and mixed-race and black women, have relied heavily on this myth, without questioning its effects. Dias writes that this "myth of the absent white lady" actually provided support for the social values of domination in Brazil's colonial society. Accordingly, "The myth of the absent lady is part of the apparatus of repression of attempts to make the act of concubinage with women of other races formal or public" (54). Since this colonial legacy later transformed itself into the naturalization of the role of the slave and then the domestic worker as a (sexual) mistress, Brazilian elites have viewed their own special case of "interracial sexuality" as less racist and have ignored the implied power relations between slave and master, and later between employer and employee. Giacomini's (1988) work seems to draw from Dias's formulation, engaging with Freyre's (1986[1933]) work and pointing out the limits to his elite, white, male perspective, one that in many respects is uncritical of the problematic nature of this unequal relationship.

27. A biographical article about Freyre by the historian Jeffrey Needell (1995a:57–58) suggests that Freyre's (1986[1933]) idealization of race relations in Brazil can be partly explained by his experiences of racism in the United States and his determination to contrast Brazil with North America. Needell argues that much of Freyre's celebration of miscegenation "derives from an evocation of the sexual relationship between privileged white boys and *mulata* servants" (1995a:69)—a relationship that Freyre boasts of having experienced firsthand.

28. Scholars tend to interpret Freyre in varied ways, depending on the focus of their scholarship. His works certainly contain contradictory images and interpretations of Afro-Brazilian women living within the slave/patriarchal system. Parker (1991) notes the ambiguity of Freyre's discussion of slave sexuality but interprets his work as promoting a generally positive perspective on the nature of sexual interaction and racial mixture. Hanchard (1994b), following the line of argument that began with black activist and scholar Abdias do Nascimento (1979), notes the absence of rape from Freyre's discussion of slave sexuality and questions the accuracy of his descriptions of consensual sex. This attention to Freyre derives from the general recognition that his work promoted the idea of racial democracy in Brazil (Skidmore 1993[1974]).

29. In an obituary of Freyre, Skidmore (1988) argues that Freyre's training with the anthropologist Franz Boas gave him the perspective to write in this particular antiracist vein. As a fellow anthropologist, I cannot help but be curious about Freyre's response to Boasian propositions on race.

30. In the 1950s, UNESCO sponsored research on racial democracy in Brazil. Although they recognized the existence of racial prejudice in Brazil, the researchers nevertheless maintained that it was relatively insignificant vis-à-vis class prejudice and discrimination. This is especially true of the North American researchers. See Wagley (1963 [1952]) for one of the more significant anthropological publications derived from this research. See also Fernandes and Bastide

(1955); Fernandes (1969); and Harris (1964b). Since these early studies, numerous others have explored race as separate from class. For examples, see Andrews (1991); Hasenbalg and Silva (1988); and Silva and Hasenbalg (1992). See Winant (1994) for an excellent summary and interpretation of the race relations literature in Brazil.

31. Corrêa (1996) argues that the mulata has been created as a mythic figure in the Brazilian national imaginary; she is "desirable," "sensual," "pure body," or "sex."

32. One would assume that if such claims were true, there would be an overwhelming number of interracial marriages. In fact, there seem to be many fewer interracial unions than most people assume. Hasenbalg, Silva, and Barcelos (1992) found that in Rio de Janeiro, "same-race" unions are more common than not: 55.9 percent of pairs are white-white, 14.5 percent of pairs include partners who are both mixed race, and 6.3 percent of pairs are black-black. See also Telles (1993).

33. See the writings of the sociologist Robert E. Park in Hughes et al. (1950). Park portrayed famous male mulattos—Frederick Douglass, Booker T. Washington, and W. E. B. Du Bois—as prototypes of the tragic because of being trapped in two cultural and economic systems.

34. See, for example, Fry (1982b); Gaspar (1985); Muraro (1983); Parker (1991); Trevisan (1986); Vainfas (1986, 1989).

35. Despite the undisputed importance of Fry's (1982a) and Parker's (1991) studies on sexuality in Brazil, their work reinforces the image of Brazil as an erotic paradise where gendered and racialized dimensions of the system, locations where inequality definitely exists, are downplayed or altogether ignored.

36. See also, for example, Brown (1998); Young (1995); Hyam (1986).

37. Only with Néstor Perlongher's O Negócio do Michê: Prostituição Viril em São Paulo (1987; The Business of the Michê: Male Prostitution in São Paulo) does race reenter scholarly discussions of Brazilian sexuality. Building upon the work of Fry, this ethnography examines the economies of desire (both literal and symbolic) within the world of male prostitution in São Paulo. Perlongher highlights the fact that the michês (males who prostitute for other males) are for the most part young, poor, and black or mixed race, while their clients are generally older, richer, and whiter. His ethnography illustrates how racial discrimination functions in this particular world among both michês and clients. For Perlongher, the "business of the michê" is simultaneously a sexual, racial, and economic transaction. Perlongher's ethnography, while limited to one particular population, highlights the intersection of race, class, and sexuality and describes how power is inscribed in the construction of these relations. It also illustrates the situational nature of racial "Othering": in one situation, prostitutes use their blackness to advertise their virility to whiter-skinned clients and thereby obtain higher prices, whereas in other situations, darker-skinned clients are viewed as less desirable because of their color. While Perlongher's work addresses race and sex together, it shares with Fry (and Parker) an almost exclusive focus on male sexuality. This fact clearly limits these studies' usefulness in framing a broader discussion of sexuality in Brazil. See also Kulick (1997, 1998).

38. See chapter 6. See also Goldstein (1992, 1994a, 1994b, 1996).

39. Silence, however, cannot be conflated with hegemony and should not be read as an absence of political consciousness or knowledge. Sheriff (2000) rightly argues that in our recent scholarly pursuit of the discursive landscape, we have failed to look at the significance of communal forms of silence. She calls the communal silence about the subject of racism among poor Brazilians of African descent a form of "cultural censorship" and describes it as being "constituted through and circumscribed by the political interests of dominant groups" (114). Silence itself may be an "adaptive" response to domination. She concludes: "A fuller critique of domination, I would argue, requires our sustained attention to those forms of power that are indeed successful, in particular locations and historical moments, in suppressing narratives of resistance. As both an index and a product of such domination, silence and its consequences must be exposed" (129).

40. I say this here because there are other discourses, not within the scope of the themes addressed in this chapter, which show that there are strong moments of racial consciousness, such as in people's descriptions of looking for work. In these discourses, there is a strong sense that their color is a factor that holds them back from social mobility.

41. *Comadre* refers to the friendship resulting from Isadora's role as godparent to Zeca, one of Glória's children.

42. Literally coffee, but this is Glória's reference to the mixture of coffee and *cachaça* (sugarcane brandy) she usually drinks.

43. She is also one of the richest women in the world. See Simpson (1993) for a more detailed analysis of the Xuxa phenomenon. It is interesting to note that Xuxa's career was catapulted through her liaison with Pelé, the black soccer star, but her television show and modeling school lack a multiracial representation of Brazilian beauty (at least through the early 1990s).

44. See Winant (1994).

45. See Silva (1992).

46. Using the Brazilian census data for 1980, Nelson do Valle Silva (1992) tested the hypothesis that there would be a "status compensation" in cases of interracial marriages but found that this was not confirmed by the data, even in the cases where the man was of darker skin color than his wife.

47. In the context of male prostitution, black male sexuality is valued in the prostitute but not in the client (Perlongher 1987).

48. This inequality has parallels within same-race, same-sex, and same-class relationships.

49. This broad strategy of economic survival also pertained to a complicated sexual interest in foreigners. See also, for example, Bourgois (1995); Kuznesof (1991).

50. One telenovela that played during the 1990–91 season, *Dono do Mundo,* depicted various versions of cross-class sexual transgressions, including the opening episodes in which the central character, a wealthy plastic surgeon, titillated by the alleged virginity of the fiancée of one of his employees, bets that he can "deflower" the future bride before her husband. Many of the subplots revolve around the poor characters' use of their beauty and sensuality in exchanges with the wealthy.

51. It is not within the scope of this work to address directly the abuse of domestic workers by their employers, but I do want to mention here that this kind of abuse, or harassment, is commonplace.

52. I want to mention here the possibility that my presence and my interest in Brazilian racial inequality may have triggered Glória to view this situation as a serious case of racism. Obviously, the fact that he offered me the two kisses upon arrival and at departure provided a basis for comparing his behavior toward each of us.

53. I use "black" in this line as a translation of *preta*. *Preta* is often used by a speaker to mean dark black skin color. Because of the complex racial identity politics in Brazil, however, people do not necessarily use the term often among friends.

54. *Moreno* is the "polite" term most often used by people in the shantytown to describe themselves or others who may span the color spectrum from various shades of white to black, but it often denotes people of African descent.

55. In Brazil, military service is obligatory for men. Men are required to register for the draft at age seventeen and then serve at age eighteen. About 75 percent of those who register receive deferments. It is well known that middle- and upper-class men find ways to defer, whereas members of the lower classes wind up becoming recruits. Those who do serve usually spend about one year at an army garrison near their home. This was Roberto's case. See the Brazil country study of the Federal Research Division of the Library of Congress at the Web site memory.loc.gov/frd/cs/brtoc.html#bro128.

56. See Sheriff (2001).

57. See, for example, Hasenbalg (1985, 1996); Hasenbalg and Silva (1988, 1993).

58. See, for example, Silva (1985, 1988, 1992).

59. See Hanchard (1994b:104–9) for a more complete history of this group.

60. The citation for this study does not appear in their bibliography.

61. One of Sheriff's (2001:214) black activist informants, Mario, makes an interesting and perhaps critical point about black activists. Although many activists are dark-skinned and grew up in working-class homes—a point Sheriff makes quite clearly—Mario commented on the tendency many of them have to allow themselves to be "seduced by the insularity of the middle-class world, and like their white counterparts, they have refused to cross the class frontier."

62. See, for example, "Black, Proud and Brazilian," *Boston Globe,* September 21, 1996, A2.

63. GELEDÉS is also one of the organizations that has taken on the kinds of representational issues I have discussed in this chapter.

64. I believe this is the same survey titled "Collective Identities and Democratization: The 1986 Elections in São Paulo," cited by Hasenbalg and Silva (1999) and mentioned earlier in this chapter.

CHAPTER 4. NO TIME FOR CHILDHOOD

1. The Praça XV de Novembro is a plaza that is a historical landmark.

2. I am referring to Comando Vermelho and Terceiro Comando, gangs that

have bases in the larger center favelas in Rio de Janeiro, possess sophisticated arms and weapons, and have a reputation for invading other smaller territories to bring them under their control.

3. Ilha Grande (Big Island) Prison, also known as Cândido Mendes Penal Institution and the Devil's Cauldron, was located on an island just off the coast of the state of Rio de Janeiro. It was destroyed by the government in March 1994, and the island now caters mostly to tourists. In the late 1960s and 1970s it was known as a place where political prisoners and drug-trafficking prisoners of the Red Command network were held together. It is a point of theoretical contention whether or not these distinct groups had any influence on one another.

The timing of my own visit was just prior to the 1992 massacre of 111 inmates in the São Paulo prison Carandiru. In February 2001, an uprising of prisoners began at Carandiru during conjugal visits. The uprising led to a series of riots in prisons throughout the state and resulted in the death of 15 inmates. Human Rights Watch issued a report in 1998 on prison conditions in Brazil. See "Behind Bars in Brazil," available at www.hrw.org/reports98/brazil/. See Ilha Grande (Big Island) on maps 2, 3, and 4 of Rio de Janeiro.

4. In Brazilian Portuguese, this was said in an affectionate tone, with the *inha* attached to *Nega*.

5. In Brazilian Portuguese, this was *não falta nada*.

6. Pedro Paulo still had some time left to serve when Ilha Grande was destroyed; he probably was transferred to the penitentiary of Vincente Piragibe in the city of Rio until 1995.

7. Glória most often referred to the state institution where Pedro Paulo spent part of his childhood as FUNABEM (National Foundation for the Well-Being of the Minor). These state-level institutions are often referred to as FEBEMs (State Foundations for the Well-Being of the Minor).

8. Calligaris's book *Hello Brasil! Notas de um Psicanalista Europeu Viajando ao Brasil* (1991; *Hello Brazil: Notes of a European Psychoanalyst Traveling to Brazil*) is written in a style paralleling the European travel writers who have visited and commented on Brazil consistently since the early colonial period. His work was not meant to be a serious study of the Brazilian middle class; nevertheless, his impressionistic descriptions of the everyday culture of the middle class are thoughtful and penetrating. Calligaris recounts, for example, how he was surprised that the domestic workers in homes he frequented would serve food to their employers and their children before serving food to their own often very young children. This etiquette, an obvious leftover of slave relations, is not extraordinary in the least, yet it effectively denies the children of the poor the privileges they might otherwise receive merely for being children. Poor children learn very early on that their needs are secondary to those of the rich. In contrast, the children of the upper classes are superprivileged: they are welcomed at social functions and are generously accepted and appreciated in public spaces, certainly more than their counterparts are in comparative settings in Western Europe and the United States. See Goldstein (1998).

9. James Brooke, "Gunmen in Police Uniforms Kill 7 Street Children in Brazil." *New York Times*, July 24, 1993, 1, 3.

10. "Dead End Kids," *Newsweek*, May 25, 1992, 12–19.

11. The Brazilian reference is often made to *meninos de rua,* or "street children," meaning many categories of children, including not only those who actually live and sleep on the street but also poor children who work occasional jobs on the street and do have a home to go to.

12. See Stephens (1995) for an analysis of the depiction of children in mainstream and global media.

13. In Brazil, the state police are divided into two nearly autonomous entities, the civil and the military police. Both forces are under the control of the state governor, though the military police are also auxiliary and reserve units of the army. The military police is a uniformed force that patrols the streets, maintains public order, and may arrest suspects caught in the act of committing crimes (although, in practice, they arrest suspects beyond this legitimate legal basis). Under Brazilian law, criminal suspects may be arrested only if they are caught in the act of committing a crime (in *flagrante delicto*) or pursuant to an arrest warrant issued by a judge. It is usually the military police who respond to crimes while they are in progress; the civil police investigate crimes after they have occurred. Once the military police arrest a suspect, they are required to transport him to the appropriate civil police precinct *(delegacia)* for processing. At this point, the military police ordinarily have no further participation in the related criminal investigation. The civil police are authorized to perform investigations and, in practice, to oversee the operation of precincts. Each precinct is run by a *delegado,* who by law must hold a law degree. In some rural areas, however, these police precinct chiefs have no legal training. Both civil and military police officers are charged with many serious human rights abuses. See "Brazil Country Report on Human Rights Practices for 1996" at www.state.gov/www/global/human_rights/1996_hrp_report/brazil.html.

14. Under the Estatuto da Criança e do Adolescente (Children and Adolescents Act), the law instituted in 1990 to replace the Código do Menor (Minor's Code) that addresses infractions by those under eighteen years of age and stipulates the application of corrective measures, it is difficult to process cases involving children under the age of twelve. In 1992, there was some movement to change the age restriction so that individuals under eighteen would be criminally responsible for their acts. See "Técnicos Querem Penalizar Menores de 18," *Folha de São Paulo,* October 25, 1992, section 4, p. 2. In 1996, there has been further concern about the infractions of minors, which may eventually lead to a change in the statute. So far, the definition of minor in Brazil has remained the same, with eighteen being the age at which one can be criminally prosecuted as an adult. See the Brazilian Service of Justice and Peace Web site for more information, www.oneworld.org/sejup/469.htm.

15. In Brazilian cities, guarding cars is a unique occupational niche for young boys. They are responsible for making sure that nobody robs or bothers a car while the patron is conducting other business.

16. This news was talked about for days and sent a message to the poor that the rule of the gangs was absolute.

17. In Portuguese, the word used for killing "street children" is *limpando,* or "cleaning." This construction makes some sense given that what is out on the street is often seen as dirty, including the children. Thus, killing them is a form

of cleansing. See Da Matta (1991a) for an analysis of the "street" and the "house" as Brazilian cultural categories.

18. See chapter 5.

19. Hansen's disease is another name for leprosy, a chronic, mildly contagious disease characterized by ulceration of the skin, loss of sensation, paralysis, gangrene, and deformation.

20. *Colégio interno* literally means a boarding school, but here it refers to FUNABEM.

21. For a more recent analysis of the role of institutions in the lives of street children in São Paulo, see Gregori (2000), especially chap. 4, "A Trama Institucional."

22. The completion of primário in Brazil is considered the completion of first through eighth grade.

23. This idiomatic expression does not translate directly, but it refers to the fact that this person changed dramatically. In this case, it translates literally as "only having seen you [before] would I recognize you." He was very thin and wasting away. Here it means something like "you're so thin you almost disappeared," or that "you are gone in the blink of an eye."

24. He mentioned coffee in describing a potion that cast an evil deathly spell over him. He apparently thought that a woman was trying to get revenge on him. Freyre (1986[1933]) refers to the important role of coffee in Afro-Brazilian sexual magic, referred to as coffee with a spell placed on it, usually as a love potion.

25. This is an Afro-Brazilian religion or religious ceremony.

26. Glória is talking in 1992 about an event that took place in the 1980s but is speaking in terms of the *conto,* an earlier form of currency. She is most likely referring to *cruzeiro novo* (currency in use between 1967 and 1986) or *cruzado* (the currency in 1986) notes here.

27. Brazilian Portuguese makes use of forms of "you" that signify varying degrees of respect. In Glória's household, she demanded the highly formal *a senhora* (formal address to an older woman) as a form of address from her children. The use of *você* was a sign of disrespect on the part of the daughter. It is interesting to note that among middle- and upper-class informants, children commonly address their parents with *você.*

28. For a collection of essays that deals with the "psychoanalytic culture" and psychologization of various sectors of Brazilian society, see Figueira (1985). In the opening essay, Figueira writes: "These articles present an unexpected and undisputed effect of the psychology *boom* in Brazil, particularly of psychoanalysis. It created a 'psychoanalytical culture,' which led to the psychologization of various sectors of the Brazilian social life" (7).

29. Owensby (1999) writes the following:

As individual, middle-class Cariocas and Paulistanos, and likely others as well, had acquired a stake in a modernizing nation, but having lost their bid to articulate populism on middle-class terms, they distrusted political elites and recoiled from undifferentiated absorption into the people. This was why the middle class as such was largely absent from the explicit political representation of class at the national level, unlike organized workers and employers. Middle-class people benefited enormously from expanding white-collar labor markets, growing educational opportunities, rising incomes, and greater access to consumer goods. Yet none of these seemed to flow

from any politics they had undertaken, but from the wellspring of modernization itself. As a result, the pressure their everyday lives exerted on those who wielded
power remained invisible. Beneficiaries of modernization, they could feel themselves
victims of a process that never seemed to deliver quite what it promised and over
which they felt themselves to have little influence. (240)

30. See Owensby (1999:248).
31. See Manhães (1988) for a brief history of child and adolescent psychoanalysis in Rio de Janeiro.
32. Foucault (1975) notes that the birth of scientific psychology accompanied the changes in discipline and punishment associated with a transformed
penal system.
33. Bourdieu (1984:368) elaborates on the importance of therapeutic discourse in transformations in child-rearing practices.
34. See Zaluar (1994[1985]) for a similar finding on the division of the world
into bandits and honest workers.
35. Bourgois (1995:chap. 4) makes the additional point that these young
men suffer a form of "cultural dislocation" in the service economy, meaning that
they feel too close to the dominant culture, where they are made to feel inadequate. My sense is that the situation in Rio de Janeiro may be different.
36. See Vianna (1988) and Sansone (1998, 2001) for analyses of the galeras
in the periphery of Rio de Janeiro. Both of these authors backed away from suggesting that the funk dances represent a form of rising black consciousness.
While the attendance at these dances was perceived to be rising—Vianna (1988)
reported that every weekend there were more than seven hundred dances with
funk music, with anywhere from five hundred to ten thousand dancers attending (one million total in the greater metropolitan area of Rio de Janeiro)—and
most of the participants were black youth, he did not see these events as a place
where black consciousness politicization was taking place. Sansone's (2001)
more recent work confirms these findings and urges social scientists to be more
careful in assessing whether or not these events can be taken as sites of resistance.
He warns that "we must remain wary of any a priori direct link between rage,
revolt, violence, gangs, and funk" (143).

CHAPTER 5. STATE TERROR, GANGS, AND
EVERYDAY VIOLENCE

This chapter appeared in Portuguese in a much earlier form. See Goldstein
(2000b).
1. Crime narratives is one of the ways in which Caldeira (2000) gets at the
talk of crime: "Most narratives of crime introduce the episode by stating the
exact time at which it happened. They also always give details about the place,
circumstances and routine character of what was going on just beforehand, creating a precise mark of rupture through the elaboration of small details. They
represent an event that had the power to interrupt the uneventful flux of everyday life, changing its quality for ever—an event that stands out because of its absurdity and gratuitousness" (27).
2. I draw here from Pereira's (1997) working definition of the rule of law:

The ideal of the rule of law is not simply that the actions of those who control the state are legal in some technical sense. Instead, it is that law forms a complex and interlocking pyramid of rules in which the state itself is bound, and in which the constitution is the ultimate authority to which subordinate statutes, regulations, administrative rules, and judicial sentences are in compliance. State power is exercised within this pyramid of rules, from which it derives its legitimacy. Laws are clear, publicly available, and consistently applied, and they reflect some degree of popular consensus and normative allegiance. Rather than being merely the rationalization of the prerogatives of those who rule, the rule of law represents a fusion of and compromise between the "people's" and the "state's" law. (2)

3. U.S. Department of State, *Brazil Country Report on Human Rights Practices for 1996, Department of State Human Rights Country Report* (Washington, D.C.: Bureau of Democracy, Human Rights and Labor, 1997), 25. See www.state.gov/www/global/human_rights/1996_hrp_report/brazil.html.

4. Increasingly, the large gangs such as Comando Vermelho (Red Command, also known as Falange) and Terceiro Comando (Third Command) appear to be at least as well armed as the civil and military police forces. Indeed, Leeds (1996) notes:

Although journalist reports of the scope of the Falange or Comando Vermelho should be read with skepticism, they nevertheless convey some sense of its power. Carlos Amorim reported a 1990 Globo figure estimating that 90 percent of Rio's 480 *favelas* were dominated by the group, some two and a half million residents of Rio (see Amorim 1993, 29). A more realistic assessment of the current situation, based on interviews with *favela* leaders in July 1994, suggests a pattern of alliances rather than any strict organization, with allegiances currently split between two prison or crime organizations, the Comando Vermelho and the Terceiro Comando. Groups of favela drug-dealing organizations tend to ally themselves with one group or the other without strict or all-encompassing control. (56, note 25)

5. Operation Rio is one example of the Brazilian state's only partial success at institutionalizing democratic procedures in the political system (Holston and Caldeira 1998:266) and at attempting to gain control of territories it had considered lost from its control. Not long after Fernando Henrique Cardoso's inauguration as president in 1994, Operation Rio began as an attempt by the Rio state government to combat crime and drug trafficking through a joint army-police occupation of specific favelas throughout the city. During the operation, the army was deployed to help fight drug-trafficking gangs "precisely because of the notorious violence and corruption of Rio's police" (Human Rights Watch/Americas 1996). Residents of the favelas occupied during this time were terrified by the simultaneous presence of armed military police and equally well-armed local drug traffickers. Residents spoke bitterly about this time, and when I returned to Rio in 1995, many of the central favelas were still occupied by military forces with sophisticated automatic weaponry. In Felicidade Eterna, residents spoke of a child in a nearby favela who, during Operation Rio, was killed by a bullet to the left eye in the cross fire between gangs and the military police. See Human Rights Watch/Americas (1996:7).

Mingardi, who writes about police corruption in São Paulo, describes Operation Rio as "a complete failure" because no trafficker was imprisoned (or, at least, no important trafficker), less than one hundred kilos of cocaine were confiscated (in four months), and the quantity of heavy arms retrieved was small compared with the amount usually retrieved in a similar time frame (1998:203). On the other hand, the armed presence affected thousands of ordinary residents, and entire neighborhoods were under siege. According to a Human Rights Watch/Americas report from 1996:

> Operation Rio was punctuated by torture, arbitrary detentions and warrantless searches and at least one unnecessary use of lethal force. Some of these abuses, such as subjecting entire neighborhoods to house-by-house searches, were expressly authorized and, indeed, were demanded by the strategic goals adopted for the operation. Other abuses, such as torture, were not openly included in Operation Rio's design. Nevertheless, the failure of civilian and military authorities to respond swiftly and decisively to complaints of abuse as Operation Rio unfolded, as well as public statements by officials commonly understood to condone "excesses" during the operation and the absence to date of convictions for the abuses endured by many *favela* residents suggest appalling indifference by Brazilian authorities to the violation of human rights. At worst, they suggest tacit acquiescence in those violations. (3)

Operation Rio coincided with the appointment of Nilton Cerqueira as secretary of the security forces (civil police), who, in November 1995, instituted a series of "bravery" awards and promotions offered to police for the capture of criminals. In 1997, the Superior Institute of Religious Studies (ISER) and author Ignacio Cano (1997) studied the effects of the bravery awards and promotions on Rio de Janeiro's intentional homicide rate (in those cases involving the police forces). There had been cursory evidence that this particular policy accounted for the increase in Rio's already high homicide rate, and the study confirmed this evidence.

6. See Kowarick (1979).

7. Making a place dirty means to kill or steal from people inside the community itself. This is the idea of not dirtying one's own nest.

8. Civil police officers in Brazil usually do not wear uniforms, so many residents assumed that they could have been members of the civil police.

9. The Human Rights Watch/Americas publication titled "Police Brutality in Urban Brazil" (1997:17–18) distinguishes between five types of police brutality. What is talked about at the local level as "police-bandits" correlates exactly with what the publication describes as the fourth type; for obvious reasons, it is the most difficult to document because the events happen while the police are off duty. The first involves the police use of deadly force in the course of massive raids into favelas. The second involves individual instances of police killings that suggest the use of deadly force, often accounted for as "resisting arrest," while the third involves extrajudicial executions in non-life-threatening situations. The fourth form involves police who kill while off duty, "either to resolve personal vendettas or in response to some minor provocation or inconvenience." The fifth form involves the cases of criminal suspects who "disappear" from police custody.

10. He said, "*Eu não vou engordar elas para outros comerem. Eu vou comer mesmo.*"

11. This attitude is an extension of the stereotype of the Northeasterner as a country bumpkin or, more extremely, too "stupid" to take action.

12. See also Zaluar (1993).

13. In 1998, they were in the process of building themselves a large house a few miles from the favela on asphalted (non-favela) streets.

14. *Justa causa* translates as "just cause," meaning here a legal action.

15. See the *New York Times*, 2 April, 1997, A3.

16. In a classic paper on the development of citizenship and social class, T. H. Marshall (1964[1949]) outlines three kinds of citizenship that have developed in succession during the past three centuries. Political citizenship arose during the nineteenth century and social citizenship during the twentieth century. Civil citizenship developed during the eighteenth century and involves a set of individual rights, including liberty, freedom of speech, the right to own property, and equality before the law. These civil citizenship rights developed in parallel to capitalism and industrialization, and thus they have been awarded during periods of increasing class stratification. The acknowledgment of class-stratified civil citizenship rights would, of course, imply that our standard definitions of political democracy and democratic citizenship as measured in the characteristics of the party system and electoral politics are necessarily flawed, as O'Donnell (1993) and Holston and Caldeira (1998) have pointed out.

17. CEDEC is its acronym in Portuguese; it stands for Centro de Estudos de Cultura Contemporânea.

18. See CEDEC (1997:4).

19. See CEDEC (1997:4, table 1).

20. According to another recent study, youths experience the highest risk of violence. Cardia (1997), citing a study by Vermelho and Mello Jorge (1996), finds that homicide is the first cause of mortality of youths between the ages of fifteen and twenty-four.

21. The two are defined by the authors of the map in the following manner: *Homicídio doloso* is the legal term that means intentional homicide. The study registered the number of victims who suffered this crime. *Homicídio culposo*, or culpable homicide, refers to accidental homicide; this type was excluded from the study. Also, *lesões dolosas* (intentionally caused injuries) were accounted for, and *lesões culposas* (accidental injuries) were not (CEDEC 1997:8).

22. What follows here, for the benefit of the non-Brazilian reader, is a helpful summary (put out by the U.S. Department of State) describing these two police forces in Brazil: "Police forces fall primarily under the control of the states. State police are divided into two forces: The civil police, who have an investigative role, and the uniformed police, known locally as the 'Military Police,' who are responsible for maintaining public order. Although controlled by the individual state governments, the Constitution provides that the uniformed police can be called into active military service in the event of an emergency, and they maintain some residual military privileges, including a separate judicial system. The federal police force is very small and plays little role in maintaining internal security. State police officers are charged with many serious human rights abuses." U.S. Department of State, *Brazil Country Report on Human Rights Practices for 1996, Department of State Human Rights Country Reports* (Washington, D.C.: Bureau of Democracy, Human Rights and Labor, 1997), 1; www.state.gov/www/global/human_rights/1996_hrp_report/brazil.html.

The U.S. Department of State, *Brazil Country Report on Human Rights Practices for 1997* reports the following:

> Extrajudicial killings continued to be a serious problem throughout the country. In urban areas, high crime rates, failure to apprehend most criminals, and an inept and inefficient criminal justice system all contribute to public acquiescence in police brutality and killings of criminal suspects. . . . The number of citizens killed in conflicts with police fell in São Paulo but continued to rise in Rio de Janeiro. A study by the Institute for Religious Studies (ISER) concluded that 10 percent of all Rio de Janeiro homicides were civilians killed by police. The ISER study also documented that in a sample of 697 cases of fatal police shootings between 1993 and 1996, Rio de Janeiro police officers rarely fired to immobilize rather than kill; half the victims were killed with four or more bullets, and the majority of victims were shot in either the shoulders or the head. Forty cases clearly demonstrated execution-style deaths, where victims were first immobilized and then shot at close range. Victims were generally young, black, and without criminal records. (www.state.gov/www.global/human_rights/1997_hrp_report/brazil.html, 2–3)

The ISER study referred to by the U.S. Department of State is the one written by Cano (1997). It covered the period between January 1993 and July 1996 in the city of Rio de Janeiro, and 1,171 police incident reports and 64 military police inquiries were examined. Among the more interesting comparative findings was the fact that police operations in Rio de Janeiro normally produce dramatically more deaths than police action in America's most violent and dangerous cities: "The police forces in Rio kill, per year, almost as many people as the combined police forces of the United States (a nation with more than 250 million inhabitants)" (Cano 1997:32). In Rio, one in every ten victims of intentional homicide is the result of police work. The study noted that of the fatalities that resulted from military police operations, 64 percent were characterized by at least one bullet wound to the head or the back. Cano (1997:64–65) also notes that the lethality index in favelas (3.6) is more than twice that of asphalted areas (1.6), indicating a clear intent to kill on the part of police in their actions in the poorer areas of the city.

23. Zaluar (1994:101) makes a similar observation.

24. This song, "Banditismo por Uma Questão de Classe," or "Banditry for Reasons of Class," by Chico Science, relates the attraction of banditry to those innocents who are deprived of decent lives, ones free of police violence and hunger.

25. Holloway (1993) further underlines the paradoxical development of lower-class police officers in charge of repressing their own class peers for financial rewards—rewards that ensure them a minimal expected standard of living. Thus it became, and continues to be, the duty of the poor to patrol other poor and, by definition, to mete out punishment directly to those from similar economic circumstances as themselves:

> The history of what today is called police brutality is not the unintended result of attracting amoral sadists into an unsavory branch of public service. The police expected to play that role as disciplinary agent over minor transgressions and especially over people who did not matter to those at the top of this highly segmented and stratified society except as a problem to be controlled. A disciplinary function, with punishment meted out by the police themselves, was for a long time explicitly incorporated into operating procedures. From 1808 to 1831 it was still part of the

broader definition of police, necessary for keeping things working, along with provisioning, providing water, and paving streets. (283)

26. *Jogo do bicho* is an illegal animal lottery game that is popular throughout Brazil.

27. Perhaps one of the most well-known events relating to death squads in Brazil reached the international press in July 1993. At the time, both Brazilian and international media gave a fair amount of attention to the killing of eight street children in central Rio. The Human Rights Watch/Americas report (1994) offered some insights into this event, which became known as the Candelária killings:

> The Candelária killings also reflect the larger pattern of perpetrators and motives. In many cases, homicides of children are committed by on-duty police or by private death squads (known in Brazil as *grupos de extermínio*), which are frequently composed of off-duty policemen. The killings frequently occur because poor children are perceived as menaces and criminals, who must be eliminated, or because criminal deals made between children and police or organized gangs go awry. (ix–x)

28. Foucault (1991) defines governmentality as the following: "The ensemble formed by the institutions, procedures, analyses and reflections, the calculations and tactics that allow the exercise of this very specific albeit complete form of power, which has as its target population, as its principal form of knowledge political economy, and as its essential technical means apparatuses of security" (102).

29. Sociologist Paulo Sérgio Pinheiro (1991), in an attempt to explain the development of a corrupt military police in the contemporary Brazilian context, argues that the military police adopted the armed forces' mentality of working against the internal political enemy, an approach developed during the military dictatorship of 1968. Following from Pinheiro's argument is the point that unrestricted police powers were fortified during the dictatorship by a national security ideology. When confrontation with urban guerrillas ended in Brazil, the military police expanded the war on crime, using the same techniques they had employed against the guerrillas. Pinheiro sees the implicit political content of policing—how it is used for the defense and protection of the ruling classes—as a manner of stemming protest by the lower classes: "The military police are deeply concerned with crimes of the lower classes (theft, robbery, murder) while ignoring such organized and white-collar crimes as embezzlement, fraud, and illegal financial operations—these together constitute the sum of common crimes against national property" (179). See also Fausto (1984) for a similar argument concerning the relationship between police and the lower classes.

30. See, for example, Soares, Milito, and Silva (1996:194).

31. See Aureliano Biancarelli, "27% Dos Policiais Evitam Sair de Farda," *Folha de São Paulo,* April 6, 1997, sec. 3, p. 5.

32. The Baixada Fluminense region is a flat drainage basin about twenty miles north of metropolitan Rio de Janeiro that includes a number of suburbs, many of which are considered extremely dangerous. Duque de Caxias is its own municipality. See maps 3 and 4.

33. Leeds (1996) notes that leaders of residents associations are automati-

cally in danger, having to negotiate a precarious role between the gangs and the police. For an interesting history of the relationship between community organization and political elites in two Rio favelas, see Gay (1994).

34. In Brazilian Portuguese this would translate as *Mataram uma mulher crente com barriga.*

35. See Goldstein (2000a) for a full review of Burdick (1998).

36. In his book *Cidade Partida* (*Divided City*), the journalist Zuenir Ventura (1994:127) writes a personal account of the Viva Rio movement, and he makes a similar point. Ventura argues that these religious groups are the only ones providing a counterculture to that of the gangs.

37. This body of work on the rise of evangelical religions is growing and can be traced back to Stoll's (1990) work. For examples of works that address gender-related issues, see Burdick (1993, 1998); Chestnut (1997); Brusco (1995).

38. Sister Iara herself was a relatively recent member of the church as well, having "found God" only in 1990, when she discovered she had AIDS and assumed she would die; instead, Sister Iara considers herself to be "cured" of AIDS and cites as proof of this her healthy survival well into 1998. Sister Iara inspired many people in Felicidade Eterna to join her fledgling congregation. The perception that she had been "cured of AIDS" was seen as proof of both her belief in God and her healing powers. In addition, she motivated congregation members to lend time and resources to one another and, perhaps just as important, discouraged the use of vengeance as a solution to interpersonal problems. She also came to Soneca's and Filomena's rescue many times by offering to babysit their children free of charge.

39. Burdick (1998) writes about the conversion process during times of crisis. In this example, there seems to be a rhythm or cyclical nature to an individual's decision to join and leave any one particular religious group, which may be related to other social phenomena occurring in that individual's community. Crises may simply bring about the desire for, rather than simply provoke, a one-way conversion process. One would need long-term longitudinal data on a number of individuals and/or families to explore this issue more thoroughly.

40. See, for example, Caldeira (2000); Scheper-Hughes (1992).

CHAPTER 6. PARTIAL TRUTHS

1. A partial listing of major works that deal with the question of sexuality in Brazil includes Batinga (1981); Freyre (1986[1933]); Fry (1982a); Gaspar (1985); Mott (1988); Muraro (1983); Parker (1991); Perlongher (1987); Trevisan (1986); Vainfas (1986, 1989).

2. The film was named after the collection of poems of the same title that was published posthumously under the poet Drummond de Andrade's name.

3. Carlos Drummond de Andrade (1902–87), one of Brazil's most prolific poets, wrote a series of erotic poems that remained unpublished during his lifetime because he feared they would be deemed pornographic. These same poems form the centerpiece around which the characters in the film read and respond. See Andrade (1998[1992]).

4. Some of the numerous words used to describe the buttocks or *bunda* are *bum-bum, nádegas, edi, cú, bundão, bundinha.* One could have a *bunda imp-*

inada (a buttock that is slung high on the body) or a *bunda de geleía* (a buttock that moves like jelly). Many negative expressions associated with the buttock are used. Somebody who is considered an idiot, for example, may be called a *bunda mole* (soft-ass).

5. In this sense, the humor is similar to the poetry of the women discussed in Abu-Lughod's moving ethnography *Veiled Sentiments: Honor and Poetry in a Bedouin Society* (1986).

6. Elis lived in Felicidade Eterna as a woman married to a man, although in her conversations she also referred to herself as a bicha. See Kulick's (1998) ethnography of a subculture of travestis who work as transgendered prostitutes in Salvador Bahia. See also Silva (1993).

7. Here, as will be discussed in later sections of the chapter, is the reference to *comer* (to eat); in this case it is being used to denote someone "going native." *Comer* is also a highly "sexualized" verb in the sense that in Brazilian Portuguese, "to eat someone" is to experience them sexually.

8. Parker describes what he perceives as a uniquely Brazilian cultural grammar where *comer* and *dar* structure sexuality into a set of hierarchies. Parker demonstrates how these hierarchies define sexual meanings in both heterosexual and homosexual encounters: men are active penetrators and women, bichas, and viados (deer; doe; derogatory reference to gay men) are passive recipients in this structure.

9. As Parker (1999) himself recently points out, this is but one more traditional construction among a number of emerging male homoerotic communities, but one that is still popular among the lower classes.

10. In this construction, also popular throughout the Mediterranean region (see, for example, Peristiany 1966; Blok 1981; Brandes 1981), male honor is constructed through the sexuality of close females, in this case, of one's partner. An adulteress has the power to put horns on her man, thereby symbolically turning a man into an animal such as the *veado,* a horned, deerlike animal that also refers to a homosexual or pansy (and spelled *viado*). To be cuckolded is to be symbolically transformed into a woman.

11. Social anthropologists have long expressed an interest in the relationship between eating and sexuality more generally, arguing, for example, that there is a universal tendency to make a ritual association between eating and sexual intercourse. Leach (1964), for example, tried to understand the relationship between edibility and animal abuse terms and the ritual values embedded in the choice of specific animal categories. In his discussion, it is the anomalous categories that have ritual value and become taboo. He claimed that understanding these categories would help us to understand a wide variety of nonrational behavior. Brandes (1984) sees the animal metaphors as communicative strategies of social control, as providing people with terms that can reinforce the social and moral order.

12. *"Morreram depois de haver me comido,"* is what Sarlete said.

13. These are foods from Northeast Brazil.

14. In focus group and individual interviews with working-class men and women in Rio and São Paulo, I found that this was the case. It held true in Felicidade Eterna as well.

15. Virginity is a complicated issue that I cannot explain in depth here. Shantytowns in Rio de Janeiro hold a diversity of immigrants from other regions of Brazil and ideas of how one ought to experience sexuality. In Felicidade Eterna, for example, there were families from Ceará, Pernambuco, Minas Gerais, and the interior regions to the west of Rio de Janeiro. Not everyone agreed about the codes and rules concerning sexual honor or virginity. There are class-specific issues relevant here as well. In a Data Folha survey taken from a sample of upper-middle-class Paulistanos between the ages of sixteen and forty-five in February 1991, 96 percent of the men and 83 percent of the women interviewed said that they had had sexual relations before marriage. This indicates that, among the elite, men and women were acting, at least, as if virginity was no longer an important concept. Later in the year, however, the same pollsters conducted a socioeconomically stratified survey taken among a broad universe of Paulistanos sixteen years of age and older; they found that 70 percent think men should not marry as virgins, while only 47 percent think women should not marry as virgins. In other words, 53 percent of respondents still feel that women should marry as virgins or that virginity for women is still an issue. In terms of class divisions, of those who earned up to five minimum salaries, 39 percent say that one should marry as a virgin (they did not specify male or female virginity, but let us assume that in this context the question implies female virginity), whereas only 13 percent of those who earn twenty minimum salaries or more feel that one ought to marry as a virgin. See "Mulher é Menos Convencional No Casamento," *Folha de São Paulo,* October 1, 1991. Pitt-Rivers (1966:65) also suggests that there is a class element related to notions concerning sexual honor and that in Spain the upper and upper-middle classes were able to move away from the popular class concern for sexual honor, thus leading to greater freedom of action for the married women of the upper class. There are also historical differences noted by authors looking at virginity in São Paulo and in Rio de Janeiro. Two books about the construction of love during the belle époque in São Paulo and in Rio de Janeiro reach opposite conclusions about the importance of virginity at the beginning of the twentieth century. Esteves (1989) believes that in 1900 lower-class women in Rio de Janeiro were already becoming less concerned with elite notions of female chastity and hygiene and were, in fact, rebelling, especially against cultural attitudes toward virginity. She argues that these women were creating their own subculture, which placed less importance on virginity than did the elite culture. She notes that her opinion differs from that of Fausto (1984), who, based on an analysis of archives in São Paulo, claims that virginity was indeed highly valued at that time and in all social classes. Their disagreement may actually document a real difference between São Paulo and the Rio de Janeiro milieu, rather than a difference in the interpretation of data. My research found similar differences between the two cities.

16. See Parker (1991).

17. See Buckley (2000).

18. See U.S. Department of State, *Brazil Country Report on Human Rights Practices for 1997;* Christie (1996).

19. See Brown (1994) for an excellent study of Umbanda.

20. We ought to approach this second explanation, however, with some cau-

tion. As Vicki Bell (1993) and Judith Butler (1990) point out in their feminist critiques of the incest prohibition, the incest taboo often exists as a discursive rule. In these matrifocal settings where biological fathers are in fact rare, the version of the incest taboo that emerges is one that assumes that biological fathers will not abuse their own kin.

21. Hecht (1998) has found that female children who are on the street are perceived as sexually experienced women merely because they are living on the street.

22. See Da Matta's (1991a) casa-rua distinction.

23. This sense of unprotectedness and of being "ruined" came up repeatedly in interviews I conducted in São Paulo as well. One young male factory worker from Ceará, a state in Northeast Brazil, told me about his clandestine sexual relation with a woman who had come from his hometown, an interior city of the state. This woman had been raped by a soldier and then sent away by her family to labor as a domestic worker in São Paulo. Because of the rape, she was deemed "unmarriageable," despite the fact that the rape was recognized as such by everyone in the town and had been beyond her control. The factory worker describing the woman's fate made it quite clear that he was not interested in marrying her—she was not his type. He explained that within their shared community in the Northeast, she was seen as tainted and unclean, as a woman not worthy of respect, but to him, a more cosmopolitan Paulista, she was *uma mulher limpa* (a clean woman, not a prostitute, honorable). One of the intriguing aspects about this interview was that he referred to his sexual relation with the woman as if he were doing her a great personal kindness—merely by being willing to be her lover. Despite her new life in São Paulo, her connection to this worker's family prevented her from creating a new identity, one removed from her rape and from her construction as a "ruined" woman. And the factory worker congratulated himself for not imposing his native Northeastern culture on this situation, treating her as a mistress rather than as a prostitute.

24. According to Kulick (1998:46–52), episodes of early sexual abuse are common among travestis who are sex workers. Travestis often remember these early sexual encounters as formative experiences leading to the realization of their own homoerotic desires. See also Silva (1993) for more on Brazilian travestis.

CHAPTER 7. WHAT'S SO FUNNY ABOUT RAPE?

1. Despite the fact that men move in and out of women's households frequently, a sacred notion of the biological father still persists in discourse.

2. See Rebhun (1999) for a fascinating ethnography on love, romance, intimacy, and economics in Northeast Brazil.

3. See Fausto (1984) for the case of São Paulo during the belle époque. Fausto reaches the opposite conclusions.

4. See also Huggins (1991); O'Donnell (1992).

5. In this case the word is meant literally as having screwed her daughters. For a detailed examination of the concept of sacanagem, see chapter 6.

Glossary

abertura political opening
ABIA (Associação Brasileira Interdisciplinar de AIDS) Brazilian Interdisciplinary AIDS Association
Alemães Germans
ama wet nurse
ama de leite milk mother
amarelo yellow
amigo friend
anemia falciforme sickle-cell anemia
angu corn or manioc mush
apaixonada passionate (for); in love
arma firearm
arrastão taking or dragging in of a fishing net
assassina assassin
aventura love affair
avião (aviãozinho) airplane; drug deliverer
avoada flighty; loose; tricky

babá nanny
bacana nice; swell; great; super; attractive
(os) bacanas group of people who enjoy the good life
baiana Bahian; from Salvador, Bahia
baile funk funk dance
bairro nobre literally "noble" neighborhood, meaning wealthy neighborhood
bandidos bandits; gang members; criminals
baralho card game; cards
barraco hut; cottage; refers to store that sells supplies

barreira barrier; limit; boundary
barriga stomach; belly
bicha slang for gay; derogatory, meaning small animal; wormlike creature; faggot
boa aparência good appearance; reference to color, white-skinned
boca de fumo mouth of smoke; area of sale for drugs
boca fechada a closed mouth; silent
bom papo good talk; good conversation
bombon candy
bondade goodness
(de) boné with headgear, hat, headpiece, cap
botequim bar; taphouse
branco(a) white
brasilidade the act of being Brazilian; Brazilianness
brincar to joke, tease
buceta vagina
bunda buttocks
bundinha little buttocks

cabelo ruim bad hair; most often applied to Afro-Brazilians
cachaça sugarcane brandy; (white) rum
café coffee; prepared alcoholic drink
cafuné massaging of the scalp
Candelária church in central Rio
capim a coarse grass used as fodder
capuzados hooded; masked
Carioca native or resident of Rio de Janeiro
carnaval Shrovetide; carnival; season of merrymaking just before Lent
carne seca dried beef
carteira (de identidade) Brazilian identity card
carteira (de trabalho) Brazilian social security card
casa house; home
casa grande big house (as in master's house)
catuaba plant
cesta básica basket of basic goods
chato lousy
chefe boss
chouriço sausage
cidade maravilhosa marvelous city; Rio de Janeiro
claro(a) light
Clube dos Paraplégicos Paraplegics Club
colegial high school student
colégio (elementary or high) school
colégio interno boarding school; correctional institution for minors
Coletivo Feminista Sexualidade e Saúde Feminist Health and Sexuality Collective (women's organization in São Paulo)
colônia colony
comadre godmother, in relationship to one's child

Comando Vermelho Red Command (drug-trafficking gang in Rio de Janeiro)
comer to eat; to experience someone sexually; to go native
compadre godfather, in relationship to another person's child
conto number; thousand cruzeiros note (formerly milréis)
copeira domestic worker with serving and cleaning duties and/or waitress duties
copeiro domestic worker with butler and/or waiter duties
Corcovado the mountain where the Christ the Redeemer statue is located
cornear act of cuckolding; betrayal through infidelity
corno horn; man who is a cuckold
cornudo cornute; horned
coroa old person; crown, sovereignty; older, middle- or upper-class person
cozinheira cook
crente believer; someone who joins new Protestant religious group
criança em circulação child shifting; child circulation
criminoso criminal
crioulo creole; originally a home-born slave
cruzado Brazilian monetary unit (1986–90)
cruzeiro Brazilian monetary unit (1990–93)
cura cure

dar to give; also in relation to sexual act
delegacia civil police precinct
democracia racial racial democracy
desabafar let out feelings
dissolvedor dissolver; to break up; separate parts
doido mad; crazy; insane; enthusiastic
doloso intentional
dom do samba knowledge of how to dance samba
Dona before a female name means Mrs.; respectful title; mistress of a household
dono owner; boss

empregada domestic worker
engenho mill (sugar)
enredo theme; ballad
errado wrong
escola de samba samba school
escopeta a short rifle or carbine
escuro dark
esquentar a cabeça get hotheaded
Estado Novo New State; Vargas dictatorship from 1937 to 1945
estômago stomach
exaltados exalted; angry; political group
exús ambiguous spirits thought of as mischievous or devil-like in Afro-Brazilian
    religions

falecida deceased
fantasia costume; fantasy

favela urban shantytown
favelados shantytown dweller (can be derogatory)
faxineira heavy-duty day cleaner, usually paid a wage on a daily basis
fazenda large farm
fechado closed
feder to stink, reek; to smell badly
feijão bean staple dish
Felicidade Eterna Eternal Happiness
filha daughter; can be used affectionately as form of address
(em) flagrante in the act
forró Brazilian musical form
fresco effeminate boy or man; sissy
fricote Brazilian musical form
fubá maize flour; couscous
funk funk music

galera gang based on funk dance membership
galinha chicken; derogatory reference to woman with more than one partner;
    flirtatious woman
garagista person who cares for cars in public garages
geledés Black Women's Institute, São Paulo
gente people; folk; population; humanity
golpe do baú marriage for economic interest; treasure chest coup
gordo fat
grana money
gringo foreigner; white person

herança inheritance
homem (homens) man (men)
homicídio homicide; murder

Iemanjá goddess of the sea; Afro-Brazilian divinity
Ilha Grande Big Island; island off Rio de Janeiro
inhame yam

jangadeiro fisherman (Northeast Brazil)
jogo do bicho animal lottery game; illegal
justa causa just cause; legal action

lagoa lake
lazer recreation
ligar pay attention to; attach importance to
limpar to clean

macaco monkey; monkey wrench used for fixing tire
maconha pot; marijuana
maconheiro pothead; person who smokes quantities of maconha

macumba Afro-Brazilian religion
macumbeiro one who practices macumba
madama madam; polite form for mistress of a household; reference to middle-
  or upper-class woman; can also refer to prostitute
mãe, mamãe mother
mãe preta black mother
malandro scoundrel; thief
marginal marginal; criminal
menina(o) girl (boy)
menor youngster; minor; person under legal age
mestiçagem mixed-race
mestiço(a) mestizo, mixed-race
metido have a hand in; involved; meddling
michê male who prostitutes for other males
Minas Gerais a state to the north of Rio de Janeiro
mingau porridge with wheat or manioc grains
mínimo minimum
moça young girl; virgin
moço young man; servant
mocotó soup made from the hoof of the cow
moreno(a) ambiguous color term often used to denote African descent
morrer to die
morro favela hill
Movimento dos Trabalhadores Rurais Sem Terra Struggle of the Landless (social movement)
Movimento Negro Black Consciousness Movement
mucama chamber maid
mulato(a) mixed-race (black and white)
mulher woman
mulher da rua woman of the street; prostitute

namorar court; date seriously; philander; to court a girl and become sweet-
  hearts
nariz chato flat nose
nega(o), negra(o) black person (can be derogative)
neguinha(o) little blackie; term of endearment
Nordestino(a) person from Northeast Brazil
novela soap opera (referring to telenovela)

orelhão literally, big ear, meaning public telephone
orixá African divinity
oxente exclamation, "You all"

padastro stepfather
padrinho godfather
pagode popular samba form; popular samba club
papo (bater) chatter; talk

paraplégico paraplegic
pardo(a) mulatto
Partido dos Trabalhadores Workers Party
pastora female pastor
patroa (ões) mistress; matron; madam; boss (plural)
Paulistano, Paulista person from São Paulo
piranha piranha; meat-eating fish; can be derogatory for "active" woman
Plano Real Real Plan; economic program
pobre poor
polenguinho soft processed cheese available in triangular packages
povo people; folk; nation; race; mob; rabble
prefeitura city hall
pretinho(a) little black
preto(a) black
primário primary school; elementary school
Programa Bolsa-Escola School Bursary Program
propósito purpose, intention, aim, object
puxa from puxar (to pull); damn; darn

quadrilha local gang
queijo minas salty aged cheese that crumbles at the touch
quintal backyard

real currency in place in Brazil since 1994
requeijão liquid cheese spread; yogurt-like consistency
revoltado(a) disgusted; shocked; angry
rico (os) rich; the rich
ronda game of chance with cards
rua street

sacanagem filthy behavior; unfairness; foul play
safadez sexual misdeeds
safado shameless; trickster; screwed up
salário salary
samba samba
Sambódromo Sambadrome; stadium where Rio Carnival takes place
sapatão lesbian; large shoe
sarará freckled; refers to mixed-race combination
sargento sergeant
seca (sequinha) dried out; wasted (a little dried out or wasted)
segundo grau high school
segurança security guard
senhora Mrs.; mistress; formal address; pronoun "you"
sesmaria large estate
seu colloquial reduced form of senhor; polite form of address to a male
sexo é bom sex is good

sindicato union
sujar a área literally, dirty an area; to commit a crime (on one's own territory)

telenovela soap opera on television
terreiro temple or congregation
tia aunt; also form of address to older woman
trabalhador worker
travesti literally means disguise; male who dresses as a female; transgendered person
treinta-oitão big .38 pistol
triagem selection and sorting
trio elétrico mobile truck with live music on top
turma group of friends

União Democrática Nacional National Democratic Union, political party
urubu black vulture

vagabundo vagrant
vai tomar no cú literally go take it in the ass, but can also generally mean "don't bother me," "go away," or "cut it out." In ending a conversation, it can also mean, "Don't you take me for a sucker."
vapor drug delivery person
veado deer, doe; homosexual
velho old man
vestibular admissions examination to higher education
viado derogatory reference to homosexual man, slang spelling
viciado addict
(a) vida literally, the life, sometimes referring to crime or prostitution
você you; thou
vovó grandmother
vovô grandfather

zoava get rowdy
Zona Norte North Zone, outskirts of Rio de Janeiro
Zona Oeste West Zone, outskirts of Rio de Janeiro
Zona Sul South Zone, beach community where wealthy people in Rio live

References

BOOKS AND ARTICLES

"A Cinderela Negra." 1993. *Veja*, July 7, 66–73.

Abu-Lughod, Lila. 1986. *Veiled Sentiments: Honor and Poetry in a Bedouin Society*. Berkeley and Los Angeles: University of California Press.

Alvarez, Sonia E. 1990. *Engendering Democracy in Brazil*. Princeton, N.J.: Princeton University Press.

Alvarez, Sonia E., Evelina Dagnino, and Arturo Escobar, eds. 1998. *Cultures of Politics/Politics of Culture: Revisioning Latin American Social Movements*. Boulder, Colo.: Westview Press.

Alvarez, Sonia E., and Arturo Escobar, eds. 1992. *The Making of Social Movements in Latin America: Identity, Strategy and Democracy*. Boulder, Colo.: Westview Press.

Amorim, Carlos. 1993. *Comando Vermelho: A História Secreta do Crime Organizado*. 4th ed. Rio de Janeiro: Record.

Anderson, Benedict. 1983. *Imagined Communities: Reflections on the Origin and Spread of Nationalism*. London: Verso.

Andrade, Carlos Drummond de. 1998 [1992]. *O Amor Natural*. Rio de Janeiro: Editora Record.

Andrade, Oswald de. 1970 [1928]. "Manifesto Antropófago." In *Obras Completas: Do Pau-Brasil à Antropofagia e às Utopias*. Rio de Janeiro: Civilização Brasileira.

Andrews, George Reid. 1991. *Blacks and Whites in São Paulo Brazil, 1888–1988*. Madison: University of Wisconsin Press.

———. 1992. "Racial Inequality in Brazil and the United States: A Statistical Comparison." *Journal of Social History* (winter): 229–63.

Apte, Michael L. 1985. *Humour and Laughter: An Anthropological Approach*. Ithaca, N.Y.: Cornell University Press.

Araújo, Joel Zito. 2000. *A Negação do Brasil: O Negro na Telenovela Brasileira.* São Paulo: Editora SENAC.

Ardaillon, Danielle, and Guita Debert. 1987. *Quando a Vitima é Mulher: Análise de Julgamentos de Crimes de Estupro, Espancamento e Homocídio.* Brasília: Conselho Nacional dos Direitos da Mulher.

"Arruaça Na Areia." 1992. *Veja,* October 28, 18–22.

Azevedo, Aluísio. 2000. *The Slum.* Trans. David H. Rosenthal. Oxford: Oxford University Press.

Baer, Werner. 1983. *The Brazilian Economy: Growth and Development.* 2d ed. New York: Praeger.

"Baixa Escolaridade Realimenta a Discriminação." 2001. Folha Cotidiano, C1, *Folha de São Paulo,* Domingo, January 14.

Bakhtin, Mikhail. 1981. *The Dialogic Imagination.* Trans. Caryl Emerson and Michael Holquist. Austin: University of Texas Press.

———. 1984 [1965]. *Rabelais and His World.* Trans. Helene Iswolsky. Bloomington: Indiana University Press.

Bartlett, John. 1980. *Familiar Quotations.* 15th ed. Boston: Little, Brown.

Batinga, Fernando. 1981. *A Outra Banda da Mulher: Encontros Sobre a Sexualidade Feminina.* Rio de Janeiro: Editora Codecri.

Bell, Vicki. 1993. *Interrogating Incest: Feminism, Foucault and the Law.* London: Routledge.

Benjamin, Medea, and Maisa Mendonça. 1997. *Benedita da Silva: An Afro-Brazilian Woman's Story of Politics and Love.* Oakland, Calif.: Institute for Food and Development Policy.

Benjamin, Walter. 1978a. "The Author as Producer." In *Reflections: Essays, Aphorisms, Autobiographical Writings.* Edited and with an introduction by Peter Demetz. Trans. Edmund Jephcott. New York: Harcourt Brace Jovanovich.

———. 1978b. "A Berlin Chronicle." In *Reflections: Essays, Aphorisms, Autobiographical Writings.* Edited and with an introduction by Peter Demetz. Trans. Edmund Jephcott. New York: Harcourt Brace Jovanovich.

Bergson, Henri. 1956 [1911]. "Laughter." In *Comedy: An Essay on Comedy by George Meredith and Laughter by Henri Bergson,* with an introduction and appendix by Wylie Sypher. Garden City, N.Y.: Doubleday Anchor.

Besançon, Alain. 1974. *Éducation et Société en Russie dans le Second Tiers du XIXe Siècle.* Paris: Mouton.

Biancarelli, Aureliano. 1997. "27% dos Policiais Evitam Sair de Farda." *Folha de São Paulo,* April 8, 5.

"Black, Proud and Brazilian." 1996. *Boston Globe,* September 21, A2.

Blok, Anton. 1974. *The Mafia of a Sicilian Village, 1860–1960: A Study of Violent Peasant Entrepreneurs.* Prospect Heights, Ill.: Waveland Press.

———. 1981. "Rams and Billy-Goats: A Key to the Mediterranean Code of Honor." *Man* 16 (3): 427–40.

Bordo, Susan. 1993. "Feminism, Foucault and the Politics of the Body." In *Up against Foucault: Explorations of Some Tensions between Foucault and Feminism,* edited by Caroline Ramazanoglu, 179–202. London: Routledge.

Bourdieu, Pierre. 1977. *Outline of a Theory of Practice*. Cambridge: Cambridge University Press.

———. 1984. *Distinction: A Social Critique of the Judgement of Taste*. Cambridge, Mass.: Harvard University Press.

———. 1991. *Language and Symbolic Power*. Edited and introduced by John B. Thompson. Cambridge, Mass.: Harvard University Press.

———. 1993. *La Misere du Monde*. Paris: Seuil.

Bourdieu, Pierre, and J.-C. Passeron. 1977. *Reproduction in Education, Society, and Culture*. Beverly Hills, Calif.: Sage.

Bourgois, Philippe. 1995. *In Search of Respect: Selling Crack in El Barrio*. Cambridge: Cambridge University Press.

Bowen, Elenore Smith. 1954. *Return to Laughter*. New York: Harper.

Brandes, Stanley. 1981. "Like Wounded Stags: Male Sexual Ideology in an Andalusian Town." In *Sexual Meanings: The Cultural Construction of Gender and Sexuality*, edited by Sherry B. Ortner and Harriet Whitehead, 216–39. Cambridge: Cambridge University Press.

———. 1984. "Animal Metaphors and Social Control in Tzintzuntzan." *Ethnology* 23:207–15.

Breton, André. 1966. *Anthologie de l'Humour Noir*. Paris: J.-J. Pauvert.

———. 1978 [1936]. "What Is Surrealism?" In *What Is Surrealism? Selected Writings: André Breton*, edited and introduced by Franklin Rosemont, 112–41. New York: Pathfinder Press.

Brites, Jurema. 2000. "Afeto, Desigualdade e Rebeldia: Bastidores do Serviço Doméstico." Ph.D. diss., Instituto de Filosofia e Ciências Humanas, Programa de Pós-Graduação em Antropologia Social, Universidade Federal do Rio Grande do Sul.

Brooke, James. 1993. "Gunmen in Police Uniforms Kill 7 Street Children in Brazil." *New York Times,* July 24, 1, 3.

Brown, Diana DeGroat. 1994. *Umbanda: Religion and Politics in Urban Brazil*. New York: Columbia University Press.

Brown, Jacqueline Nassy. 1998. "Black Liverpool, Black America, and the Gendering of Diasporic Space." *Cultural Anthropology* 13 (3): 291–325.

Brusco, Elizabeth. 1995. *The Reformation of Machismo: Evangelical Conversion and Gender in Colombia*. Austin: University of Texas Press.

Buarque, Cristovam. 1992. *A Revolução na Esquerda e a Invenção do Brasil*. Rio de Janeiro: Editora Paz e Terra.

Buckley, Stephen. 2000. "Birthrate among Teens Shows Brazil May Be Too Sexy: Attempts at Education Seem to Have Failed." *Washington Post,* January 14.

Burdick, John. 1993. *Looking for God in Brazil: The Progressive Catholic Church in Urban Brazil's Religious Arena*. Berkeley and Los Angeles: University of California Press.

———. 1998. *Blessed Anastácia: Women, Race and Popular Christianity in Brazil*. New York: Routledge.

Burke, Peter. 1978. *Popular Culture in Early Modern Europe*. New York: Harper and Row.

Burns, E. Bradford. 1993. *A History of Brazil*. 3d ed. New York: Columbia University Press.

Butler, Judith. 1990. *Gender Trouble: Feminism and the Subversion of Identity.* New York: Routledge.

Cain, Maureen. 1993. "Foucault, Feminism and Feeling: What Foucault Can and Cannot Contribute to Feminist Epistemology." In *Up against Foucault: Explorations of Some Tensions between Foucault and Feminism,* edited by C. Ramazanoglu, 73–96. London: Routledge.

Caldeira, Teresa Pires do Rio. 1991. "Direitos Humanos ou 'Privilégios de Bandidos'? Desventuras da Democratização Brasileira." *Novos Estudos CEBRAP* 30 (July): 162–74.

———. 2000. *City of Walls: Crime, Segregation, and Citizenship in São Paulo.* Berkeley and Los Angeles: University of California Press.

Calligaris, Contardo. 1991. *Hello Brasil! Notas de um Psicanalista Europeu Viajando ao Brasil.* São Paulo: Escuta.

Cano, Ignacio. 1997. *The Use of Lethal Force by Police in Rio de Janeiro.* Rio de Janeiro: ISER (Instituto de Estudos da Religião).

Capécia, Mayotte. 1997. *I Am a Martinican Woman.* Pueblo, Colo.: Passegiata Press.

Cardia, Nancy. 1997. "A Violência Urbana e a Escola." *Contemporaneidade e Educação* Ano II, no. 2: 26–69.

Cardoso, Fernando Henrique, and Enzo Faletto. 1979. *Dependency and Development in Latin America.* Berkeley and Los Angeles: University of California Press.

Caulfield, Sueann. 2000. *In Defense of Honor: Sexual Morality, Modernity, and Nation in Early Twentieth-Century Brazil.* Durham, N.C.: Duke University Press.

CEDEC. 1997. *Mapa de Risco da Violência: Cidade do Rio de Janeiro.*

Chaney, Elsa M., and Mary Garcia Castro. 1989. "A New Field for Research and Action." In *Muchachas No More: Household Workers in Latin America and the Caribbean,* edited by Elsa M. Chaney and Mary Garcia Castro, 3–13. Philadelphia: Temple University Press.

Chestnut, Andrew. 1997. *Born Again in Brazil: The Pentecostal Boom and the Pathogens of Poverty.* New Brunswick, N.J.: Rutgers University Press.

Christie, Michael. 1996. "Brazil Debates If 12-Year-Olds Can Decide on Sex." *Reuters North American Wire,* May 28.

Clifford, James, and George E. Marcus, eds. 1986. *Writing Culture: The Poetics and Politics of Ethnography.* Berkeley and Los Angeles: University of California Press.

Collins, Patricia Hill. 1990. *Black Feminist Thought: Knowledge, Consciousness, and the Politics of Empowerment.* Cambridge, Mass.: Unwin Hyman.

Comaroff, John, and Jean Comaroff. 1992. *Ethnography and the Historical Imagination.* Boulder, Colo.: Westview Press.

Corrêa, Mariza. 1996. "Sobre a Invenção da Mulata." *Raça e Gênero* 6–7:35–50.

Da Cunha, Euclides. 1944. *Rebellion in the Backlands.* Chicago: University of Chicago Press.

Da Matta, Roberto. 1973. "O Carnaval Como um Rito de Passagem." In *En-*

saios de Antropologia Estrutural, edited by Roberto Da Matta, 121–68. Petrópolis: Vozes.

———. 1978. *Carnavais, Malandros e Heróis: Para uma Sociologia do Dilema Brasileiro.* Rio de Janeiro: Zahar Editores.

———. 1991a. *A Casa & Rua.* Rio de Janeiro: Editora Guanabara Koogan.

———. 1991b. *Carnivals, Rogues, and Heroes: An Interpretation of the Brazilian Dilemma.* Trans. John Drury. Notre Dame, Ind.: University of Notre Dame Press.

———. 1994. "Treze Pontos Riscados em Torno da Cultura Popular." *Anuário Antropológico/92.*

Darnton, Robert. 1991. "Workers Revolt: The Great Cat Massacre of the Rue Saint-Séverin." In *Rethinking Popular Culture,* edited by Chandra Mukerji and Michael Schudson, 97–120. Berkeley and Los Angeles: University of California Press.

Davis, Murray S. 1995. "The Sociology of Humor: A Stillborn Field?" *Sociological Forum* 10 (2): 327–39.

De Jesus, Carolina Maria. 1960. *Quarto de Despejo.* Rio de Janeiro: Livraria Francisco Alves.

———. 1962. *Child of the Dark: The Diary of Carolina Maria de Jesus.* New York: Dutton (Translation of *Quarto de Despejo.*)

De Souza, Julia Filet-Abrey. 1980. "Paid Domestic Service in Brazil." *Latin American Perspectives* 7 (1): 35–63.

"Dead End Kids." 1992. *Newsweek,* May 25, 12–19.

Debert, Guita Grin. 1979. *Ideologia e Populismo: A. de Barros, M. Arraes, C. Lacerda, L. Brizola.* São Paulo: T. A. Queiroz, Editor.

Degler, Carl N. 1971. *Neither Black Nor White: Slavery and Race Relations in Brazil and the United States.* New York: Macmillan.

Dias, Maria Odila Leite da Silva. 1995 [1984]. *Power and Everyday Life: The Lives of Working Women in Nineteenth-Century Brazil.* New Brunswick, N.J.: Rutgers University Press.

Dimenstein, Gilberto. 1990. *A Guerra dos Meninos.* São Paulo: Brasiliense.

Douglas, Mary. 1966. *Purity and Danger: An Analysis of the Concepts of Pollution and Taboo.* London: Routledge and Kegan Paul.

Dundes, Alan. 1985. "The J.A.P. and the J.A.M. in American Jokelore." *Journal of American Folklore* 98 (390): 456–75.

———. 1987. *Cracking Jokes: Studies of Sick Humor Cycles and Stereotypes.* Berkeley: Ten Speed Press.

Dundes, Alan, and Thomas Hauschild. 1983. Auschwitz Jokes. *Western Folklore* 42 (4): 249–60.

Dunn, Christopher. 2001. "Tropicália, Counterculture, and the Diasporic Imagination in Brazil." In *Brazilian Popular Music and Globalization,* edited by Charles A. Perrone and Christopher Dunn, 72–95. Gainesville: University Press of Florida.

Ehrenreich, Barbara. 1987. "The New Right Attack on Welfare." In *The Mean Season: The Attack on the Welfare State,* edited by F. Block et al., 161–95. New York: Pantheon.

————. 2001. *Nickel and Dimed: On (Not) Getting By in America*. New York: Metropolitan Books.

Escobar, Arturo. 1995. *Encountering Development: The Making and Unmaking of the Third World*. Princeton, N.J.: Princeton University Press.

Esteves, Martha de Abreu. 1989. *Meninas Perdidas: Os Populares e o Cotidiano do Amor no Rio de Janeiro de Belle Époque*. Rio de Janeiro: Paz e Terra.

Fanon, Frantz. 1967 [1952]. *Black Skin, White Masks*. New York: Grove Press.

Fausto, Boris. 1984. *Crime e Cotidiano: A Criminalidade em São Paulo (1800–1924)*. São Paulo, Brasiliense.

Fernandes, Florestan. 1969. *The Negro in Brazilian Society*. New York: Columbia University Press.

Fernandes, Florestan, and Roger Bastide. 1955. *Relações Raciais Entre Negros e Brancos em São Paulo*. São Paulo: Editora Anhembi.

Fernandes, Ismael. 1997 [1982]. *Memória da Telenovela Brasileira*. 4th ed. São Paulo: Editora Brasiliense.

Figueira, Sérvulo A., org. 1985. *Cultura da Psicanálise*. São Paulo: Editora Brasiliense.

Firth, Raymond. 1975. "Social Anthropology and Marxist Views on Society." In *Marxist Analyses and Social Anthropology*, edited by Maurice Bloch, 29–60. London: Malaby.

Fonseca, Claudia. 1986. "Orphanages, Foundlings and Foster Mothers: The System of Child Circulation in a Brazilian Squatter Settlement." *Anthropological Quarterly* 59 (1): 15–27.

————. 1992. "Honra, Humor e Relações de Gênero: Um Estudo de Caso." In *Uma Questão de Gênero*, organized by Albertina de Oliveira Costa and Cristina Bruschini. São Paulo: Editora Rosa dos Tempos.

————. 1995. *Caminhos da Adoção*. São Paulo: Cortez Editora.

Fonseca, Manuel A. R. da. 1998. "Brazil's Real Plan." *Journal of Latin American Studies* 30:619–39.

Foucault, Michel. 1975. *Discipline and Punish: The Birth of a Prison*. New York: Vintage.

————. 1980 [1978]. *The History of Sexuality: Volume 1: An Introduction*. New York: Vintage Books.

————. 1980. *Power/Knowledge: Selected Interviews and Other Writings*. Ed. Colin Gordon. New York: Pantheon.

————. 1991. "Governmentality." In *The Foucault Effect: Studies in Governmentality*, edited by Graham Burchell, Colin Gordon, and Peter Miller, 87–104. Chicago: University of Chicago Press.

Francis, Paulo. 1980. *O Afeto Que Se Encerra: Memórias*. Rio de Janeiro: Civilização Brasileira.

Frank, André Gunder. 1967. *Capitalism and Underdevelopment in Latin America: Historical Studies of Chile and Brazil*. New York: Monthly Review Press.

Freud, Sigmund. 1963 [1905]. *Jokes and Their Relation to the Unconscious*. New York: Norton.

Freyre, Gilberto. 1986 [1933]. *The Masters and the Slaves*. Berkeley and Los Angeles: University of California Press.

―――. 1986 [1936]. *The Mansions and the Shanties*. Berkeley and Los Angeles: University of California Press.

Friedan, Betty. 1963. *The Feminine Mystique*. New York: Norton.

Fry, Peter. 1982a. "Da Hierarquia à Igualdade: A Construção da Homosexualidade no Brasil." In *Para Inglês Ver: Identidade e Política na Cultura Brasileira*, 87–115. Rio de Janeiro: Zahar Editores.

―――. 1982b. "Homossexualidade Masculina e Cultos Afro-Brasileiros." In *Para Inglês Ver: Identidade e Política na Cultura Brasileira*, 55–85. Rio de Janeiro: Zahar Editores.

―――. 1982c. *Para Inglês Ver: Identidade e Política na Cultura Brasileira*. Rio de Janeiro: Zahar Editores.

―――. 1995. "Why Brazil Is Different." *Times Literary Supplement*, December 8, 6–7.

―――. 1995/1996. "O Que a Cinderela Negra Tem a Dizer Sobre a 'Politica Racial' no Brasil." *Revista USP* 28:122–35.

Fussell, Paul. 1983. *Class: A Guide through the American Status System*. New York: Summit Books.

Gaspar, Maria Dulce. 1985. *Garotas de Programa: Prostituição em Copacabana e Identidade Social*. Rio de Janeiro: Jorge Zahar Editor.

Gay, Peter. 1993. "The Bite of Wit." In *The Bourgeois Experience: Victoria to Freud*. Vol. 3, *The Cultivation of Hatred*, 368–423. New York: Norton.

Gay, Robert. 1994. *Popular Organization and Democracy in Rio de Janeiro: A Tale of Two Favelas*. Philadelphia: Temple University Press.

Geertz, Clifford. 1973. "Thick Description." In *The Interpretation of Cultures: Selected Essays*, 3–30. New York: Basic Books.

Giacomini, Sonia Maria. 1988. *Mulher e Escrava: Uma Introdução Histórica da Mulher Negra no Brasil*. Petrópolis: Vozes.

―――. 1990. "Aprendendo a Ser Mulata: Um Estudo Sobre a Identidade de Mulata Profissional." Programa de Pós-Graduação em Antropologia Social do Museu Nacional/UFRJ.

Gilliam, Angela. 1998. "The Brazilian *Mulata*: Images in the Global Economy." *Race and Class* 40 (1): 57–69.

Gilliam, Angela, and Onik'a Gilliam. 1999. "Negotiating the Subjectivity of Mulata Identity in Brazil." *Latin American Perspectives* 26 (3): 60–84.

Gilman, Sander. 1985. "Black Bodies, White Bodies: Toward an Iconography of Female Sexuality in Late Nineteenth-Century Art, Medicine, and Literature." In *Race, Writing, and Difference*, edited by Henry Louis Gates Jr., 223–61. Chicago: University of Chicago Press.

Ginzburg, Carlo. 1976. *The Cheese and the Worms*. New York: Penguin.

Gois, Antônio Gois. 2001. "Provão Revela Barreira Racial no Ensino." *Folha Cotidiano*, C1, *Folha de São Paulo*, Domingo, January 14.

Goldstein, Donna. 1992. "From Condom Literacy to Women's Empowerment: AIDS and Women in Brazil." *Proteus* 9 (2): 25–34.

―――. 1994a. "AIDS and Women in Brazil: The Emerging Problem." *Social Science and Medicine* 39 (7): 919–30.

―――. 1994b. "Women and AIDS in Brazil: The Class, Cultural, Racial, Sexual, and Gender Politics of Modern Disease." Ph.D. diss., University of California, Berkeley.

———. 1995a. *The Cultural, Class, and Gender Politics of a Modern Disease: Women and AIDS in Brazil*. International Center for Research on Women, Women and AIDS Research Program. Research Report Series No. 6.

———. 1995b. "From Yellow Star to Red Star: Anti-Semitism, Anti-Communism, and the Jews of Hungary." *Polar: Journal of Political and Legal Anthropology* 18 (1): 1–12.

———. 1996. "O Lugar da Mulher no Discurso Sobre AIDS no Brasil." In *Quebrando o Silêncio: Mulheres e AIDS no Brasil,* organized by Richard Parker and Jane Galvão, 137–52. Rio de Janeiro: Relume Dumará Editores.

———. 1997. "Re-imagining the Jew in Hungary: The Reconstruction of Ethnicity through Political Affiliation." In *Rethinking Nationalism and Ethnicity: The Struggle for Meaning and Order in Europe,* edited by H.-R. Wicker, 193–210. Oxford: Berg.

———. 1998. "Nothing Bad Intended: Child Discipline, Punishment, and Survival in a Shantytown in Rio de Janeiro, Brazil." In *Small Wars: The Cultural Politics of Childhood,* edited by Nancy Scheper-Hughes and Carolyn Sargent, 389–415. Berkeley and Los Angeles: University of California Press.

———. 1999. " 'Interracial' Sex and Racial Democracy in Brazil: Twin Concepts?" *American Anthropologist* 101 (3): 563–78.

———. 2000a. Book Review. "Blessed Anastácia: Women, Race, and Popular Christianity in Brazil. John Burdick." *American Anthropologist* 102 (1): 186–87.

———. 2000b. "Por Que os Homens Não Envelhecem? Violência, Morte, Conversão Religiosa e a Vida Cotidiana nas Favelas do Rio de Janeiro." In *Políticas do Corpo e o Curso da Vida,* organized by Guita Debert and Donna Goldstein, 17–48. São Paulo: Editora Sumaré.

Graham, Sandra Lauderdale. 1995 [1988]. *House and Street: The Domestic World of Servants and Masters in Nineteenth-Century Rio*. Austin: University of Texas Press.

Gramsci, Antonio. 1971. *The Prison Notebooks*. New York: International Publishers.

Green, James N. 1999. *Beyond Carnival: Male Homosexuality in Twentieth-Century Brazil*. Chicago: University of Chicago.

Gregori, Maria Filomena. 2000. *Viração: Experiências de Meninos nas Ruas*. São Paulo: Companhia das Letras.

Guillermoprieto, Alma. 1990. *Samba*. London: Jonathan Cape.

Hall, Stuart. 1991a. "The Local and the Global: Globalization and Ethnicity." In *Culture, Globalization and the World-System,* edited by Anthony King, 19–39. London: Macmillan Education.

———. 1991b. "Old and New Identities, Old and New Ethnicities." In *Culture, Globalization and the World-System,* edited by Anthony King, 45–67. London: Macmillan Education.

Hamburger, Esther. 1999. "Politics and Intimacy in Brazilian Telenovelas." Ph.D. diss., University of Chicago.

Hanchard, Michael G. 1994a. "Black Cinderella? Race and the Public Sphere in Brazil." *Public Culture* 7:165–85.

———. 1994b. *Orpheus and Power: The Movimento Negro of Rio de Janeiro and São Paulo, Brazil, 1945–1988.* Princeton, N.J.: Princeton University Press.

Harris, Marvin. 1964a. "The Myth of the Friendly Master." In *Patterns of Race in the Americas,* 65–78. New York: Walker and Company.

———. 1964b. "Racial Identity in Brazil." *Luso-Brazilian Review* 1:24–28.

Harris, Marvin, Josildeth Gomes Consorte, Joseph Lang, and Bryan Byrne. 1993. "Who Are the Whites? Imposed Census Categories and the Racial Demography of Brazil." *Social Forces* 72 (2): 451–62.

Harvey, David L., and Michael H. Reed. 1996. "The Culture of Poverty: An Ideological Analysis." *Sociological Perspectives* 39 (4): 465–595.

Hasenbalg, Carlos A. 1985. "Race and Socioeconomic Inequalities in Brazil." In *Race, Class and Power in Brazil,* edited by Pierre-Michel Fontaine, 25–41. Los Angeles: University of California, Center for Afro-American Studies.

———. 1996. "Racial Inequalities in Brazil and throughout Latin America: Timid Responses to Disguised Racism." In *Constructing Democracy: Human Rights, Citizenship, and Society in Latin America,* edited by Elizabeth Jelin and Eric Hershberg, 161–76. Boulder, Colo.: Westview Press.

Hasenbalg, Carlos, and Nelson do Valle Silva. 1988. *Estrutura Social, Mobilidade e Raça.* São Paulo: Vertice e IUPERJ.

———. 1993. "Notas Sobre Desigualdade Racial e Política no Brasil." *Estudos Afro-Asiáticos* 25:141–59.

———. 1999. "Notes on Racial and Political Inequality in Brazil." In *Racial Politics in Contemporary Brazil,* edited by Michael G. Hanchard, 154–78. Durham, N.C.: Duke University Press.

Hasenbalg, Carlos A., Nelson do Valle Silva, and Luiz Claudio Barcelos. 1992. "Notas Sobre Miscigenação Racial no Brasil." In *Relações Raciais no Brasil Contemporâneo,* edited by Nelson do Valle Silva and Carlos Hasenbalg, 67–77. Rio de Janeiro: Rio Fundo Editora.

Hecht, Tobias. 1998. *At Home in the Street.* Cambridge: Cambridge University Press.

Hobsbawm, Eric J. 1959. *Primitive Rebels.* New York: Norton.

Holloway, Thomas H. 1993. *Policing Rio de Janeiro: Repression and Resistance in a Nineteenth-Century City.* Stanford, Calif.: Stanford University Press.

Holston, James. 1989. *The Modernist City: An Anthropological Critique of Brasília.* Chicago: University of Chicago Press.

Holston, James, and Teresa P. R. Caldeira. 1998. "Democracy, Law, and Violence: Disjunctions of Brazilian Citizenship." In *Fault Lines of Democracy in Post-Transition Latin America,* edited by Felipe Agüero and Jeffrey Stark, 263–96. Coral Gables, Fla.: North-South Center Press at the University of Miami.

Holy Bible (Authorized or King James version). 1955 [1951]. Red Letter Edition. Chicago: J. A. Hertel for International Sunday School League.

Horowitz, C. 1997. "Are American Jews Disappearing?" *New York Magazine,* July 14, 30–37, 101, 108.

Huggins, Martha. 1991. "Introduction: Vigilantism and the State—A Look South and North." In *Vigilantism and the State in Modern Latin America: Essays in Extra Legal Violence,* edited by Martha Huggins, 1–18. New York: Praeger.

Hughes, Everett C., et al., eds. 1950. *The Collected Papers of Robert Ezra Park: Race and Culture.* Vol. 1. Glencoe, Ill.: Free Press.

Human Rights Watch/Americas. 1994. *Final Justice: Police and Death Squad Homicides of Adolescents in Brazil.* New York: Human Rights Watch.

———. 1996. *Brazil: Fighting Violence with Violence: Human Rights Abuse and Criminality in Rio de Janeiro.* New York: Human Rights Watch.

———. 1997. *Police Brutality in Urban Brazil.* New York: Human Rights Watch.

Hyam, Ronald. 1986. "Empire and Sexual Opportunity." *Journal of Imperial and Commonwealth History* 14 (2): 34–90.

IBGE. 1996. *Retratos Municipais: Região Metropolitana do Rio de Janeiro/IBGE, Departamento de População e Indicadores Sociais.* Rio de Janeiro: IBGE.

———. 1997a. *Brazil in Figures.* Vol. 5. Ministério do Planejamento e Orçamento, Instituto Brasileiro de Geografia e Estatística.

———. 1997b. *Pesquisa Nacional por Amostra de Domicílios: Rio de Janeiro e Região Metropolitana do Rio de Janeiro.* Vol. 18, No. 25.

ISER, Núcleo de Pesquisa. 1996. *Censo Institucional Evangélico.* Rio de Janeiro: ISER.

JanMohamed, Abdul R. 1990. "Sexuality on/of the Racial Border: Foucault, Wright and the Articulation of 'Racialized Sexuality.' " In *Discourses of Sexuality from Aristotle to AIDS,* edited by Domna C. Stanton, 94–116. Cambridge, Mass.: Harvard University Press.

Jelin, Elizabeth. 1980. "The Bahiana in the Labor Force in Salvador, Brazil." In *Sex and Class in Latin America,* edited by June Nash and Helen Safa, 129–46. New York: Praeger.

Kant de Lima, Roberto. 1986. "Legal Theory and Judicial Practice: Paradoxes of Police Work in the Rio de Janeiro City." Ph.D. diss., Harvard University.

———. 1987. *Cultura Jurídica e Práticas Policiais. A Produção e a Reprodução da Ética Policial no Rio de Janeiro.* Belo Horizonte: Mimeo.

Koestler, Arthur. 1989 [1964]. *The Act of Creation.* London: Arkana Penguin Books.

Kofes, Maria Suely. 1990. "Mulher: Mulheres. Diferença e Identidade nas Armadilhas da Igualdade e Desigualdade: Interação e Relação Entre Patroas e Empregadas Domésticas." Ph.D. diss., Universidade de São Paulo.

Koller, M. R. 1988. *Humor and Society: Explorations in the Sociology of Humor.* Houston: Cap and Gown Press.

Kottak, Conrad. 1963. "Race Relations in a Bahian Fishing Village." *Luso-Brazilian Review* 4 (2): 35–52.

Kowarick, L. 1979. *A Espoliação Urbana.* Rio de Janeiro: Paz e Terra.

Kulick, Don. 1997. "The Gender of Brazilian Transgendered Prostitutes." *American Antropologist* 99 (3): 574–85.

————. 1998. *Travesti: Sex, Gender, and Culture among Brazilian Transgendered Prostitutes.* Chicago: University of Chicago Press.

Kulick, Don, and Margaret Willson, eds. 1995. *Taboo: Sex, Identity, and Erotic Subjectivity in Anthropological Fieldwork.* New York: Routledge.

Kuznesof, Elizabeth Anne. 1991. "Sexual Politics, Race and Bastard-Bearing in Nineteenth-Century Brazil: A Question of Culture or Power?" *Journal of Family History* 16 (3): 241–60.

Lakoff, Robin Tolmach. 1975. *Language and Woman's Place.* New York: Harper and Row.

Lassalle, Yvonne M., and Maureen O'Dougherty. 1997. "In Search of Weeping Worlds: Economies of Agency and Politics of Representation in the Ethnography of Inequality." *Radical History Review* 69:243–60.

Lavinas, Lena, Bila Sorj, Leila Linhares, and Angela Jorge. 2001. *Home Work in Brazil: New Contractual Arrangements.* Series on Homeworkers in the Global Economy. Geneva: International Labour Office Book source. Web site: www.ilo.org/public/english/employment/ent/sed/publ/wp7.htm.

Leach, Edmund. 1964. "Anthropological Aspects of Language: Animal Categories and Verbal Abuse." In *New Directions in the Study of Language,* edited by Eric H. Lennenberg. Cambridge, Mass.: MIT Press.

Leacock, Eleanor, ed. 1971. *The Culture of Poverty: A Critique.* New York: Simon and Schuster.

Leal, Ondina Fachel. 1990 [1985]. *A Leitura Social da Novela das Oito.* 2d ed. Petrópolis: Vozes.

————. 1995. "Sangue, Fertilidade e Práticas Contraceptivas." In *Corpo e Significado: Ensaios de Antropologia Social,* organized by Ondina Fachel Leal, 13–35. Porto Alegre: Editora da Universidade/UFRGS.

Leeds, Elizabeth. 1996. "Cocaine and Parallel Polities in the Brazilian Urban Periphery: Constraints on Local-Level Democratization." *Latin American Research Review* 31 (3): 47–83.

Levine, Robert M. 1994. "The Cautionary Tale of Carolina Maria de Jesus." *Latin American Research Review* 29 (1): 55–83.

Levine, Robert M., and José Carlos Sebe Bom Meihy. 1995. *The Life and Death of Carolina Maria de Jesus.* Albuquerque: University of New Mexico Press.

Lewis, Oscar. 1959. *Five Families: Mexican Case Studies in the Culture of Poverty.* New York: Basic Books.

————. 1963. *The Children of Sanchez.* New York: Vintage.

————. 1965. *La Vida: A Puerto Rican Family in the Culture of Poverty—San Juan and New York.* New York: Random House.

————. 1966. "The Culture of Poverty." *Scientific American* 215 (4): 19–25.

Lluch, Constantino. 1979. "Employment, Earnings and Income Distribution." In *Annex II of Human Resources Special Report: Brazil.* Washington, D.C.: World Bank.

Lobato, Lenaura, and Luciene Burlandy. 2000. "The Context and Process of Health Care Reform in Brazil." In *Reshaping Health Care in Latin America: A Comparative Analysis of Health Care Reform in Argentina, Brazil, and Mexico,* edited by Sonia Fleury Teixeira, Susana Belmartino, and Enis Baris, 79–102. Ottowa, Canada: International Development Research Centre.

Lock, Margaret. 1993. *Encounters with Aging: Mythologies of Menopause in Japan and North America*. Berkeley and Los Angeles: University of California Press.

Lovell, Peggy. 2000. "Gender, Race, and the Struggle for Social Justice in Brazil." *Latin American Perspectives* 6 (115): 85–102.

Machado, Maria das Dores C., and Cecília L. Mariz. 1997. "Mulheres e Prática Religiosa nas Classes Populares: Uma Comparação entre as Igrejas Pentecostais, as Comunidades Eclesiais de Base e os Grupos Carismáticos." *Revista Brasileira de Ciências Sociais* 12 (34): 71–87.

MacRae, Edward. 1992. "Homosexual Identities in Transitional Brazilian Politics." In *The Making of Social Movements in Latin America: Identity, Strategy and Democracy*, edited by Arturo Escobar and Sonia E. Alvarez, 185–203. Boulder, Colo.: Westview Press.

Maggie, Yvonne. 1988. "O Que Se Cala Quando Se Fala do Negro no Brasil." Mimeo, June.

Manhães, Maria P. 1988. "Sociedade Psicanalítica do Rio de Janeiro." *Revista Brasileira de Psicanálise* 22 (4): 678–84.

Marcus, George E., and Michael M. J. Fischer. 1986. *Anthropology As Cultural Critique: An Experimental Moment in the Human Sciences*. Chicago: University of Chicago Press.

Marshall, T. H. 1964 [1949]. "Citizenship and Social Class." In *Class, Citizenship, and Social Development*, 71–134. Garden City, N.Y.: Doubleday.

Marx, Karl. 1906–1909. *Capital: A Critique of Political Economy*. 3 vols. Chicago: C. H. Kerr.

McGhee, P. E., and J. H. Goldstein, eds. 1983. *Handbook of Humor Research*. 2 vols. New York: Springer-Verlag.

McLaughlin, M. E. 1997. "Toward Real Welfare Reform: Decoding Race and Myths." In *Removing Risk from Children: Shifting the Paradigm*, edited by A. Carten and J. Dempson, 83–111. Silver Springs, Md.: Beckman House.

Mingardi, Guaracy. 1992. *Tiras, Gansos e Trutas — Cotidiano e Reforma na Polícia Civil*. São Paulo: Scritta.

———. 1998. *O Estado e o Crime Organizado*. São Paulo: IBCCrim.

Mintz, Sidney. 1960. *Worker in the Cane*. New Haven, Conn.: Yale University Press.

———. 1985. *Sweetness and Power: The Place of Sugar in Modern History*. New York: Penguin.

Morreall, John, ed. 1987. *The Philosophy of Laughter and Humor*. Albany: State University of New York Press.

Morris, David B. 1991. *The Culture of Pain*. Berkeley and Los Angeles: University of California Press.

Mott, Luiz. 1988. *Escravidão, Homossexualidade, e Demonologia*. São Paulo: Ícone.

Mukerji, Chandra, and Michael Schudson. 1991. "Introduction: Rethinking Popular Culture." In *Rethinking Popular Culture*, edited by Chandra Mukerji and Michael Schudson, 1–61. Berkeley and Los Angeles: University of California Press.

"Mulher é Menos Convencional no Casamento." 1991. *Folha de São Paulo*, October 1, sec. 4, p. 4.

Mulkay, Michael. 1988. *On Humor: Its Nature and Its Place in Modern Society*. Oxford: Basil Blackwell.

Muraro, Rose Marie. 1983. *Sexualidade da Mulher Brasileira: Corpo e Classe Social no Brasil*. Petrópolis: Vozes.

Nascimento, Abdias do. 1979. *Brazil: Mixture or Massacre: Essays on the Genocide of a Black People*. Dover, Mass.: Majority Press.

Needell, Jeffrey D. 1987. *A Tropical Belle Epoque: Elite Culture and Society in Turn-of-the-Century Rio de Janeiro*. Cambridge: Cambridge University Press.

———. 1995a. "Identity, Race, Gender, and Modernity in the Origins of Gilberto Freyre's Oeuvre." *American Historical Review* 100 (1): 51–77.

———. 1995b. "Rio de Janeiro and Buenos Aires: Public Space and Public Consciousness in *Fin-de-Siècle* Latin America." *Comparative Studies in Society and History* 37 (3): 519–40.

Neto, [Henrique Maximiliano] Coelho. 1908. "Os Sertanejos." *A Notícia* (Rio de Janeiro), November 29, 3.

Novo Michaelis. 1961. Vol. 2, Português-Inglês. 43d edition. São Paulo: Comp. Melhoramentos de São Paulo.

O'Donnell, Guillermo. 1992. "Transitions, Continuities, and Paradoxes." In *Issues in Democratic Consolidation*, edited by Scott Mainwaring, Guillermo O'Donnell, and J. Samuel Valenzuela, 17–56. Notre Dame, Ind.: University of Notre Dame Press.

———. 1993. "On the State, Democratization and Some Conceptual Problems: A Latin American View with Glances at Some Postcommunist Countries." *World Development* 21 (8): 1355–69.

Ondaatje, Michael. 2000. *Anil's Ghost*. New York: Knopf.

Oring, Elliot. 1984. *The Jokes of Sigmund Freud*. Philadelphia: University of Pennsylvania Press.

———. 1992. *Jokes and Their Relations*. Lexington: University Press of Kentucky.

———. 1994. "Humor and the Suppression of Sentiment." *Humor* 7 (1): 7–26.

Ortiz, Renato. 1986. *Cultura Brasileira e Identidade Nacional*. 2d ed. São Paulo: Brasiliense.

Ortner, Sherry B. 1995. "Resistance and the Problem of Ethnographic Refusal." *Comparative Studies in Society and History* 37 (1): 173–93.

———. 1998. "Identities: The Hidden Life of Class." *Journal of Anthropological Research* 54 (1): 1–17.

"Outcry over Police Brutality in Brazil." 1997. *New York Times*, April 2, A3.

Owensby, Brian P. 1999. *Intimate Ironies: Modernity and the Making of Middle-Class Lives in Brazil*. Stanford, Calif.: Stanford University Press.

Park, Robert E. 1931. "Mentality of Racial Hybrids." *American Journal of Sociology* 36 (4): 534–51.

Parker, Richard G. 1991. *Bodies, Pleasures, and Passions: Sexual Culture in Contemporary Brazil*. Boston: Beacon Press.

———. 1999. *Beneath the Equator: Cultures of Desire, Male Homosexuality, and Emerging Gay Communities in Brazil*. New York: Routledge.

Parkin, Robert. 1993. "The Joking Relationship and Kinship: Charting a Theoretical Dependency." *Journal of the Anthropological Society of Oxford* 24 (3): 251–63.

Pastore, José. 1982. *Inequality and Social Mobility in Brazil*. Madison: University of Wisconsin Press.

Patai, Daphne. 1991. "Florisa Verucci: Introduction." *Feminist Studies* 17 (3): 551–56.

Peacock, Thomas Love. 1970 [1836]. *Memoirs of Shelley, and Other Essays and Reviews*. Ed. Howard Mills. London: Hart-Davis.

Pereira, Anthony. 1997. "Elitist Liberalism: Citizenship, State Violence, and the Rule of Law in Brazil." Paper presented at the XX International Congress of the Latin American Studies Association, April, Guadalajara, Mexico.

Pereira de Melo, H. 1989. "Feminists and Domestic Workers in Rio de Janeiro." In *Muchachas No More: Household Workers in Latin America and the Caribbean*, edited by Else M. Chaney and Mary Garcia Castro, 245–67. Philadelphia: Temple University Press.

Peristiany, John G. 1966. *Honour and Shame: The Values of Mediterranean Society*. Chicago: University of Chicago Press.

Perlman, Janice E. 1976. *The Myth of Marginality: Urban Poverty and Politics in Rio de Janeiro*. Berkeley and Los Angeles: University of California Press.

Perlongher, Néstor. 1987. *O Negócio do Michê: Prostituição Viril em São Paulo*. São Paulo: Editora Brasiliense.

Pinheiro, Paulo Sérgio. 1991. "Police and Political Crisis: The Case of the Military Police." In *Vigilantism and the State in Latin America: Essays on Extralegal Violence*, edited by Martha Huggins, 167–88. New York: Praeger.

Pino, Julio César. 1997a. *Family and Favela: The Reproduction of Poverty in Rio de Janeiro*. Westport, Conn.: Greenwood Press.

———. 1997b. "Sources on the History of Favelas in Rio de Janeiro." *Latin American Research Review* 32 (3): 111–22.

Pitt-Rivers, J. 1966. "Honour and Social Status." In *Honour and Shame: The Values of Mediterranean Society*, edited by John G. Peristiany, 19–77. Chicago: University of Chicago Press.

Podesta, Don. 1993. "Black Slums Belie Brazil's Self-Image: Equality Is the Law, Inequality Is the Fact." *Washington Post*, August 17, A12.

Powell, Chris, and George E. C. Paton, eds. 1988. *Humour in Society: Resistance and Control*. New York: St. Martin's Press.

Prado, Paulo. 1972 [1928]. *Retrato do Brasil: Ensaio Sôbre a Tristeza Brasileira*. In *Coleção Documentos Brasileiros*. Vol. 152. 7th ed. Rio de Janeiro: Livraria José Olympio Editôra.

Pratt, Alan. 1993. *Black Humor: Critical Essays*. New York: Garland Press.

Radner, Joan N., ed. 1993. *Strategies of Coding in Women's Cultures: Coding in Women's Folklore*. Urbana: University of Illinois Press.

Ramazanoglu, Caroline. 1993. "Introduction." In *Up against Foucault: Explorations of Some Tensions between Foucault and Feminism*, edited by Caroline Ramazanoglu, 1–25. London: Routledge.

Rebhun, L. A. 1999. *The Heart Is Unknown Country: Love in the Changing Economy of Northeast Brazil.* Stanford, Calif.: Stanford University Press.

Roseberry, William. 1988. "Political Economy." *Annual Review of Anthropology* 17:161-85.

Rostow, W. W. 1960. *The Stages of Economic Growth.* Cambridge: Cambridge University Press.

Rubbo, Anna, and Michael Taussig. 1977. "Up Off Their Knees: Servanthood in Southwest Colombia." *Michigan Discussions in Anthropology* 3:41–65.

Sabatini, Rafael. 1999 [1921]. *Scaramouche: A Romance of the French Revolution.* Washington, D.C.: Regnery.

Saffiotti, H. I. B. 1978. *Emprego Doméstico e Capitalismo.* Petrópolis: Vozes.

Sahlins, Marshall. 1999. "What Is Anthropological Enlightenment? Some Lessons of the Twentieth Century." *Annual Review of Anthropology* 28:i–xxiii.

———. 1999 [1993]. *Waiting for Foucault.* Cambridge, England: Prickly Pear Press.

Sanjek, Roger. 1971. "Brazilian Racial Terms: Some Aspects of Meaning and Learning." *American Anthropologist* 73:1126–43.

Sansone, Livio. 1998. "Funk Baiano: Uma Versão Local de um Fenômeno Global?" In *Ritmos em Trânsito: Sócio-Antropologia da Música Baiana,* organized by Livio Sansone and Jocélio Teles dos Santos, 219–40. São Paulo: Editora Dynamis.

———. 2001. "The Localization of Global Funk in Bahia and in Rio." In *Brazilian Popular Music and Globalization,* edited by Charles A. Perrone and Christopher Dunn, 136–60. Gainesville: University Press of Florida.

Scheper-Hughes, Nancy. 1992. *Death without Weeping: The Violence of Everyday Life in Northeast Brazil.* Berkeley and Los Angeles: University of California Press.

Schiffman, Bonnie, and Bill Zehme. 1991. *The Rolling Stone Book of Comedy.* Boston: Little, Brown.

Scott, James C. 1985. *Weapons of the Weak: Everyday Forms of Peasant Resistance.* New Haven, Conn.: Yale University Press.

———. 1989. "Prestige as the Public Discourse of Domination." *Cultural Critique* 12:146–66.

———. 1990. *Domination and the Arts of Resistance.* New Haven, Conn.: Yale University Press.

Seabrook, John. 2000. *Nobrow: The Culture of Marketing, the Marketing of Culture.* New York: Knopf.

Shapiro, Dolores. 1996. " 'A Barriga Limpa': Metaphors of Race and Strategies of Class Mobility in Northeastern Brazil." Paper presented at the meeting of the American Anthropological Association, San Francisco, November.

Sheppard, Alice. 1986. "From Kate Sanborn to Feminist Psychology: The Social Context of Women's Humor 1885–1985." *Psychology of Women Quarterly* 10:155–70.

Sheriff, Robin. 2000. "Exposing Silence as Cultural Censorship: A Brazilian Case." *American Anthropologist* 102 (1): 114–32.

———. 2001. *Dreaming Equality: Color, Race, and Racism in Urban Brazil.* New Brunswick, N.J.: Rutgers University Press.

Shirley, Robert W. 1990. "Recreating Communities: The Formation of Community in a Brazilian Shantytown." *Urban Anthropology* 19 (3): 255–76.

Silva, Hélio. 1993. *Travesti: A Invenção do Feminino.* Rio de Janeiro: Relume Dumará.

Silva, Nelson do Valle. 1985. "Updating the Cost of Not Being White in Brazil." In *Race, Class, and Power in Brazil,* edited by Pierre-Michel Fontaine, 42–55. Los Angeles: University of California, Center for Afro-American Studies.

———. 1988. "Cor e Processo de Realização Sócio-Econômica." In *Estrutura Social, Mobilidade, e Raça,* edited by Carlos A. Hasenbalg and Nelson do Valle Silva, 144–63. Rio de Janeiro: Editora Revista Dos Tribunais.

———. 1992. "Distância Social e Casamento Inter-Racial no Brasil." In *Relações Raciais no Brasil Contemporâneo,* edited by Carlos A. Hasenbalg and Nelson Do Valle Silva, 17–52. Rio de Janeiro: Rio Fundo Editora.

Silva, Nelson do Valle, and Carlos A. Hasenbalg. 1992. *Relações Raciais no Brasil Contemporâneo.* Rio de Janeiro: Rio Fundo Editora.

Simpson, Amelia. 1993. *Xuxa: The Mega-Marketing of Gender, Race, and Modernity.* Philadelphia: Temple University Press.

Skidmore, Thomas. 1988. "Obituary Gilberto Freyre (1900–1987)." *Hispanic American Historical Review* 68:803–05.

———. 1993 [1974]. *Black into White: Race and Nationality in Brazilian Thought.* New York: Oxford University Press.

———. 1999. *Brazil: Five Centuries of Change.* New York: Oxford University Press.

Soares, Luis Eduardo, Cláudia Milito, and Hélio R. S. Silva. 1996. "Homicídios Dolosos Praticados Contra Crianças e Adolescentes no Estado do Rio de Janeiro-1991 a Julho de 1993." In *Violência e Política no Rio de Janeiro,* organized by Soares e colaboradores, 189–215. Rio de Janeiro: Relume Dumará: ISER.

Soper, Kate. 1993. "Productive Contradictions." In *Up against Foucault: Explorations of Some Tensions between Foucault and Feminism,* edited by Caroline Ramazanoglu, 29–50. London: Routledge.

Souza, Neusa Santos. 1983. *Tornar-Se Negro ou as Vicissitudes da Identidade do Negro Brasileiro em Ascensão Social.* Rio de Janeiro: Graal.

Stallybrass, Peter, and Allon White 1986. *The Politics and Poetics of Transgression.* Ithaca, N.Y.: Cornell University Press.

Stam, Robert. 1989. *Subversive Pleasures.* Baltimore: Johns Hopkins University Press.

———. 1997. *Tropical Multiculturalism: A Comparative History of Race in Brazilian Cinema and Culture.* Durham, N.C.: Duke University Press.

Stephens, Sharon. 1995. "Children and the Politics of Culture in 'Late Capitalism.' " In *Children and the Politics of Culture,* edited by Sharon Stephens, 3–48. Princeton, N.J.: Princeton University Press.

Stoler, Ann Laura. 1989. "Making Empire Respectable: The Politics of Race and Sexual Morality in Twentieth-Century Colonial Cultures." *American Ethnologist* 16 (4): 634- 60.

———. 1995. *Race and the Education of Desire: Foucault's History of Sexuality and the Colonial Order of Things.* Durham, N.C.: Duke University Press.

————. 1997. "Racial Histories and Their Regimes of Truth." *Political Power and Social Theory* 11:183–206.

Stoll, David. 1990. *Is Latin America Turning Protestant? The Politics of Evangelical Growth*. Berkeley and Los Angeles: University of California Press.

Tannen, Deborah. 1990. *You Just Don't Understand: Women and Men in Conversation*. New York: Ballantine.

Tannenbaum, Frank. 1947. *Slave and Citizen*. New York: Knopf.

Taussig, Michael. 1989. "History as Commodity: In Some Recent American (Anthropological) Literature." *Critique of Anthropology* 9 (1): 7–23.

"Técnicos Querem Penalizar Menores de 18." 1992. *Folha de São Paulo*, October 25, sec. 4, p. 2.

Telander, Rick. 1995 [1988]. *Heaven Is a Playground*. Lincoln: University of Nebraska Press.

Telles, Eduardo. 1993. "Racial Distance and Region in Brazil: Intermarriage in Brazilian Urban Areas." *Latin American Research Review* 28 (2): 141–62.

Thompson, E. P. 1963. *The Making of the English Working Class*. New York: Vintage.

————. 1974. "Patrician Society, Plebian Culture." *Journal of Social History* 7 (4): 382–405.

————. 1978. "Folklore, Anthropology, and Social History." *Indian Historical Review* 3 (2): 247–66.

Tolosa, H. 1996. "Rio de Janeiro: Urban Expansion and Structural Change." In *The Megacity in Latin America*, edited by Alan Gilbert, 203–23. New York: United Nations University Press.

Trevisan, J. 1986. *Perverts in Paradise*. London: GMP Publishers.

Turner, Victor. 1995 [1969]. *The Ritual Process: Structure and Anti-Structure*. New York: Aldine De Gruyter.

Twain, Mark. 1897. "Pudd'nhead Wilson's New Calendar." In *Following the Equator*. 2 vols. Hartford, Conn.: American Publishing Company.

Twine, France Winddance. 1996. "O Hiato de Gênero nas Percepções de Racismo—O Caso dos Afro-Brasileiros Socialmente Ascendentes." *Estudos Afro-Asiáticos* 29:37–54.

————. 1998. *Racism in a Racial Democracy: The Maintenance of White Supremacy in Brazil*. New Brunswick, N.J.: Rutgers University Press.

UNICEF. 1985. *Rocinha, Mães e Vidas—Depoimentos*. Rio de Janeiro: Editorial Alhambra.

Vainfas, R. 1989. *Trópico dos Pecados: Moral Sexualidade e Inquisição no Brasil*. Rio de Janeiro: Editora Campus.

————, ed. 1986. *História e Sexualidade no Brasil*. Biblioteca de Historia. Rio de Janeiro: Edições Graal.

Valentine, Charles. 1968. *Culture and Poverty: Critique and Counter-Proposals*. Chicago: University of Chicago Press.

Ventura, Zuenir. 1994. *A Cidade Partida*. São Paulo, Editora Schwarz.

Vermelho, L., and Mello Jorge, Maria H. P. 1996. "Mortalidade de Jovens: Análise do Período de 1930 a 1991 (a Transição Epidemiológica Para a Violência)." *Revista Saúde Pública* 30 (4): 319–31.

Vianna, Hermano. 1988. *O Mundo Funk Carioca*. Rio de Janeiro: Jorge Zahar.

Wagley, Charles, ed. 1963 [1952]. *Race and Class in Rural Brazil.* New York: UNESCO/Columbia University Press.

Wallerstein, Immanuel. 1974. *The Modern World System: Capitalist Agriculture and the Origins of the European World-Economy in the Sixteenth Century.* New York: Academic Press.

Williams, Brackette. 1987. "Humor, Linguistic Ambiguity, and Disputing in a Guyanese Community." *International Journal of the Sociology of Language* 65:79–94.

Willis, Paul. 1977. *Learning to Labor: How Working Class Kids Get Working Class Jobs.* Farnborough: Axon House.

Winant, Howard. 1994. *Racial Conditions: Theories, Politics and Comparisons.* Minneapolis: University of Minnesota Press.

Wolf, Diane, ed. 1996. *Feminist Dilemmas in Fieldwork.* Boulder, Colo.: Westview Press.

Wolf, Eric. 1982. *Europe and the People without History.* Berkeley and Los Angeles: University of California Press.

Wood, Charles H., and José Alberto Magno de Carvalho. 1988. *The Demography of Inequality in Brazil.* Cambridge: Cambridge University Press.

Young, Robert J. C. 1995. *Colonial Desire: Hybridity in Theory, Culture and Race.* London: Routledge.

Zaluar, Alba. 1993. "Mulher de Bandido: Crônica de Uma Cidade Menos Musical." *Estudos Feministas* 1 (1): 135–42.

———. 1994 [1985]. *A Máquina e a Revolta: As Organizações e o Significado da Pobreza.* 2d ed. São Paulo: Brasiliense.

———. 1994. *Condomínio do Diabo.* Rio de Janeiro: Revan/UFRJ.

———. 1995. "The Drug Trade, Crime and Policies of Repression in Brazil." *Dialectical Anthropology* 20 (1): 95–108.

WEB SITES

The dates sites were accessed appear in brackets following the URL.

"A Fundação Oswaldocruz-FIOCRUZ." www.fiocruz.br/ [December 16, 2002].

"Apprendiz: Cristoua Buarque." www.uol.com.br/aprendiz/n_colunas/c_buarque [July 27, 2001].

"Brazil—A Country Study." memory.loc.gov/frd/cs/brtoc.html#bro128 [December 16, 2002].

Britannica.com.Inc. www.britannica.com/seo/s/scaramouche/ [July 20, 2001].

"Human Rights Watch Report. Behind Bars in Brazil." www.hrw.org/reports98/brazil/ [December 16, 2002].

"Rocinha." www.rocinha.com.br/ [December 16, 2002].

"United Nations Website on National Information on Sustainable Development." www.un.org/esa/agenda21/natlinfo/index.html [December 16, 2002].

"U.S. Census Bureau Website: Questions and Answers for Census 2000 Data on Race." www.census.gov/Press-Release/www/2001/raceqandas.html [September 3, 2001].

U.S. Department of State. *Brazil Country Report on Human Rights Practices for 1996.* Department of State Human Rights Country Reports, February 1997,

Washington, D.C.: Bureau of Democracy, Human Rights and Labor, 1997. www.state.gov/www/global/human_rights/1996_hrp_report/brazil.html [July 20, 2001].

———. *Brazil Country Report on Human Rights Practices for 1997.* www .state.gov/www/global/human_rights/1997_hrp_report/brazil.html [July 29, 2001].

WORKS CITED IN THE 2013 PREFACE

Biondi, Karina. 2010. *Junto e misturado: Uma etnografia do PCC.* São Paulo: Editora Terceiro Nome.
Bourdieu, Pierre. 1984. *Distinction: A Social Critique of the Judgement of Taste.* Cambridge, Mass.: Harvard University Press.
Byrne, Leo. 2012. "Brazil Raises 2013 Minimum Wage: Daily." *Rio Times,* December 18. http://riotimesonline.com/brazil-news/rio-politics/brazil-to-increase -2013-minimum-wage [accessed February 23, 2013].
Dobzhansky, Theodosius. 1951 [1937]. *Genetics and the Origin of the Species.* New York: Columbia University Press.
"Focus: Brazil." 2011. *The Economist* online, November 1. www.economist.com/ blogs/dailychart/2011/11/focus [accessed February 23, 2013].
Geertz, Clifford. 2001. "Life among the Anthros." *New York Review of Books,* February 8.
Gianatasio, David. 2011. "Johnnie Walker Awakens a Gentle Giant in Brazil: Neogama BBH Spot Stirs National Pride." *Adweek,* October 12. www.adweek .com/adfreak/johnnie-walker-awakens-gentle-giant-brazil-135736 [accessed February 23, 2013].
Goldstein, Donna M. 2000. "Por que os homens não envelhecem? Violência, morte, conversão religiosa e a vida cotidiana nas favelas do Rio de Janeiro." In *Políticas do corpo e o curso da vida,* edited by Guita Debert and Donna Goldstein, 15–48. São Paulo: Editora Sumaré.
———. 2007a. "Gun Politics: Reflections on Brazil's Failed Gun Ban Referendum in Rio de Janeiro." In *Open Fire: Understanding Global Gun Cultures,* edited by Charles Fruehling Springwood, 28–41. Oxford: Berg.
———. 2007b. "Life or Profit?: Structural Violence, Moral Psychology, and Pharmaceutical Politics." In "The Location of Culture and Politics in Latin American and Caribbeanist Anthropology," special issue, *Anthropology in Action* 14 (3): 44–58.
———. 2012. "Experimentalité: Pharmaceutical Insights into Anthropology's Epistemologically Fractured Self." In *Medicine and the Politics of Knowledge,* edited by Susan Levine, 118–51. Cape Town, South Africa: Human Sciences Research Council.
Herzfeld, Michael. 2009. *Evicted from Eternity: The Restructuring of Modern Rome.* Chicago: University of Chicago Press.
Rapoza, Kenneth. 2013. "Brazil's 'Poor' Middle Class, and the Poor That No Longer Serve Them." *Forbes,* January 22. www.forbes.com/sites/kenrapoza/ 2013/01/22/brazils-poor-middle-class-and-the-poor-that-no-longer-serve- them [accessed February 23, 2013].

Regalado, Antonio. 2012. "Playing Rio." *National Geographic,* October, 72–89.
Tavener, Ben. 2013. "Angra Nuclear Plans Restarted in Brazil." *Rio Times,*
    February 12. http://riotimesonline.com/brazil-news/rio-business/brazil-nuclear
    -plans-restarted-in-angra [accessed February 23, 2013].
Tierney, Patrick. 2000. *Darkness in El Dorado: How Scientists and Journalists
    Devastated the Amazon.* New York: Norton.
Žižek, Slavoj. 2008. "The Violence of Liberal Utopia." *Distinktion* 17:9–25.

Index

CALIFORNIA SERIES IN PUBLIC ANTHROPOLOGY

The California Series in Public Anthropology emphasizes the anthropologist's role as an engaged intellectual. It continues anthropology's commitment to being an ethnographic witness, to describing, in human terms, how life is lived beyond the borders of many readers' experiences. But it also adds a commitment, through ethnography, to reframing the terms of public debate—transforming received, accepted understandings of social issues with new insights, new framings.

SERIES EDITOR: Robert Borofsky (Hawaii Pacific University)

CONTRIBUTING EDITORS: Philippe Bourgois (University of Pennsylvania), Paul Farmer (Partners in Health), Alex Hinton (Rutgers University), Carolyn Nordstrom (University of Notre Dame), and Nancy Scheper-Hughes (UC Berkeley)

UNIVERSITY OF CALIFORNIA PRESS EDITOR: Naomi Schneider